YOUNG CHARLES LAMB 1775–1802

Charles Lamb at 29, dressed as a Venetian Senator; by William Hazlitt, 1804. One of Hazlitt's most sensitive portraits before he gave up painting for writing. (Hazlitt first met Lamb in 1803)

National Portrait Gallery

YOUNG CHARLES LAMB
1775–1802

Winifred F. Courtney

MACMILLAN PRESS
LONDON

First Edition 1982
Reprinted 1984

Published by
THE MACMILLAN PRESS LTD
London and Basingstoke
Companies and representatives
throughout the world

ISBN 0 333 31534 0 (hardcover)
ISBN 0 333 36379 5 (papercover)

Printed in Hong Kong

For Denis

I had no notion what an exquisite writer Lamb is; and thus I have a juster opinion of Miss V. S.: and God knows how I shall have the courage to dip my pen tomorrow.

–Virginia Woolf (as Miss Stephen) to Clive Bell, 1908, from *The Flight of the Mind*, Volume 1 of *The Letters of Virginia Woolf*, edited by Nigel Nicolson (Harcourt Brace Jovanovich Inc. and Hogarth Press Ltd, 1975)

Contents

List of Illustrations

Acknowledgments

This book has been assisted and encouraged in countless ways by generous friends and professionals: Victor Allen, Barbara Bannon, F. L. Beaty, Michael Biddle, W. H. Bond, A. Day Bradley, Donald Breidt, Helen Burnham, Marchette Chute (who said, 'Yes, write it', over her own rose-hip tea), Kathleen Coburn (who allowed me to work in the Coleridge Collection, Victoria College Library, Toronto), my son Stephen Courtney, Jill Davies and Richard Pankhurst of the Royal Asiatic Society, Judith Damkoehler, Helen Duncan, Helen Einhorn, Kenneth Garlick, Marilyn Gaull, Janice Johnson, Betty Karpoff, Jessie Kitching, V. J. Kite, Molly Lefebure, R. F. Lloyd, Lillian McClintock, Sian Morgan, Leslie Parris of the Tate Gallery, W. Hugh Peal, Jean Peters, Miriam Phelps, Thoreau Raymond, Lynne Robinson, Duane Schneider, Aileen Ward, Carl Woodring, and Richard Wordsworth, whose Annual Wordsworth Summer Conference in the Lake District has twice provided information, stimulus and valuable friendship.

I record with sorrow the death before this book appeared of Dr Sam M. Seitz, psychiatrist, who provided voluntary and penetrating modern professional interpretations of the psychological problems of Mary Lamb, Charles Lamb and Charles Lloyd and who became through this association a close personal friend.

Especial thanks goes to Marguerite Bodycombe for her voluntary, indefatigable typing of the first lengthy draft; to Malcolm C. Johnson, who encouraged this book from an early stage, and long thereafter; to Carl H. Pforzheimer, Jr, who offered me the use of the Carl H. Pforzheimer Library, and Donald H. Reiman, editor and scholar, whom I found there and who suggested many fruitful avenues of research, as well as Mihai M. Handrea, librarian, and the editorial and library staff of the Pforzheimer. The staff of the Royal Commission on Historical Manuscripts provided research facilities, as did the Croton Free Library through its statewide borrowing system, and the R. R. Bowker Company Library in New York. The British Library kindly provided microfilm.

It was good to meet the Charles Lamb Society in London, of whom Florence Reeves and Basil Savage were particularly helpful; helpful also were the A. D. G. Cheynes, the Sidney Halls, Mary R. Wedd and Mr D. O. Pam and the staff of the Edmonton Main Library, where the Society's Charles Lamb Library was housed until recently (it is now in the Guildhall, London).

Edwin W. Marrs, Jr, editor of the fine new *Letters of Charles and Mary Anne Lamb*, has been most prompt and kind in providing information. I am grateful to the staff of the New York Public Library, where most of my research was done, and to Lola L. Szladits, Curator of its Berg Collection, who allowed me to study the Keats marginalia in a book by Charles Lamb (acknowledged below) and provided other assistance. Burton R. Pollin was kind enough to send me copies of his many articles on members of Lamb's circle. Mr T. R. T. Manning and his aunt Miss Ruth B. Manning were gracious hosts in Norfolk and Suffolk, providing the opportunity to look at the family memorabilia of Thomas Manning. Anne Lonsdale of Oxford University's Oriental Institute, now writing a much-needed biography of Manning, was most generous in sharing her knowledge.

Clement Alexandre spent many hours going over earlier versions of the manuscript and providing editorial advice, sometimes severe and therefore immensely valuable. David V. Erdman gave much time and lent his own unpublished notes on the history of the *Albion* newspaper, for which Lamb wrote, as well as other material and assistance for my three-part article which provides the basis for much of Chapter 26. E. P. Thompson kindly provided me with an interesting sidelight on Lamb and John Thelwall.

My husband, Denis A. Courtney, read and proof-read all chapters in several versions, offering valuable suggestions, helped me in retyping the final manuscript and in countless other chores, besides providing inestimable moral (and financial!) support. Richard Garnett, T. M. Farmiloe, Julia Tame and others at Macmillan have been patient, prompt and responsive.

I am also indebted to the following firms and individuals: Cornell University and Cornell University Press for permission to quote extensively from *The Letters of Charles and Mary Anne Lamb*, edited by Edwin W. Marrs, Jr, Volume I, copyright © 1975 by Cornell University, Volume II, copyright © 1976 by Cornell University, Volume III, copyright © 1978 by Cornell University; and to Cornell University and its Press for permission to quote from *The Letters of*

John Wordsworth, edited by Carl H. Ketcham, 1969; to Roger Robson Maddison of Knapp-Fishers, Solicitors, London, and his co-trustee for the Estate of the late E. V. Lucas, and Associated Book Publishers (UK) Ltd for permission to quote from Volumes I, II and III of *The Letters of Charles and Mary Lamb*, edited by E. V. Lucas, 1935; to Lord Abinger for permission to read and to quote from William Godwin's unpublished diaries, recorded on microfilm at the Carl H. Pforzheimer Library; to Oxford University Press and Mr A. H. B. Coleridge for permission to quote from Volume I of *The Collected Letters of Samuel Taylor Coleridge*, edited by Earl Leslie Griggs, 1956; to Columbia University Press and Professor Kenneth Curry on behalf of the late Mrs F. F. Boult for permission to quote from Volumes I and II of *New Letters of Robert Southey*, edited by Kenneth Curry, 1965; to the Charles Lamb Society, London, for permission to quote from two (then) unpublished articles in its possession, and *The Charles Lamb Bulletin* (formerly *The Charles Lamb Society Bulletin*) for quotation from published articles including two of my own (all specifically acknowledged in the text); to the British Library, Department of Manuscripts, for permission to quote from a letter of Sir John Stoddart; to the Henry W. and Albert A. Berg Collection of the New York Public Library, Astor, Lenox and Tilden Foundations, for the Keats marginalia in Lamb's *Specimens of English Dramatic Poets Who Lived About the Time of Shakespeare*; to *Studies in Romanticism* for quotations from Burton R. Pollin's 'Charles Lamb and Charles Lloyd as Jacobins and Anti-Jacobins' in its Summer 1973 issue; to the Carl and Lily Pforzheimer Foundation, Inc., for permission to quote from Volume I of *Shelley and His Circle*, edited by Kenneth Neill Cameron, 1961; to the Author's Literary Estate, Harcourt Brace Jovanovich, Inc., and the Hogarth Press Ltd for permission to quote from Virginia Woolf's *The Common Reader: Second Series*, and *The Flight of the Mind*, Volume I of *The Letters of Virginia Woolf*, edited by Nigel Nicolson.

If there are any inadvertent omissions, my repentant apologies. All errors are, of course, entirely my own responsibility. The search for copyright owners of three of the illustrations (of Charles Lloyd, Robert Lloyd and Hester Savory) has been unavailing; I should welcome their claims.

Croton-on-Hudson, NY   WINIFRED F. COURTNEY
November 1980

Note on Referencing

Displayed extracts are followed by the name of the author, or an abbreviation, and the relevant page numbers. Publication details can then be found in the Selected Bibliography (alphabetized to include abbreviations). For extracts which are not displayed an endnote gives the name of the author, or an abbreviation, and the page numbers. Again, full details can be found in the Selected Bibliography.

Genealogical Trees

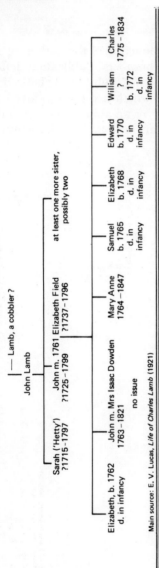

THE LAMB FAMILY (Lincolnshire)

— Lamb, a cobbler ?

John Lamb

Sarah ('Hetty')
?1715–1797 — John m. 1761 Elizabeth Field
?1725–1799   ?1737–1796

at least one more sister,
possibly two

Elizabeth, b. 1762
d. in infancy

John m. Mrs Isaac Dowden
1763–1821
no issue

Mary Anne
1764–1847

Samuel
b. 1765
d. in
infancy

Elizabeth
b. 1768
d. in
infancy

Edward
b. 1770
d. in
infancy

William
?
b. 1772
d. in
infancy

Charles
1775–1834

Main source: E. V. Lucas, *Life of Charles Lamb* (1921)

FIELDS, BRUTONS, GLADMANS (Hertfordshire)

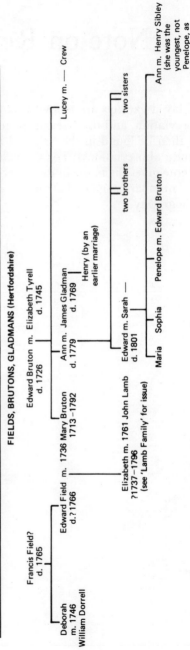

Edward Bruton m. Elizabeth Tyrrell
d. 1726   d. 1745

Francis Field?
d. 1765

Edward Field m. 1736 Mary Bruton
d. ?1766   1713–1792

Deborah
m. 1746
William Dorrell

Elizabeth m. 1761 John Lamb
?1737–1796
(see 'Lamb Family' for issue)

Ann m.
d. 1769
James Gladman
d. 1779

Henry (by an
earlier marriage)

Lucey m. — Crew

Edward m. Sarah —
d. 1801

Penelope m. Edward Bruton

two brothers

two sisters

Ann m. Henry Sibley
(she was the
youngest, not
Penelope, as
Lamb has it)

Maria   Sophia

Main source: Phyllis G. Mann — see notes to Chapter 3

xiv

THE PLUMERS OF BLAKESWARE AND GILSTON NEW PLACE (Hertfordshire)

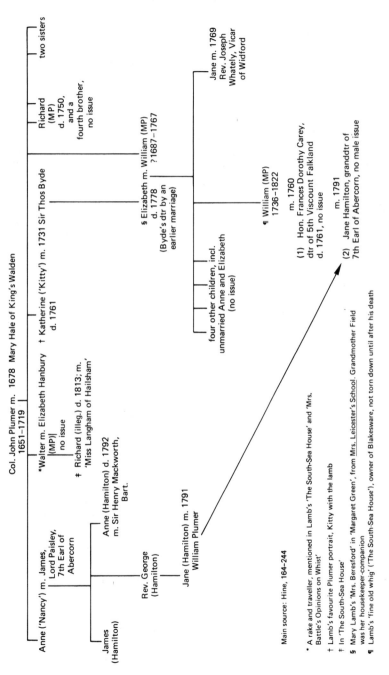

Col. John Plumer m. 1678 Mary Hale of King's Walden
1651–1719

*Walter m. Elizabeth Hanbury   † Katherine ('Kitty') m. 1731 Sir Thos Byde   Richard   two sisters
  |(MP)| d. 1761   (MP)
  no issue   d. 1750,
                                                                              and a
  ‡ Richard (illeg.) d. 1813; m.   fourth brother,
    'Miss Langham of Hailsham'   no issue

Anne ('Nancy') m. James,   § Elizabeth m. William (MP)   Jane m. 1769
  Lord Paisley,   d. 1778   ?1687–1767   Rev. Joseph
  7th Earl of   (Byde's dtr by an   Whately, Vicar
  Abercorn   earlier marriage)   of Widford

Anne (Hamilton) d. 1792
  m. Sir Henry Mackworth,
  Bart.

James
(Hamilton)

Rev. George   four other children, incl.   ¶ William (MP)
(Hamilton)   unmarried Anne and Elizabeth   1736–1822
                                    (no issue)
Jane (Hamilton) m. 1791   m. 1760
  William Plumer   (1) Hon. Frances Dorothy Carey,
                                                                        dtr of 5th Viscount Falkland
                                                                        d. 1761, no issue

                                                                    m. 1791
                                                                    (2) Jane Hamilton, granddtr of
                                                                        7th Earl of Abercorn, no male issue

Main source: Hine, 164–244

* A rake and traveller, mentioned in Lamb's 'The South-Sea House' and 'Mrs.
  Battle's Opinions on Whist'

† Lamb's favourite Plumer portrait, Kitty with the lamb

‡ In 'The South-Sea House'

§ Mary Lamb's 'Mrs. Beresford' in 'Margaret Green', from Mrs. Leicester's School. Grandmother Field
  was her housekeeper-companion

¶ Lamb's 'fine old whig' ('The South-Sea House'), owner of Blakesware, not torn down until after his death

xv

Introduction

Had Mary Lamb not stabbed their mother to the heart in 1796 in a
fit of madness, would her brother Charles have reaped so much
success with his 'Elia' essays in the *London Magazine* of the 1820s?
Was the tension of tragedy required to make him an enduring figure
in English literature? The old question is intriguing – and beyond
our power to answer. But the man who at twenty-one promised to
look after his sister for life, to keep her out of Bedlam, and did so,
maintaining her at home where she could be as independent as she
chose (but subject to recurring periods of unreason), cannot fail to
move us and arouse our curiosity.

When 'Elia' appeared in the *London* and the reading public took
him to their hearts, it was as a quirkish bachelor of forty-five,
informal, witty, sentimental, sharp, scholarly, wise, original, a
'reasonable Romantic' who could say a great deal in brief space and
who enjoyed his fellows, the odder the better. Lamb is a little out of
fashion today, though the informal essay is returning – with E. B.
White's recent collection, the Op-Ed page of the *New York Times*,
and other manifestations. But he continues to attract enthusiasts; he
stands up as a writer still. There is a flourishing Charles Lamb
Society in London with an international membership. When I
recommended him to a young woman she immediately began to
encounter him in the New York City of 1978. There was even a
Charles Lamb Restaurant then, on East 88th Street. And until it
gave up the building on West 44th Street, also in the 1970s, the
Lambs' Club displayed portraits and mementos of Charles and
Mary – because they so loved actors and the stage.

If you cannot bear whimsy, Lamb has important essays free of it.
Then there are the fine letters, now appearing in a new edition,
which reveal several Lambs, some straightforward and *un*sentimental as distinct from Elia, with whom the real Lamb shares a
good many traits but not all. There is even a political Lamb, whose
existence has been little noticed until recently.

Lamb had no grandiose purpose in the matter of English prose. If
he occasionally seems long-winded and overfond of the archaisms of

Burton's *Anatomy of Melancholy*, of Isaak Walton and Sir Thomas Browne, he sought in his essays merely to entertain, or to arrive at some modest truths in the context of his own era – and of 'antiquity'. 'His serious conversation, like his serious writing, is his best', said William Hazlitt. His very defects are engaging, for he was a bundle of frailties – shy, depressive, belligerent, a heavy smoker, and sometimes tipsy – all of which Elia knew how to exploit as literary capital. There was, too, a kind of fine madness in his own balance and sense of proportion. If things were too solemn, he wanted to laugh, if pompous, he wanted to puncture. Hence his puns and jokes, which were the other side of despair, and an outlet for it.

Lamb often turns up in quotation. His characterization of Coleridge as an 'Archangel, slightly damaged' has suggested the title for a recent book on that poet. 'Get the Writings of John Woolman by heart; and love the early Quakers' echoes into our time – and gives us his view on slavery. Roast pork is the more succulent because he wrote about it. Charles and Mary's *Tales from Shakespear* seem never to have been out of print since first publication. The illustrator Grabianski has embellished in colour *Ten Tales from Shakespeare* (Dent) as lately as 1969.

Lamb survives because within his small frame the core was diamond – his determination to live his constricted life and to enable Mary to live hers with all the artistry and happiness they could muster. His quick eye is directed outward, now amused, now sardonic, on the scenes and people he daily encounters, or remembers. What makes them tick? and contradict themselves? Elia is hero, but more often antihero, victim of ignorances, accidents and malignant forces. Or he is the serious critic of art and manners. Looking at people through his eyes, we understand them as he did. They are alive; we have seen and met them.

His originality lies in *how* they come alive to us; his treatment of character brought several steps closer some of the methods of the modern novelist. Geoffrey Tillotson says,

> I must confess that in my own case it was an accident that drew me back to him – a fortunate accident if only because it enabled me to see that for anyone working in the mid-nineteenth-century field Lamb is as important as Wordsworth and Coleridge, Keats and Shelley, Jane Austen and Scott. His essays were of the very mind of his successors, whose work in poetry and the novel we are coming to value more truly. We know how much Dickens

admired him. . . . Thackeray also admired the essays, as did Charlotte Brontë, and Browning, and Le Fanu. . . .

I take it that the essays are irremovable masterpieces in their own right, but I am looking at some of them here mainly as a reminder that Lamb's work in this particular field is vital to our proper understanding of the great things that followed in the mid-nineteenth century. (Tillotson, 89–90)

John Keats, who knew Charles Lamb, gave his fiancée, Fanny Brawne, Lamb's *Specimens of English Dramatic Poets* (1808) – excerpts, with commentary, from the Elizabethans – as what proved the poet's last birthday gift to Fanny, from his own library. (It is now in the Berg Collection of the New York Public Library.) Below one of Lamb's comments he wrote, 'This is the most acute deep sighted and spiritual piece of criticism ever penned.' Modern scholars are according fresh tribute to Lamb as critic of literature, drama and painting.

Lamb went to an office daily and experienced a time of rapid change not unlike our own. Who were his friends and what were the forces that moulded him? When we learn that he knew in his youth some of the most important radicals of his day we cannot suppose him altogether immune to politics. Nor was he, in spite of his care for his sister, immune to love. Lamb grew, of course, out of his age, and it is as a man and writer of his age that this book attempts to see him.

The last 'definitive' biography of Lamb, by E. V. Lucas, appeared in its fifth edition in 1921. A new one is sorely needed. *Young Charles Lamb* (even as Volume 1) does not pretend to fill that gap. It is, rather, an effort to interest the modern general reader in the man and writer from some new perspectives related to our own times.

A final note: I have quoted Lamb and his friends freely and often because I as reader like to know what *they* said of each other and their lives, not what someone says they said. The manner and tone of voice of people speaking and writing most quickly brings to us the real essence of a time, of a society long gone. They do not talk – they do not even think – as we do. What better way to arrive at some comprehension of their world than by listening to them directly?

9 July 1980   W. F. C.

CHAPTER ONE

Starting Off

I am a Christian, Englishman, Londoner, Templar. Lamb to Robert Southey (M III, 155)

Streets, streets, streets, markets, theatres, churches, Covent Gardens, Shops sparkling with pretty faces of industrious milliners, neat sempstresses, Ladies cheapening, Gentlemen behind counters lying, Authors in the street, with spectacles, . . . Lamps lit at night, Pastry cook & Silver smith shops, Beautiful Quakers of Pentonville, noise of coaches, drowsy cry of mechanic watchmen at night, with Bucks reeling home drunk if you happen to wake at midnight, cries of fire & stop thief, Inns of court (with their learned air and halls and Butteries just like Cambridge colleges), old Book stalls, Jeremy Taylors, Burtons on melancholy, and Religio Medici's on every stall—. These are thy Pleasures O London with the many sins . . . Lamb to Thomas Manning (M I, 248)

London lies at the heart of England, and the Temple – where Charles Lamb was born on 10 February 1775 – at the heart of London, just within the original City. The Temple was a place of venerable red brick buildings and green gardens directly touching on the river Thames at their foot.

A property once owned by the medieval order of the Knights Templar, it comprises two of the four Inns of Court – the Inner Temple and the Middle Temple. These are legal societies so old, and so informal at first, that no records of their exact origins survive. Their members were (in Lamb's time) students, barristers and Masters of the Bench, or Benchers. Some sixty Benchers ran the Society of the Inner Temple, with which Lamb would be concerned; one of its functions was the training of lawyers. Most senior members occupied Temple chambers – residential flats combined with offices – though residence within the Temple was not confined to members of the legal profession.

You approached the Temple from Fleet Street, near Temple Bar, a handsome stone gateway by Christopher Wren marking the City border. Two of its glories were the Elizabethan Middle Temple

Hall with its hammerbeam roof and fine oak screen (where *Twelfth Night* was performed in Shakespeare's lifetime), and the Temple Church (where all the Lamb children were christened) with its squat round tower dating from Norman times – sadly decayed and neglected at the time of Lamb's birth. Effigies of Templar Knights in armour, hands at prayer, legs crossed or not, then lay outside the church in darkened marble, so casually as to be almost a living presence. (They are now within it.) Oliver Goldsmith had been buried in the churchyard only in 1774. Dr Johnson, once a Temple dweller, still toiled at his *Lives of the Poets* not far away.

'Sweet Themmes runne softly, till I end my Song' was the refrain of Edmund Spenser, soon to be one of Lamb's literary favourites, and to Lamb's child eyes, 'What was this king of rivers to me but a stream that watered our pleasant places?'[1] In his reminiscent essay 'Old Benchers of the Inner Temple' he recalls the Hall, the sundials, and the fountain he used to make rise and fall to astonish other young urchins. In manhood he brooded on fountains, then disappearing elsewhere:

> The fashion, they tell me, is gone by, and these things are esteemed childish. Why not then gratify children, by letting them stand? Lawyers, I suppose, were children once. . . . Why must every thing smack of man and mannish? Is the world all grown up? Is childhood dead? Or is there not in the bosoms of the wisest and best some of the child's heart left, to respond to its earliest enchantments? (*Elia*, 84)

Later lawyers have acknowledged that this is so and around 1900 erected a new fountain in the Inner Temple garden as a memorial to Lamb. Childhood and autobiography were to permeate many of the 'Elia' essays, even if Elia was not quite Charles Lamb. Elia wrote in 'New Year's Eve',

> That I am fond of indulging, beyond a hope of sympathy, in such retrospection, may be the symptom of some sickly idiosyncrasy. Or is it owing to another cause; simply, that being without wife or family, I have not learned to project myself out of myself; and having no offspring of my own to dally with, I turn back upon memory, and adopt my own early idea, as my heir and favourite? (*Elia*, 28)

He was born on the ground floor at No. 2, Crown Office Row, opposite the fine iron gateway to the Inner Temple garden. From his front door the boy Charles could run easily to the river wall.

Thames waters then were full of incident. Annually there passed that way the Lord Mayor's river procession in barges of gold, their high sterns elegantly carved, canopied in blue and scarlet and flying bright flags, propelled by as many as twenty oarsmen as the City's first official took his way from Crane Stairs near St. Paul's to be sworn in at Westminster Hall. The King's Birthday procession was even grander. George III, like other English kings, found public panoply essential to government.

Most immediate was the daily sight of the Old Benchers, the lawyers Lamb later described in his essay, taking their morning promenade near Crown Office Row and arousing in the small boy the relish for odd characters that never left him. One such was Thomas Coventry, 'a close hunks'.

> By taking care of the pence, he is often enabled to part with the pounds, upon a scale that leaves us careless generous fellows halting at an immeasurable distance behind. . . . His housekeeping was severely looked after, but he kept the table of a gentleman. (*Elia*, 87)

Coventry

> made a solitude of children wherever he came, for they fled his insufferable presence, as they would have shunned an Elisha bear. His growl was as thunder to their ears, whether he spake to them in mirth or in rebuke, his invitatory notes being, indeed, of all, the most repulsive and horrid. Clouds of snuff, aggravating the natural terrors of his speech, broke from each majestic nostril, darkening the air. (*Elia*, 85)

There were others: 'Omniscient' Jackson, source of inaccurate information; 'Mingay with the iron hand' (a hook), who blustered and was noisy; Baron Maseres, who walked in the outmoded 'costume of the reign of George the Second'.[2] All were real Benchers of the day, even to their names.

Chief of them in Lamb's recollection was the genial Samuel Salt. Charles's father, John Lamb, was Salt's general factotum of some fifty-five years – valet, scribe, clerk, protector, and friend. The elder

Lamb had come to Salt in the 1750s, before the lawyer's move from the Paper Buildings (also in the Temple) to Crown Office Row in 1768. Salt had been Whig Member of the House of Commons from Liskeard for over a dozen years, also from 1768.[3] Charles Lamb was surrounded by Whigs from the cradle.

Salt had possession of two sets of Temple chambers, as well as others he maintained for worthy relatives; he lived directly above the Lambs in Crown Office Row. He owned a carriage and employed two indoor servants. He had also collected a fine library to which the Lambs, including the children, had access.

'You could not ruffle Samuel Salt,' wrote Lamb, who refers to John Lamb his father as 'Lovel' in the 'Old Benchers' essay:

> S. had the reputation of being a very clever man, and of excellent discernment in the chamber practice of the law. I suspect his knowledge did not amount to much. When a case of difficult disposition of money, testamentary or otherwise, came before him, he ordinarily handed it over with a few instructions to his man Lovel, who was a quick little fellow, and would despatch it out of hand by the light of natural understanding, of which he had an uncommon share. It was incredible what repute for talents S. enjoyed by the mere trick of gravity. . . . (*Elia*, 86)

Salt had been widowed long ago and chose to remain so, but he had not failed to note one Susan Peirson's devotion – she was the sister of Old Bencher Peter Peirson (Lamb spells him Pierson). He left her £500, his silver inkstand, and books he especially valued in his will. He served in Lamb's childhood on the governing boards of innumerable 'hospitals' (charitable institutions of all kinds), was a Deputy Governor of the South Sea Company, and had earlier been Subtreasurer of the Temple itself. He took a more than kindly interest in his assistant's children.

John Lamb had come to London as a youth from the cathedral city of Lincoln, having probably grown up in the fen country near Stamford. His family, whom Charles never knew except for an aunt – or possibly two aunts – in London, descended from rural folk of small means whom Charles visualized as shepherds in his poem 'The Family Name'. His Lamb grandfather was said by Charles to have been a cobbler, probably in or near Stamford. In time the family[4] moved to the cathedral town of Lincoln and came up in the world a little.

After brief schooling in Lincoln, John left home to seek his fortune. He was a footman in fashionable Bath Spa for a while, earning perhaps £10 a year. By 1746 he had made his way to London and soon after his arrival entered the employ of Samuel Salt. By 1756 he had been made Second Waiter for the barristers' dinners served in Inner Temple Hall, next to Crown Office Row, and in 1772 First Waiter to the end of his life, adding an extra £32 to the family's annual income. He was competent to draw up a will, as he did for his wife's Aunt Ann Gladman in 1772. Salt and the Lambs moved within the Temple to Crown Office Row in the late 1760s – after Mary's birth but before Charles's.

John wrote light verses, which he published (1777?) as *Poetical Pieces on Several Occasions*. He dedicated these to his 'Friendly Society' of fifty males who held meetings at the Devil Tavern and arranged financial aid for the widows and orphans of its members. Several are moral tales about birds. 'The Sparrow's Wedding' suggests that John Lamb valued a tranquil, kindly home life. Another describes the life of a footman, presumably from John's own experience.

His literary bent was inherited by all three of his surviving children. John's family was said to have a history of 'lunacy', as it was then called, though it skipped John himself. Was this known in the beginning to his statuesque and lovely wife, the dark Elizabeth Field from nearby Hertfordshire?

Elizabeth's forebears had been gardeners, farmers, and farm labourers. Her mother, Mary Field, was – for some fifty years – employed in domestic service by William Plumer of Blakesware, a large house near the village of Widford and the town of Ware in Hertfordshire. Plumer was a Whig Member of Parliament and good friend of Samuel Salt. After Plumer's death in 1767 his son William (another MP) kept Mrs Field on as his mother's housekeeper-companion, then as caretaker of Blakesware, empty after old Elizabeth Plumer's passing. Elizabeth Field may have met John Lamb through the Plumer–Salt connection. They were married in London on 29 March 1761, at St. Dunstan's-in-the-West, Fleet Street, when Elizabeth was about twenty-four and John perhaps thirty-six.

Charles's classic description of his father (as Lovel) appears in the 'Old Benchers' essay. 'Lovel' was honest to a fault, chivalrous in defence of the oppressed, 'the liveliest little fellow breathing'. He 'had a face as gay as [David] Garrick's, whom he was said greatly to resemble'. He was a fisherman, and he

> possessed a fine turn for humorous poetry—next to Swift and Prior—moulded heads in clay or plaster of Paris to admiration, by the dint of natural genius merely; turned cribbage boards, and such small cabinet toys, to perfection; took a hand at quadrille or bowls with equal facility; made punch better than any man of his degree in England; had the merriest quips and conceits, and was altogether as brimful of rogueries and inventions as you could desire. (*Elia*, 88)

For Samuel Salt

> Lovel took care of every thing. He was at once his clerk, his good servant, his dresser, his friend, his "flapper," his guide, stop-watch, auditor, treasurer. He did nothing without consulting Lovel, or failed in any thing without expecting and fearing his admonishing. He put himself almost too much in his hands, had they not been the purest in the world. (*Elia*, 87)

Elizabeth Lamb remains a shadowy figure, in part because of her tragic end, which suppressed her children's recollection of her in most of the writings which came after. One senses in her a strong current of bitterness.

Elizabeth lost her first child, another Elizabeth, as a baby, but the next, the junior John, born in 1763, grew up to be strong, sturdy, spirited, and handsome – his mother's and Grandmother Field's unconcealed favourite. The girl Mary followed on 3 December 1764; she was less robust and probably something of a care from the first. Though we know of no puzzling illnesses before 1794 – when she was twenty-nine – she had shown in childhood the first signs of mental instability. Lamb writes in 1796 of Grandmother Field's unthinking and repeated reproach to the little girl: 'Polly, what are those poor crazy moyther'd brains of yours thinking of always?'[5] Throughout her life Mary normally appeared rational, sensible, highly intelligent, and calm, her reserve masking great control. No one who knew her mentions any physical charms beyond a winning smile, so we may assume these were negligible, and indeed the portraits we have of her in advancing years are not those of a former beauty.

Elizabeth was baffled and made uneasy by her plain queer daughter. Mary was superior to Elizabeth in intelligence, a quality hard for certain mothers to countenance in a girl. Such a daughter does not marry easily; she must be prepared, in view of the family's modest means, to support herself.

More children followed, two boys (or possibly three[6]) and a girl, all dying in infancy. One was a second Elizabeth, of whom Mary wrote in condolence to a friend mourning a child:

> Together with the recollection of your dear baby, the image of a little sister I once had comes fresh into my mind as if I had seen her as lately. A little cap with white satin ribbon, grown yellow with long keeping, and a lock of light hair, were the only relics left of her. The sight of them always brought her pretty, fair face to my view, that to this day I seem to have a perfect recollection of her features. (CL II, 272)

The pain of loss, at four or five, had been Mary's too, and again for a brother Edward some two years later. She must have felt the edge of her mother's sorrow and by this time well understood her own place in the scheme of things. In a rare moment of revelation, Charles wrote at twenty-one to Samuel Taylor Coleridge:

> —Poor Mary, my mother indeed *never understood* her right. She loved her, as she loved us all with a Mother's love, but in opinion, in feeling, & sentiment, & disposition, bore so distant a resemblance to her daughter, that she never understood her right. Never could believe how much *she* loved her—but met her caresses, her protestations of filial affection, too frequently with coldness & repulse,—Still she was a good mother, God forbid I should think of her but *most* respectfully, *most* affectionately. Yet she would always love my brother above Mary, who was not worthy of one tenth of that affection, which Mary had a right to claim. But it is my Sister's gratifying recollection, that every act of duty & of love she could pay, every kindness (& I speak true, when I say to the hurting of her health, & most probably in great part to the derangement of her senses) thro' a long course of infirmities & sickness, she could shew her, she ever did. (M I, 52)

The boy John became the typical mother's darling, though circumstances dictated his departure to the London boarding school Christ's Hospital, at the age of five, weaning him early from too close dependence on his family. Indeed, he managed to remain pretty detached throughout his career, solving the family problems for himself by ignoring them. He became very masculine and self-assertive at an early age and not, therefore, closely bound to a sister with whom he had little in common.

No wonder then that when on 10 February 1775, the last child, Charles, appeared, the ten-year-old Mary found an outlet for emotional deprivation in caring for the boy. Though somewhat sickly and physically underdeveloped, he had a charming dark curly head and ready laugh. Now she fitted most happily into the role of mother's helper, and Elizabeth must have breathed a sigh of relief to observe the two runts of her brood so taken up with each other. Mary taught Charles his letters before he could speak (or so Charles said later) and when he spoke it was with a stammer which showed that he too knew where the maternal preference lay;[7] it stayed with him for life.

Mary had already begun to devour all the reading matter she could find. 'She was tumbled early, by accident or design, into a spacious closet of good old English reading'[8] – Salt's library – and Charles followed suit, seeking in books adventure and refuge. Both remained diminutive and dark, while John shot up and was blond. Both had the quick sympathy and sensitivity that often goes with literary gifts. Neither was ever to escape the close bonds and strong affection that then took root, and it was fortunate for Mary that the affection was real and enduring for both.

In their London wanderings it was inevitable that they should practise Charles's reading in some of the pleasant, yew-sheltered churchyards in which the city abounds. Charles one day, wondering at the many virtues celebrated on stone memorials, looked up at his sister and asked, 'Mary, where are the naughty people buried?'[9] Years later he would say of himself, 'He never greatly cared for the society of what are called good people';[10] the bad were far more interesting and less apt to be hypocritical.

For Elizabeth the family life was ingrown. Samuel Salt's welfare was their joint care, and their own apartment rather tightly inhabited by three children and three adults – for John Lamb's elderly sister, twenty years Elizabeth's senior, lived with them almost from the start. If Elizabeth lacked true understanding of her younger children, she was a dutiful wife, mother – and sister-in-law to 'Hetty', as old Sarah Lamb was called. Hetty contributed money for room and board to the family but not much else as Elizabeth saw it. Lamb is perhaps exaggerating when he says of his aunt in 'My Relations',

> The only secular employment I remember to have seen her engaged in, was the splitting of French beans and dropping them into a china basin of fair water. The odour of these tender vegetables to this day comes back upon my senses, redolent of sustaining recollections. Certainly it is the most delicate of culinary operations. (*Elia*, 71)

Mary wrote to a friend in 1803:

> My father had a sister lived with us, of course lived with my Mother her sister-in-law, they were in their different ways the best creatures in the world—but they set out wrong at first. They made each other miserable for full twenty years of their lives—my Mother was a perfect gentlewoman, my Aunty as unlike a gentlewoman as you can possibly imagine a good old woman to be, so that my dear Mother (who though you do not know it, is always in my poor head and heart) used to distress and weary her with incessant & unceasing attentions, and politeness to gain her affection, The Old woman could not return this in kind, and did not know what to make of it—thought it all deceit, and used to hate my Mother with a bitter hatred, which of course was soon returned with interest, a little frankness and looking into each others characters at first would have spared all this, and they would have lived as they died fond of each other, for the last few years of their life when we grew up & harmonised them a little they sincerely loved each other. (M ii, 123–4)

(The gift of being able to 'harmonise', which her brother shared, is expanded a sentence or two later, when Mary remarks on 'a knack I know I have of looking into peoples real characters, and . . . never expecting another to do as I would do in the same case'.)

Charles too understood his mother, though his ambivalence comes through in a poem to her written in 1798:

Thou should'st have longer liv'd and to the grave
Have peacefully gone down in full old age!
Thy children would have tended thy gray hairs.
We might have sat, as we have often done,
By our fireside, and talk'd whole nights away,
Old times, old friends, and old events recalling;
With many a circumstance, of trivial note,
To memory dear, and of importance grown.
How shall we tell them in a stranger's ear?
A wayward son ofttimes was I to thee;
And yet, in all our little bickerings,
Domestic jars, there was, I know not what,
Of tender feeling, that were ill exchang'd
For this world's chilling friendships, and their smiles
Familiar, whom the heart calls strangers still.

                                                              (*P*, 22)

Lamb speaks of 'maids' telling him stories or bringing him goodies at school, and perhaps there was a maid solely at the Lambs' disposal, but one servant was little enough in the primitive kitchens of the eighteenth century and Mary must have been her mother's chief family assistant; indeed this is apparent in the quiet skill with which she later managed her brother's spare and tidy quarters.

John Lamb the younger confirmed Elizabeth's Christian nurture when (in a letter to Leigh Hunt's *Examiner* of 1818) he wrote,

> I am happy in having been brought up an humble but sincere follower of the Nazarene: I love to consider Christ as my Redeemer and would not give up my belief in him for the choicest gifts of fortune. When a child, I have had my feelings so affected by his sufferings, that I never can give up his dying for me upon the dreadful cross. (*Life*, 592)

Even John had his sensitivities – and in manhood the interest in fine paintings shared by Charles, though he could afford to collect them, as Charles could not.

John lacked the humorous perspective on self so evident in Charles and only a little less in Mary. He cared for the poor (subject of the *Examiner* letter) and, more ardently, for the sufferings of animals. He wrote and published impassioned pleas for dumb creatures: his concern for eels skinned alive was once the subject of a page-long sentence. His sympathies were strongest beyond the confines of home. Probably from their father, all three children absorbed the liberal, 'benevolent' strain based on the twin currents of Reform in politics and Dissent in religion.

Charles in later years looked upon his brother with astonishment and amusement – John had a head for figures and got on in the world – but also with great affection. In 'Dream Children' he recalls a time when he, Charles, was 'lame-footed', a circumstance which caused John to 'carry me upon his back'; and he says of John's death (in 1821), 'I missed him all day long, and knew not till then how much I had loved him. I missed his kindness, and I missed his crossness, and wished him to be alive again, to be quarrelling with him (for we quarreled sometimes), rather than not have him again . . .'[11]

John in his odd way returned the affection, though he rarely, if at all, showed it in the form of cash for the struggling pair in their early days. But he kept in touch with brother and sister throughout his life, and though his wife survived him (with an income of her own), left them everything in his will. At least one of Charles's friends, Henry Crabb Robinson, disliked John intensely for his boorishness. Charles's understanding ran deeper: John was simply blind in some ways.

CHAPTER TWO

A Company of Witches

The night-time solitude, and the dark, were my hell. The sufferings I endured in this nature would justify the expression. I never laid my head on my pillow, I suppose, from the fourth to the seventh or eighth year of my life . . . without an assurance, which realized its own prophecy, of seeing some frightful spectre. (Elia, 67)

Gorgons, and Hydras, and Chimaeras . . . may reproduce themselves in the brain of superstition—but they were there before. They are transcripts, types— the archetypes are in us, and eternal . . . Both from 'Witches, and Other Night-Fears' (*Elia*, 68)

Elizabeth's thorn-in-the-flesh, Aunt Hetty, doted on Charles from the moment he was born, thereby incidentally defying those who fell upon his brother John with admiration and indulgence.[1] Old Sarah Lamb was an eccentric figure, perhaps herself slightly touched by the Lamb mental weakness, but no more than to make her difficult and somewhat strange, left to herself as she often was in self-imposed exile from the rest of the household. When she was thus out of the way she occupied herself with reading. This was largely of Roman Catholic texts, but in practice she enjoyed at various times Catholicism, the Church of England, and Non-Conformity without much distinction – except on the part of Elizabeth, who was leery of Papists.

Mary by the age of fourteen or fifteen would have many household responsibilities and was perhaps already apprenticed to a dressmaker. So little Charles was often left to his aunt, 'a dear and good one' in his memory.

She was one whom single blessedness had soured to the world. She often used to say, that I was the only thing in it which she loved; and, when she thought I was quitting it, she grieved over me with mother's tears. . . . I think, at one period of her life, she told me, she had read with great satisfaction the Adventures of an Unfortunate Young Nobleman. Finding the door of the [Unitarian] chapel in Essex-street open one day—it was in the infancy of that heresy—she went in, liked the sermon, and the manner of worship, and frequented it at intervals for some time after. . . . She was a woman of strong sense, and a shrewd mind—extraordinary at a *repartee*; one of the few occasions of her breaking silence—else she did not much value wit. (*Elia*, 70–1)

The Unitarian 'heresy' was the only formal religion Lamb ever came close to accepting, well before the deftly ironic portrait in 'My Relations' was written. The suggestion that young Charles had once been gravely ill is supported by his mention elsewhere of having had smallpox at five – though he often invented or switched such details – and by his father's grateful verse to a doctor whose 'clysters, potions, helped to save/Our infant lambkin from the grave'[2] – but *which* lambkin is not specified. Charles was not pockmarked as far as we know; his disease may have been infantile paralysis (poliomyelitis), since his very thin legs and 'plantigrade' shuffling walk are frequently noted by his friends and we have seen him claim in 'Dream-Children' that for a while in childhood he was 'lame-footed'. Illness almost never kept him from his office in later life, and he became – perhaps in defiance of natural disability – a prodigious walker.

Although he loved Aunt Hetty in return, 'almost . . . better than both my parents put together',[3] she became associated in his mind with an early terror. 'From my childhood,' he writes, 'I was extremely inquisitive about witches and witch-stories. My maid, and more legendary aunt, supplied me with good store.'[4] Samuel Salt's 'book-closet' contained Fox's *Book of Martyrs* and *Philosophical Considerations Touching Witches and Witchcraft*, by Joseph Glanville (1666), as well as Thomas Stackhouse's *New History of the Holy Bible*, illustrated (1737).[5] The study of these became a pastime for Charles. A children's story Charles wrote for Mary's *Mrs. Leicester's School* (1809) is of interest here. The volume consists of stories about themselves told by young girls at school on the prompting of their teacher, as a means of getting acquainted. Charles Lamb writes as 'Maria Howe'. In the 'book-closet' says Maria, 'I was eternally fond of being shut up by myself, to take down whatever volumes I pleased, and pore upon them, no matter whether they were fit for my years or whether I understood them.' Here she 'stayed for hours together, till the loneliness which pleased

me so at first, has at length become quite frightful',[6] and she rushed
out for the sight of a human face. An aunt who corresponds in every
detail to Lamb's Aunt Hetty would blame her terrified state on
those *'nasty books*: so she used to call my favourite volumes, which I
would not have parted with, no not with one of the least of them'.[7]
Maria relished the illustration of Noah's Ark in Stackhouse. But

Stackhouse contained one picture which made more impression
upon my childish understanding than all the rest. It was the
picture of the raising up of Samuel, which I used to call the Witch
of Endor picture. I was always very fond of picking up stories
about witches. . . . Glanvil on Witches used to lie about in this
closet; it was thumbed about, and shewed it had been much read
in former times. This was my treasure. Here I used to pick out the
strangest stories. My not being able to read them very well
probably made them appear more strange and out of the way to
me. But I could collect enough to understand that witches were
old women who gave themselves up to do mischief;—how, by the
help of spirits as bad as themselves, they lamed cattle, and made
the corn not grow; and how they made images of wax to stand for
people that had done them any injury. . . . One night that I had
been terrified in my sleep with my imaginations, I got out of bed,
and crept softly to the adjoining room. My room was next to
where my aunt usually sat when she was alone. Into her room I
crept for relief from my fears. The old lady was not yet retired to
rest, but was sitting with her eyes half open, half closed; her
spectacles tottering upon her nose; her head nodding over her
prayer-book; her lips mumbling the words as she read them, or
half read them, in her dozing posture: her grotesque appearance;
her old-fashioned dress, resembling what I had seen in that fatal
picture in Stackhouse; all this, with the dead time of night, as it
seemed to me, (for I had gone through my first sleep,) all joined to
produce a wicked fancy in me, that the form which I had beheld
was not my aunt, but some witch. Her mumbling of her prayers
confirmed me in this shocking idea. I had read in Glanvil of those
wicked creatures reading their prayers *backwards*, and I thought
that this was the operation which her lips were at this time
employed about. Instead of flying to her friendly lap for that
protection which I had so often experienced, . . . I shrunk back
terrified and bewildered to my bed, where I lay in broken sleeps
and miserable fancies, till the morning. . . . (*Chil.*, 321–2)

At thirty-three, when he wrote this, Lamb could re-create his feelings and experiences as a child without any trouble at all. A few years later he wrote, 'A child's nature is too serious a thing to admit of its being regarded as a mere appendage to another being, and to be loved or hated accordingly; they stand with me upon their own stock, as much as men and women do.'[8]

The idea of witches continued to fascinate him. In his critical writing on Elizabethan drama he comments on three separate varieties – the 'foul anomalies' of *Macbeth*, who 'come with thunder and lightning, and vanish to airy music', those of Thomas Middleton, raising 'jars, jealousies, strifes', and that of *The Witch of Edmonton* – 'the plain traditional old woman witch of our ancestors; poor, deformed, and ignorant; the terror of villages, herself amenable to a justice'. 'On a Passage in *The Tempest*' concerns Prospero's cryptic mention ('how have I pondered over this when a boy!') that the witch Sycorax had done one *good* thing, for which her life was spared.[9] A witch that did good! The contradiction charmed him.

In the essay 'Witches, and Other Night-Fears', which suggests that the experience of Stackhouse was his own, Lamb speculates about the primeval nature of the fears which created witches 'when no law of agency was understood'.[10] 'It is not,' he says, 'book or picture, or the stories of foolish servants, which create these terrors in children. They can at most but give them direction.' Even a child he knows who has been sheltered from frightening tales starts up at night 'in sweats to which the reveries of the cell-damned murderer are tranquillity. Gorgons, and Hydras, and Chimaeras . . . may reproduce themselves in the brain of superstition—but they were there before. They are transcripts, types—the archetypes are in us, and eternal. [They afford us] a peep at least into the shadow-land of pre-existence.'[11]

Lamb the psychologist (how closely his theory verges on Jung's archetypes) has plumbed Lamb the child – and pleads here for an understanding of children's fears. Adults must not leave children to tremble alone in the dark, he says quite firmly.

His own early life was no more unhappy than that of millions of other children, but in him was the seed of an ordering perception which caught the hard look in Elizabeth's eye, the bitterness in Aunt Hetty's, and the frightening 'moyther'd' quality in Mary's, on occasion: with these observations came the first intimations of evil, and the sense of the dread importance of evil in life. The ordering perception related books to life, and imagination made terrors of the night shadows. Who can say that the child exaggerates in fearing evil, when all is said and done?

Virginia Woolf speaks of Lamb's essays as haunting the mind, and as growing out of a 'mind at harmony with itself'. His reticence, she says, 'springs from composure'.[12] If we remember the temperamental ups and downs, the depressions and wild gaieties of Charles Lamb in maturity we may at first resist these comments. What she means, of course, is that he developed his *art* to its finest pitch by bringing under control the fruits of a strong imagination. Having overcome his most terrible imagined fears he could face genuine horrors and live them down.

It is an indication of the close correspondence of brother and sister that Mary Lamb, too, chose to write in *Mrs. Leicester's School* of a childhood terror. This occurs to little 'Margaret Green' visiting a fictional Blakesware. In the story its caretaker is Margaret's mother rather than grandmother and 'Mrs Beresford' her mother's old and blind charge. In the library of the great house the little girl comes on a book called *Mahometism Explained*, the only readable one she can find there. She spends much of her time in solitude, since, 'following the example of her patroness', her mother 'has almost wholly discontinued talking to me'.[13] This very odd statement (if we risk construing it as autobiography) seems more plausible as applied to a grandmother than a mother. If it were true of Mrs Field – who had, in fact, made the tactless 'poor moyther'd brains' remark – it adds yet another element to the typical family attitude to the manic depressive, dutiful but not very loving of a particular child. Condemnation to total silence (except for the servants greeting her in the halls) drove Margaret Green, at any rate, to the library for refuge, where she read the book on Islam and 'concluded that I must be a Mahometan, for I believed every word I read'.

> At length I met with something which I also believed, though I trembled as I read it:—this was, that after we are dead, we are to pass over a narrow bridge, which crosses a bottomless gulf. The bridge was described to be no wider than a silk thread; and it said, that all who were not Mahometans would slip on one side of this bridge, and drop into the tremendous gulf that had no bottom. I considered myself as a Mahometan, yet I was perfectly giddy whenever I thought of passing over this bridge.

One day, seeing the old lady totter across the room, a sudden terror seized me, for I thought, how would she ever be able to get over the bridge. Then too it was, that I first recollected that my mother would also be in imminent danger; for I imagined she had never heard the name of Mahomet. . . . (*Chil.*, 309)

The resulting anxiety 'threw me into a fever'; the child became so ill and incoherent that a doctor was sent for. Explanations restored the little girl to sanity and she went for a change of scene to a house full of children. (Did Mary Lamb go to her great-aunt's farm?)

The fear of witches and bottomless gulfs are not uncommon – they are the very stuff of nightmare – but a writer's first encounter with evil can have interesting consequences for literature. Aunt Hetty was in Lamb's child eyes the personification of both evil and good. She was the human paradox full-blown. Indeed, in all four women who most sheltered Lamb's childhood – the cold-warm Elizabeth, the witch-angel Aunt Hetty, the harsh-kind Mary Field, and the mad-sane Mary Lamb – contradiction was rife. No wonder Lamb grew up with a relish for eccentricity.

And these four did for him one other thing: they gave him an abiding respect for women as his equals. For the rest of his days he preferred character, warmth, and intelligence in women to the mere beauty of what he called 'furniture wives'.[14]

CHAPTER THREE

Diversions

Snug firesides—the low-built roof—parlours ten feet by ten—frugal boards, and all the homeliness of home—these were the conditions of my birth—the wholesome soil which I was planted in. 'Blakesmoor in H---shire' (*Elia,* 155)

The toga virilis *never sate gracefully on his shoulders. The impressions of infancy had burnt into him, and he resented the impertinence of manhood. These were weaknesses; but as they were, they are a key to explicate some of his writings.* Lamb on Lamb, 'Preface to the Last Essays of Elia' (*Elia,* 153)

Beyond the immediate household there were other figures of Charles's childhood: Randal Norris of the Temple, Charles's godfathers Fielde and Henshaw, and Charles Lovekin. These lived most of their lives in or near London. In Hertfordshire, a county just to the north of (London's) Middlesex and bordering on it, were Grandmother Mary Field,[1] old Mrs Plumer, and a host of casual acquaintances in the village of Widford and the town of Ware near the great house Blakesware; also Great-Aunt Ann Gladman, Grandmother Field's sister, at a farm called Mackery End, near Wheathampstead.

And in the dim distance were others, no longer seen. Francis Field, Lamb's maternal great-grandfather, had been a 'gardener' (according to church records), who also kept the Bridewell, or House of Correction, at Hitchin.[2] His son, Grandfather Edward Field, husband of Mary the Blakesware housekeeper, was also a gardener, dying in 1766 – also buried at Hitchin. Both had survived long enough to know of John Lamb's marriage in 1761 to young Elizabeth, but her father was not present at the wedding. In Edward's place at St. Dunstan's-in-the-West stood William Dorrell, husband for fifteen years of Edward's sister Deborah. Originally from Oxfordshire, he now had a thriving grocer's shop in Lincoln's Inn Fields, London. Dorrell also witnessed John Lamb's will at this time, and he soon proved expert at forging another family will, or so Lamb was told by his upright parents.

The swindle had grave consequences for the Temple Lambs, and Charles twice publicly reported it when Dorrell was dead and gone. Once in the essay 'New Year's Eve': 'It was better that our family should have missed that legacy, which old Dorell cheated us out of, than that I should have at this moment two thousand pounds *in banco*, and be without the idea of that specious old rogue.'[3] And in a grimly jovial set of verses from 1827, on Widford and other folk living and dead, 'Gone or Going', he characterized 'wicked old Dorrell' as groaning in his coffin and thereafter sojourning in Hell, 'Where will-forgers enter/Amid the dark Powers'.[4]

Charles Lovekin both Charles and Mary spoke of as 'my cousin the bookbinder', or 'my poor relation the bookbinder'. 'Poor relation' was irony. Lovekin, five years Lamb's junior, was eventually rich enough to lend money to St. Bride's Church in Fleet Street, a favourite one with the book trade, where he was buried in the end.[5] Charles and Mary kept in touch with him – there is a copy of Lamb's 1818 *Works* inscribed 'To Mr. C. Lovekin from his friend and cousin the Author'[6] – but they did not like him very well. He was not only rich but *mean*, a quality which put Lamb off.

As my poor cousin, the bookbinder, now with God, told me, most sentimentally, that having purchased a picture of a fish at a dead man's sale, his heart ached to see how the widow grieved to part with it, being her dead husband's favourite; and he almost apologized for his generosity by saying he could not help telling the widow that she was 'welcome to come and look at it'—e.g. at *his house*—'as often as she pleased.' There was the germ of generosity in an uneducated mind. He had just *reading* enough from the backs of books . . . —had he read the inside, the same impulse would have led him to give back the two-guinea thing— with a request to see it, now and then, at *her* house. (CL III, 137)

Lovekin may have been more unimaginative than illiterate, for Lamb claims to have borrowed a 'Life of Nelson' from him in 1809.

Another friend or relative was Francis Fielde, Lamb's godfather at his christening in Temple Church. Fielde was an 'oilman' with a shop at No. 62, High Holborn. Lamb describes him as tall and grave, 'with pretensions above his rank'.[7] He moved in theatrical circles and professed himself a close friend of Richard Brinsley

Sheridan, through whom he could command free tickets to the Drury Lane Theatre. He became an overseer of St. Andrew's Church, Holborn, and climbed the economic ladder far enough to take up quarters in fashionable New Cavendish Street.[8] He owned, too, a charming country cottage known as 'Button Snap', still standing today near Westmill in Hertfordshire, which Fielde left to Lamb in his will. A second godfather, called Henshaw, died at ninety-nine in 1822; he was a gunsmith.

Then there was old 'Mr Billet' of Lamb's essay 'Poor Relations', his father's impecunious cousin and schoolmate from Lincoln, who worked, Lamb said, for the Mint.

> Once only I saw the old gentleman really ruffled, and I remembered with anguish the thought that came over me: "Perhaps he will never come here again." He had been pressed to take another plate of the viand, which I have already mentioned as the indispensable concomitant of his visits. He had refused, with a resistance amounting to rigour—when my aunt, an old Lincolnian, but who . . . would sometimes press civility out of season—uttered the following memorable application—"Do take another slice, Mr. Billet, for you do not get pudding every day." The old gentleman said nothing at the time—but he took occasion in the course of the evening, when some argument had intervened between them, to utter with an emphasis which chilled the company, and which chills me now as I write it— "Woman, you are superannuated." (*Elia*, 162)

Christmas night the Lambs always joined young Randal Norris, thirty in 1781, also of the Temple and 'the kindliest of human creatures', with 'the old plainness of manners and singleness of heart'.[9] Norris had been articled early to a lawyer in the Paper Buildings. He became Subtreasurer of the Inner Temple and its librarian; much later he married a bride who had grown up in Widford. Norris died the same year as Charles Lovekin, 1827, but the difference in Lamb's feeling is considerable:

> He was my friend and my father's friend all the life I can remember . . . in his eyes I was still the child he knew me. To the last he called me Charley. I have none to call me Charley

now. . . . Letters he knew nothing of. . . . Yet there was a pride of literature about him from being amongst books (he was librarian), and from some scraps of doubtful Latin which he had picked up in his office of entering students, that gave him very diverting airs of pedantry. Can I forget the erudite look with which, when he had been in vain trying to make out a black-letter text of Chaucer in the Temple Library, he laid it down and told me that—'in those old books, Charley, there is sometimes a deal of very indifferent spelling.' (CL III, 67)

He had his perennial jokes and on Christmas night he regularly sang a song:

It was an old thing, and spoke of the flat bottoms of our foes and the possibility of their coming over in darkness, and alluded to threats of an invasion many years blown over; and when he came to the part

We'll still make 'em run, and we'll still make 'em sweat,
In spite of the devil and Brussels Gazette!

his eyes would sparkle as with the freshness of an impending event. And what is the 'Brussels Gazette' now? I cry while I enumerate these trifles.(CL III , 67–8)[10]

The song was David Garrick's 'Hearts of Oak' from his pantomime *Harlequin's Invasion* (1759), and 'these trifles' were of first importance to Charles Lamb.

The scene conveys the warmth of family life at its best to which Charles returned again and again. If all was not harmony, Charles nevertheless found in his family the source of good humour and cheerfulness he liked to spread, and the sense of what a frail thing is a child. Here he became incurably attached to the arts of making a home.

'The oldest thing I remember', wrote Lamb, reporting after a return visit,

is Mackery End; or Mackerel End, as it is spelt, perhaps more properly, in some old maps of Hertfordshire; a farm-house,— delightfully situated within a gentle walk from Wheathampstead.

I can just remember having been there, on a visit to a great-aunt, when I was a child, under the care of [Mary]; who . . . is older than myself by some ten years. . . . The house was at that time in the occupation of a substantial yeoman, who had married my grandmother's sister. His name was Gladman. My grandmother was a Bruton, married to a Field. . . . We had been talking about Mackery End all our lives. (*Elia*, 77)

The house was that leased to the Gladman family by the gentry at Mackery End House, just then Thomas Hawkins. Several of Lamb's kin married earlier-and-later Hawkinses and Sibleys, related to the great-house incumbents, but great-aunt Ann Bruton Gladman was housekeeper to this Hawkins, as well as tenant of his farm.[11]

With the possible exception, then, of distant kindred, who verged on gentry or became gentry by marriage, all Lamb's near, adult relatives were of the superior servant class or in trade, a state of life which kept him from ever identifying with the prejudices and habits of those with independent incomes.

Mary's memories of Mackery End – she probably went there several times – were still vivid when she wrote the stories in *Mrs. Leicester's School*. In 'Louisa Manners' the little girl goes to the farm of her 'grandmama', where she visits the barn, sees a man threshing, gets to know the ducks in the pond and the chickens. 'Grandmama says a hen is not esteemed a very wise bird.' Fruit trees are in blossom – and 'butter-cups and cowslips, and daffodils, and blue-bells,' which Louisa picks, and falls down with. She admires the vegetable garden, the beehives, the cows being milked, makes friends with a particular cow, picks violets for her 'grandmama'.[12]

The children enjoyed the day the hay was made but were distressed to find the wild flowers destroyed 'by the cruel scythe of the mower'. The sheep-shearing supper was an annual occasion, second only to the harvest home, and 'there was no want at all of either beef or plum-pudding'. The children watched – and surely partook of – that fragrant meal, though not with the company at the 'long oak table, which was finely carved, and as bright as a looking-glass'.[13]

The common supper that we had every night was very cheerful. Just before the men came out of the field, a large faggot was flung on the fire; the wood used to crackle and blaze, and smell delightfully; and then the crickets, for they loved the fire,

they used to sing, and old Spot, the shepherd, who loved the fire
as well as the crickets did, he used to take his place in the chimney
corner; after the hottest day in summer, there old Spot used to sit.
It was a seat within the fire-place, quite under the chimney, and
over his head the bacon hung.

When old Spot was seated, the milk was hung in a skillet over
the fire and then the men used to come and sit down at the long
white table. (*Chil.*, 288)

Little Charles experienced the joys of farm life at Aunt
Gladman's only once. His memories were dim because he can have
been only three or four years old at the time: Ann Gladman died
suddenly at the end of July, 1779.[14]

The great house near Widford, some twenty miles to the east of
Mackery End (both were twenty-five miles north of London)
offered another kind of delight. In the huge, rambling, rich man's
mansion of Blakesware, empty after Lamb was three except for
Grandmother Field and a handful of servants, he and Mary could
explore the setting for generations of aristocratic family life and the
relics of a cultural past, antiquated and growing musty. Here,
content as each was to be a little solitary, their lively, bookish
imaginations had free rein. 'The solitude of childhood,' wrote
Charles, 'is not so much the mother of thought as it is the feeder of
love, and silence, and admiration.'[15] Blakesware became material
for both their pens – Charles's in half a dozen pieces, but most
directly as 'Blakesmoor in H---shire', Mary's in the story of 'The
Young Mahometan'.

Mary gives us first the Marble Hall, where the busts of the twelve
Caesars hung against the wall, the inscriptions under each to be
read by climbing a chair. Charles, 'young reader of faces, as I was',
wondered at 'the frowning beauty of Nero', but 'the mild Galba had
my love'.[16] In this echoing chamber with mosaic floor hung also the
prints of William Hogarth. That chronicler of London won Lamb
for life before the little boy could understand the complex message
of the artist. And

Certain it is that the whole story of the children [in the Wood] and
their cruel uncle was to be seen fairly carved out in wood upon the
chimney-piece of the great hall, the whole story down to the

Robin Redbreasts, till a foolish rich person pulled it down to set up a marble one of modern invention in its stead, with no story upon it. . . . (*Elia*, 101)

Here or upstairs in the silent nursery (wrote Mary) they came across 'an old broken battledore, and some shuttlecocks with most of the feathers missing', once volleyed by children long gone.[17]

Opening from the Marble Hall was the family portrait gallery, where earlier children, stiffly caparisoned, could be seen – who, Mary fancied, might step out of their frames to play with her. A blonde young girl – Kitty Plumer – with a bunch of roses was Charles's 'Beauty with the cool pastoral drapery, and a lamb—that hung next to the great bay window'.[18]

Lonely Charles soon 'wandered and worshipped everywhere'.[19] The old family became his own. Sometimes he crept into the

cheerful store-room, in whose hot window-seat I used to sit and read Cowley[20], with the grass-plat before, and the hum and flappings of that one solitary wasp that ever haunted it about me—it is in mine ears now, as oft as summer returns. (*Elia*, 154)

Or he would seek, upstairs, the 'tapestried bed-rooms'. He lifted their coverings and saw 'all Ovid on the walls' and the Greek gods.[21] Mary found Biblical scenes: Hagar and Ishmael (her favourite) – and Nebuchadnezzar, long of claw, eating grass.

When one tired of the house, there were the grounds, and in his various descriptions Charles the city-lover gives way to the nature-smitten poet. In the essay 'Dream-Children' he recalls

how I never could be tired with roaming about that huge mansion, with its vast empty rooms, with their worn-out hangings, fluttering tapestry, and carved oaken pannels, with the gilding almost rubbed out—sometimes in the spacious old-fashioned gardens, which I had almost to myself, unless when now and then a solitary gardening man would cross me—and how the nectarines and peaches hung upon the walls, without my ever offering to pluck them, because they were forbidden fruit, unless now and then,—and because I had more pleasure in strolling about among the old melancholy-looking yew trees, or the firs, and picking up the red berries, and the fir apples, which were good for nothing but to look at—or in lying about upon the fresh grass, with all the fine garden smells around me. (*Elia*, 102)

'The Last Peach' records the consequence of picking it. No sooner had he done so than the sky darkened and let loose 'some few raindrops'

> and I was a type of our first parents. . . . I felt myself naked and ashamed; stripped of my virtue, spiritless. The downy fruit, whose sight rather than savour had tempted me, dropt from my hand, never to be tasted. (*Misc.*, 284)

He had imagined a lake beyond a point which a 'spell' prevented his crossing. As a middle-aged man he dared to break the spell, and found 'to my astonishment, a pretty, brawling brook'.[22]

When old Mrs Plumer died in 1778, her son William had already moved to his family's other large house at Gilston, a few miles away. Though (early and long) a widower, the son did not choose to come home except for the occasional dutiful visit. One sister, Jane, having married the Rector of Widford Church in 1769, the two others, Anne and Elizabeth, lived on with their mother at Blakesware until her death, making a sizeable household for Mary Field to superintend.

William Plumer the younger's distinguished Parliamentary career was lifelong, spanning fifty-four years. He is Lamb's 'fine old whig' of the 'South-Sea House' essay. Samuel Salt was his friend, long ago a trustee at his marriage. On old Mrs Plumer's death Plumer settled Mary Field's future by keeping her on as caretaker of Blakesware while moving his sisters to a smaller house elsewhere. Thus he delayed coming to a decision about the house that had been his family's seat since the Restoration: it was only after his death in 1820 that Blakesware was torn down.

We have seen Grandmother Field talking of Mary's queer brains, and there is one more uncompromising picture of the old lady in Lamb's commentary on a picture called 'Saturday Night' by Sir David Wilkie, his contemporary. The scene is a mother (or grandmother?) washing a child's face rather too vigorously.

> The tender mercies of the wicked are cruel. I am always disposed to add, so are those of Grandmothers. *Mine*—the Print

has made her look rather too young—had never-failing pretexts
of tormenting children for their good. I was a chit then; and I well
remember when a fly had got into a corner of my eye, and I was
complaining of it to her, the old Lady deliberately pounded two
ounces or more of the finest loaf sugar that could be got, and
making me hold open the eye as wide as I could—all innocent of
her purpose—she blew from delicate white paper, with a full
breath, the whole saccharine contents into the part afflicted,
saying, "There, now the fly is out." 'Twas most true—a legion of
blue-bottles, with the prince of flies at their head, must have
dislodged with the torrent and deluge of tears which followed. I
kept my own counsel, and my fly in my eye when I had got one, in
future, without troubling her dulcet applications for the remedy.
(*Misc.*, 324–5)

But he admired the dignified, hard-working, and courageous
Mrs Field. Imagining himself a father, Lamb as Elia tells his
'Dream-Children' that she was a good and

religious woman; so good indeed that she knew all the Psaltery by
heart, ay, and a great part of the Testament besides. . . . Then I
told what a tall, upright, and graceful person their great-
grandmother Field once was; and how in her youth she was
esteemed the best dancer . . . till a cruel disease, called a cancer,
came, and bowed her down with pain; but it could never bend
her good spirits, or make them stoop. . . . Then I told how she
used to sleep by herself in a lone chamber of the great lone house;
and how she believed that an apparition of two infants was to be
seen at midnight gliding up and down the great staircase near
where she slept, but she said "those innocents would do her no
harm;" and how frightened I used to be, though in those days I
had my maid to sleep with me, because I was never half so good or
religious as she—and yet I never saw the infants. (*Elia*, 101)

Brother John was her joy:

I told how, though their great-grandmother Field loved all her
grand-children, yet in an especial manner she might be said to
love their uncle, John L---, because he was so handsome and
spirited a youth, and a king to the rest of us; and, instead of
moping about in solitary corners, like some of us, he would mount

the most mettlesome horse he could get, when but an imp no bigger than themselves, and make it carry him half over the county in a morning, and join the hunters when there were any out—and yet he loved the old great house and gardens too, but had too much spirit to be always pent up within their boundaries. (*Elia*, 102)

Whether Charles and Mary went to Blakesware in the summer of 1780, when Lamb was five, is problematical; they certainly went frequently thereafter, if not again to Mackery End. One wonders, however, where Charles and Mary were at the time of the Gordon Riots in June, which shook all London and threatened the Temple with destruction. Charles's only reference to them is remote and impersonal, as if he had not experienced or heard much about them. One need not speculate further: they occurred, and had an impact on the entire nation. We shall look at them shortly.

On 1 December 1780, as the air grew chill and damp and the pall of smoke hung low over London, Charles went for the first time to the theatre, as he tells in 'My First Play'.

At the north end of Cross-court there yet stands a portal, of some architectural pretensions, though reduced to humble use, serving at present for an entrance to a printing-office. This old door-way, if you are young, reader, you may not know was the identical pit entrance to Old Drury—Garrick's Drury—all of it that is left. I never pass it without shaking some forty years from off my shoulders, recurring to the evening when I passed through it to see *my first play*. The afternoon had been wet, and the condition of our going (the elder folks and myself) was, that the rain should cease. With what a beating heart did I watch from the window the puddles, from the stillness of which I was taught to prognosticate the desired cessation! I seem to remember the last spurt, and the glee with which I ran to announce it. (*Elia*, 97)

Godfather Francis Fielde was the source of the tickets.

To the Theatre Royal, Drury Lane, went the parents and little Charles, walking the short three-quarters of a mile from home in the smoky darkness, past bright shop fronts, past Bow Street and such police as then existed. London, though still a city of vast Hogarthian slums to the east, was well lit at its centre and beginning to be paved (Paris was dark and dirty by comparison).

Arrived at the theatre, they waited at the inner door for the stampede that preceded the days of booking seats: 'O when shall I be such an expectant again!' Vending girls cried, 'Chase some oranges, chase some nonpareils, chase a bill of the play', – chase for choose. At a quarter past five they were admitted – for a quarter past six performance. Charles sat on Elizabeth's lap – in the pit.

> The boxes at that time, full of well-dressed women of quality, projected over the pit; and the pilasters reaching down were adorned with a glistening substance . . . resembling . . . sugar candy. . . . The orchestra lights at length arose. . . . Once the bell sounded. It was to ring out yet once again—and, incapable of the anticipation, I reposed my shut eyes in a sort of resignation upon the maternal lap. It rang the second time. The curtain drew up—I was not past six years old—and the play was Artaxerxes! (*Elia*, 98)

Artaxerxes, by Dr Arne, was an English opera admired by Haydn. Even at that tender age, Charles

> had dabbled a little in the Universal History—the ancient part of it—and here was the court of Persia. It was being admitted to a sight of the past. I took no proper interest in the action going on, for I understood not its import—but I heard the word Darius, and I was in the midst of Daniel. All feeling was absorbed in vision. . . . No such pleasure has since visited me but in dreams.—Harlequin's Invasion followed. (*Elia*, 98–9)

'Daniel' was of course the Biblical book, and *Harlequin's Invasion* by David Garrick the source of Randal Norris's Christmas patriotic song. The part of Abram in it was played by an actor called Thomas Holcroft.

Charles saw other plays in the winter of 1781–2, including *Robinson Crusoe* and *The Way of the World*. Then schooling intervened, and after the seven crucial years at Christ's Hospital he claimed that his excitement was never quite the same: 'I had left the Temple a devotee and was returned a rationalist.[23] But *Artaxerxes* seen at the age of five had made Charles Lamb a devotee of the theatre for life.

The Times: No Popery, 1780

Thomas Holcroft, the actor in *Harlequin's Invasion* and Lamb's future friend, was, and was to be, many things besides an actor. He was already a published writer in his own name; in 1780 he produced a pamphlet under the pen name 'William Vincent, of Gray's Inn' entitled *A Plain and Succinct Narrative of the Late Riots and Disturbances in the Cities of London and Westminster, and Borough of Southwark.*[1] These were the anti-Catholic Gordon Riots, which took place in a curiously permissive atmosphere until London itself faced destruction. (The traditional fear of Catholics had recently been given impetus by a vast influx of poor Irish, much resented by native Londoners.)

The affair, as Holcroft tells it, began with the Parliamentary repeal of certain repressive provisions of an Act 'for further preventing the Growth of Popery', dating from William III. The 1780 repeal allowed priests again to celebrate Mass, and believers to educate their young in Catholic schools and to own land, provided that every Catholic affected, aged twenty-one or over, swore to uphold the King against any claims on England by the Pope or a Catholic pretender. Sir George Savile's motion, wrote Holcroft, 'was received with universal approbation, and a bill was accordingly brought and passed without a single negative'.

Outside Parliament, however, the new Act, says Holcroft,

> greatly alarmed many people, some on religious, and others on political principles. . . . Bills were dispersed, and advertisements inserted in the news-papers, inviting those who wished well to the cause, to unite under the title of the Protestant Association, and Lord George Gordon, who had been so active at the head of the Malcontents in Scotland was chosen president. Little notice was taken of these societies and the president, whose eccentric and desultory character and speeches in the House of Commons tended rather [to put matters of import] in a ludicrous than in a serious point of view. He has the manners and the air of a modern Puritan; his figure is tall and meagre, his hair strait, and his dress plain. (p. 11)

On 2 June 1780, Lord George led more than 40,000 followers and hangers-on wearing blue cockades in their hats, with a petition against the repeal, 'before both Houses of Parliament, on which occasion they gave a general shout'. Lord George had not, however, counted on the kind of rabble he would collect, and things almost immediately got out of his control.

> They obliged almost all the Members to put blue cockades in their hats and call out "No Popery!" . . . They took possession of all the avenues from the outer door to the very door of the House of Commons, which they twice attempted to force open. The like attempt was made at the House of Lords; but . . . it did not succeed. The Archbishop of York was one of the first they attacked. As soon as his coach was known coming down Parliament Street, he was saluted with hisses, groans, and hootings; and when he got out of his carriage, to avoid greater mischief, was obliged to say (which he did in a piteous and enfeebled voice) "No Popery, No Popery!" The Lord President of the Council, Lord Bathurst, they pushed about in the rudest manner, and kicked violently on the legs. Lord Mansfield [the Lord Chief Justice] had the glasses of his carriage broken, the pannels beat in, and narrowly escaped with his life. The Duke of Northumberland was exceedingly ill treated, and had his pocket picked of his watch. (pp. 16–17)

In the course of events a Colonel Gordon, Lord George's near relation,

> went up to him and accosted him in the following manner: "My Lord George, do you intend to bring your rascally adherents into the House of Commons? If you do,—the first man of them that enters, I will plunge my sword not into his, but into your body!" (p. 20)

Eventually the Commons voted – without the debate sought by the crowd – six for the petition and 192 against it. A party of horse and foot guards dispersed the mob and the House adjourned.

But far worse was to come. On Sunday afternoon, after a weekend lull, the houses, shops, and chapels of Catholics in and near Moorfields (where lived many of the Irish) were attacked and burned. This continued throughout the week until the very Jews wrote 'This house is a true Protestant' on their shutters. The homes of MPs, including Sir George Savile, were gutted and sacked. Lord Chief Justice Mansfield lost his house, his law manuscripts, and a valuable collection of pictures in Bloomsbury Square, he and Lady Mansfield escaping by the back door in the nick of time. Their new Adam residence by Caen Wood on Hampstead Heath nearly suffered the same fate, saved by the quick thinking of local authorities, who sent a 'party of Horse' just in time – and, it is said, of a tavern keeper nearby who kept the would-be attackers imbibing.

The house of the Prime Minister, Lord North, was also approached, 'and only preserved by the exertion of a party of Light Horse'. The notorious rake Lord Sandwich, then First Lord of the Admiralty, 'was wounded in attempting to go down to the Parliament House to attend his duty, his carriage demolished, and himself rescued by the military with difficulty'.

On Wednesday, after due notice, a mob burned down the King's Bench and Fleet Prisons, releasing the inmates. Newgate Prison was next followed by the toll gates of Blackfriars Bridge, not far from the Temple. Now the rioters threatened

> to destroy the Bank, Gray's Inn, Temple, Lincoln's Inn, the Grand Arsenal at Woolwich, and Royal Palaces. A universal stupor had seized the minds of men: They looked at one another, and waited with a resigned consternation for the events that were to follow. (p. 31)

Even the city's water supply, at New River Head in Islington, was in danger.

By this time, when fire and chaos had reigned for five or six days, there had been more than a little bloodshed, 'but powder and ball do not seem to have been so fatal to [the rioters] as their own inordinate appetites'. The stocks of wine and spirits from rich men's cellars, from the prisons and other establishments were being steadily consumed, fanning the mad passions of the plunderers.

> Numbers, it is said, and at various places, died with inebriation, especially at the distilleries of the unfortunate Mr. Langdale, from whose vessels the liquor ran down the middle of the street, was taken up by pailfuls, and held to the mouths of the besotted multitude; many of whom killed themselves with drinking non-rectified spirits, and were burnt or buried in the ruins. (p. 36)

These included boys, and women with babes in arms.

As, on Wednesday, events reached their climax, the Lord Mayor at last called for help and the King ordered the military to suppress the riots. This was not at all the welcome move one might suppose, for

> Virtuous citizens . . . had their terrors greatly increased at a report, which every where prevailed, that Martial Law was proclaimed. . . . the possibility of abuse, the being but an hour under the controul of a Military Force, was humiliating, derogatory, and alarming. (pp. 39–41)

Champions of freedom, and the Aldermen of London who were at loggerheads with King and Tory government, and even Edmund Burke, the great Whig MP, disliked the use of soldiery. Charles James Fox, the Whig leader, said that he would 'much rather be governed by a mob than a standing army'.[2] But there hardly seemed any alternative: the Bank and other focal points were now held by the military against the rioters. After *requesting* citizens to refrain from wearing blue cockades, the government at last got matters in hand, and on Friday, 9 June (the day the *Morning Post* belatedly reported that 'The barristers and students of the Temple . . . have armed themselves for the defence of that inn of court, and are spiritually determined to hazard their lives in its protection'[3]) a kindly Black chandler informed the eminent sculptor Joseph Nollekens, his visitor, 'I am sure you will be pleased to learn that Lord George Gordon is taken, and that a party of guards is now escorting him in an old ramshackled coach to the Tower.'[4]

The role of government is admirably represented by the 'old ramshackled coach'; when Lord Mayor Kennet's role was investigated, he 'seemed to have no pain at declaring he thought *fear* a very sufficient excuse for his want of activity'.[5] Several hundred people lost their lives in this week, four prisons and seventy houses were destroyed, and the damages ran into millions of pounds (of 1780).

The feelings on all sides were complex, including the feelings of those in authority and of those who really thought they were preventing Popery. The fears of the latter group derived from the time of the Catholic James II, of Bloody Mary, and of the massacre of Huguenots in France. These fears had recently been fanned by the flamboyant John Wilkes, protagonist of the voteless common man under the rallying cry of 'Wilkes and Liberty!' But Alderman Wilkes (as he now was) did not sanction wanton destruction and himself led the rescue of the Bank.

As for Lord George, he wore black velvet to his trial in the Court of King's Bench, where the address to the jury by the much-injured Lord Mansfield was eminently fair. That jury found Gordon innocent of inciting to violence with intention to coerce the Legislature – and acquitted.

A dozen years later, as Charles Lamb grew to manhood, the government was supine no longer when the populace ran amok. By then the King and ruling class had seen what a mob could do to their counterparts across the Channel, and had drawn what they considered the appropriate lesson. The debate over what exactly *was* the lesson of the French Revolution consumed the ardours of Lamb's generation: no one could escape it.

CHAPTER FOUR

Schooling and Schoolfellows

The Christ's Hospital or Blue-coat boy, has a distinctive character of his own, as far removed from the abject qualities of a common charity-boy as it is from the disgusting forwardness of a lad brought up at some other of the public schools. There is pride *in it . . . ; and there is a* restraining modesty.   Lamb's 'Recollections of Christ's Hospital' (*Misc.*, 141)

I have a strong recollection, that in my time there were two boys, one of whom went up into the drawing-room to his father, the master of the house; and the other, down into the kitchen to his *father, the coachman. . . . The boys themselves . . . had no sort of feeling of the difference of one another's ranks. . . . The cleverest boy was the noblest, let his father be who he might.*   Leigh Hunt on Christ's Hospital, in his *Autobiography* (Hunt, 55)

In thinking back upon his schooldays at Christ's Hospital, Lamb quoted from Juvenal, the Roman poet, 'Not easily do they rise, whose abilities are hampered by straitened means at home.'[1] But John Lamb had a way out of that for both his sons, if not his daughter. For Samuel Salt was a governor of Christ's Hospital, and Christ's Hospital was the best thing that ever happened to Charles Lamb. It gave him a liberal education, sensitive to moral issues, and it gave him gifted friends, chief of whom was Samuel Taylor Coleridge.

Charles had had some earlier schooling, first from Mary, who taught him to read, then from a Mrs Reynolds, *née* Chambers, early separated from her husband. Daughter of one of Salt's clerks, she had grown up in the Temple. She had even been acquainted with the Temple-dweller Oliver Goldsmith, who had lent her his copy of *The Deserted Village*, or so she always claimed. Charles and Mary never lost sight of her until she died in 1832. She profited from and contributed to the Lambs' later literary 'evenings', even when (as Lamb later wrote)

34

. . . prim Betsey Chambers,
Decay'd in her members,
No longer remembers
Things as she once did . . .
(*P,* 72)

William Hazlitt said that, 'being of a quiet turn', Mrs Reynolds 'loved to hear a noisy debate';[2] Thomas Hood that at these gatherings

you occasionally saw an elderly lady, formal, fair, and flaxen-wigged, looking remarkably like an animated wax doll. . . . When she spoke, it was as if by an artificial apparatus, through some defect in her palate, and she had a slight limp and a twist in her figure occasioned . . . by running down Greenwich Hill![3]

In her decline, Hood points out, 'this antiquated personage' received from Lamb annually a contribution of £32, today worth some £320 or $720.[4] Hood deprecated her learning, but she knew Alexander Pope's work and personal history as well as Goldsmith's. She was a cultured woman of sorts – and by these accounts an engaging one – certainly equal to teaching a very intelligent small boy his first formal lessons.

These could not have lasted very long, probably no more than a year, for soon Charles was attending the school of one Mr Bird, off Fetter Lane, a very short walk from the Temple. Girls were taken in the evenings, and Mary's entire schooling, here undergone, was brief indeed. Years later, aroused by an account of the memoirs of an oddity named 'Captain' William Starkey, recently deceased, in William Hone's *Every-Day Book*, Lamb wrote a letter to the periodical about his and Mary's joint recollections of Bird's school, where Starkey had been an assistant in Mary's day. He was then a mere lad in his teens whom Mary remembered as having cried out regularly to her classes, 'Ladies, if you will not hold your peace, not all the powers in heaven can make you.' He once ran away from his job for a day or two; 'A little old unhappy-looking man brought him back – it was his father.' He moped in a corner that day and 'the girls, his tormentors, in pity for his case, for the rest of that day forbore to annoy him'.[5]

In his memoirs Starkey described himself as 'apprentice to Mr. William Bird, an eminent writer and teacher of languages and mathematics, in Fetter-Lane, Holborn',[6] and his later life was similarly unremarkable. Lamb responded, 'Heaven knows what"languages" were taught in Bird's school then; I am sure that neither my Sister nor myself brought any out of it, but a little of our native English. By "mathematics," reader, must be understood "cyphering" '.[7] Starkey's successor in Charles's day was Bird's nephew, a Mr Cook with acting ambitions. Lamb goes on:

> I well remember Bird. He was a squat, corpulent, middle-sized man, with something of the gentleman about him, and that peculiar mild tone—especially while he was inflicting punishment—which is so much more terrible to children, than the angriest looks and gestures. Whippings were not frequent; but when they took place, the correction was performed in a private room adjoining, whence we could only hear the plaints, but saw nothing. This heightened the decorum and the solemnity. But the ordinary public chastisement was the bastinado, a stroke or two on the palm with that almost obsolete weapon now—the ferule.   (*Misc.*, 300)

Otherwise he found Bird 'in the main a humane and judicious master'. Lamb tried to learn handwriting at Bird's school, crowded too close to his fellows. All were assigned to copy 'Art Improves Nature'–a popular theory of the day, soon to be reversed by Romantics. Lamb won a spelling prize, 'which almost turned my head'.[8]

Christ's Hospital was quite another affair–a large school of high reputation which still exists, though no longer in London. It was then in Newgate Street, opposite the forbidding pile of the rebuilt prison. Its Grammar School was Lamb's awesome destination. Beyond the school buildings to the north was the ancient St. Bartholomew's Hospital (for the sick) and its two associated churches, facing the great open area of the Smithfield Meat Market, whither cattle were brought for sale from the surrounding countryside. This was also the site, in autumn, of St. Bartholomew's Fair, which Lamb loved, and to which he introduced William Wordsworth.

Christ's Hospital was founded in 1552 by Edward VI,

to take out of the streets all the fatherless and other poor men's children that were not able to keep them and to bring them to the late dissolved house of the Greyfriars, which they devised to be a Hospital for them, where they should have meat, drink, and clothes, lodging and learning, and officers to attend upon them.[9]

John Lamb, a 'Scrivener', appears on the application for Charles's admission of 30 March 1781. The petitioner 'has a Wife and three child^n.; and he finds it difficult to maintain and educate his Family without some Assist^{ce}.'[10] Though a Christ's Hospital education was considered so good that it occasionally attracted the sons of the wealthy, these paid their own fees, far beyond John Lamb's means. Every applicant had to produce a sponsor from the Board of Governors, each of whom was allowed two applicants: a sponsor signed a bond of £100 against any damage a pupil might cause. Since Salt's pupil quota was filled, it was Governor Timothy Yeats, a well-to-do dealer in hops and brandy, who sponsored Charles, surely with Salt's cooperation.

Charles was seven before he was formally entered at Christ's Hospital on 7 July 1782, the same day as Coleridge, though Coleridge, already nine, went to the Junior School at Hertford before joining the London establishment a month before Charles, in September. Coleridge has left a succinct account of Christ's: a strong and lingering impression was the meagreness of its diet, which left him always hungry.

Places were scarce and Lamb was sent home to await a vacancy, which occurred on 9 October of that year, recorded as the day he was 'Cloathed'. It was Aunt Hetty's pride and delight that he recalled when she died:

>   . . . I have not forgot
> How thou didst love thy Charles, when he was yet
> A prating schoolboy: I have not forgot
> The busy joy on that important day,
> When, child-like, the poor wanderer was content
> To leave the bosom of parental love,
> His childhood's play-place, and his early home,
> For the rude fosterings of a stranger's hand,
> Hard uncouth tasks, and school-boy's scanty fare.
> How did thine eyes peruse him round and round,

And hardly know him in his yellow coats,
Red leathern belt, and gown of russet blue!

(*P*, 19-20)

This distinctive garb was well known to Londoners, who regarded it in general with respect. For both the King and the Lord Mayor took particular interest in the school. The King's Boys, mathematical students destined for the Navy, were received every year at Court, and the entire student body annually heard the Spital Sermon given in their church by an eminent divine, in the presence of other hospitallers, the Lord Mayor, City Aldermen, and school Governors. Afterwards the scrubbed Bluecoat faces appeared in parade as they marched to the Mansion House for Mayoral hospitality and the singing of an anthem of school composition.

Lamb went as a boarding student in spite of his nearness to home. If school meals were meagre, they were taken in the magnificent surroundings of the 130-foot Great Hall. Above the carved panelling hung a Holbein *Henry VIII* – for he it was that seized the Franciscan monastery whose core was the school's cloister – and a huge Antonio Verrio, almost the length of the inner long wall, which showed the King's Boys being received by James II.

Living quarters were sparse and Spartan – high-ceilinged dormitories which Lamb called 'airy', but where the very small entering boy was never alone at night. Sometimes not even in bed; with some sixty boys to a ward, there were not always beds to go round. From time to time the Governors became concerned and cut down on admissions to reduce crowding.

The Reverend James Boyer presided over the Grammar School from 1778 to 1799 and did its most effective teaching of the older boys, a least those who were both bright and resilient. Hunt says that 'th ugh he had a leaning to the servile [pupils], and, perhaps, to the ons of rich people, . . . he would persecute others in a manne truly frightful.'[11] When one day Boyer knocked out one of Hunt's teeth (a loose one) with the

bacl of a Homer, in a fit of impatience at my stammering . . . the bloc rushed out . . . he turned pale, and on my proposing to go out nd wash the mouth, he said "Go, child" in a tone of voice amc inting to the paternal. Now "Go, child," from Boyer, was wor a dozen tender speeches from anyone else. (Hunt, 83)

Coleridge suggests that Boyer's teaching was important for English Romanticism:

> I learnt from him that poetry, even that of the loftiest and . . . wildest odes, had a logic of its own as severe as that of science; and more difficult, because more subtle, more complex, and dependent on more and more fugitive causes. In the truly great poets, he would say, there is a reason assignable, not only for every word, but for the position of every word. . . .
>
> In our own English compositions . . . he showed no mercy to phrase, metaphor or image unsupported by a sound sense, or where the same sense might have been conveyed with equal force and dignity in plainer words. . . . In fancy, I can almost hear him now, exclaiming, "Harp? Harp? Lyre? Pen and ink, boy, you mean! Muse, boy, muse? Your nurse's daughter, you mean! Pierian spring? Oh, aye! the cloister-pump, I suppose!" (BL, 3–4)

Boyer kept a book of the best work of Christ's pupils: in it Coleridge was asked to copy four poems (and seven prose pieces), Hunt none, Lamb one, an interesting indication of Boyer's prescience in regard to these three. Lamb's *Mille Viae Mortis* describes a dream.

> What time in bands of slumber all were laid,
> To Death's dark court, methought I was convey'd;
> In realms it lay far hid from mortal sight,
> And gloomy tapers scarce kept out the night.
>
> On ebon throne the King of Terrors sate . . .
> (Life, 66)

Around him were pallid Fear, dark Despair, Fever, Dropsy, Gout, Madness, and Plague,

> but chief in honour stood
> More-wasting War, insatiable of blood . . .

The poet addresses the King, praising his power; Death decries his flattery and cries, 'Hence, or thou feel'st my dart!' The poet is terrified, 'the vision fled'. This first effort scans, rhymes, rises to a climax, is reasonably direct, and has a certain power in the heavily personified archaic mode. (Romantics would resist personification but not archaisms.) The precocious fourteen-year-old broods, as adolescents must, on the horrors to be encountered in life, and on life's end. We may laugh at the ponderous solemnity of the schoolboy aping his elders, but with this early encouragement Boyer must have bolstered Lamb's self-confidence as a writer at a crucial moment.

His friend Valentine Le Grice has written of their schooldays,[12]

> Lamb was an amiable quiet boy, very sensitive and keenly observing: his countenance was mild, his complexion clear brown with an expression that he might have been taken to be of Jewish parentage . . . his step was plantigrade, which made him [*sic*] walk as a boy very slow and peculiar.

He was a

> quiet, gentle, studious boy, a looker on rather than a participator in the frolics of others. He enjoyed their mirth extremely, but his delicate frame, and his difficult utterance, which was increased by agitation, unfitted him for joining in the usual sports of boys. The description which he gives in his Recollections of Christ's Hospital of the habits and feelings of the schoolboy is a deliniation of himself:—the feelings were all in his own heart: while others were all fire and play, he "stole along with all the self-concentration of a young monk": this habit and these feelings were awakened and cherished from some peculiar circumstances. He had been born and bred in the Temple, so that he passed from cloister to cloister, and this was all the change the young man knew. On every holiday, in ten minutes he was in the gardens, or in the cloisters, or on the terrace, or at the fountain of the Temple. . . . Here he had a happy home, and a sister who watched him with the tenderest solicitude, and he also had access to the library of . . . Mr. Salt . . . (*CLB*, Apr. 1974, 116–17)

Lamb makes little of the differences which set him apart. He was likeable, and his fellows abstained from teasing him. Says Le Grice,

I never heard his name mentioned without the addition of Charles, although as there was no other boy of the name of Lamb, the addition was unnecessary; but there was an implied kindness in it, and it was a proof that his gentle manners excited that kindness. (Blunden, *Lamb . . . Recorded*, 19)

But it is to Lamb we must go. Lamb wrote two essays – 'Recollections of Christ's Hospital' in 1813, while Boyer still lived, and 'Christ's Hospital Five-and-Thirty Years Ago' in 1820, as Elia. The first extols the school in serious vein, the second, in part humorous, sets the record straight on school weaknesses.

'The Christ's Hospital boy is a religious character,' says Lamb in the first, though 'leaning towards an over-belief' in this regard, which Hunt lays to too much *church*. They also, Lamb continues, have a 'turn for romance above most other boys', devouring the *Arabian Nights* and other tales 'of a still wilder cast. . . .' There were a good many opportunities to go off unattended on whole holidays – thirty-odd saints' and patriotic days and alternate Wednesdays. Lamb remembered leading a long, long walk along the New River in search of its source – which was never found but provided much joy in the searching.

'The Christ's Hospital boy's sense of right and wrong is peculiarly tender and apprehensive,' Lamb observes. This 'pervading moral sense'[13] certainly remained with Lamb. Leigh Hunt discovered at Christ's that although he tended to be a coward in his own behalf, the spectacle of injustice to a companion gave him unearthly courage. As for Coleridge, the vision of Boyer – who beat him for professing religious doubt, for wanting to become a cobbler, and other felonies – haunted his dreams and nightmares, became his living conscience for years after.

In 'Christ's Hospital Five-and-Thirty Years Ago' Lamb treats at some length the more severe punishments – as of runaway Bluecoats, by incarcerating them, fettered, in 'little square Bedlam cells, where a boy could just lie at his length upon straw and a blanket' in dim daylight, 'barely enough to read by'. A second offence brought night-time incarceration, also solitary, but since done away with 'after one or two instances of lunacy, or attempted suicide'. 'This fancy of dungeons for children'[14] and the public disgrace following a third offence – whipping and expulsion – sickened Lamb then and always. (Had he exaggerated, others would have corrected him; we do not hear of any who protested.)

The Grecians, or top boys, were awesome figures to the younger lads. They were

> waiting the expiration of the period when they should be sent, at the charges of the Hospital, to one or other of our Universities, but more frequently to Cambridge. These youths, from their superior acquirements . . . age, and stature, . . . may be considered as the spiritual power. (*Misc.*, 146-7)

Lamb's 'Recollections' finishes with his warmest memories:

> The time would fail me if I were to attempt to enumerate all those circumstances, some pleasant, some attended with some pain, which, seen through the mist of distance, come sweetly softened to the memory. But I must crave leave to remember our transcending superiority in those invigorating sports, leap-frog, and basting the bear; our delightful excursions in the summer holidays to the New River, near Newington, where, like otters, we would live the long day in the water, never caring for dressing ourselves when we had once stripped; our savoury meals afterwards, when we came home almost famished with staying out all day without our dinners. (*Misc.*, 148)

He remembers their visits to the Tower of London, their 'solemn processions through the City at Easter, with the Lord Mayor's largess of buns, wine, and a shilling', the 'civic pleasantries' of the Aldermen; the singing of hymns, the occasional funeral of a fellow scholar, and

> the festivities at Christmas, when the richest of us would club our stock to have a gaudy day, sitting round the fire, replenished to the height with logs, and the penniless, and he that could contribute nothing, partook in all the mirth, and in some of the substantialities of the feasting; the carol sung by night at that time of the year, which, when a young boy, I have so often lain awake to hear from seven (the hour of going to bed) till ten, when it was sung by the older boys and monitors, and have listened to it, in their rude chanting, till I have been transported in fancy to the fields of Bethlehem, and the song which was sung at that season by angels' voices to the shepherds. (*Misc.*, 148-9)

The second essay, 'Christ's Hospital Five-and-Thirty Years Ago', starts off in the 'lie' mode, as if Lamb were Coleridge describing the happy situation of his friend Charles Lamb:

> In Mr. Lamb's "Works," published a year or two since, I find a magnificent eulogy on my old school, such as it was, or now appears to him to have been, between the years 1782 and 1789. . . .
>
> I remember L. at school; and can well recollect that he had some peculiar advantages, which I and others of his schoolfellows had not. His friends lived in town, and were near at hand; and he had the privilege of going to see them, almost as often as he wished, through some invidious distinction, which was denied to us. The present worthy sub-treasurer to the Inner Temple can explain how that happened. He had his tea and hot rolls in a morning, while we were battening upon our quarter of a penny loaf—our *crug*—moistened with attenuated small beer, in wooden piggins, smacking of the pitched leathern jack it was poured from. Our Monday's milk porritch, blue and tasteless, and the pease soup of Saturday, coarse and choking, were enriched for him with a slice of "extraordinary bread and butter," from the hot-loaf of the Temple. (*Elia*, 12)

Randal Norris was, of course, the subtreasurer to the Temple, and, as Lamb later implies, it was Salt – a Governor under his own roof, as it were – whose propinquity kept the school especially generous to one boy. To supplement the school diet, Lamb

> had his hot plate of roast veal, or the more tempting griskin (exotics unknown to our palates), cooked in the paternal kitchen (a great thing), and brought him daily by his maid or aunt! I remember the good old relative (in whom love forbade pride) squatting down upon some odd stone in a by-nook of the cloisters, disclosing the viands, . . . and the contending passions of L. at the unfolding. There was love for the bringer; shame for the thing brought, and the manner of its bringing; sympathy for those who were too many to share in it; and, at top of all, hunger (eldest, strongest of the passions!) predominant, breaking down the stony fences of shame, and awkwardness, and a troubling over-consciousness. (*Elia*, 13)

One day his aunt's kindness had a sequel:

My good old aunt, who never parted from me at the end of a
holiday without stuffing a sweet-meat, or some nice thing, into
my pocket, had dismissed me one evening with a smoking plum-
cake, fresh from the oven. In my way to school (it was over
London bridge)[15] a grey-headed old beggar saluted me (I have
no doubt at this time of day that he was a counterfeit). I had no
pence to console him with and in the vanity of self-denial, . . .
school-boy-like, I made him a present of—the whole cake! I
walked on a little, buoyed up, as one is on such occasions, with a
sweet soothing of self-satisfaction; but before I had got to the end
of the bridge, my better feelings returned, and I burst into tears,
thinking how ungrateful I had been to my good aunt . . .—and
the odour of that spicy cake came back upon my recollection, and
the pleasure and the curiosity I had taken in seeing her make it,
and her joy when she sent it to the oven, and how disappointed
she would feel that I had never had a bit of it in my mouth at
last—and I blamed . . . my out-of-place hypocrisy of goodness,
and above all I wished never to see the face again of that insidious,
good-for-nothing, old grey impostor. (*Elia*, 125)

This is one of the episodes that haunt the mind – the amalgam in a
single act of goodness and badness, elation and despair, as confusing
to the generous child as to any sensitive adult. (Lamb would say
elsewhere, 'The greatest pleasure I know, is to do a good deed by
stealth and to have it found out by accident.'[16])

The beggar episode comes from another essay. In 'Christ's
Hospital' Lamb goes on to contrast his own happy lot with
Coleridge's. Coming from distant Ottery St. Mary in Devon,
Coleridge was on free days often exceedingly lonely. The talkative,
brilliant, stocky lad was soon attracted to the other new boy with the
stammer – kind, ready to listen, and in love with books and
learning.

Because of this stammer, which unfitted him for the clergy, Lamb
had to be content as 'deputy Grecian'. In the main his days were
spent under a schoolmaster as different from Boyer as night from
day, the Reverend Matthew Field.[17] Field had won the
Chancellor's Gold Medal for Latin verse at Cambridge, so he was
not devoid of learning – nor was he at all interested, except absent-

mindedly, in teaching. (One would barely believe Lamb's portrait were it not corroborated by Leigh Hunt.)

The Upper and Lower Grammer School were held in the same huge room. Lamb says of Field's classes:

> We lived a life as careless as birds. We talked and did just what we pleased, and nobody molested us. We carried . . . a grammar, for form; but, for any trouble it gave us, we might take two years in getting through the verbs deponent, and another two in forgetting all that we had learned about them. There was now and then the formality of saying a lesson, but if you had not learned it, a brush across the shoulders (just enough to disturb a fly) was the sole remonstrance.

Field, 'a good easy man', retired to his private room when the going got too rough.

> Our mirth and uproar went on. We had classics of our own, without being beholden to "insolent Greece or haughty Rome," that passed current among us—Peter Wilkins—the Adventures of the Hon. Capt. Robert Boyle—the Fortunate Blue Coat Boy— and the like. Or we cultivated a turn for mechanic or scientific operations; making little sun-dials of paper; or weaving those ingenious parentheses, called, *cat-cradles*; or making dry peas to dance upon the end of a tin pipe; or studying the art military over that laudable game "French and English," and a hundred other such devices to pass away the time—mixing the useful with the agreeable—as would have made the souls of Rousseau and John Locke chuckle to have seen us. (*Elia*, 18)

Boyer, whose 'storms came near, but never touched us,' would 'sometimes, with ironic deference, send to borrow a rod of the Under Master,' then remark 'with Sardonic grin, . . . "how neat and fresh the twigs looked" '.[18] Otherwise he did not interfere.

Lamb describes his school friends. T. S. Middleton, later Bishop of Calcutta, was to send Coleridge from Cambridge the poems of the Reverend William Lisle Bowles, whose sonnets made a strong impression on Coleridge, Lamb, and Wordsworth. Middleton was said to have discovered Coleridge reading Virgil when other boys were playing and told Boyer about it. Boyer became interested in the abilities of what he called 'that sensible fool, Coleridge,'[19] whom Lamb soon worshipped:

> Come back into memory, like as thou wert in the day-spring of thy fancies, with hope like a fiery column before thee—the dark pillar not yet turned—Samuel Taylor Coleridge—Logician, Metaphysician, Bard!—How have I seen the casual passer through the Cloisters stand still, intranced with admiration (while he weighed the disproportion between the *speech* and the *garb* of the young Mirandula), to hear thee unfold, in thy deep and sweet intonations, the mysteries of Jamblichus, or Plotinus (for even in those years thou waxedst not pale at such philosophic draughts), or reciting Homer in his Greek, or Pindar— —while the walls of the old Grey Friars re-echoed to the accents of the *inspired charity-boy!*— (*Elia*, 21)

Few were the boys who could hold their own against Coleridge in 'wit-combats'; one was Charles Valentine Le Grice. In 'Grace Before Meat' Lamb tells how 'C. V. L., when importuned for a grace, used to inquire, first slyly leering down the table, "Is there no clergyman here?"—significantly adding, "Thank G—".'[20] Val was not only a wag but an inveterate punster. At Cambridge he won a prize for declamation, and later now and then appeared in print. An early work, it was said, treated the art of poking a fire. He was known to his contemporaries as the translator of the Latin poet Longus.

He did very well for himself, going to Cornwall as tutor to the son of a wealthy widow in 1796, and – now himself a clergyman – enjoying a comfortable church living with an early marriage to the widow. Thereafter he stayed in Penzance and never saw Lamb again until 1834, the year of Lamb's death, when Val took him out to dinner at the Bell in Edmonton.

Val was a Grecian and so was his brother Sam. Sam was still at school in Hunt's day; he was one of those few who knew how to disarm Boyer. Lamb found him 'sanguine, volatile, sweet-natured,' and of a 'roving temper'.[21] Says Hunt:

> He was the maddest of all the great boys in my time; clever, full of address, and not hampered with modesty. Remote humours, not lightly to be heard, fell on our ears, respecting pranks of his amongst the nurses' daughters. He had a fair handsome face, with

delicate aquiline nose, and twinkling eyes. I remember his astounding me when I was "a new boy", with sending me for a bottle of water, which he proceeded to pour down the back of G., a grave Deputy Grecian. . . . The boys adored him. (Hunt, 72)

Robert Favell Lamb characterizes as 'dogged, faithful, antici-pative of insult, warm-hearted, with something of the old Roman height about him'. Then there was Bob Allen:

Nor shalt thou, their compeer, be quickly forgotten, Allen, with the cordial smile, and still more cordial laugh, with which thou wert wont to make the old Cloisters shake, in thy cognition of some poignant jest of theirs; or the anticipation of some more material, and, peradventure, practical one, of thine own. Extinct are those smiles, with that beautiful countenance, with which . . . in the days of thy maturer waggery, thou didst disarm the wrath of infuriated town-damsel, who, incensed by provoking pinch, turning tigress-like round, suddenly converted by thy angel-look, exchanged the half-formed terrible *"bl—"* for a gentler greeting—*"bless thy handsome face!"* (*Elia*, 22)

Allen's life was brief and faltering. After a period as an Army surgeon in Portugal he married, became a journalist, flitting from job to job, and died of apoplexy in 1805.

Marmaduke Thompson, eventually the 'mildest of missionaries', was the friend to whom Lamb dedicated his early novella *Rosamund Gray*, while Thompson was still at Cambridge. He became Senior Chaplain to the East India Company at Madras.

Leigh Hunt says of his schoolmates,

Those who became Grecians always went to the University, though not always into the Church; which was reckoned a departure from the contract. When I first came to the school, at seven years old [1791, after Lamb and Coleridge had departed], the names of the Grecians were Allen, Favell, Thompson, and Le Grice, brother of the Le Grice above mentioned, and now a clergyman in Cornwall. (Hunt, 74)

Lamb and Coleridge had gravitated naturally to the group of top boys. Leadership at Christ's, it is clear, meant intellectual distinction.

Two others, James White, who became a school employee, and John Matthew Gutch were Lamb's steady friends for some time, and we shall see them again.

Otherwise there was the firm-but-kindly steward; the matrons and nurses; William Wales, the mathematics master who had been round the world with Captain Cook and who had managed, with courage and persuasive 'remonstrances' to save Christ's Hospital from invasion by the Gordon rioters; and Mrs Boyer, whose beauty, spirit, and tenderness made her as popular as her husband was feared.

In spite of brutalities and the casual Field Christ's Hospital provided an extraordinary education, as so many of its students proved. What did they learn there? In English literature the Bible, Milton, and Shakespeare. The (rather informal) requirements for Cambridge were largely the Classics. The classical rules of rhetoric were taught. In Latin, Caesar, Cicero, Virgil, Horace, and Terence were to be read at sight and students should be able to compose Latin prose and verse. Lamb could meet this test. Deputy Grecians at Christ's had studied the Greek Testament, Homer, Demosthenes, and perhaps Xenophon, but if they left school early, as Lamb did, they were not yet Greek scholars. At Cambridge the main study – following the great tradition of Isaac Newton – was now mathematics, and the philosophy of the admired William Paley. But if one tried, there was opportunity to learn widely even at an Oxford and Cambridge then in the doldrums, and University training opened many doors to ex-students as well as to graduates. Stammerers could not be clergymen, however, and must therefore leave Christ's early. Both Lamb and Hunt felt the deprivation keenly.

Lamb never forgot the Latin he had learned at Christ's – nor his English poets nor his Bible nor his Shakespeare. The earlier writers fed his interest in the past, which was to become stronger as time went on. At Christ's, too, Lamb learned to write.[22]

Christ's Hospital had provided Lamb with fodder for an awakening mind and friends who shared his love of intellectual pursuits. It was the microcosm of a world outside where punishment was cruel in similar proportion: petty larceny in England could mean death or deportation.

Lamb became first student among the Deputy Grecians. He was intensely happy at Christ's Hospital, as happy he was ever to be again.

His feelings on leaving school when nearly fifteen are not recorded, but they must have coincided with Leigh Hunt's. Like Hunt he had spent eight years there. Hunt was

> fifteen when I put off my band and blue skirts for a coat and neckcloth. I was then first Deputy Grecian, and I had the honour of going out of the school in the same rank, at the same age, and for the same reason, as my friend Charles Lamb. The reason was, that I hesitated in my speech. . . . It was understood that a Grecian was bound to deliver a public speech before he left school, and to go into the Church afterwards; and as I could do neither of these things, a Grecian I could not be. So I put on my coat and waistcoat, and, what was stranger, my hat; a very uncomfortable addition to my sensations.
>
> . . . I had now a vague sense of worldly trouble, and of a great and serious change in my condition; besides which, I had to quit my old cloisters, and my playmates, and long habits of all sorts; so that what was a very happy moment to schoolboys in general, was to me one of the most painful of my life. . . . I took leave of my books, of my friends, of my seat in the grammar-school, of my good-hearted nurse and her daughter, of my bed, of the cloisters, and of the very pump out of which I had taken so many delicious draughts, as if I should never see them again . . . The fatal hat was put on; my father was come to fetch me.[23] (Hunt, 107)

The Times: The New Men and Women

The world into which Lamb emerged in 1789 was a rapidly changing one, the momentous event of this year being the fall of the Bastille across the Channel in France on 14 July. The earlier eighteenth century was far from being the quiet classical age into which it has sometimes been pigeonholed: Britain had been involved in a succession of small wars and other embroilments throughout. British interests were far-flung, especially in Asia, where the East India Company, a private trading venture, the source of wealth for merchants and sea captains, grew ever more powerful and began to be subject to government restriction. The small island was rapidly becoming a world power. France was the traditional enemy throughout the century in Europe; in America, where it fought for a continent and lost; in the West Indies; in India, and elsewhere.

By 1789 the 'democratick' or radical tide which had its origins within the old order was well underway in England. In the seventeenth century Parliament had asserted its prerogative against the remnants of absolute monarchy: it had executed one king (Charles I) and deposed another (James II) for failing to do its will. The Gordon Riots were an extreme example, among many, of the populace taking the law into its own hands. The American colonies had revolted against taxation without representation and broken away from the mother country. (They had had their Whig sympathizers in Britain.)

The German Hanoverians, now represented by George III (recovering from his first bout of insanity[1]) reigned for most of this turbulent century. Though sometimes autocratic in expressing their will or dismissing ministers, in general they respected the Parliament. Under Prime Minister William Pitt the Younger[2] the power of Parliament grew as steadily as the influence of Britain in world affairs. It was 'representative' only by ancient standards; in fact it was ruled by the small aristocratic oligarchy of Whigs and

Tories. The powerful Whig landowners (led by Charles James Fox) together with the old-line Tory aristocrats (favoured by George III) controlled constituencies and traded pocket boroughs whose population had sometimes altogether disappeared, as in Old Sarum. Whigs had ruled earlier in the century, but young Pitt the Whig had turned New Tory; even now half the Whigs were conservative. Others, secure in their handsome houses and profitable estates, could afford with Fox their liberal principles – they were to oppose the French war from 1793. A few, like Lord Stanhope, soon to be known as 'Citizen' Stanhope in the French manner, were radicals.

The call for Parliamentary reform was in the air. Pitt himself had tried and failed to legislate it in 1785. Pitt was a fine debater who won his first political laurels in his early twenties – a coolly brilliant man who drank much port and fell into personal debt but never married. Cartoonists portrayed him as a sort of pallid stick, very thin and bending from the hips. His major interest was in fiscal reform. He knew how to lead, knew how to organize, and he gained steadily in the general esteem, though he cared little about the grinding poverty on which privilege rested. The equally brilliant Fox was short and round, with slanting dark brows and heavy jowls. A drinker too, he was ready to gamble all night, and much loved by his friends. During Lamb's life he was almost always out of office, leader of the Opposition. Interested in social and political reform, he distrusted radicals.

Middle-class intellectual radicals were those who read the French 'philosophers' – Voltaire and Rousseau in particular (both dead by 1778) – to find their own models of social justice. The goal of universal suffrage was beginning to take root in a constitutional monarchy where only a few thousand British males were voters. The new industrial centres of Birmingham and Manchester had no representation at all. Such inequities were becoming glaringly apparent even to the artisan class, who were forming societies for Parliamentary Reform, basis for the new radicalism. Many of the middle and lower classes sought new religion in Methodism (still a movement within the Church) and Unitarianism.[3]

The exploration of 'natural science' and mechanical engineering following upon the recent discoveries of Isaac Newton (d. 1727) was bringing about a revolution in the way people lived. Scientific agriculture (pursued by gentleman farmers), the enclosure of common lands, and the rise of the machine put some people out of work, drew many to the cities and factory employment under conditions dictated by employers. Working hours were inhuman, especially for children. Slavery – opposed by Pitt when he had time – was important in the British West Indian sugar industry. (Caribbean slave revolts and the ravages of tropical disease among British soldiers were among the reverses abroad that beset Pitt's ministry.) Catholics suffered severe restrictions, as we have seen.

Yet during Lamb's lifetime – by 1834 – Parliament would be reformed, British slavery would be abolished altogether, and Catholics emancipated in line with the most ardent hopes of many of his friends of the 1790s. The currents were strong even in 1789, though often forced to go underground thereafter. And now the French had overthrown despotism with violence. French despotism was proverbial: for the moment Pitt hoped to maintain British neutrality and favoured peace with France.

The intellectuals attracted by the new social and political ideas were, of course, very often writers. By the end of the century Thomas Holcroft had to his credit several novels with social themes. There were other such novels, too didactic and thin for our taste. William Godwin's *Caleb Williams* is one that can still be read. Poets brought up on verse which looked to the models of the Greek and Roman classics, best represented in the work of Alexander Pope and John Dryden, began the quest for the 'natural' virtues extolled by Rousseau, at first mildly, in the classical mode, then exuberantly with Robert Burns and William Blake.

There is much to be said and argued about Romanticism, but to place Lamb among the Romantics, where he stands, we must know that he and his friends

> grew up in an environment of democratic ideas: the natural goodness of man as opposed to the doctrine of original sin, natural rights derived from natural law, the universality of individual freedom and equality, social contract, mixed government in an ideal commonwealth, tolerance for every sect and individual . . . and the greatest good for the greatest number. All these ideas descended into the romantic period from or through the eighteenth-century rational *philosophes*. Fraternity, equality, and associated ideals of the French Revolution derived from a belief in the possession of reason by all men, or . . . the fundamental equality of men, because all are equally capable of reason, and the associated Protestant . . . insistence upon the inalienable right of the individual to free inquiry for the salvation of his soul.[4]

At the risk of oversimplification we may say that in general Romantics resisted the worship of the classics which had too long imposed a straitjacket on the arts. They distrusted the old *rule* of reason while seeking to reinterpret human life from a rational basis tempered by sympathy and emotion, by respect for the mystery of things, for the grandeur and oneness and healing power of nature, for the strange, the aberrant, the remote in time and place. They rejected the old static and mechanistic concepts of life and literature. Should not the whole of life be seen as indivisible unity, they reasoned – ever changing through growth and progress? Man and woman might, through the power of *imagination* applied to personal experience, arrive at truths and capabilities hitherto undreamt of and thereby achieve a moral and rewarding life for everyone – through understanding, education, the abolition of social prejudice and convention. Government by wealth and hereditary privilege, and the accompanying political corruption, must go. If this sounds grandiose in regard to Lamb, whose pleasure it was to fasten on 'particulars' and who loved cities, he falls none the less in this stream. The new men and women were individualists – individualists with social consciences. They were egoists: what happens to *me* has universal significance and is important for the whole of society. Here we *can* see Lamb. His 'egoistic' essays of the 1820s brought him his reputation, yet had the breadth of vision and universality of appeal to survive.

Lamb could not avoid being caught up in the exciting times, though it was his University friends Coleridge and Allen who were in closest touch with the tides of radicalism. These friends had links with young Robert Southey at Oxford, and soon with William Wordsworth, a Cambridge graduate who by 1795 had been to France and knew William Godwin. Godwin (one day, like the others, to be Lamb's friend), with Holcroft and the feminist Mary Wollstonecraft, were public figures who knew Tom Paine, the Englishman whose *Common Sense* had been seminal for the American Revolution.

Lamb was to follow Coleridge, briefly, into the Dissenting sect of Unitarianism – briefly because Lamb's profound religious sense soon detached itself from any institution. By 1796 one of his chief admirations would be for the Unitarian clergyman Joseph Priestley, radical political thinker and discoverer of oxygen. Priestley's close friend was Dr Richard Price, also a Unitarian minister, whose political gifts had earlier brought him close to government. In

November 1789, soon after Bastille Day, Price addressed a meeting of the Society for Commemorating the (1688 'glorious') Revolution (against James II). It was chaired by the radical Lord Stanhope.[5] In the course of Price's long disquisition, which welcomed developments in France, he described the cornerstone of the 1688 reforms as being the right to religious liberty of conscience, the right to resist power when abused, the right to choose, frame, and cashier a government. This sounds like the beginning of modern times and so it was; but tempest and struggle lay ahead. Price's climax was audacious and full of fire:

> Tremble all ye oppressors of the world! Take warning all ye supporters of slavish governments, and slavish hierarchies! . . . You cannot now hold the world in darkness. . . . Restore to mankind their rights; and consent to the correction of abuses before they and you are destroyed together.[6]

The great Whig Edmund Burke, who had sympathized with the American revolt, took note, trembled, and in answer to Price wrote his *Reflections on the Revolution in France* (1790). As a practical politician he felt that France was physically too near England for comfort. He feared the contagion and warned against Price's doctrines.

Burke's eloquent book brought forth many rebuttals, two being Mary Wollstonecraft's *Vindication of the Rights of Men* and Paine's *The Rights of Man*. Mary Wollstonecraft was an attractive woman whose feminism was born of harsh experience in her personal life. Dr Price had been her first friend among clear-thinking radicals, and she rose in his defence to Burke's challenge: 'Security of property!' she wrote, 'Behold . . . the definition of English liberty.'[7] Her reasoning was bold, but Paine's was inspired and spread like wildfire. Paine had been elected to the French Convention by the dominant, relatively moderate Girondin faction; he fled to Paris before sentence of treason was passed upon him in England – only to languish in a French jail with the rise of Robespierre and his Montagnards, escaping the guillotine by a hair. His book was banned in England as seditious libel.

Wollstonecraft went on to write her *Vindication of the Rights of Woman* (1792) – elaboration of an element in her reply to Burke – which won the praise of the American Aaron Burr.[8] It was published by Joseph Johnson, the radical bookseller of St. Paul's

Churchyard who had set Paine's book in type but dared not publish it. His circle of writers and artists, known in the 1790s as the 'Liberty Boys', met for Sunday dinner in Johnson's bachelor quarters over the shop. Among them Wollstonecraft was accorded the dignity due to any self-supporting man. At various times the group included Paine, Priestley, Price, William Blake, Holcroft – and William Godwin. Godwin became the next great enthusiasm of radicals in 1793 with his *Enquiry Concerning Political Justice*, a detailed political philosophy arising from conversations with his friend Holcroft.

An expensive work to buy, *Political Justice* made its impact particularly on University students, though Godwin, a thoughtful little man of serene demeanor with a rather long nose, was not the type of a popular hero. William Wordsworth greeted the book with fervour and is said to have told a young friend to 'throw aside your books of chemistry and read Godwin on Necessity!'[8] Whole groups of readers banded together to buy *Political Justice* and read it aloud.

Political Justice built an ideal society on the already widely held theory that men and women are perfectible. When proper education and economic equality have brought out the native 'benevolence' in all human beings, said Godwin, government would be replaced by temporary, voluntary associations of free men and women doing the right thing almost automatically – for Godwin was a philosophic anarchist, one who did not approve of violence. He saw the power of property – confined to the few – as the reason for political repression. His doctrine of Necessity was not new; Coleridge and Lamb embraced it in Priestley's theology. (But they did not jump on the Godwin bandwagon, for Godwin had declared himself an atheist.) 'Necessity' recognized human progress as inevitable, 'all things, past, present, and to come,' said Godwin, 'forming links in an indissoluble chain'. It was the descendant of Calvinist predestination (as opposed to free will) and ultimately, of course, proved too rigid to detain Romantics for long.

Between Godwin and Mary Wollstonecraft – who had seen France in the Terror of 1794 – there soon began the intense friendship which 'melted into love', as Godwin wrote.

Mary Wollstonecraft speaks from the eighteenth century with the voice of the twentieth:

> I may excite laughter, by dropping a hint, which I mean to pursue, some future time, for I really think that women ought to have representatives, instead of being arbitrarily governed

without having any direct share allowed them in the deliber-
ations of government. (Cameron, 1, 58)

There were other bluestockings among the radicals – women who
lived by their intellect and pens, among them Mary Hays, another
feminist writer, Mrs Barbauld, author of children's books, and Mrs
Inchbald, successful novelist, actress, and playwright. (Lamb called
them the two bald women.) There was also the formidable Hannah
More of the Evangelical Anglicans, educator and writer. Women
were asserting themselves then as now, against much greater odds.

To glance ahead a little, early in 1793 the English political situation
changed with the execution of Louis XVI and the immediate
French declaration of war against Great Britain, Holland, and
Spain, with the consequent tightening – as Robespierre pursued his
Reign of Terror – of British government attitudes against those
suspected of reformist or 'Jacobin'[10] tendencies. Godwin and his
associates were immediately under a cloud. In the general disil-
lusion with France brought on by the Terror, *Political Justice* fell of
its own weight. Godwin revised it, humanizing some of its harsher
statements. Humanity broke through more effectively in the novel
he next wrote – *Caleb Williams*, illustrating particularly his theories
on crime and punishment. It was an immediate success.

Caleb Williams, like *Political Justice*, was probably little read by the
'swinish multitude', an expression Edmund Burke let slip. The
radical multitude preferred Paine. But there were other multitudes.
A Church and King rabble, suspecting Joseph Priestley of
reformism, in 1791 burned down his house, his library, and his
laboratory, and drove him (finally) to the shores of the
Susquehanna in far-off Pennsylvania, a move which had a considerable impact on the life of Coleridge.

While Charles Lamb, with certain exceptions, avoided precise
political reference in his own writing, he was well aware of the
events of his time and was soon to feel at one with Coleridge,
Southey, and Wordsworth in the new understanding of the worth
and dignity of the lowliest human being. The lessons of the
American and French revolutions were for Lamb's generation
deeply moral, and it is the morality informing his irony, his humour,
and his deep seriousness that makes the *Essays of Elia* all of a piece
and gives us the sense of the man behind them. The Lamb so often

called 'apolitical' by later writers was political not only in that he held specific beliefs which are not too difficult to unearth, but in the profoundest sense of the word: he cared how his fellows treated each other, and he chose as his friends those who also cared.

CHAPTER FIVE

Young City Man

Joseph Paice, of Bread-street-hill, merchant, and one of the Directors of the South-Sea company—the same to whom Edwards, the Shakspeare commentator, has addressed a fine sonnet—was the only pattern of consistent gallantry I have met with. He took me under his shelter at an early age, and bestowed some pains upon me. 'Modern Gallantry' (*Elia*, 80)

. . . somehow or other my cousin contrives to wheedle me once in three or four seasons to a watering place. Old attachments cling to her in spite of experience. 'The Old Margate Hoy' (*Elia*, 177)

Such is the SOUTH-SEA HOUSE. *At least, such it was forty years ago, when I knew it,—a magnificent relic!* 'The South-Sea House' (*Elia*, 2)

Released from the confines of Christ's Hospital, Charles lived at home again. He also went to the theatre, a good many times in those years. Sarah Kemble Siddons had taken London by storm in 1782 and was now a permanent star of the Drury Lane; Charles's first published sonnet, a very minor one, was addressed to her. It ends, 'Ev'n so, thou, SIDDONS, meltest my sad heart!' Coleridge had a hand in it too, and printed it as his own in the *Morning Chronicle* of 29 December 1794, later as Lamb's, and again as his own.[1] For a shilling, and a short walk with Jem White, J. M. Gutch, or Mary, Charles could see her when he wished.

Lamb now saw little of Coleridge, though he was still in London: he did not leave Christ's Hospital till 1791. Coleridge was preoccupied with the deaths of a brother and his only sister, with illness of his own, and with a happy London family, the Evanses, who took him to its bosom. With the eldest daughter, Mary, he fell in love. Lamb himself was preoccupied with the necessity of earning a living, borne in upon him daily in the household where Samuel Salt was sometimes ill and beginning to fail. Elizabeth nursed Salt, but worn down by hard work and many childbearings, she also was not well. John Lamb was approaching seventy and growing feeble, and Aunt Hetty no less odd with advancing years. Young John had presumably left home by now for lodgings where, at twenty-six, he could be his own man. Mary, in her late twenties and still without suitors, was deep in dressmaking. A scene of Lamb's from 'Detached Thoughts on Books and Reading' suggests what her life must then have been like. Old books, he says,

> speak of the thousand thumbs, that have turned over their pages with delight!—of the lone sempstress, whom they may have cheered (milliner or harder-working mantua-maker) after her long day's needle-toil, running far into midnight, when she has snatched an hour, ill spared from sleep, to steep her cares, as in some Lethean cup, in spelling out their enchanting contents! (*Elia*, 173)

Salt and his friends had an eye out for Charles's future. Thomas Coventry – the old Bencher who terrified little children with his snuff and snortings – had a kind merchant friend called Joseph Paice, who said to Coventry, 'Let him have the run of my counting-house till something better offers.'[2] So Lamb was soon engaged in the City at 27 Bread Street Hill in learning from Paice's 'precepts and example whatever there is of the man of business (and that is not much) in my composition. It was not his fault I did not profit more.'[3] Now he began his daily trudge eastward – along bustling Fleet Street and up Ludgate Hill to St. Paul's. A few crossings beyond found him at Paice's, in a street off Cheapside.

Joseph Paice was a stroke of luck for Lamb – Paice was a businessman who was also literary. One of his relatives writes that 'his memory was stored, with poetic treasures of the Elizabethan era, for which he manifested even a religious reverence'.[4] He had known Samuel Richardson the novelist. Casual conversations with Mr Paice among the stacks of account-books in the musty offices may first have sent Lamb to look into Shakespeare's playwright contemporaries.

For Lamb continued to read and think about literature. Besides the Latin classics, Milton, the Bible, and Shakespeare, by 1796 (date of his first letter to Coleridge) he had read all the modern poets, especially Robert Burns, Cowper, Bowles the sonneteer, Shenstone, and many others. He was even reading novels, which he later affected to despise, though he had managed to acquire a good knowledge of Defoe's novels, *Tristram Shandy*, *Tom Jones*, and

Richardson's *Pamela*. There is a pleasant recollection of an encounter at about this time:

> I do not remember a more whimsical surprise than having been once detected—by a familiar damsel—reclined at my ease upon the grass, on Primrose Hill . . . , reading—*Pamela*. There was nothing in the book to make a man seriously ashamed at the exposure; but as she seated herself down by me, and seemed determined to read in company, I could have wished it had been—any other book. We read on very sociably for a few pages; and, not finding the author much to her taste, she got up, and—went away. Gentle casuist, I leave it to thee to conjecture, whether the blush (for there was one between us) was the property of the nymph or the swain in this dilemma. From me you shall never get the secret. (*Elia*, 176)

By 1796 he was reading, too, some of the new reviews just then proliferating and publishing young writers. And by 1796 he had become, like Paice, an enthusiast for Beaumont and Fletcher, as well as Massinger and other earlier playwrights. Beyond all these he knew intimately John Bunyan's *Pilgrim's Progress* and Isaak Walton's *Compleat Angler*, the favourites from his youth – and was dipping into theologians.

So the two bookish associates, man and boy, got on well. But Joseph Paice had other virtues. He showed Charles that a man of business could also be an admirable human being. The essay in which Paice appears, 'Modern Gallantry', begins on a note, rare for Elia, of sober earnestness – injustice always stirred him.

> In comparing modern with ancient manners, we are pleased to compliment ourselves upon the point of gallantry; a certain obsequiousness, or deferential respect, which we are supposed to pay to females, as females.
>
> I shall believe that this principle actuates our conduct, when I can forget, that in the nineteenth century of the era from which we date our civility, we are but just beginning to leave off the very frequent practice of whipping females in public, in common with the coarsest male offenders.
>
> I shall believe it to be influential, when I can shut my eyes to the fact, that in England women are still occasionally—hanged.

I shall believe in it, when actresses are no longer subject to be hissed off a stage by gentlemen.

I shall believe in it, when Dorimant hands a fish-wife across the kennel; or assists the apple-woman to pick up her wandering fruit, which some unlucky dray, has just dissipated. . . .

I shall begin to believe that there is some such principle influencing our conduct, when more than one-half of the drudgery and coarse servitude of the world shall cease to be performed by women. . . .

I shall believe it to be something more than a name, when a well-dressed gentleman in a well-dressed company can advert to the topic of *female old age* without exciting, and intending to excite, a sneer:—when the phrases "antiquated virginity," and such a one has "overstood her market," pronounced in good company, shall raise immediate offence in man, or woman, that shall hear them spoken. (*Elia*, 79–80)

How close he is to Wollstonecraft's ironic observation, 'A lively writer, I cannot recollect his name, asks what business women turned of forty have to do in the world?'[5] Lamb does not, like her, reject gallantry altogether – *she* has to keep a firm hold over herself when a man leaps to open a door for her. He is concerned with the worth of the individual and with hypocrisy.

Joseph Paice, he goes on, had learned a lesson from his long-dead fiancée, who had once overheard her lover speak roughly to a woman of no standing and had lectured him severely. He took the lesson to heart:

Though bred a Presbyterian, and brought up a merchant, he was the finest gentleman of his time. He had not *one* system of attention to females in the drawing-room, and *another* in the shop, or at the stall. . . . I have seen him—nay, smile not—tenderly escorting a market-woman, whom he had encountered in a shower, exalting his umbrella over her poor basket of fruit, that it might receive no damage, with as much carefulness as if she had been a Countess. To the reverend form of Female Eld he would yield the wall (though it were to an ancient beggar-woman) with more ceremony than we can afford to show our grandams. (*Elia*, 80–1)

And so Paice helped prepare the way for Charles's instant response to the question of his twenty-first year: 'Is a woman's life worth a

man's?' Lamb ends the essay wishing that more women would stand
up for themselves in the world. If women accept ignominy, that is
what they will get.

In October, 1790, when Charles was fifteen and Mary twenty-
five, they managed to go on holiday together. From London they
took a sailing boat called a *hoy*, which carried them to Margate, the
seaside resort. Again there is an Elia essay, 'The Old Margate Hoy',
to commemorate the occasion. In it Mary becomes his 'cousin' for
literary purposes.

> We have been dull at Worthing one summer, duller at Brighton
> another, dullest at Eastbourn a third, and are at this moment
> doing dreary penance at—Hastings!—and all because we were
> happy many years ago for a brief week at—Margate. That was
> our first sea-side experiment, and many circumstances combined
> to make it the most agreeable holyday of my life. We had neither
> of us seen the sea, and we had never been from home so long
> together in company . . . (*Elia*, 177)

Mary, he says, is the one who favours the sea. The voyage appealed
to their youth and high spirits.

> Can I forget thee, thou old Margate Hoy, with thy weather-
> beaten, sun-burnt captain, and his rough accommodations—ill
> exchanged for the foppery and fresh-water niceness of the modern
> steam-packet. . . . Thy course was natural, not forced, as in a
> hot-bed, nor didst thou go poisoning the breath of ocean with
> sulphureous smoke . . . (*Elia*, 177)

The eager travellers plied the crew with questions about the
mysteries of a sailing vessel, went below for cordials at the invitation
of the steward, and listened to the travel tales of a magnificent liar.

His first trip by water stirred the adolescent Charles, who knew at
least by reputation some of the things that moved the Romantic
hero of Goethe's novel *The Sorrows of Werther* (it had swept Europe
the year before Charles was born). This was the sort of experience
which brought forth sonnets, and Lamb forthwith produced one in
the contemporary vein. At the back of his mind was Coleridge's
dictum that 'In a Sonnet . . . we require a development of some
lonely feeling, by whatever cause it may have been excited; but

those Sonnets appear to me the most exquisite, in which moral Sentiments, Affections, or Feelings, are deduced from, and associated with, the Scenery of Nature.'[6]

In looking at Lamb's early poetry, it is easy to say at once that he is remembered, after all, for his prose. He tried very hard to be a poet, and though much of his verse is less than memorable, it is well to recall that his more successful friends Coleridge, Southey, and Wordsworth also wrote bad poetry, then and later. Southey's verses were so immensely popular that he became Poet Laureate of England in 1813, yet little of his output has stood the test of time. Coleridge was to produce great poetry only briefly; Wordsworth's stature has been confirmed by a considerable body of work that still has power to move us. But before the late 1790s the future was still in doubt. For some years Lamb the poet could be mentioned in the same breath with Coleridge and often was, together with their friend the now forgotten poet Charles Lloyd. The three published together; all were read and talked about. It is to Lamb's credit that he realized in the course of time that poetry was not his *métier*. Had it been, he would surely have transcended his early minor efforts, as did his later friend John Keats. But it was as poet that Lamb first got into print. Reading much poetry, he thought about it as critic. Here his gifts – and the assistance he gave to Coleridge – were impressive.

So after the period covered by this book Lamb gave up trying to be a serious poet, though (with Mary) he later wrote children's verse for money and would now and then drop into rhyme for comic or political or friendly purposes to the end of his life, even publishing more of it than was strictly wise (it is hard to give up an old love).

His poetry can be divided roughly into four categories: the juvenile sonnets; experiment with story ballads and poetic drama; 'blank verse'; and the miscellaneous humorous verse, political epigrams, and 'album verses' for friends. The most interesting group for the biographer are those in blank verse, which contemplate his tragedies and hurts from a deeply serious base. Lamb wrote only two poems that have survived – 'The Old Familiar Faces' and 'Hester'.[7]

The new poetry looked to the past, to the very beginnings of poetry in English, particularly those found in the miscellaneous collection of ballads published by Bishop Thomas Percy in his *Reliques of Ancient English Poetry* (1765),[8] but also to Shakespeare, now being rediscovered. Shakespeare, it was observed, had not written by classical rules, and he had composed many sonnets, the form derived from yet earlier poets in Italy. The sonnet had returned with a vengeance;[9] in the new sonnets sentiment played a part which now seems to us mannered and false. Coleridge wrote his fair share; the young Keats, especially under the influence of Leigh Hunt, found sentiment difficult to shake off even at a later period, but did so triumphantly. As sonnet writer Charles Lamb never progressed beyond it. Yet one of his juvenile sonnets, on 'Innocence', was admired and translated by the great French critic Sainte-Beuve, demonstrating that even great critics find it difficult to predict what in the work of their contemporaries will endure.

The poem arising from Lamb's Margate experience begins with the poet on shipboard ready to laugh *and* weep, somewhat histrionically. Wild-eyed Phantasy is personified – straight out of the classical poetry young bards were now rejecting. The bark is winged, the hour is drear, the poet unbonneted or hatless, as well as wet and 'chilly'; the winds rave, the poet gazes. It does not strike us as original; we have heard it all before – much of it in poetry since Lamb's time, however. The mood is that of Keats in a better poem: 'Now more than ever seems it rich to die.' Despairing and exultant both at once, the poet Lamb is capable of 'enthusiasm'. Seen in the context of the times, it is not a bad start for a sonneteer: Coleridge was delighted with the Margate poem. In general, such efforts prepared the way for the superb sonnets of Wordsworth and Keats; we must exercise a little tolerance for the young writer finding his voice. Here, then, is Lamb's 'Written at Midnight, by the Seaside, After a Voyage':

> O! I could laugh to hear the midnight wind,
> That, rushing on its way with careless sweep,
> Scatters the ocean waves. And I could weep
> Like to a child. For now to my raised mind
> On wings of winds comes wild-eyed Phantasy,
> And her rude visions give severe delight.
> O winged bark! how swift along the night
> Pass'd thy proud keel! nor shall I let go by
> Lightly of that drear hour the memory,
> When wet and chilly on thy deck I stood,
> Unbonnetted, and gazed upon the flood,
> Even till it seemed a pleasant thing to die,—

> To be resolv'd into th' elemental wave,
> Or take my portion with the winds that rave.
>
> (*P,* 4)

The Elia essay 'The Margate Hoy' takes time to evoke other elements in what the sea means to the Romantic traveller (Lamb's poetry in prose):

> He comes to it for the first time—all that he had been reading of it all his life, and *that* the most enthusiastic part of life,—all he has gathered from narratives of wandering seamen; what he has gained from true voyages, and what he cherishes as credulously from romance and poetry. . . . He thinks of the great deep, and of those who go down unto it; of its thousand isles, and of the vast continents it washes; of its receiving the mighty Plata or Orellana, into its bosom, without disturbance . . . ; of Biscay swells . . . of fatal rocks . . . of great whirl-pools, and the water-spout; of sunken ships, and sumless treasures swallowed up in the unrestoring depths: of fishes and quaint monsters . . . of naked savages, and Juan Fernandez; of pearls and shells; of coral beds, and of enchanted isles; of mermaids' grots — . . . (*Elia,* 181)

Seeing it at last, he is disappointed; and he is faced with Margate, resort of *stockbrokers*. He feels hemmed in just looking at the sea – he wants to be on it and away. He would prefer to meet smugglers in a fishing village, go in their boats and help them smuggle; they rob 'nothing but the revenue—an abstraction I never greatly cared about'.[10]

But at fifteen he has enjoyed it all and so has his sister. They returned, after a little week, refreshed and relaxed and full of their adventures.

Whether before or after this experience, a better job for Charles did turn up, at the South Sea House, of which Paice was a director, Salt Deputy Governor, and young John Lamb an increasingly important employee as Deputy Accountant. Charles's may have been a temporary position, but in general the South Sea Company offered permanence, decent pay, a pension, and the sense of participating in large affairs. Many a literary man has been thankful for such a post. 'Forty years' later (in reality nearer thirty) Lamb was able to get considerable fun out of it in 'The South-Sea House', the first essay he wrote for the *London Magazine,* in 1820.

When he came to work there the offices had shrunk considerably for lack of trade and offered a fine source of nostalgia. It was

> —a magnificent relic! What alterations may have been made in it since, I have had no opportunities of verifying. Time, I take for granted, has not freshened it. No wind has resuscitated the face of the sleeping waters. A thicker crust by this time stagnates upon it. The moths; that were then battening upon its obsolete ledgers and day-books, have rested from their depredations, but other light generations have succeeded, making fine fretwork among their single and double entries. Layers of dust have accumulated (a superfœtation of dirt!) upon the old layers, that seldom used to be disturbed, save by some curious finger, now and then, inquisitive to explore the mode of book-keeping in Queen Anne's reign . . . (*Elia*, 2)

The South Sea offices were inhabited, if we are to believe Elia, largely by musical bachelors. These he proceeds to dissect in the manner of the 'Old Benchers' essay, with mocking affection. The names are real ones from real clerks of the time, and Lamb's embroidery is only on the edges. There was even a 'fine rattling, rattleheaded Plumer' there, 'uncle—bachelor uncle, to the fine old whig still living, who has represented the county in so many successive parliaments, and has a fine old mansion near Ware. . . . But, besides his family pretensions, Plumer was an engaging fellow, and sang gloriously.—'[11] Lamb has muddled Plumer's history, intentionally. Figures like these would one day people *The Pickwick Papers* and other works of Charles Dickens,[12] who loved Elia.[13]

Whether because the job was temporary or because of the decline and death of Samuel Salt which took place this year, Charles was again unemployed in February 1792, when there is a record of his receiving £12 15s. 6d. for twenty-three weeks of work – at half a guinea a week. His next position, as clerk with the East India Company, did not begin until 5 April, when he was eighteen. (This appointment he also owed to Paice, through Sir Francis Baring, the Company's chairman.)

It is not clear exactly when, after Salt's death and the relinquishing of his Temple chambers, the family moved to No. 7 Little Queen

Street, Lincoln's Inn Fields, a very short walk from their old
habitation, and a house which they shared for a while with a couple
called Weight, who moved away in 1794. The Lambs were still in
the Temple, however, when an episode occurred which is described
in Le Grice's letter of memoirs[14] to Talfourd:

> After he quitted school he kept up a constant intimacy with his
> contemporaries whose companion he would have been if he had
> remained on the University List, spending his hours of recreation
> and his evenings with them. It was during this intimacy that he
> obtained the Sobriquet of Guy of which he was as familiarly
> known among them in after life, as by his real name: of this I met a
> notable proof within the last few days. A clergyman of the city
> observed to me I have no recollection of Lamb: there was a gent
> called Guy to whom you once introduced me, and with whom I
> was in the habit of interchanging Nods for twenty years, but how
> is it that I never knew Lamb?; If ever I was introduced to Lamb,
> I wonder we never came in contact during my residence at
> Edmonton. Imagine the Gentleman's surprise when I told him
> that he had been nodding to Lamb for thirty years. He obtained
> this Nickname from the following circumstances: In the very
> first years of his clerkship he came one evening, the 5th of
> November,[15] and spent the evening with some of his con-
> temporaries. His hat happened to be of peculiar large brim,
> and his late schoolmates pinned up the sides of it to form a three
> cocked hat: instead of taking out the pins he walked home in it;
> and as he was going down Ludgate Hill in his usual slow pace
> some young men exclaimed Here is the veritable Guy Fawkes in
> propria persona—no man of straw—Guy himself:—they took
> him up in their arms and carried him as far as St. Paul's Yard—
> sat him on a post—gave him three cheers . . . and left him. This
> was the story Lamb told and so seriously that we believed it to be
> true, and he retained the name ever after. His facetious friend
> James White whose humour was the constant theme of his eulogy
> and for recollection to the last days of his existence never
> addressed him by another. (*CLB*, Apr. 1974, 117)

The idea of Guy Fawkes as an underdog – because he failed in his
attempt to blow up the British Parliament and was thereafter
universally despised – rather appealed to Lamb in the days before
widespread terrorism made such figures less amusing. Lamb even

wrote an essay on the theme in 1811, with suitable apologies for his
levity and the hope that the distance in time from Fawkes's day
allowed it. The thought of losing the aristocracy (the Lords) and the
lawmakers (the Commons) in one blow, had Fawkes succeeded, was
interesting to speculate upon. Lamb quite enjoyed his identification
with Guy and did nothing to allay the confusion it caused.

Leigh Hunt is an eyewitness for the impression the young man
now made upon others – probably after the death of his mother in
September 1796 and before Leigh Hunt left school in 1799:

> Lamb I recollect coming to see the boys, with a pensive, brown,
> handsome, and kindly face, and a gait advancing with a motion
> from side to side, between involuntary consciousness and attem-
> pted ease. His brown complexion may have been owing to a visit
> in the country; his air of uneasiness to a great burden of sorrow.
> He dressed with a Quaker-like plainness. I did not know him as
> Lamb: I took him for a Mr. "Guy," having heard somebody
> address him by that appellative, I suppose in jest. (Hunt, 102)

The Quakerlike plainness was the dark suiting encouraged for
lower-echelon employees of the East India Company. Lamb found
it congenial as well as frugal.

CHAPTER SIX

· Ann Simmons

I loved a love once, fairest among women.—'The Old Familiar Faces'

The year 1792 was a crucial one for the Lamb family. Samuel Salt and Mary Field were both desperately ill. It seems likely[1] that soon after he left the South Sea House on 8 February Charles was sent as emissary and consoler to old Mrs Field, dying at Blakesware of breast cancer, while Elizabeth and John, with what help Mary could spare from dressmaking, coped with the illness of the kindly Salt. Charles would not be with his grandmother every moment, though the bond was close: she was often in pain and the Plumer family would have provided her with an attendant. He would have time for pretty, yellow-haired Ann Simmons, by others called Nancy, but to Lamb always Ann, Anna, or (for disguise in the essays) Alice W—n.

We know at any rate that he was in love with her and that he may have known her from the age of fourteen, like the hero of his brief novel published six years later, *Rosamund Gray*. Now he was seventeen and – in the freshness of an English country springtime – ripe for experience. Ann lived with her mother and a sister Maria in a cottage of a group called 'Blenheims' half a mile from the Plumer mansion. The records of her life are fragmentary, but there is a good deal in Lamb's sonnets, letters, and essays, to suggest what the love affair was like if we remember that closely autobiographical writing was characteristic of him from the beginning; the mystifying 'lie' mode came later.

A Tale of Rosamund Gray and Old Blind Margaret (1798) takes place at Widford and is about a girl who lived in just such a cottage as Ann's – with her grandmother. The story is slight indeed, in the manner of Henry Mackenzie, author of *The Man of Feeling* and *Julia de Roubigné*, whose sentimental novels were then exceedingly popular – the kind to be satirized by Jane Austen in *Sense and Sensibility* soon after. The poet Shelley was to be charmed with it and Keats to be lectured on religion by the editor John Scott, using *Rosamund Gray* as an example. Keats, said Scott, 'must surely feel the gentle poetical beauty which is infused into the starlight tale of Rosamund Gray through its vein of "natural piety". What would that tale be without the Grandmother's Bible?'[2]

Rosamund resembles Ann Simmons, the 'mild-eyed maid' of Lamb's sonnet:

> Rosamund Gray was the most beautiful young creature that eyes ever beheld. Her face had the sweetest expression in it—a gentleness—a modesty—a timidity—a certain charm—a grace without a name. . . . Young Allan Clare, when but a boy, sighed for her.

Allan Clare is like Charles, though he is a 'rich young gentleman';[3] and Lamb's hair was black, perhaps with a chestnut tinge.[4]

> There was a fine openness in his countenance—the character of it somewhat resembled Rosamund's—except that more fire and enthusiasm were discernible in Allan's—his eyes were of a darker blue than Rosamund's—his hair was of a chesnut colour—his cheeks ruddy, and tinged with brown. There was a cordial sweetness in Allan's smile, the like to which I never saw in any other face. (*Misc.*, 9–10)

Lamb's own smile (a touch of vanity) is often so described by his friends.

> Allan Clare was just two years elder than Rosamund. He was a boy of fourteen, when he first became acquainted with her—it was soon after she had come to reside with her grandmother at Widford.
>
> He met her by chance one day, carrying a pitcher in her hand, which she had been filling from a neighbouring well—the pitcher was heavy, and she seemed to be bending with its weight.
>
> Allan insisted on carrying it for her—for he thought it a sin, that a delicate young maid, like her, should be so employed, and he stand idle by.
>
> Allan had a propensity to do little kind offices for every body—but at the sight of Rosamund Gray his first fire was kindled—his young mind seemed to have found an object, and his enthusiasm was from that time forth awakened. His visits, from that day, were pretty frequent at the cottage.

He was never happier than when he could get Rosamund to walk out with him. He would make her admire the scenes he admired—fancy the wild flowers he fancied—watch the clouds he was watching—and not unfrequently repeat to her poetry, which he loved, and make her love it. . . . (*Misc.*, 7–8)

They fell in love:

Rosamund was one day reading the tale of "Julia de Roubigné"—a book which young Clare had lent her.

Allan was standing by, looking over her, with one hand thrown round her neck, and a finger of the other pointing to a passage in Julia's third letter.

"Maria! in my hours of visionary indulgence, I have sometimes painted to myself a *husband*—no matter whom—comforting me amidst the distresses, which fortune had laid upon us. I have smiled upon him through my tears; tears, not of anguish, but of tenderness;—our children were playing around us, unconscious of misfortune; we had taught them to be humble, and to be happy; our little shed was reserved to us, and their smiles to cheer it.—I have imagined the luxury of such a scene, and affliction became a part of my dream of happiness."

The girl blushed as she read, and trembled—she had a sort of confused sensation, that Allan was noticing her—yet she durst not lift her eyes from the book, but continued reading, scarce knowing what she read.

Allan guessed the cause of her confusion. Allan trembled too— his colour came and went—his feeling became impetuous—and, flinging both arms round her neck, he kissed his young favourite.

Rosamund was vexed and pleased, soothed and frightened, all in a moment—a fit of tears came to her relief. . . . (*Misc.*, 8–9)

Allan and Rosamund were thenceforth rather shy with each other.

There is a *mysterious character*, heightened indeed by fancy and passion, but not without foundation in reality and observation, which true lovers have ever imputed to the object of their affections. This character Rosamund had now acquired with Allan—something *angelic, perfect, exceeding nature.*

Young Clare dwelt very near to the cottage. He had lost his parents, who were rather wealthy, early in life; and was left to the care of a sister, some ten years older than himself.

Elinor Clare was an excellent young lady—discreet, intelligent, and affectionate. Allan revered her as a parent, while he loved her as his own familiar friend. He told all the little secrets of his heart to her—but there was *one*, which he had hitherto unaccountably concealed from her—namely, the extent of his regard for Rosamund.

Elinor knew of his visits to the cottage, and was no stranger to the persons of Margaret and her grandaughter. . . . (*Misc.*, 9)

Elinor has visions of her dead mother very similar to Mary Lamb's. Allan and Rosamund entertain the grandmother – who is not only blind but ill – by the hour. They love her and are understanding: Rosamund does not argue with her, nor complain when told the same story for the umpteenth time. In the cottage are books that Lamb himself loved – Bunyan, Walton, the poet George Wither, the Bible.

Rosamund had not read many books beside these; or if any, they had been only occasional companions. . . . [Her] mind was pensive and reflective, rather than what passes usually for *clever* or *acute*. From a child she was remarkably shy and thoughtful—this was taken for stupidity and want of feeling; and the child has been sometimes whipt for being a *stubborn thing*, when her little heart was almost bursting with affection. (*Misc.*, 2–3)

The narrator of the story – Allan's close friend – is a Coleridge figure who describes Elinor as 'the kindest of sisters'.[5] There is even a recollection of Lamb's childhood question in the cemetery as to 'where be all the *bad* people buried?'[6] In later chapters the narrator visits Blakesware and its Wilderness, though it is not named.

The first part of *Rosamund Gray* has the delicate quality imparted by its author's almost feminine perception. Unfortunately Lamb was always weak on plot, and the story loses credibility as the young author leaves what he knows and plunges into a rapid denouement: Rosamund's rape by a villain is followed by her death, her grandmother's, and Elinor's. Matravis the villain dies last, in Allan's presence.

In a group of sonnets written mostly in 1795 'Anna' has already assumed the aura of the girl loved and lost. Probably 'madness in the

Lamb family' was a cause; Lamb's youth and poverty, too, hardly recommended him as husband. Possibly, as E. V. Lucas suggests, the alarm was sounded by his ill and anxious grandmother. Or perhaps the trouble had another source, since the real break did not come for two years, until 1794, when Mary had a serious illness of a kind not specified. By 1796 the 'madness' had declared itself to all who knew the Lambs.

The sonnets Charles wrote about Anna were, like his Margate poem, in the manner of W. L. Bowles. He eventually published four of them. They are young (written at nineteen and twenty), sprinkled with 'methoughts' and other archaisms.

The poet has lost his Anna –

> mild-eyed maid!
> Beloved! I were well content to play
> With thy free tresses all a summer's day,
> Losing the time beneath the greenwood shade.
>
> (*P*, 4)

He has

> passed the little cottage which she loved,
> That cottage which did once my all contain;
> It spake of days which ne'er must come again,
> Spake to my heart, and much my heart was moved.
>
> (*P*, 7)

Here is one complete:

> Was it some sweet device of Faery
> That mocked my steps with many a lonely glade,
> And fancied wanderings with a fair-hair'd maid?
> Have these things been? or what rare witchery,
> Impregning with delights the charmed air,
> Enlighted up the semblance of a smile
> In those fine eyes? methought they spake the while
> Soft soothing things, which might enforce despair
> To drop the murdering knife, and let go by
> His foul resolve. And does the lonely glade
> Still court the foot-steps of the fair-hair'd maid?
> Still in her locks the gales of summer sigh?

> While I forlorn do wander reckless where,
> And 'mid my wanderings meet no Anna there
>
> (*P*, 3)

Another shows him walking to Hertfordshire, recalling 'merrier days', 'Kindling afresh the flames of past desire'[7] and, in a rare moment, rejecting the city. It demonstrates that the preoccupation of the young men of his generation with political liberty was also his.

> I turn my back on thy detested walls,
> Proud City! and thy sons I leave behind,
> A sordid, selfish, money-getting kind;
> Brute things, who shut their ears when Freedom calls.
>
> (*P*, 14)

These partake of all the weaknesses we have noted in the Margate poem. If they do not carry us away, they are in the mood of the early chapters of *Rosamund Gray* and reflect, I think, real feeling. They do not suggest to me that Lamb was merely in love with love (though this is a likely element in any first love affair). They are also an exercise in being a poet: when discussing them with Coleridge, Lamb considers their mood, technique, and poetical qualities as one poet to another.

Two other poems of this period (1795–6) are not directly addressed to Anna, but composed in the mood of the troubled lover yearning for the time when life was less complicated. The sonnet 'We were two pretty babes, the youngest she' refers not to Anna but to the poet's Innocence, lost when

> I left the garb and manners of a child
> And my first love for man's society,
> Defiling with the world my virgin heart—
>
> (*P*, 8)[8]

An eleven-line poem called 'Childhood'[9] and unrhymed, looks wistfully back to the time when the poet was happy to roll downhill, 'to pluck gay flowers', then throw them away, and to frolic lightly on a lawn – without a care, is the implication.

I see no reason to doubt that Lamb really was in love with Ann, and that though he later realized she was not *intelligent* enough for him, the trauma at being cut off from her in 1794 went very deep.

He speaks in another love sonnet of his 'care-crazed mind'[10] – and it is hardly far-fetched to assume that he saw in the outcome a portent of his own sexual future.

But rejection, *Rosamund Gray*, and the sonnets still lay in the future. Leaving Widford early in 1792,[11] Lamb had sorrows enough in the partings from Ann and from his dying grandmother, not knowing how soon, if ever, he would see the old lady again. She herself would know her prospects and find it hard to let him go. No doubt he found some relief in the new job at the East India House, begun on 5 April.

Samuel Salt breathed his last on 27 July and Grandmother Field on the thirty-first. Now an uncertain future loomed for the Lamb family.

Until recently, Lamb was thought to have seen no more of Ann Simmons after 1794, or at latest 1795, when Coleridge left London to marry. We can only guess about the preceding two years, when there must have been meetings and possibly letters exchanged. Surely Charles was present at his grandmother's funeral in August 1792, when 'a concourse of all the poor, and some of the gentry, too, of the neighbourhood for many miles round' came 'to show their respect for her memory'.[12] She was buried in the Widford churchyard. During the year and a half which followed, the love affair was still very much alive.

But with the end of 1794 – perhaps by letter and probably because of Simmons family pressures – the frequent meetings with Ann came to an end, and Lamb soon after wrote to Coleridge that when Coleridge left London, 'I found myself cut off at one and the same time from the two most dear to me.'[13] The sonnets of 1795 indicate that Ann was the other loss.

We next hear of her in Charles's sonnet written to Mary during his breakdown at the end of that year, in which he says Mary would often

> lend
> An ear to the desponding, love-sick Lay
> Weeping my sorrows with me . . .
> (M 1, 4)

In time he tried to forget Ann Simmons, with firm statements of purpose. In November 1796, when Coleridge was about to print the

'Anna' sonnets with poems of his own, following upon the tragedy of Elizabeth Lamb's death, Lamb wrote to him:

> And pray admit or reject these fragments, as you like or dislike them, without ceremony. Call 'em Sketches, Fragments, or what you will, but do not entitle any of my *things* Love Sonnets, as I told you to call 'em; 'twill only make me look little in my own eyes; for it is a passion of which I retain *nothing*, 'twas a weakness, concerning which I may say, in the words of Petrarch (whose life is now open before me), 'if it drew me out of some vices, it also prevented the growth of many virtues, filling me with the love of the creature rather than the Creator, which is the death of the soul.' Thank God, the folly has left me for ever; not even a review of my love verses renews one wayward wish in me . . .
>
> (M 1, 60)

In December he says that along with a general burning and renunciation of poetry (because of his mother's death), he 'burned a little journal of my foolish passion which I had a long time kept'.[14] But in January 1798 the flame is still not dead. Two poignant lines from his best-known poem, 'The Old Familiar Faces', run:

> I loved a love once, fairest among women;
> Closed are her doors to me, I must not see her . . .
>
> (P, 23)

He must not see her either because of the original prohibition or because she is now betrothed or married to John Thomas Bartrum or Bartram (a name of Widford farmers). By 1799 she was Mrs Bartram and had moved to London, where her husband was a silversmith who also kept a pawnshop, near Leicester Square. As his business prospered she gave him a son and three daughters, one of whom eventually (1840) married the eminent surgeon Dr William Coulson, who was known to Lamb (but the union occurred after Lamb's death).[15]

Lamb's biographers have paid scant attention to the report of William Hazlitt's grandson, W.C. Hazlitt, that 'Lamb was seen by Hazlitt, subsequent to his Alice becoming Mrs. Bartrum, to wander up and down outside the shop, in the hope of catching a glimpse of the object of his passion.'[16] Hazlitt, we may note, did not *meet* Lamb until 1803, eleven years from the likely flowering of his love in 1792, ten years since its end. There are further fascinating links in the chain, after Ann was married but before Hazlitt knew Lamb. One took place in May, 1799, a month after the elder Lamb's death, when Mary had just joined Charles in a house in Pentonville. Robert Southey, with whom Lamb had been corresponding, wrote to his wife, the former Edith Fricker, on 16 May:

> I went to the India house. Among other things Lamb told me he dined last week twice with his Anna—who is married, and he laughed and said she was a stupid girl. There is something quite unnatural in Lambs levity. If he never loved her why did he publish those sonnets? if he did why talk of it with bravado laughter, or why talk of it at all? My opinions are for the world but my feelings are to myself. I would proclaim the one under the gallows, but shrink from the indulgence of the other in the presence of my nearest friends. This is not generally the case, and therefore the world is so full of amiable people who are rogues. Lamb loves to laugh at every thing—he speaks of every body in a joke except Bishop Taylor. . . . (NL, 190)

Bishop Taylor was Jeremy Taylor, author of *Holy Living* and *Holy Dying*, to which Coleridge had recommended him. But Anna was now Mrs Bartram. Whatever the reason, the remark is in strong contrast to the tender lyricism of *Rosamund Gray*, published only a few months earlier.

Here we must take into consideration Lamb's complex – often contrary – nature. The other face of the sentimental young writer was the cynic who did not temper his language when with male companions, who could mock at people sharply as well as amiably, the man who blurted things out, sometimes harshly, and wanted to laugh in intense situations.

Lamb's later friend P.G. Patmore is illuminating on the contrast. He finds in Lamb a peculiarity he has not seen mentioned in the recollections of other friends. Behind Lamb's real 'pervading sweetness and gentleness', says Patmore, is the intimation that these qualities were 'preserved and persevered in, in spite of opposing and contradictory feelings within, that struggled in vain for mastery'.

> I am sure that the peculiarity I speak of was there. . . . The truth then is, that Lamb was . . . a gentle, amiable, and tender-hearted misanthrope. He hated and despised man with his mind

and judgment, in proportion as (and precisely because) he loved and yearned toward them in his heart; and individually, he loved those best whom everybody else hated, and for the very reasons for which others hated them. (Patmore, 9–10)

Lamb's sensitive antennae were, then, always under a good deal of tension and he tended to take on the colour of the company he was in. As Patmore points out, he did not care for making small talk or indulging in 'conventional cant'. 'He would do anything to gratify his guests but that. He would joke or mystify or pun, or play the buffoon. . . . '

The consequence was, that to those who did not know him, or knowing, did not or could not appreciate him, Lamb often passed for something between an imbecile, a brute, and a buffoon; and the first impression he made on ordinary people was always unfavourable—sometimes to a violent and repulsive degree. (Patmore, 12)

Much later he would have this effect on Carlyle. The various masks were, we may surmise, a form of self-defence against the unknown – an outlet unavailable to Mary, whose suppressions were to exhibit themselves in madness. Charles was luckier.

Southey was not known for his perception, but the incident he records gives rise to a host of questions. Had Lamb run into Mrs Bartram in the street and been invited by both Bartrams twice in one week because they were sorry for all the family tragedies? Or had Southey written 'last week' in mistake for 'last month', meaning April, which might take the invitations back to the period just after John Lamb's death on the thirteenth, when Lamb was moving to a new address in preparation for Mary's joining him and would have had an upset household? (Mary had joined him by 23 April.) But if John Bartram knew of the published novel and amorous sonnets, would he have been eager to invite Lamb? Was he at home when Lamb came? Was Charles's jeering at Ann in retrospect merely sour grapes, a mask for hurt? Or had Ann said or done something Lamb really didn't like?

Southey's anecdote would seem more out of character had we not Lamb's 'Curious Fragments, Extracted from a common-place book which belonged to Robert Burton, the famous Author of the *Anatomy of Melancholy*' – and one of Lamb's passionate favourites among early writers. These he produced as imitations of Burton in 1800 and published in 1802. There are three Fragments, and the third is certainly autobiographical – the description of a beggar's funeral he developed for the essay 'Complaint of the Decay of Beggars'. Fragment 1 concerns a rejected lover, and strikes, I think, very close to the bone, even if we take it as in no sense fact, merely as the real pain Lamb left out of *Rosamund Gray* and the sonnets. Here are two passages:

> My fine Sir is a lover, an *inamorato*, a Pyramus, a Romeo; he walks seven years disconsolate, moping, because he cannot enjoy his miss, *insanus amor* is his melancholy, the man is mad; . . . all this while his Glycera is rude, spiteful, not to be entreated, churlish, spits at him yet exceeding fair, gentle eyes, (which is beauty,) hair lustrous and *smiling*. . . . in conclusion she is wedded to his rival, a boore, a *Corydon*, a rustic, [an ignoramus], yet haughty, fantastic, *opinionatre*. (*Misc.*, 32)

The lover travels to forget her, comes back in seven years to find her

> a widow having children, grown willing, prompt, amorous, shewing no such great dislike to second nuptials, he might have her for the asking, no such thing, his mind is changed, he loathes his former meat, had liever eat ratsbane, aconite, his humour is to die a bachelour. . . . (*Misc.*, 32)

For seven more years he feels this way until he finds himself once again possessed by the image of his sweetheart (now grown old and ugly) as she once was; and 'that which hee thought her to be, in former times, how beautiful! torments him, frets him, follows him, makes him that he wishes to die'.[17]

Certain phrases and echoes in this fragment reflect Lamb's own perturbation of spirit and inability to shake the vision of Ann as he had once known her: 'seven years'; 'the man is mad'; 'exceeding fair, gentle eyes . . . hair lustrous and *smiling*'; 'wedded to his rival'; 'die a bachelour'; 'solitude is but a hell'; and the final statement that the lover 'wishes to die'.

Surely the hurt twenty-five-year-old is here expressing his own torment, trying to rid himself of it in mockery. (And perhaps Ann Simmons *had* proved less than he once thought her.) If Hazlitt's vignette is true, he failed. But his long bondage to Ann was far more, we may conclude, than the calf-love daydream it has sometimes been considered. 'Anna', or 'Alice', glows like a firefly, now here, now there, in Lamb's life and works. In his poem 'Written a Year After the Events' (surrounding his mother's death), he asks the Lord's forgiveness for 'Vain loves and wanderings with a fair-hair'd maid' which kept his 'captive heart steeped in idolatry/ And creature-loves'.[18] When he published 'The Londoner' in a *Morning Post* of 1802 he recalled the 'period in which I had set my affections upon a charming young woman'[19] as the only time he had, like all lovers, preferred country to city.

Most interesting is the fact that among the attested relics of Charles Lamb's library, Reginald L. Hine found a book which according to its spine was a treatise on Savings Banks. Lamb, who often bought secondhand volumes boardless, sometimes inserted them between the covers of other books disembowelled for the purpose. In this case the inside book is called *Love's Lyrics, or Cupid's Carnival*, a collection of poems Hine considered 'erotic' or 'bawdy': 'This may account for the fact that four of the pages have been torn out.'

> Still more curious, and to Elians fascinating, is the fact that the inamorata of these 'effusions' is called Anna. In amongst verses *To a Clergyman not very Exemplary*; *Lines sent to a Lady with an Almanack in a Silver Case*; *On Holding a Glass of exquisite Wine*; *The Standard Value of a Kiss*, there are no fewer than eleven addressed to Anna, the lady-love of J. Scott Byerley. . . . Once again we are left wondering. Upon what London bookstall did Lamb light upon this bargain? Was the poet – he bears a Widford name – known to him? Was Charles drawn to the book out of continuing love and affection for *his* Anna? Its date is 1806, twelve years after his 'disappointed hope,' and eleven years after the sonnets which he wrote with his life's blood and with an aching heart . . . (Hine, 123–4)

'Anticipated Rapture' ran

> O, come my Anna, or I die,
> O come and close my swimming eyes,
> And let my soul's ecstatic sighs
> Love's boiling ardour sink to rest,
> And I expire upon thy breast.
>
> (Hine, 125)

Hine finds 'three passable poems', one 'To Anna on her asking the author, why he did not write oftener.' The two others are underlined in pencil – by Lamb or another owner. One reads:

> *Hodie mihi cras tibi.*
> To-day she's mine,
> To-morrow thine.
> (Hine, 125)

The last verse of the third reads,

> Fairest, do your nature right,
> Yield your soul to Love's delight,
> Come, and in my faithful arms,
> Taste the soft and sweet alarms
> Of mutual love.
> (Hine, 125)

We are hardly to be shocked by these today – rather amused at the Savings Bank subterfuge, protective alike against friend and sister. But Anna again!

There remain his references to her in the Elia essays, where in the 1820s the idyll reappears, softened and mellowed. The hurt – except for a literary wistfulness – is over.

In 'The Old and the New Schoolmaster' the beloved wife at the end is 'Anna'.

In 'Blakesmoor in H---shire' Elia has worshipped the painting of the 'Beauty with the cool blue pastoral drapery, and a lamb – that hung next the great bay window – with the bright yellow H---shire hair, and eye of watchet hue – so like my Alice!'[20]

In 'New Year's Eve': 'Methinks, it is better that I should have pined away seven of my goldenest years, when I was thrall to the fair hair, and fairer eyes, of Alice W—n, than that so passionate a love-adventure should be lost.[21]

In 'A Chapter on Ears', concerning a young woman who sang to a harpsichord:

Why should I hesitate to name Mrs. S—, once the blooming Fanny Weatheral of the Temple—who had power to thrill the soul of Elia, small imp as he was. . . ; and to make him glow, tremble, and blush with a passion, that not faintly indicated the day-spring of that absorbing sentiment, which was afterwards destined to overwhelm and subdue his nature quite, for Alice W—n. (*Elia*, 38)

And in 'Dream-Children', the fantasy of his having married his Alice:

Here Alice put on one of her dear mother's looks, too tender to be called upbraiding. . . . Then I told how for seven long years, in hope sometimes, sometimes in despair, yet persisting ever, I courted the fair Alice W—n; and, as much as children could understand, I explained to them what coyness, and difficulty, and denial meant in maidens—when suddenly, turning to Alice, the soul of the first Alice looked out of her eyes with such a reality of re-presentment, that I became in doubt which of them stood before me, or whose that bright hair was; and while I stood gazing, both the children grew fainter to my view, receding. . . . 'We are not [they seem to say] of Alice, nor of thee, nor are we children at all. The children of Alice call Bartrum father. We are nothing; less than nothing and dreams. We are only what might have been. . .' (*Elia*, 101–3)

The ageing bachelor shakes himself awake to see his cousin Bridget – that is, Mary Lamb – sitting near him as before.

And did Ann Simmons Bartram not read these pieces in the *London Magazine*? When all London was discussing their author it would have been strange if she had not. By now Lamb's heart was elsewhere engaged, but it pleased him always to go back to things.

Sometime in the 1830s, probably after Lamb's death in 1834, Ann Simmons was recalled by Mrs Tween, daughter of Randal Norris of the Temple whose wife had come from Widford:

The last time I went to see Mrs. Bartram, the "fair haired maiden" so frequently alluded to and ever cherished in af- fectionate remembrance . . . she was then a widow residing in Fitzroy Street, Fitzroy Square, with her three daughters before Maria her second daughter was married to Dr. Coulson. (*Life*, 101)[22]

Ann Simmons was of very great concern to Charles, then, from his fourteenth to his thirty-first year – perhaps even beyond. In memory her golden wraith – rather than the living, greying lady of Fitzroy Street – came to represent his lost youth to him, and the happiness he had felt before everything crashed about him. The fair-haired girl of the fields and woodlands around Blakesware would be forever a figure in his imaginative landscape.

CHAPTER SEVEN

Coleridge

I cannot think a thought, I cannot make a criticism on men or books, without an ineffectual turning and reference to him. He was the proof and touchstone of all my cogitations. He was a Grecian . . . at Christ's Hospital, where I was deputy Grecian; and the same subordination and deference to him I have preserved through a life-long acquaintance. Lamb on Coleridge's death, 1834 (*Misc.*, 351)

'An idea starts up in my head,' he explained to Godwin; 'away I follow it thro' thick & thin, Wood & Marsh, Brake and Briar.' E. L. Griggs, Introduction to Coleridge's *Collected Letters* (p. xxxv)

Lamb has too long been thought of as the humble clerk far removed from the currents of world affairs, with which he did not concern himself. In fact he took a substantial interest in politics in so far as they turned upon permanent questions of good and evil, justice and injustice. It would, for example, be hard to outdo for virulence his first known newspaper epigram – that on James Mackintosh.[1] Nor did he mellow politically as long as he engaged in journalism; his sonnet to Matthew Wood of 1820 is equally bitter about George Canning. Such attacks proceed from strong feeling. The strong feeling, proceeding *to* political convictions, began, with Lamb as with everyone, in adolescence, through the strong radical bent of his Christ's Hospital friends, especially those who went on to Cambridge University. The most influential of these was Samuel Taylor Coleridge.

If Charles Lamb was, on the surface, full of contradictions, how much more so was his friend Coleridge, in retrospect the giant of his age, whose very modern perceptions in poetry, criticism, religion, and philosophy continue to stimulate scholars today as they did the young disciples of his later years. 'The class of thinkers has scarcely yet arisen by whom he is to be judged,' wrote John Stuart Mill in 1840.[2]

Author of a handful of superb poems – and many lesser ones – his

84

range of interest was as vast as was his effort to see and understand all things in the world in *relation* to one another. He was also a prolific journalist and commentator on his times, a 'slothful' man (he said) who could walk thirty miles and more in a day and who read and jotted incessantly. He was a plagiarist (but discard the true plagiarisms and the giant remains), a breaker of promises, political apostate, avoider of duties, a prey to pain and nightmare. Yet to William Wordsworth, who knew all this, Coleridge was the most wonderful man he had ever known.

From a child he could express himself brilliantly. Lamb said, 'He would talk from morn to dewy eve, nor cease till far midnight. . . . He had the tact of making the unintelligible seem plain.'[3]

His relations with his family were often difficult, and before he left school his father and five of the siblings he had grown up with had died. Of the survivors he wrote in 1799, 'I have three Brothers/that is to say, relations by Gore—two are Parsons and one is a Colonel—George & the Colonel good men as times go—very good men; but alas! we have neither Tastes or Feelings in common.'[4] A few years later he failed to visit his ageing mother as he had talked of doing; often he did not open letters from home. The ambivalent family feelings saddled him with a constant and exaggerated sense of guilt, which led to foolish deceptions on the one hand, and remorse, confession, and self-abasement on the other. The resultant tangles could be appalling, though he had the capacity to rally and survive. A growing addiction to opium, taken first as laudanum on prescription at school, and easily obtainable, was not the least of what he had to survive.

A sense of humour helped in this – and drew Lamb to him: Coleridge not only made you think, he made you laugh. In hall at Cambridge when the main dish proved somewhat coarse, he answered an inquiry: 'We have veal, Sir, tottering on the verge of beef!'[5] His 'Summer has set in with its usual severity' still strikes a responsive chord in the breast of the tourist in England.

A friend's cousin, Charlotte Poole, thought him (at twenty-three) 'clever, and a very short acquaintance will unfold he is extremely vain of it'.[6] Her cool eyes saw him as 'a young man of brilliant understanding, great eloquence, desperate fortune, democratick principles, and entirely led away by the feelings of the moment'.[7] He made quite a different impression on an admirer, the Reverend Leapidge Smith:

. . . a tall, dark, handsome young man, with long, black, flowing hair; eyes not merely dark, but black, and keenly penetrating; a fine forehead, a deep-toned, harmonious voice; a manner . . . full of life, vivacity, and kindness; dignified in person.[8]

In his latter schoolboy years, happy with the Evans family as he had never been with his own, his more attractive side began to flourish alongside the bumptious, tiresome, and bungling one. He was then a Grecian, enjoying his seniority and finding that he could charm, instruct, and amuse not only his juniors but also enlightened contemporaries. His spirits took on a new buoyancy as he extended his horizons, through lending libraries, through earnest discussions with clergymen casually met, and through the intelligent Mary Evans.

Freed at last from the disciplines of Christ's Hospital, he went up to Jesus College, Cambridge, in October 1791. At Cambridge he found his school friend Middleton a good influence. There too was his old adversary Val Le Grice. Coleridge early won a prize for a Greek Ode – on the slave trade! – though a scholarship for which he competed went to another.

As Charles Lamb went through the ordeals of the Salt and Field deaths and toiled away on his lofty perch at the India House, entering the bolts of cotton, indigo dyes, teas, and spices in large ledgers and hating every minute of it, Coleridge fell into debt and found new stimulus in the republican ideas that were then rife at Cambridge. The Christmas holidays of 1792 he spent happily with the Evans family.

The following spring occurred the University trial of William Frend, Fellow of Jesus, under fire both as radical and blasphemer for his pamphlet *Peace and Union*. Coleridge and the entire undergraduate body were behind Frend.

It was a low time for Cambridge, when much learning was catch-as-catch-can, when mere residence brought degrees to the rich and titled, when professorial absence and student over-drinking were the order of the day. Intellectual students now took heart from Godwin's *Political Justice*. Its concept of Benevolence developed and supplanted the Cambridge philosopher William Paley's smug theory of self-interest as the motivating force in human society: young idealists had at last their champion. Godwin's ideas – deprecating formal marriage and formal government, scornful of such emotions as gratitude – were revolutionary but his method pacific. Human perfectibility would operate inevitably if his principles were heeded. There was no need of an English revolution to bring it about. Godwin's theories encouraged students to think, write, or even – like George Tierney of Peterhouse – to go into Parliament, but kept them from the radical Painite political action which was by 1793 increasingly risky.

Richard Porson of Trinity, now Regius Professor of Greek, mostly resident in London, was one of the many Cambridge men who admired Godwin. Coleridge's Classics prowess brought him into contact with Porson, who published searing satires in defence of William Frend. Porson met Godwin late in 1793 and became his intimate.

Coleridge's friend George Dyer, another Cambridge man with a mission, was a poet, polemicist, biographer, historian, and reformer who was absent-minded to the point of folly and motivated by real benevolence and compassion in generous measure. He too had come to know Godwin, early in 1793.

The Godwin brushfire burned fiercely: an analysis by Ben Ross Schneider, Jr., of Godwin's diary shows that 'between 1787 and 1799, he saw thirty-three known Cambridge men more than 400 times altogether'.[9] It was a small world in those days, and the radicals were generally known to one another, though there was more than one centre. In London there were two principal literary-intellectual circles, that of Johnson, verging on the Painite, though Godwin frequented it, and that of Perry, Porson, Horne Tooke, and others, who also dined regularly together, very often with Holcroft and Godwin.

Coleridge's college room was now the centre for nightly gatherings of young 'Jacobins'. At a time when 'pamphlets swarmed from the press' (said Val Le Grice), 'Coleridge had read them all'; every evening his photographic memory enabled him to 'repeat whole pages verbatim' – 'we had them *viva voce* gloriously'.[10] Tom Middleton of Christ's Hospital was in the group, but, barred from a Fellowship for *his* republicanism, he soon left Cambridge to pursue the unlikely path that made him first Anglican Bishop of Calcutta.

The loss of Middleton had a weakening effect on the unstable Coleridge. It may also have been in 1793 that the first break with Mary Evans came, at her initiative. One thing led to another, and by the autumn of 1793 he had begun to collect experiences rather wildly, attending drinking parties, joining a literary society, 'learning' the violin, and neglecting his studies. Up to his ears in debt, Coleridge panicked. Desperately he dashed to London to buy a ticket in the Irish Lottery – and drew a blank. He was walking in Chancery Lane in deep despair when he happened to encounter a recruiting officer for His Majesty's Fifteenth Light Dragoons. Suddenly he saw a way out. In a moment, one of the few Englishmen who 'had all his life "a violent antipathy to soldiers and horses" '[11] had sold his soul to the British Army, as Silas Tomkyn Comberbache or Comberback (variously spelled). He made an impossible soldier, and by February 1794 he was writing to the Reverend George Coleridge, 'My more than Brother, . . . I have been a fool even to madness. . . . O that without guilt I might ask of my Maker Annihilation!'[12] His Army brother James achieved his release early in April, and back to Cambridge the errant student went, promising reform.[13] His brothers took care of his debts.

He was soon, however, carried away by an enthusiasm – a plan for escape from England's political hopelessness and mounting tyranny (now that the war with France had begun) to the shores of the Susquehanna in America where Joseph Priestley had taken refuge. Here a choice group of young people from England – with their *wives* – would set up a model community based on 'Pantisocracy', which combined the benefits of real democracy (even to the equality of women) and communal ownership.

Bob Allen at Oxford had been one of Coleridge's few confidants in the army adventure, and had in compassion visited him twice and sent him food, money, and consolation. So when in June Coleridge set forth on a walking tour of Wales, he stopped at Oxford to see Allen, and was introduced to Bob's new friend Robert Southey, who was also aglow with democratick zeal. Coleridge, Southey, and their two friends Robert Lovell, a Quaker, and George Burnett, a former student and temporary farmer, had soon hatched the Pantisocracy plan. They would emigrate, buy and clear land for farming, and live a wholesome life based on a few hours of work a day, as Godwin and Adam Smith had shown to be possible for such a group if it were truly efficient. The rest of the time would be spent – by the women too, who would share child-rearing – in cultural activities. The provider of women was to be the entire family called Fricker – a widow, five daughters, and a son – of Bristol, where Southey lived. All were prepared to undertake the journey. Southey was already engaged to Edith, Lovell to Mary. And Coleridge sometime in August became impetuously engaged to the eldest daughter, Sara. By August, too, he had written with Southey a play in blank verse called *The Fall of Robespierre*. With that tyrant dead, France again offered hope for civilization.

The two poets' letters to friends and relatives about their undertaking make enchanting reading. Wrote Southey in August:

> Calmly and firmly—after long deliberation I pronounce—I am going to America. . . . Should the resolution of others fail, Coleridge and I will go together, and either find repose in an Indian wig-wam—or from an Indian tomahawk. . . . By this day twelvemonths the Pantisocratic society . . . will be settled on the banks of the Susquehannah. . . . When Coleridge and I are sawing down a tree we shall discuss metaphysics; criticise poetry when hunting a buffalo, and write sonnets whilst following the plough. (NL 1, 70–2)

But in May 1794, at the height of the French Terror, the war going badly for England and prices soaring, a man called Robert Watt had confessed at the moment of dying that as leader of a Scottish artisan-and-weaver reformist group he had been planning armed revolt in Edinburgh, Dublin, and London. A few crude weapons were found. Pitt had panicked, suspended Habeas Corpus, and began his attack on all such societies.[14] (In 1795, when the poor of England were threatened with famine, he said he would lose his head in six months should he resign – a palpable overstatement of the British case.) By October terrible impetus was given to the Pantisocrats' plan of escape by the trial for high treason of the leadership of the London Corresponding Society, a reform group, but an innocent one,[15] of artisans, small tradesmen, and intellectuals. They sometimes allowed themselves extravagant rhetoric and had been planning a 'Convention' – now a sinister word from the French use of it. Since May, twelve of the society's leaders had been confined to Newgate and the Tower. The penalty was hanging. Among them were Thomas Holcroft, newly famous as author of the successful play *The Road to Ruin*; Thomas Hardy, the Society's shoemaker founder; John Thelwall, its courageous theorist and lecturer; and John Horne Tooke, a polished older radical and philologist. Their brilliant advocate Thomas Erskine (a Cambridge man) outdid himself in their defence, knowing the consequence to free-born Englishmen if they were to die. But at least one of their number laid his rescue to the timely and beautifully reasoned letter to the *Morning Chronicle* – later circulated as a pamphlet – from the personal friend of nearly all the defendants, William Godwin.

The English jury deliberated Hardy's case for three hours – and acquitted. Acquittals for all followed. Some time later Horne Tooke kissed Godwin's hand publicly in a flamboyant expression of gratitude. England might well have done the same.[16] In the near future Thelwall, Godwin, Tooke, and Holcroft would be personally known to Lamb. Lamb certainly knew of Godwin's role and admired it, as did William Wordsworth, who sought Godwin out in London in 1795. It was the kind of thing both never forgot.

Mary Evans now begged Coleridge to give up his Susquehanna scheme for the sake of his friends and his country. He tried to cure one love with another – a Miss Brunton – to no avail. He found it impossible to write to Sara Fricker, whom he did not love. He was 'wretched'.[17]

Then Coleridge returned to Cambridge and took up carpentry.

The money for the American scheme was clearly not going to be found by March, the Pantisocrats' departure date, and Southey now began to think of Wales as the best spot for their plan: his rich aunt, who had raised him, had disinherited him the moment *she* heard of the Susquehanna project.

Lamb had, no doubt, seen something of Coleridge during the latter's London visit of September, over drinks at the Salutation and Cat, a relief for his own troubles. The elder Lamb had received £500 in South-Sea stock from Salt at his death and £10 a year for handling Salt's exchequer annuities; Elizabeth Lamb £200, in part for her care of Salt during an illness. (The two Johns had put up a £500 bond each for Charles as he entered the East India House. Old Peter Peirson was the third guarantor.) By January of 1793 John Lamb the elder had had to petition to retire from the one position that he retained – that of First Waiter in the Temple Hall, 'setting forth that he had been a servant to the House near Forty years, and that he had nearly lost the use of his left hand, and was otherwise very infirm,'[18] according to the official record. (This suggests he had suffered a stroke.) The parents' capital could not have lasted more than a year or so. Charles's first three years at the India House were considered apprenticeship and brought only a £30 gratuity. This threw both earning and nursing heavily on Mary, the humble mantua-maker. Small wonder that by December of 1794 she too was ill under the severe strains she had to undergo. Lamb, therefore, was in no situation to join the Susquehanna scheme, even had he wished to.

Coleridge stayed in Cambridge until the end of the term and returned to London in mid-December, after pulling up his Jesus College stakes more or less for good. Now he and Lamb met nightly at the ale-house, 'drinking egg-hot and smoking Oronooko,'[19] and regretting their lost loves. Coleridge wrote 'On a Discovery Made Too Late' about Mary Evans, and Lamb cogitated his 'Anna' sonnets: there was much to discuss about love and poetry, politics and Pantisocracy, philosophy and religion. Both were seeking a personal and artistic credo and Lamb willingly followed his older friend's lead.

Coleridge needed no more than hint of encouragement to expand upon his own philosophical explorations. He could now discourse to an interested hearer about his most recent enthusiasm – the philosophy of David Hartley, who encompassed within the doctrine of Necessity a whole theory of the development of the human mind through sense impressions and the association of ideas – a 'scientific' framework which allowed for artistic and literary creation and was important to Romantics. Lamb himself was more interested in Joseph Priestley's Unitarianism. Both, while admiring certain of their political ideas, despised Holcroft and Godwin for their religious unbelief.

In poetry Coleridge was still no more than the accomplished amateur, like many literary young men of his day. His true line of work, when he found it, must bring in money for Pantisocracy. He would lecture, or teach, or become a journalist, or preach for the Unitarians. But he had written minor poetry on nearly every subject that touched his life, in a fine medley of styles and moods. Just now he was contributing a series of sonnets to James Perry's *Morning Chronicle* – tributes to Lafayette, Priestley, Koskiusko, the radical Lord Stanhope – and William Godwin, while Burke and Pitt came in for searing scorn. The series included the Lamb–Coleridge sonnet to Siddons and one to Richard Brinsley Sheridan.

The new political poet inevitably attracted his new editor's attention, and on 16 December Perry invited Coleridge to dinner – with Thomas Holcroft, who 'absolutely infests you with *Atheism*'[20] and was shockingly contemptuous of Bowles. Nor did Holcroft approve of the Pantisocracy proposal. One can hear Coleridge recounting the scene to Lamb (as he wrote it to Southey), in the firelight of the smoky-drinky Salutation and Cat:

> I had the honour of *working* H. a little—and by my great *coolness* and command of impressive Language certainly *did him over*. . . . Sir! (said he) I never knew so much real wisdom—& so much rank Error met in one mind before! Which (answered I) means, I suppose—that in some things, Sir! I agree with you and in others I do not.— (Griggs 1, 138-9)

He invokes the Cambridge Classics Professor. 'Compare him with Porson!,' Coleridge exclaims. 'My God! to hear Porson *crush* Godwin, Holcroft &c.—They absolutely tremble before him!'[21]

Holcroft was forty-nine and fresh from prison; the brash undergraduate was just twenty-two. Nevertheless, Holcroft had invited Coleridge to meet Godwin the following Sunday. On that occasion Porson was present too. Coleridge began to swim with the radical tide.

Coleridge was also writing poetical tributes of a private nature, including one to Charles Lamb. In talking of Lamb to Southey, Coleridge commends him as ' a man of uncommon Genius—Have you seen his divine Sonnet of—O! I could *laugh* to hear the winter winds & c?'[22]–the Margate sonnet. Lamb lost some companionable evenings in December nursing Mary. Coleridge told Southey,

> His Sister has lately been very unwell—confined to her Bed dangerously—She is all his Comfort—he her's . They dote on each other. Her mind is elegantly stored—her Heart feeling—Her illness preyed a good deal on his Spirits—though he bore it with an apparent equanimity, as beseemed him who like me is a Unitarian Christian and an Advocate for the Automatism of Man.—(Griggs 1, 147)

By which he meant that Lamb was a Necessarian. Coleridge enclosed (still to Southey) some 'careless lines which flowed from my Pen extemporaneously', labelled 'To C. Lamb', thirty-three rather laboured lines in which he visualizes Lamb creeping 'round a dear-lov'd Sister's Bed/With noiseless step . . . ' He recalls his own sister, now dead, but 'Cheerily, dear Charles!/Thou thy best Friend shalt cherish many a year . . . ' He praises Mary's 'Soul affectionate yet wise' and her 'polish'd wit', and ends on a religious note.[23]

Mary got better; the two men discussed the nature of poetry far into the night, recalling Boyer's dismissal of the sort of lines Britain's current Poet Laureate, Henry Pye, was capable of committing:

> When genial Zephyr's balmy wing
> Fans with soft plume the flowery vale . . .[24]

meaning 'When the wind blows in the valley', as Boyer would have pointed out. In strong and welcome contrast was the freshness of Bowles's quiet melancholy – 'There is strange music in the stirring wind'[25] – though his sonnets seem faded today. Besides writing a sonnet, 'My heart has thanked thee, Bowles!', Coleridge had made forty copies by hand (or so he said) of his idol's 1789 volume and could not wait to meet Bowles in person.

Lamb and Coleridge talked, too, of other poets – Spenser, Shakespeare, Milton, Lamb's own idol Robert Burns, and the 'divine chitchat' of Cowper (in Coleridge's famous expression). Then Coleridge would recommend authors from his own vast reading, many of them writers of the seventeenth century like Taylor, Wither, Browne, Burton.[26] Both poets in these evenings were sharpening their critical skills. [27] Lamb was to refer again and again in his letters to the time 'when you were repeating one of Bowles's sweet sonnets in your sweet manner, while we two were indulging sympathy, a solitary luxury, by the fireside at the Salutation. . . . I [have] no higher ideas of heaven.'[28]

They were not always alone. Sometimes Favell or Sam Le Grice or Jem White or J. M. Gutch, the Christ's Hospital cronies, were present, and sometimes others, drawn by Coleridge's eloquence. Said William Hazlitt:

> His genius at that time had angelic wings and fed on manna. He talked on forever; and you wished him to talk on for ever. His thoughts did not seem to come with labour and effort; but as if borne on the gusts of genius. . . . His voice rolled on the ear like the pealing organ, and its sound alone was the music of thought. . . .[29]

Though Charles was then 'far from being in a composed or natural state',[30] as Coleridge later recalled, he could hardly fail to be uplifted by his friend's ecstatic talk of a world so much broader than his own, in which so many things were possible, and take heart from it. And if Lamb benefited, so did Coleridge. From Lamb Coleridge got valuable criticism of his own poetry, which was to continue in correspondence.

The long arm of Duty finally reached to London and put an end to the enchanted evenings. Coleridge had tarried too long incommunicado. As Robert Southey wrote years later:

> C. did not come back to Bristol till January 1795, nor would he I believe have come back at all, if I had not gone to London to look for him. For having got there from Cambridge at the beginning of winter, there he remained, without writing to Miss F. or to me, till we actually apprehended that his friends had placed him somewhere in confinement. At last I wrote to Favell. . . . (NL II, 447)

Arrived in London in January, Southey had some difficulty locating Coleridge. He looked in the Salutation and Cat – 'a most foul stye' – before discovering that his friend on a Sunday 'was gone with Lamb to the Unitarian chapel'.[31] In the end he persuaded Coleridge to return to Bristol with him to meet his future. Could Southey have foreseen what that future would be he might have been less importunate. On his arrival at Bristol, Sara told her errant lover that she had in his absence rejected two suitors, one a man of fortune, for his sake.

Coleridge's fate was sealed, and he took, in time, the required course.

The Times: Church, State and the Young Radicals

In noting that 'Coleridge was gone with Lamb to the Unitarian chapel', Southey pointed to another area in which Lamb and Coleridge then saw eye to eye. The child Charles may have been somewhat familiar with Unitarian chapels through Aunt Hetty, but for Lamb at nineteen, as for Coleridge at twenty-two, Unitarianism was a matter of conscious choice.[1]

The Established Church in which Lamb had been brought up was, like the government of which it was an integral part, now in need of reform. While Edmund Burke, the Pitts, Fox, and the Lord Mayor of London and his Council had opposed the war against the American colonies, all too many of the Anglican clergy had supported it – and young Radicals had readily identified with American aspirations.

The Church had become careless of its moral role and so lax in organization that by 1813, it is said, half its 10,800 benefices were without a resident clergyman.[2] Underpaid curates carried the local load, and often for more than one parish, their Sunday duties sometimes requiring them to dash through a service with unseemly haste. Lamb's contemporary, Richard Watson, Bishop of Llandaff, was not only an absentee Professor of Cambridge but rector of sixteen parishes; he seldom visited his see of Llandaff in Wales. He lived most of his life comfortably with his family by the English Lakes.

Religion was all too often seen not as a spiritual calling but as an alternative for younger sons to the Army, the Navy, or the Law. Gibbon the historian comments on 'the fat slumbers of the Church' in his *Autobiography*, and a later historian, G.M. Trevelyan, points out that a clerical living was regarded as ' "a piece of patronage" awarded as a favour and enjoyed as a privilege'.[3] But (says Trevelyan), 'half the livings of England were not so endowed as to support a squire's son'.[4] The disparity in income among local clergy was acute. Bishops earned many thousands of pounds a year, and clergymen in good livings might keep a pack of hounds for foxhunting and drink as hard as the county families from which they came, their piety a thin veneer. Of course there were decent, hard-working bishops and clerics too. The witty Reverend Sydney Smith would have been a bishop had he not preferred to press for Catholic Emancipation and other reforms. As it was, none of his teacups matched and for most of his career he was financially pinched.

The Evangelicals were sincere reformers within the Church, but these were not to Lamb's taste either. An informal and distinguished group of them were known as the Clapham Sect from the part of London where some of their leaders lived. The most eminent was William Wilberforce, who pressed the anti-slavery cause in Parliament. Hannah More cared about Sunday Schools for the education of poor children. Lamb had little good to say of Wilberforce and More,[5] who were blind to the wage-slavery of the English worker, supported the Combination Acts which prevented the formation of trade unions, and attempted to lecture the English working class into submission to autocratic employers.

Among Dissenters Lamb found the Unitarians and Quakers most sympathetic, as we have seen. At Cambridge Unitarianism was strong among undergraduates; Coleridge had been converted to it by William Frend. Derived from Faustus Socinus in the sixteenth century, it was undergoing a kind of rebirth among those intellectual rebels who were not prepared to become atheists or agnostics. Socinus had rejected the doctrine of the Trinity, the divinity of Jesus, and the use of formal creeds. The questioning attitude which quickened scientific advance had led many to embrace a religious belief which also questioned, and which claimed to base itself on reason rather than blind faith. The exiled Unitarian Joseph Priestley, barred for religious reasons from ever teaching at Oxford or Cambridge, already enjoyed an international reputation outstripping most of his English contemporaries. Lamb and Coleridge understood his persecuted brilliance, valued his sympathy for the underdog, and took his religious and political teaching to their hearts. For the time being Priestley became Lamb's idol. He read everything of Priestley's he could get hold of.

Coleridge's immediate destiny after Southey retrieved him was shared lodgings in Bristol with Southey and George Burnett, a bright young man with little self-discipline who had been one of the original Pantisocrats – he would soon be known to Lamb. Their goal had to be the making of money, and soon Coleridge and Southey were making a little by giving political and historical lectures. These were of a flaming radicalism, both lecturers eulogizing Tom Paine as they went, quite oblivious to the risks they ran. William Wordsworth had been duly cautious in suppressing his 'letter to the Bishop of Llandaff' a year earlier. He had suggested among other things that the government might have had a hand in inciting the riots against Priestley. But Coleridge thought nothing of calling the Prime Minister publicly a 'calumniated Judas Iscariot'[6] for not recognizing in the French war the libertarian principles he had supported when the Americans went to war in their defence. Coleridge published two of his lectures in 1795 as *Conciones ad Populum* (Addresses to the People), and Lamb found them 'not unfrequently sublime'.

The popular Jacobin of the hustings was still John Thelwall, no irresponsible demagogue but a level-headed member of the London Correspondence Society, soon personally known to Coleridge:

> On Hardy's [1794] arrest, he immediately rallied the society. When spies attended his lectures, he turned the tables by lecturing on the spy system; when an attempt was made to provoke riot, he led the audience quietly out of the hall. He modified intemperate resolutions and was watchful for provocations. His command over crowds was great, and when at the final demonstration against the Two Acts the cry went up of 'Soldiers, Soldiers!' he is said to have turned a wave of panic into a wave of solidarity, by preaching the society's doctrine of fraternisation with the troops. (Thompson, 158)

The Two Acts were those of December, 1795, known as the Treasonable Practices and the Seditious Assemblies Acts.

> By the first of these it became a treasonable offence to incite the people by speech or writing to hatred or contempt of King, Constitution or Government. By the second no meetings of over fifty persons could be held without notifying a magistrate, who had wide powers to stop speeches, arrest speakers, and disperse the meetings. Yet one more capital offence was added to the statute book – defiance of the magistrate's orders was punishable by death. A special clause, aimed particularly at Thelwall,

enabled reformers' lecture-rooms to be closed as 'disorderly houses'. (Thompson, 145)

Thelwall did not hesitate to speak at two enormous meetings held by his Society in protest before the bills became law. (William Frend was another speaker.) Gillray the cartoonest caricatured Thelwall with arm upraised, catching his wiry energy, his dark hair and jowls, his smouldering eye, to make him the 'dangerous' man he was not, though there was a perhaps legitimate fear, expressed by Burke, that things might get out of hand. Between the two protest meetings, each around 100,000 strong by a conservative estimate,[7] the King was jeered in the streets and a few stones thrown at his carriage; a rabble wrecked the royal mews.

The French had now overrun Belgium and Holland and were looking toward Germany and the Austrian Empire. There was growing dissension among Britain's Continental allies. By 1797 Napoleon would establish the Lombard Republic in Italy; by 1798 the French would hold Rome; by 1799 the French Consulate would govern France with Bonaparte as First Consul. British prowess was exercised mainly on the seas, but already the Mediterranean was threatened and the invasion of England an ever-present nightmare. Pitt's government intensified its campaign against the 'Jacobins' at home.

It is extraordinary that Coleridge and Southey escaped prosecution. Luckily they belonged to no organizations but were strictly self-propelled. And such was the receptivity of the Radical–Dissenter population of the newly industrialized Midlands that Coleridge had no difficulty in signing up a thousand subscribers for his literary–political periodical *The Watchman* in 1796 – an ample send-off for his day.

CHAPTER EIGHT

Difficulties

You came to Town, & I saw you at a time when your heart was yet bleeding with recent wounds. Like yourself, I was sore galled with disappointed Hope. . . . When I read in your little volume . . . I think I hear you again. I image to myself the little smoky room at the Salutation & Cat, where we have sat together thro' the winter nights, beguiling the cares of life with Poesy. When you left London I felt a dismal void in my heart, I found myself cut off at one & the same time from two most dear to me . . . Lamb to Coleridge, Thursday, 9 June 1796 (M, 1, 18)

Bereft as he was of both Ann and Coleridge, Lamb now endured one of the dreariest periods of his life – dreary because of the inconsequence of everything, the absence of nearly everything which had given his existence point.

Robert Southey had paid the Lambs one visit when he came to London in pursuit of Coleridge. He found the family 'evidently in uncomfortable circumstances. The father and mother were both living; and I have some dim recollection of the latter's invalid appearance. The father's senses had failed him before that time.' Elizabeth was only in her fifties, John about seventy. Charles showed Southey his father's poems, among them 'The Sparrow's Wedding'. 'This,' said Southey, 'was the author's favourite; he liked, in his dotage, to hear Charles read it.'[1] He also liked Charles to play cribbage with him, a good deal of it.

Lamb's painful year of 1795 is otherwise little documented, but it seems to have brought an intensifying of the drudgery at the East India House, and with it, in April, the very limited glory of being at last paid for his work. For each of the three years of his employment he had had at most a £10 annual 'gratuity' – say some £100 or $225 in purchasing power today. The twenty-year-old was required to petition for the gratuity and then for the privilege of earning a salary, which for his fourth year would amount to £40 (£400 or $900 today). From his fifth year he would earn £70 (£700 or $1575), still a pittance.

Sales of indigo by the East India Company multiplied fivefold between 1792 and 1795, but no additional staff was taken on by the Accountant's Office to cope with the heavy load. This is known to have affected the health of one of Lamb's colleagues, who was obliged to retire at forty. Before Lamb's first year of paid work ended, some of the clerks petitioned the Company for a substantial increase in pay,[2] the risk of this measure being an indication of how desperate the petitioners were. They might all have been let go, as had happened in certain well-known cases. As it was, the Company chose to heed them – but not until Lamb himself had spent six weeks in a madhouse. He was, in the course of 1795, having to do many hours of overtime work, and without dinner; he could not afford to pay for a meal away from home.

The building in which he laboured (normally from ten to four) stood at the Aldgate end of Leadenhall Street, in the City. Four stories high, it had a portico

formed of six Ionic fluted columns, supporting a triangular pediment adorned with emblematic devices representing the commerce of the East, protected by an ungainly, unwarlike figure of George III. The main entrance led into a central corridor which ran through the building; doorways on the right opened into the Proprietors' General Court Room, which was large, lofty, and oblong in shape, and into the Directors' Court Room, which was dominated by an enormous horse-shoe table round which the Directors met; on the left of the corridor were situated the Sale Room and various committee rooms; in the rear there were more committee rooms and several offices, whose business was connected with the yards and warehouses. Most of the offices, including the important department of the Examiner of Indian Correspondence, were on the upper floors. This part of the building was gloomy and dingy, intersected with long corridors and dark staircases. Charles Lamb, who served for thirty-three years (1792–1825) as a clerk in the Accountant's Department, wrote of 'the labyrinthine passages and light-excluding pent-up offices, where candles for one half of the year supplied the place of the sun's light'.[3]

The Accountant General was one William Richardson, and at the time of Lamb's arrival nearly all his fellow clerks were twice or three times his own age. Some thirty clerks toiled at various tasks within a huge room divided by seven-foot partitions into 'compounds' of six clerks – three facing three across enormously high, sloping desks before which the toilers sat on high backless stools. (A compound is a 'collection of simples' in Lamb's famous jest.) Within the compounds, and surrounding the clerks, were high metal railings, the doors to which could be locked overnight, or whenever the desks were vacant or workers exceptionally busy. Two inkwells, for black ink and red ink (clerk's blood, said Lamb), and a supply of goosequills (Lamb once supplied Coleridge with a large shipment of such pens gratis) were the tools of the trade. A reference book, *Tables of Interest*, still exists in which Lamb has written that this was a volume of 'great interest',[4] which did not much engage his sympathy. Fat ledgers contained what Lamb called his 'true works' – the endless jottings and tottings required by the vast commercial establishment the East India Company then was.

At one end of the room in winter was a great fire, not awfully effective at a distance, before which Lamb used to warm himself periodically. (He thought catarrh or other throat-and-chest ailments might well shorten his days.) 'This dead, everlasting dead desk—how it weighs the spirit of a gentleman down,' he would write, and 'I sit like Philomel all day (but not singing) with my breast against this thorn of a Desk'[5] – sentiments he repeated many times.

In the early days Lamb's tasks, like those of all clerks before the computer, involved considerable routine and repetition – and he never shook loose from all of it into a really interesting post. As the great East Indiamen came in, there would be heavy work indeed. At other periods he was able to write his friends quite comfortably in office time. The goods from the East would be brought by wagon to the dozen or so warehouses at the back of the building. All along the way accounts had to be kept – then audited – for cartage, wages and pensions, rental of warehouse space, price sold for at auction in the Sale Room – the business of Lamb's true works. Most were destroyed in 1858 with the demise of the Company, but six have been found. One of Lamb's duties, against such items as

Amount of sundry boat and sloopshire[6] to carry off 300 chests treasure to His Majesty's ship Thalia, with extra men and guard, searcher's fees and labour employed securing and shipping the same, was the writing – or initialling, for two clerks checked each item – of

> Right added
> Accots Office [and the date],

or

> This Bill is wrong added £1—should be £37 14s. 2d.,

or

> Right added, and Commission right cast.[7]

He made mistakes, and had to erase, as a colleague called Ogilvie has reported and as these accounts prove. Later Lamb did other work, such as attending the noisy tea sales and making notes on the transactions – one of the few tasks which took him from his perch. In the course of his service he had a good deal of contact with agents of various kinds, with merchants, and with sea captains who were allowed to trade on their own account. The compounds were open to the public for the answering of questions and other business.

It is worth a moment's consideration as to how the imaginative literary young man would have felt on beginning this line of work. Accounts of any kind demand constant concentration, accuracy, care, and tidiness: one must be alert every minute. All around one are apt to be people who are good at the work. Those who are not become rapidly bored and inclined to dream – a fatal indulgence even for a minor accountant. If the novice clerk conquers the tendency to dream, he still is not quick, and he will fix on, and put down, wrong numbers and have to rub them out – Lamb with his little finger, we are told. He learns to recheck himself constantly: this does not increase his speed. His whole working life at the start is a struggle to meet the standards of those really gifted for figures. Life did not offer young Charles Lamb any practical alternatives. At the end of his India House service he used to say that the fear of having made an error brought him nightmares.

There were opportunities for advancement, mostly through special work such as that of auctioneer, bringing with it extra profit or pay. Lamb's stammer precluded such an active role. He never advanced except through longevity, and was repeatedly overtaken and outrun by his juniors.

He felt himself a fish out of water, and told Coleridge, 'Not a soul loves [the poet] Bowles here; scarce one has heard of Burns; few but laugh at me for reading my Testament—they talk a language I understand not; I conceal sentiments that would be a puzzle to them.'[8]

The wear and tear of a job for which Charles Lamb was so ill fitted has been underestimated as a factor in his nervous ailments, his drinking, and his occasional very odd behaviour. And yet he did keep his job, with few absences, for thirty-three years. He was known for his honesty, his good nature, his regularity, and he rose to a substantial salary and pension through these qualities; this was his triumph. But at a price. He hated the Appearance Book in which, at the end of his service, employees were required to sign themselves in and out. He hated anyone who appeared to be running an office – even years later when he and John Keats (similarly prejudiced) made outrageous fun of Wordsworth's superior at the Stamp Office, an uninvited guest at a small party. He hated routine, he hated bureaucracy, and yet these provided more independence than the literary hack enjoyed at the hands of the bookseller/publisher – as he had the wit to recognize. He even missed the thralldom when he escaped it well before his death, with a liberal pension. By then he had made good friends at East India House, all younger than himself. There is an incomparable picture of Lamb at work only a few years later, when he had really settled down to the task. It is by Thomas De Quincey, then a callow undergraduate in love with the poetry of Coleridge and Wordsworth. Someone had given him a letter of introduction to Lamb, whom he knew to be a friend of Coleridge:

It was either late in 1804 or early in 1805 . . . that I had obtained from a literary friend a letter of introduction to Mr. Lamb [who was then twenty-nine] . . . I went, therefore, to the India House; made inquiries amongst the servants; and, after some trouble, (for *that* was early in his Leadenhall Street career, and possibly he was not much known,) I was shown into a small room, or else a small section of a large one . . . in which was a very lofty writing-desk, separated by a still higher railing from that part of the floor on which . . . the laity . . . were allowed to approach the *clerus*, or clerkly rulers of the room. Within the railing sat, to the best of my remembrance, six quill-driving gentlemen; . . . they were all too profoundly immersed in their oriental studies to have any sense of my presence. . . . I walked, therefore, into one of the two open doorways of the railing, and stood closely by the high stool of him who occupied the first place within the little aisle. I touched his arm . . . and, presenting my letter, asked if that gentleman (pointing to the address) were really a citizen of the present room; for I had been repeatedly misled . . . into wrong rooms. The gentleman smiled; it was a smile not to be forgotten. This was Lamb. . . . The seat upon which he sat, was a very high one . . . absurdly high . . . he began to dismount instantly; and, as it happened that the very first *round* of his descent obliged him to turn his back upon me as if for a sudden purpose of flight, he had an excuse for laughing; which he did heartily—saying . . . that I must not judge from first appearances; . . . that he was not going to fly; and other facetiae, which challenged a general laugh from the clerical brotherhood.

De Quincey greeted Lamb.

Lamb took my hand; did not absolutely reject it: but rather repelled my advance by his manner. This, however, long afterwards I found, was only a habit derived from his too great sensitiveness to . . . people's feelings, which run through a gamut so infinite of degrees and modes as to make it unsafe for any man who respects himself, to be too hasty in his allowances of familiarity. Lamb had, as he was entitled to have, a high self-respect; and me he probably suspected (as a young Oxonian) of some aristocratic tendencies. The letter of introduction . . . was speedily run through; and I instantly received an invitation to spend the evening with him. . . . He was, with his limited income . . . positively the most hospitable man I have known in this world. . . . (*Lit. Rem.* I, 67–70)

It was a happier Lamb that De Quincey met. A decade earlier, bereft of friend and sweetheart, galled by his daily lot, and with small comfort at home, Charles needed diversion and found a little – very occasionally with Valentine Le Grice, down from Cambridge, but more often with the second-class brains of James White, whom he thought a very amusing fellow, and John Matthew Gutch,

Christ's Hospitallers. These two, like himself, had not gone on to the University but remained in London, White in the Treasurer's office of his old school.[9] Gutch was preparing to set up as a law stationer. He later recalled that

> We were at this time in the habit of meeting at the *Feather*, in Hand Court, Holborn, to drink nips of Burton ale, as they were called. One of our friends, who was particularly fond of the beverage, was called "Nipperkin."
> White was a remarkably open-hearted, joyous companion; very intimate with the Lamb family . . . (WCH, 156)

White, who came from Worcestershire, was Lamb's exact contemporary, Gutch a year younger. Lamb and White shared a common love of Shakespeare. A pleasure of White's was, with Lamb's help, to hold annual dinners for young chimney sweeps, subject of Lamb's Elia essay 'The Praise of Chimney-Sweepers', written just after White's death in 1820. 'He carried away with him half the fun of the world when he died—of my world at least.'[10] Lamb addressed White as Jem and Jem called Lamb Guy. Jem was very much the extrovert and very kind; at Peter Peirson's death he assumed that worthy's £500 bond for Lamb, required by the East India Company. A letter from Val Le Grice[11] tells how eighteen months before Lamb's death he

> dined with Lamb at Johnny Gilpin's at Edmunton, tete-a-tete by appointment June 13th 1833, and he talked of nothing but Jemmy White. Oh! there was none like him! We shall never see his like on such days again— . . . (*CLB*, Apr. 1974, 117)

Le Grice refers to Lamb's footnote on an encounter between White and one of Lamb's favourite actors, James William Dodd, in the essay 'On Some of the Old Actors'. The same essay gives a touching picture of Dodd, whom Lamb himself met shortly before the actor's death in 1796, as both walked in the lovely gardens of Gray's Inn. Lamb did not at first recognize him:

> But could this sad thoughtful countenance be the same vacant face of folly which I had hailed so often under circumstances of gaiety; which I had never seen without a smile . . . ? Was this the

face—full of thought and carefulness—that had so often divested
itself at will of every trace of either to give me diversion, to clear
my cloudy face for two or three hours at least of its furrows?
(*Elia*, 137)

For in his dull life he could still have the theatre for a shilling in the
top gallery, and went often with White, Gutch, and one or two
others. White and Lamb sometimes worked in White's rooms[12] on
the *Original Letters, &c. of Sir John Falstaff and His Friends; Now First
Made Public by a Gentleman, a Descendant of Dame Quickly, from Genuine
Manuscripts which have been in the possession of the Quickly Family near
Four Hundred Years*, in which Lamb is thought merely to have
assisted White, but which gave him his first taste of imitation as an
amusing form of literary activity. Though he never claimed a part in
the published book, he may have written a section of its preface, in
which a short passage suggests his later 'Roast Pig' essay. It was
published in 1796. He maintained a proprietary interest in it ever
after, and pressed it on the attention of his friends.[13] (White's
fondness for 'playing' Falstaff constantly in these years must have
been somewhat tedious for his companions.)

Charles also saw Mrs Siddons as Lady Randolph in *Douglas*, by
John Home, perhaps the most popular of the tragedies modelled on
Shakespeare which were all too common in the drama of Lamb's
day.

Douglas was a Scottish tragedy much played since its debut in
1757, the young 'Norval' was its ill-starred hero, his mother the
good Lady Randolph. It was built on the customary
misunderstandings among good people and the villainy of one
Glenalvon; the Scottish setting gave it a fine, wild, poetic quality to
appeal to the admirer of Burns and Gray. Lamb a little later wrote a
poem on the *Douglas* theme, and in sending it to Coleridge for a joint
publication of 1797 remarked on 'so exquisite a pleasure as I have
often received at the performance of the tragedy of Douglas, when
Mrs Siddons has been the Lady Randolp[h]'.[14] The play made a
strong impression on him.

In London around this time was Bob Allen, but for all Bob's
kindness to soldier Coleridge, he was not a great resource for the
lonely East India clerk. Bob had now married a widow (with
children) about whom Southey was unenthusiastic. He reported her

in 1796 as consumptive, and she soon died. Allen and Southey, in the wake of the French excesses, were now so disillusioned that Southey wrote (also in 1796), 'Allen agrees with me that Man is a Beast. He verges toward misanthropy and says that a year's crusade to benefit mankind will cure any man of his prejudices in their favour. So say I, for I have been a Crusader. . . .'[15] This was rather a common development in the thinking of young English revolutionaries at this time.

Lamb had been little in touch with Coleridge recently, but presumably enough to learn of his friend's marriage to Sara Fricker in October, 1795, and to arrange for the publication of four of his own sonnets (somewhat doctored by Coleridge) in Coleridge's *Poems on Various Subjects* of March, 1796.[16] Two of these were 'Anna' sonnets. A third was that to Sarah Siddons, now signed 'C.L.' like the other three, and the fourth the Margate poem. The odd practice of including a friend's poems with one's own was quite acceptable to their readers, though among the generally favourable notices, only the *Critical Review's* noticed Lamb: 'Mr. Coleridge tells us he was indebted for three [actually four] of the Effusions to Mr. Charles Lamb, of the India House,—these are very beautiful.'[17] Coleridge in introducing them had written magnanimously, 'independently of the signature their superior merit would have sufficiently distinguished them'.[18] The Margate poem also appeared at this time in the *Monthly Magazine*, edited by Richard Phillips. So Lamb was in print at twenty-one.

It was probably not until May of 1796 that Lamb was again in touch with Coleridge on a regular basis.[19] From that month dates the first extant letter of Lamb's considerable correspondence. In the early days he kept Coleridge's letters (they have since disappeared except for one or two of which Coleridge kept copies). Later he kept none but those of his later friend Thomas Manning. He and Mary, who moved often, regularly destroyed the letters they received. Coleridge, on the other hand – whose habits were untidier and whose own moves were equally frequent in early life – kept all, or nearly all, of Lamb's letters to him, as did most of the Lambs' friends, luckily for us.

The sheer volume and length of Lamb's letters to Coleridge in 1796, and just after, he was never to equal again. They are the serious probings of a young man in search of himself and of friendship and literature and personal growth, and they are not without humour. The very first is rather an important one. After referring to a London innkeeper's bill he had paid for Coleridge and recording some chat about mutual friends Lamb says,

> Coleridge, I know not what suffering scenes you have gone through at Bristol,—my life has been somewhat diversified of late. The 6 weeks that finished last year & began this your very humble servant spent very agreeably in a mad house at Hoxton—. I am got somewhat rational now, & dont bite any one. But mad I was—& many a vagary my imagination played with me, enough to make a volume if all told— — . . .
>
> Coleridge it may convince you of my regards for you when I tell you my head ran on you in my madness as much almost as on another Person, who I am inclined to think was the more immediate cause of my temporary frenzy—. The sonnet I send you has small merit as poetry but you will be curious to read it when I tell you it was written in my prison house in one of my lucid Intervals

to my sister

> If from my lips some angry accents fell,
>   Peevish complaint, or harsh reproof unkind,
>   Twas but the Error of a sickly mind,
> And troubled thoughts, clouding the purer well,
>   & waters clear, of Reason: & for me
>   Let this my verse the poor atonement be,
> My verse, which thou to praise: wast ever inclined
>   Too highly, & with a partial eye to see
> No Blemish: thou to me didst ever shew
>   Fondest affection, & woudst oftimes lend
> An ear to the desponding, love sick Lay,
>   Weeping my sorrows with me, who repay
> But ill the mighty debt, of love I owe,
>   Mary, to thee, my sister & my friend——

> With these lines, & with that sisters kindest remembrances to C—I conclude—

Yours Sincerely
Lamb
(M I, 3–4)

The poem to Mary is sentimental ('weeping my sorrows') and sometimes laboured ('My verse, which thou to praise: wast ever inclined/Too highly'; 'harsh reproof unkind'), sometimes trite ('desponding, love sick Lay') – and, for the reader familiar with Lamb's life, quite moving.

Lamb's time in the madhouse resulted from a year of intense unhappiness, compounded by overwork at the India House, though he treats the episode lightly enough in his letter. Whether he himself took it lightly is another matter. His keepers were probably humane in a private establishment like that to which Mary was later sent by him: all madhouses in those days were not Bedlams. It offered at least a rest and escape from all that was furrowing his brow just then. There can be no question that he did undergo the experience. Southey knew of it, John Lamb the younger blamed Coleridge for it, and Valentine Le Grice writes (again in the rough draft we have seen):

I am not certain as to dates, but I think about the year 1795, poor Lamb suffered a temporary derangement of his intellects, and confinement under medical care was necessary. I remember it from this circumstance. I received a very long letter from Lamb—very well written—the main purpose of which was to advise me to [? read] Hartley on Man, one expression in it I perfectly remember. "Hartley appears to me to have had as clear an insight into all the [secrets] of the human mind as I have into the items of a Ledger—as an Accountant has—a good counting-Housical Simile you'll say, and appropos from a clerk in the India House." The very next day I received a letter from his mother to say that the supposed [letter] that I among other friends had received [had been written in a state of madness]—that she was sorry to say that a temporary confinement was necessary, and that she desired that I would make no reply to it. (*CLB*, Apr. 1974, 118)

The ages around twenty are known for suicide: adolescence may be the most difficult period that some individuals have to endure. As to his casual treatment of his breakdown, Lamb, unlike Coleridge, seldom revealed all that he felt or knew. The only thing one can deduce from his account is that he felt he had recovered and, to Coleridge at least, was not being grim about it. There are several further references to it in letters. In June of 1796, recalling Salutation and Cat days to Coleridge, he wrote,

In your conversation you had blended so many pleasant fancies, that they cheated me of my grief. But in your absence, the tide of melancholy rushd in again, & did its worst Mischief by overwhelming my Reason. I have recoverd. But feel a stupor that makes me indifferent to the hopes & fears of this life. I sometimes wish to introduce a religious turn of mind, but habits are strong things, & my religious fervors are confined alas to some fleeting moments of occasional solitary devotion—. A correspondence, opening with you has roused me a little from my lethargy. . . . Indulge me in it. I will not be very troublesome. at some future time I will amuse you with an account . . . of the strange turn my phrensy took. I look back on it at times with a gloomy kind of Envy. For while it lasted I had many many hours of pure happiness. Dream not Coleridge, of having tasted all the grandeur & wildness of Fancy, till you have gone mad. All now seems to me vapid; comparatively so. Excuse this selfish digression— (M 1, 18–19)

Southey reported that Lamb in his 'phrensy' had imagined himself to be young Norval, hero of Home's *Douglas*. Delirium, in 'normal' people too, can bring just this sense of escape, joy, comfort.

In December 1796 he tells Coleridge,

I almost burned all your letters,—I did as bad, I lent 'em to a friend to keep out of my brother's sight, should he come and make inquisition into our papers, for much as he dwelt upon your conversation while you were among us, and delighted to be with you, it has been his fashion ever since to depreciate and cry you down,—you were the cause of my madness—you and your damned foolish sensibility and melancholy—and he lamented with a true brotherly feeling that we ever met . . . (M 1, 78)

After the weight of responsibility for his family shifted from Mary to himself, however, Lamb never had another depressive episode severe enough for confinement.

In the year 1796 he was beginning again to cope with life, though he complained sometimes of illness and headache. There was the happy prospect of having more of his sonnets printed in a second edition of Coleridge's *Poems*, and Coleridge was corresponding with him magnificently in response to his plea. Lamb was replying profusely, pouring forth his reactions to his friend's letters and poems, on which he was flattered to be consulted, offering excellent friendly criticism in much detail. He was, too, sending Coleridge his own sonnets. Coleridge asked him to come to Clevedon – where he and Sara had their cottage, near Bristol – for a visit.

But this was not yet possible. In late May, after rejecting Coleridge's offer to pay the innkeeper's bill, he reports that 'my poor brother has had a sad accident, a large stone blown down by yesterday's high wind has bruised his leg in a most shocking manner', and he is under a doctor's care, and there are '10,000' other objections.[20] Coleridge has sent him a poem of Wordsworth's, just then in London, but Lamb will be 'too ill' to return it in person to that poet (a first meeting missed). 'Poor' Val Le Grice, ere setting forth to his Cornwall tutorship, has written a very witty satire on college declamations; he and Lamb have been punning together. He commiserates with Coleridge on the sudden, shocking death of Sara's brother-in-law, young Robert Lovell. He comments on some *Watchman* issues, has enjoyed especially in it some parts of Coleridge's 'Religious Musings'. Of that touching on Priestley,

> I *have* seen priestly. I love to see his name repeated in your writings. I love & honour him almost profanely. You would be charmed with his *sermons*, if you never read em,—You have doubtless read his books, illustrative of the doctrine of Necessity. Prefixed to a late work of his, in answer to Paine there is a preface given [giving] an account of the Man & his services to Men, written by [Theophilus] Lindsey, his dearest friend,—well worth your reading— (M I, 12)

In the next letter, of 8–10 June, he extols Southey's revolutionary epic: 'With Joan of Arc I have been delighted, amazed'.[21] He picks out the parts he liked best, including some lines contributed by Coleridge, and provides his usual sane criticism.[22]

John Lamb, he says, is now 'very feverish and light headed, but Cruikshanks has pronounced the symptoms favourable & gives us every hope that there will be no need of amputation. God send, not.' Their brother was staying with them.

> We are necessarily confined with him the afternoon & evening till very late, so that I am stealing a few minutes to write to you. Thank you for your frequent letters, you are the only cor-

respondent & I might add the only friend I have in the world. I go nowhere & have no acquaintance. Slow of speech, & reserved of manners, no one seeks or cares for my society & I am left alone. Allen calls very occasionally as tho' it were a duty rather, & seldom stays ten minutes. Then judge how thankful I am for your letters. Do not, however burthen yourself with the correspondence. I trouble you again so soon, only in obedience to your injunctions. Complaints apart, proceed we to our task. I am called away to tea, thence must wait upon my brother . . . Farewell— (M 1, 17)

But by his addition of the next day to this letter he has taken up Coleridge's own poetry – for several pages. Then he takes Coleridge to task for changing his – Lamb's – sonnets: 'I love my sonnets because they are the reflected images of my own feelings at different times. . . . I charge you, Col. spare my ewe lambs.'[23]

And so it went between them through the most difficult summer – with John foisted upon them – the Lambs had yet known. Charles smoked and drank to kill care ('I am writing at random, and half-tipsy'[24]) but hoped to get to the Coleridges at Clevedon for a visit soon. By 1 July, 'My mother is grown so entirely helpless (not having any use of her limbs) that Mary is necessarily confined from ever sleeping out, she being her bed fellow. She thanks you tho' & will accompany me in spirit.'[25]

Lamb may have felt he *had* to get away, to preserve his own sanity, so recently threatened. But this was not yet to be. Several men in his office were ill, and 'that execrable aristocrat & knave Richardson has given me an absolute refusal of leave!'[26] On 5 July, intimating his own utter exhaustion, he wrote the Coleridges a blank-verse lament about not going ('Was it so hard a thing?').

Next day he tells Coleridge he hopes to be able to get him a house if his friend comes to London as a journalist. He urges Coleridge to review White's *Falstaff* and describes Bob Allen refusing to become a clergyman (when White informed him of a vacant living in the gift of Christ's Hospital) on William *Godwin's* advice! – for which Lamb shows proper scorn. He asks Coleridge to look up someone in Bristol who might assist Lamb's first teacher, Mrs Reynolds, now 'in very distrest circumstances' and 'in the room at this present writing'.[27] He quotes for Coleridge his new sonnet to Cowper – 'Of England's Bards the wisest & the Best' – who has just recovered from a period of madness. It begins,

Cowper, I thank my God, that thou art heal'd.
Thine was the sorest malady of all;
And I am sad to think, that it should light
Upon thy worthy head! But thou art heal'd . . .
(**M** 1, 40–1)

The next extant letter was not written until late September, when Mary Lamb, driven over the edge of sanity by overwork and poverty and care and sleeplessness, had killed her mother with a carving knife.

CHAPTER NINE

Disaster

In one little half year's illness, and in such an illness of such a nature and of such consequences! Lamb to Coleridge, April 1797 (M 1, 106)

Lamb to Coleridge, 27 September 1796, on the events of the previous Thursday, 22 September:

> My dearest friend—
>   White or some of my friends or the public papers by this time may have informed you of the terrible calamities that have fallen on our family. I will only give you the outlines. My poor dear dearest sister in a fit of insanity has been the death of her own mother. I was at hand only time enough to snatch the knife out of her grasp. She is at present in a mad house, from whence I fear she must be moved to an hospital. God has preserved to me my senses,—I eat and drink and sleep, and have my judgment I believe very sound. My poor father was slightly wounded, and I am left to take care of him and my aunt. Mr. Norris of the Bluecoat school has been very kind to us, and we have no other friend, but thank God I am very calm and composed, and able to do the best that remains to do. Write,—as religious a letter as possible—but no mention of what is gone and done with—with me the former things are passed away, and I have something more to do tha[n] to feel—— . . .
>   mention nothing of poetry. I have destroyed every vestige of past vanities of that kind. Do as you please, but if you publish, publish mine (I give free leave) without name or initial, and never send me a book, I charge you, you[r] own judgment will convince you not to take any notice of this yet to your dear wife.— You look after your family,—I have my reason and strength left to take care of mine. I charge you don't think of coming to see me. Write. I will not see you if you come. God almighty love you and all of us——
>   (M 1, 44–5)

'Mr. Norris of the Bluecoat school' was most likely Philip Norris, who had charge of certain building work for Christ's Hospital.[1]

The newspaper account in the *Morning Chronicle* of the day before had run:

On Friday afternoon the Coroner and a respectable Jury sat on the body of a Lady in the neighbourhood of Holborn, who died in consequence of a wound from her daughter the preceding day. It appeared by the evidence adduced, that while the family were preparing for dinner, the young lady seized a case knife laying on the table, and in a menacing manner pursued a little girl, her apprentice, round the room; on the eager calls of her helpless infirm mother to forbear, she renounced her first object, and with loud shrieks approached her parent.

The child by her cries quickly brought up the landlord of the house, but too late—the dreadful scene presented to him the mother lifeless, pierced to the heart, on a chair, her daughter yet wildly standing over her with the fatal knife, and the venerable old man, her father, weeping by her side, himself bleeding at the forehead from the effects of a severe blow he received from one of the forks she had been madly hurling about the room.

For a few days prior to this the family had observed some symptoms of insanity in her, which had so much increased on the Wednesday evening, that her brother early the next morning went in quest of Dr. Pitcairn—had that gentleman been met with, the fatal catastrophe had, in all probability, been prevented.

It seems the young Lady had been once before, in her earlier years, deranged, from the harassing fatigues of too much business.—As her carriage towards her mother was ever affectionate in the extreme, it is believed that to the increased attentiveness, which her parents' infirmities called for by day and night, is to be attributed the present insanity of this ill-fated young woman.

It has been stated in some of the Morning Papers, that she has an insane brother also in confinement—this is without foundation.

The Jury of course brought in their Verdict, *Lunacy*.

(M I, 45)

The *Whitehall Evening Post* had not suppressed the name, but added,

The above unfortunate young person is a Miss Lamb, a mantua-maker, in Little Queen-street, Lincoln's-inn-fields. She has been, since, removed to Islington mad-house.   (M 1, 46)

The letter reached Coleridge by the next day, when he immediately responded with the 'religious' letter Lamb had requested, urging him not to give way to despair and to accept the terrible circumstances in the spirit of 'Father, thy will be done.'[2] (Coleridge kept a copy of the letter.)

Lamb next wrote on the third of October:

My dearest friend,
    your letter was an inestimable treasure to me. It will be a comfort to you, I know, to know that our prospects are somewhat brighter. My poor dear dearest sister, the unhappy & unconscious instrument of the Almighty's jud[g]ments to our house, is restored to her senses; to a dreadful sense & recollection of what has past, awful to her mind & impressive (as it must be to the end of life) but temper'd with religious resignation, & the reasonings of a sound judgment, which in this early stage knows how to distinguish between a deed committed in a transcient fit of frenzy, & the terrible guilt of a Mother's murther. I have seen her. I found her this morning calm & serene, far very very far from an indecent forgetful serenity; she has a most affectionate & tender concern for what has happened. Indeed from the beginning, frightful & hopeless as her disorder seemed, I had confidence enough in her strength of mind, & religious principle, to look forward to a time when *even she* might recover tranquillity.

Of himself he could say,

God be praised, Coleridge, wonderful as it is to tell, I have never once been otherwise than collected, & calm; even on the dreadful day & in the midst of the terrible scene I preserved a tranquillity, which bystanders may have construed into indifference, a tranquillity not of despair; is it folly or sin in me to say that it was a religious principle that *most* supported me? I allow much to other favourable circumstances. I felt that I had something else to do than to regret; on that first evening my Aunt was laying insensible, to all appearance like one dying,—my father, with his poor forehead plaisterd over from a wound he had received from a daughter dearly loved by him, & who loved him no less dearly,—my mother a dead & murder'd corpse in the next room—yet was I wonderfully supported. I closed not my eyes in sleep that night, but lay without terrors & without despair. I have lost no sleep since. . . . I had the whole weight of the family thrown on me, for my brother, little disposed (I speak not without tenderness for him) at any time to take care of old age & infirmities had now, with his bad leg, an exemption from such duties, & I was now left alone. One little incident may serve to make you understand my way of managing my mind. Within a day or 2 after the fatal one, we drest for dinner a tongue, which we had had salted for some weeks in the house. As I sat down a feeling like remorse struck me,—this tongue poo[r] Mary got for me, & can I partake of it now, when she is far away—a thought occurrd & relieve[d] me,—if I give into this way of feeling, there is not a chair, a room, an object in our rooms, that will not awaken the keenest griefs, I must rise above such weaknesses—. I hope this was not want of true feeling. I did not let this carry me tho' too far. On the very 2d day (I date from the day of horrors) as is usual in such cases there were a matter of 20 people I do think supping in our room—. They prevailed on me to eat *with them* (for to eat I never refused) they were all making merry! in the room,—some had come from friendship, some from busy curiosity, & some from Interest; I was going to partake with them, when my recollection came that my poor dead mother was lying in the next room, the very next room, a mother who thro' life wished nothing but her children's welfare—indignation, the rage of grief, something like remorse, rushed upon my mind in an agony of emotion,—I found my way mechanically to the adjoin[in]g room, & fell on my knees by the side of her coffin, asking forgiveness of heaven, & sometimes of her, for forgetting her so soon. Tranquillity returned, & it was the only violent emotion that master'd me, & I think it did me good.——(M 1, 47–8)

Sam Le Grice was a constant attendant for several days before his mother called him home; he was adept at

humoring my poor father. Talk'd with him, read to him, play'd at cr[ib]bage with Him (for so short is the old man's recollection, that he was playing at cards, as tho' nothing had happened, while the Coroner's Inquest was sitting over the way!) Samuel wept

tenderly when he went away. . . . Mr. Norris of Christ Hospital
has been as a father to me, Mrs. Norris as a Mother, tho' we had
few claims on them. A Gentleman brother to my Godmother,[3]
from whom we never had right or reason to expect any such
assistance, sent my father twenty pounds,—& to crown all these
God's blessings to our family at such a time, an old Lady, a cousin
of my father & Aunts, a Gentlewoman of fortune, is to take my
Aunt & make her comfortable for the short remainder of her
days.——

He makes rational plans:

My Aunt is recover'd & as well as ever, & highly pleased at
thoughts of going,—& has generously given up the interest of her
little money (which was formerly paid my Father for her board)
wholely & solely to my Sister's use. Reckoning this we have,
Daddy & I for our two selves & an old maid servant to look after
him, when I am out, which will be necessary, £170 or £180
(rather) a year out of which we can spare 50 or 60 at least for
Mary, while she stays at Islington, where she must & shall stay
during her father's life for his & her comfort. I know John will
make speeches about it, but she shall not go into an hospital. The
good Lady of the Mad house, & her daughter, an elegant sweet
behaved young Lady, love her & are taken with her amazingly,
& I know from her own mouth she loves them, & longs to be with
them as much———. Poor thing, they say she was but the other
morning saying, she knew she must go to Bethlem for life; that one
of her brother's would have it so, but the other would wish it Not,
but he obliged to go with the stream; that she had often as she
passed Bedlam thought it likely "here it may be my fate to end my
days"—conscious of a certain flightiness in her poor head
oftentimes, & mindful of more than one severe illness of that
Nature before. A Legacy of £100 which my father will have at
Xmas, & this 20 I mentioned before with what is in the house, will
much more than set us Clear,—if my father, an old servant maid,
& I cant live & live comfortably on £130 or £120 a year we ought
to burn by slow fires, & I almost would, that Mary might not go
into an hospital. Let me not leave one unfavourable impression
on your mind respecting my Brother. Since this has happened he
has been very kind & brotherly; but I fear for his mind,—he has
taken his ease in the world, & is not fit himself to struggle with

difficulties, nor has much accustomed himself to throw himself into their way,—& I know his language is already, "Charles, you must take care of yourself, you must not abridge yourself of a single pleasure you have been used to" &c &c. & in that style of talking. But you, a necessarian, can respect a difference of mind, & love what *is amiable* in a character not perfect. He has been very good, but I fear for his mind. Thank God, I can unconnect myself with him, & shall manage all my father's monies in future myself, if I take charge of Daddy, which poor John has not even hinted a wish, at any future time even, to share with me——

As to Mary,

The Lady at this Mad house assures me that I may dismiss immediately both Doctor & Apothecary, retaining occasionally an opening draught or so for a while, & there is a less expensive establishment in her house, where she will only not have a room & nurse to herself for £50 or guineas a year—the outside would be 60—. You know by œconomy how much more, even, I shall be able to spare for her comforts——

She will, I fancy, if she stays, make one of the family, rather than of the patients, & the old & young ladies I like exceedingly, & she loves dearly, & they, as the saying is take to her very extraordinaryily, if it is extraordinary that people who see my sister should love her. Of all the people I ever saw in the world my poor sister was most & throughly devoi[d] of the least tincture of selfishness—. . . .

Coleridge, continue to write but do not for ever offend me by talking of sending me cash, sincerely & on my soul we do not want it. God love you both— . . .   (M 1, 49–50)

The blow had struck, and young Charles Lamb responded with extraordinary strength and steadiness. It was as though, dazed as he was in sorrow and shock, he could stand aside from himself and bring great resources to bear on his situation, rising to the magnitude of the things demanded of him. In the course of that terrible day while his thirty-three-year-old brother trembled, the twenty-one-year old had become a man.

CHAPTER TEN

Loneliness

. . . pray, pray, write to me: if you knew with what an anxiety of joy I open such a long packet as you last sent me, you would not grudge giving a few minutes now & then to this intercourse (the only intercourse, I fear we two shall ever have) this conversation with your friend—such I boast to be called. Lamb to Coleridge, 1 December 1796 (M 1 67)

From the death of his mother to mid-1797 was a desolate period, in which Lamb clung to Coleridge's religion and Coleridge's married happiness as if to make these a sustaining part of himself. He spent long hours writing to Coleridge in the office or while his senile father dozed, pouring out his worries and hopes without self-pity. The letters concentrate on the practical and poetic matters that would interest Coleridge. Coleridge, to his everlasting credit, supported Lamb manfully from the midst of a thousand distractions.[1] And through Coleridge he made two new friends, the Jacobin John Thelwall and the young Quaker poet Charles Lloyd.

Coleridge did not think Lamb should abandon the writing of verse. From Clevedon he said as much in the poem 'To a Friend Who Had Declared his Intention of Writing No More Poetry'. It adjured Charles, 'But take thou heed:/ For thou art vulnerable, wild-eyed boy', and urged him to write a poem on his beloved Robert Burns, who had died in July. Lamb responded much later, in a letter of 10 December:

> You sent me some very sweet lines relative to Burns, but it was at a time when, in my highly agitated and perhaps distorted state of mind, I thought it a duty to read 'em hastily and burn 'em. I burned all my own verses, all my book of extracts from Beaumont and Fletcher and a thousand sources: I burned a little journal of my foolish passion which I had a long time kept . . . (M 1, 77–8)

This was the Ann Simmons journal. Then he says he almost burned Coleridge's letters in the fear that his brother would get hold of them and damn Coleridge afresh as a bad influence. Charles had lent the letters to a friend to be out of the way for a little and the friend had lost them. So those now coming from Coleridge are 'sacred things with me'.[2]

By October he was 'not quite depress'd' and able to consider the faithful Coleridge's own situation, urging him be decisive and settle his 'plans of life'. This letter provided Mary's own assessment of *her* situation:

> Mary continues serene & chearful,—I have not by me a little letter she wrote to me, for tho' I see her almost every day yet we delight to write to one another (for we can scarce see each other but in company with some of the people of the house), I have not the letter by me but will quote from memory what she wrote in it. "I have no bad terrifying dreams. At midnight when I happen to awake, the nurse sleeping by the side of me, with the noise of the poor mad people around me, I have no fear. The spirit of my mother seems to descend, & smile upon me, & bid me live to enjoy the life & reason which the Almighty has given me—. I shall see her again in heaven; she will then understand me better, my Grandmother too will understand me better, & will then say no more as she used to Do, "Polly, what are those poor crazy moyther'd brains of yours thinkg. of always? . . . (M 1, 51–2)

On 28 October the troubled Lamb chided Coleridge for being in one of his earlier, consolatory letters too 'tinctured with mystical notions and the pride of metaphysics', but he soon turned to domestic matters. He bade Coleridge to

> rejoice with me in my sister's continued reason and composedness of mind. Let us both be thankful for it. I continue to visit her very frequently, and the people of the house are vastly indulgent to her; she is likely to be as comfortably situated in all respects as those who pay twice or thrice the sum. They love her, and she loves them, and makes herself very useful to them. Benevolence sets out on her journey with a good heart, and puts a good face on it, but is apt to limp and grow feeble, unless she calls in the aid of self-interest by way of crutch. In Mary's case, as far as respects those she is with, 'tis well that these principles are so likely to co-operate. I am rather at a loss sometimes for books for her,—our reading is somewhat confined, and we have nearly exhausted our London library. She has her hands too full of work to read much,

but a little she must read; for reading was her daily bread. (M 1, 56–7)

In November (writing again to Coleridge, as always these days) Lamb recalls his mother in a passage closely parallel to his later poem, 'Written a Year After the Events' – those of 22 September:

> Oh! my friend, I think sometimes, could I recall the days that are past, which among them should I choose? not those 'merrier days,' not the 'pleasant days of hope,' not 'those wanderings with a fair hair'd maid,' which I have so often and so feelingly regretted, but the days, Coleridge, of a *mother's* fondness for her *school-boy*. What would I give to call her back to earth for *one* day, on my knees to ask her pardon for all those little asperities of temper which, from time to time, have given her gentle spirit pain; and the day, my friend, I trust will come; there will be 'time enough' for kind offices of love, if 'Heaven's eternal year' be ours. Hereafter, her meek spirit shall not reproach me. Oh, my friend, cultivate the filial feelings! and let no man think himself released from the kind 'charities' of relationship: these shall give him peace at the last; these are the best foundation for every species of benevolence. I rejoice to hear, by certain channels, that you, my friend, are reconciled with all your relations. . . . (M 1, 64)

A November letter from Coleridge to John Thelwall, one of the important 'acquitted felons' of the Treason Trials of 1794, indicates that Lamb met Thelwall at this time, when he delivered money from Coleridge to Thelwall's London address to pay for some books Thelwall had bought at Coleridge's request.[3] This was a significant meeting for one of Lamb's radical sympathies, and Lamb thereafter speaks of Thelwall as someone he knows. Thelwall was a poet as well as politico and as such the recipient of some of Coleridge's most interesting letters. But though Coleridge was corresponding regularly with Thelwall at this time, he had not yet met him. Referring to his practice of receiving letters on his friends' behalf at the office, Lamb writes to Coleridge in February 1797, 'The India *Co* is better adapted to answer the cost [of postage] than the generality of my friend's correspondents—such poor and honest dogs as John Thelwall particularly.'[4] Lamb's sympathy for this Patriot – as Jacobins liked to call each other – is already evident. (Postage was paid by the recipient in Lamb's time.)

Mary kept well into December, but other strains were apparent.

Are we never to meet again? . . . I have never met with any one,
never shall meet with any one, who could or can compensate me for
the top[5] of your Society—I have no one to talk all these matters
about to—I lack friends, I lack books to supply their absence—.
. . . I thank you, from my heart I thank you for your sollicitude
about my Sister. She is quite well,—but must not, I fear, come to
live with us yet for a good while. In the first place, because at
present it would hurt her, & hurt my father, for them to be
together: secondly from a regard to the world's good report, for I
fear, I fear, tongues will be busy *whenever* that event takes place.
Some have hinted, one man has prest it on me, that she should be
in perpetual confinement[;] what she hath done to deserve, or the
necessity of such an hardship I see not; do you? I am starving at
the India house, near 7 oClock without my dinner, & so it has
been & will be almost all the week—. I get home at night oe'r
wearied, quite faint—& then to Cards with my father, who will
not let me enjoy a meal in peace—but I must conform to my
situation, & hope I am, for the most part, not unthankful—
     I am got home at last, & after repeated games at Cribbage
have got my father's leave to write awhile: with difficulty got it,
for when I expostulated about playing any more, he very aptly
replied, 'If you wont play with me, you might as well not come
home at all!' The argument was unanswerable, & I set to afresh—.
(M 1, 65–6).

The one man who thought Mary should be put away permanently
was presumably again brother John.
     More responsibility was on the way by 9 December.

In truth Coleridge, I am perplexed & at times almost cast
down—I am beset with perplexities—the old Hag of a wealthy
relation, who took my Aunt off our hands in the beginning of
trouble, has found out that she is "indolent & mulish" I quote her
own words, & that her attachment to us is so strong that she can
never be happy apart—the Lady with delicate Irony remarks,
that if I am not an Hypocrite! I shall rejoyce to receive her
again,—& that it will be a means of making me more fond of
home, to have so dear a friend to come home to!—the fact is she is
jealous of my Aunt's bestowing any kind recollections on us while

she enjoys the patronage of her roof—she says she finds it inconsistent with her own "ease & tranquillity" to keep her any longer—& in fine summons me to fetch her home—. Now much as I should rejoyce to transplant the poor old creature from the chilling air of such patronage, yet I know how straiten'd we are already, how unable already to answer any demand which sickness or any extraordinary expence may make—. I know this, & all unused as I am to struggle with perplexities I am somewhat non plusd to say no worse—this prevents me from a through relish of what Lloyd's kindness & yours have furnish'd me with; I thank you tho' from my heart,—& feel myself not quite alone in the earth———(M 1, 73)

December saw the Coleridges' move from Clevedon to Nether Stowey in Somerset as Lamb again took Aunt Hetty under his wing. It was a dismal Christmas. Mary, who had been well earlier in the month, was 'seriously ill'[6] at the year's turn – 'with a sorethroat & a slight species of Scarlet fever'.[7] But she soon recovered, as he reported in January, asking Coleridge, 'Is it a farm you have got, & what does your worship know about farming? Coleridge, I want you to write an Epic poem'[8] – something more ample than Coleridge had attempted hitherto; so he urged his friend's poetic career forward. Coleridge valued his comments, as he had told Lloyd's publisher Joseph Cottle a little earlier: Lamb's *taste & judgment* I see reason to think more correct & philosophical than my own, which yet I place pretty high'.[9]

Throughout these bleak months, as we shall see, Lamb had continued to write a little poetry. This ceased with his expanded household, though a happy event was the publication of his Cowper sonnet in the *Monthly Magazine*. But he managed in the midnight hours to continue to read – just now yet more Joseph Priestley. Priestley's discussion of friendship sent Lamb off on another, almost despairing account of his lack of good friends nearby, and he urged Coleridge to bolster his sometimes faltering religious zeal for Necessitarianism: 'Confirm me in the faith of that great & glorious doctrine, & keep me steady in the contemplation of it.'[10] Again he begged for details of Coleridge's life.

The Coleridge household had also expanded, since October, with the addition of the first child, the baby Hartley, and nearly simultaneously, with the arrival of a young Quaker poet, Charles Lloyd, to whom Sara had taken an immediate liking. Lloyd was in revolt against banking and doctoring, two of the professions he had tried; he had first encountered Coleridge when Coleridge came to Birmingham seeking *Watchman* subscriptions. The young man, son of a member of the well-known banking firm, was entranced with his new acquaintance, his easy manner, his learning, and his eloquence, though only two years his junior. It was soon arranged that young Lloyd would live with Coleridge as his pupil – for eighty pounds a year in the ménage where Coleridge was addressing love poems to Sara and writing tender family poems as well. (The lines 'So, for the mother's sake, the child was dear,/ And dearer was the mother for the child' pleased Charles Lamb.) Lloyd had heard much from Coleridge about Lamb and had begun to take an interest in him as well. Encouraged by Coleridge, Lamb had in November, 1796, taken up poetry again in earnest, writing now in blank verse about his grandmother, Mary Field. Charles Lloyd's own grandmother, to whom he was devoted, had recently died; he too was writing poetry in her memory,[11] and before December 1796 was out, Lloyd had included Lamb's 'The Grandame' in his own elaborately printed volume, *Poems on the Death of Priscilla Farmer*. Large of format, on fine paper, with large type, this slender work caused Coleridge to comment, 'The Book is drest like a rich Quaker, in costly raiment but unornamented. The loss of [Mrs Farmer] almost killed my poor young friend: for he doted on her from his Infancy.'[12] As for Lamb, he remarked on 'the odd coincidence of two young men, in one age, carolling their grand-mothers. . . . I cannot but smile to see my Granny so gayly deck'd forth.'[13] Charles Lloyd was two days younger than Charles Lamb; they had not yet met.

'The Grandame' (in Lamb's final version) first evokes Mrs Field's last resting-place:

> On the green hill top,
> Hard by the house of prayer, a modest roof,
> And not distinguish'd from its neighbour-barn,
> Save by a slender-tapering length of spire,
> The Grandame sleeps. . . .
>
> (*P*, 5)

'Lowly born', she was of sterling character; Lamb describes her long service to her employers, 'And how the prattling tongue of garrulous age/Delighted to recount the oft-told tale/ Or anecdote domestic–

as had the grandmother of Rosamund Gray. Her talk was of her high-born (Plumer) family, its friends, marriages, relations, scandals. 'But these are not thy praises; and I wrong/ Thy honour'd memory, recording chiefly/ Things light or trivial.' He concludes with the religious zeal of 'That reverend form bent down with age and pain/ And rankling malady',[14] her faith undimmed through her sufferings. It is one of his tender tributes, the blank-verse form allowing him an expression close to prose – too close for the poetry's sake. Lamb's own integrity surely owed much to Mrs Field, whom he had dearly loved in spite of her asperities.

This marked Lamb's fourth appearance in print for 1796 as a coming poet; there was a fifth when Coleridge put together a pamphlet later in the year called *Sonnets from Various Authors*. It contained four by Lamb[15] together with a few each by Bowles, Southey, Lloyd, Coleridge himself, and others.

Throughout the months after Lamb's tragedy Coleridge and Lamb discussed Coleridge's *Poems, Second Edition*,[16] in which Lamb would have a larger place than in the first: Lamb was particularly caustic about Coleridge's tampering with his verses. Coleridge gave way and printed only what Lamb had actually written. Lamb urged Coleridge to drop 'Effusion' for 'Sonnet' in poem descriptions; with this suggestion too Coleridge complied. Lamb continued his criticism of Coleridge's own verses. 'Cultivate simplicity', he wrote, in the effort to cure Coleridge of turgidity; 'I allow no hot-beds in the gardens of Parnassus.'[17] (He objected to the expression 'foodful fruit'[18]: it seems impossible that in less than two years Coleridge would write 'The Ancient Mariner'.)

Lamb's 'Anna' sonnets, with others, were to appear in the new Coleridge edition, and just to be sure he hadn't forgotten her (after all) he found some lines from Massinger, ending 'Long did I love this lady', to precede the love sonnets in his section of the book, which was to be grandly titled, 'Poems, Chiefly Love Sonnets, by Charles Lamb, of the India House' and dedicated to Mary (It will be unexpected, and it will give her pleasure; or do you think it will look whimsical at all?'[19]). The dedication would be even grander:

THE FEW FOLLOWING POEMS,

CREATURES OF THE FANCY AND THE FEELING

IN LIFE'S MORE VACANT HOURS,

PRODUCED, FOR THE MOST PART, BY
LOVE IN IDLENESS,
ARE
WITH ALL A BROTHER'S FONDNESS,
INSCRIBED TO
MARY ANN LAMB,
THE AUTHOR'S BEST FRIEND AND SISTER.
(M I, 63)

Of the love sonnets themselves he told Coleridge:

This is the pomp and paraphernalia of parting, with which I take my leave of a passion which has reigned so royally (so long) within me; thus, with its trappings of laureatship, I fling it off, pleased and satisfied with myself that the weakness troubles me no longer. I am wedded, Coleridge, to the fortunes of my sister and my poor old father. (M I, 63–4)

Among other poems Lamb sent was 'The Tomb of Douglas', relating to the figure in Home's play. It begins

When her son, her Douglas died,
To the steep rock's fearful side
Fast the frantic Mother hied—

O'er her blooming warrior dead
Many a tear did Scotland shed . . .
(P, 9)

Minstrels come and weep, Scottish maidens are urged to drop a tear – for a young man killed untimely. 'False Glenalvon', dead too, shall not have pity wasted on him. A creditable youthful effort in the vein of Thomas Gray's 'The Bard' written some thirty years earlier, it is one of Lamb's few attempts in the ballad style – and had a special significance for him, as we have seen.

The year 1796 drew to its close with Lamb still much worried about his sister and newly encumbered with Aunt Hetty, now succumbing to her final illness. Great was his joy, then, when in mid-January Lloyd appeared unheralded on his doorstep, like an emissary from

Coleridge's ideal household. Immediately Lamb wrote a poem, 'To Charles Lloyd, an Unexpected Visitor', which began with himself, 'Alone, obscure, without a friend,/ A cheerless, solitary thing'. Lamb wonders what Lloyd could find in him, Lamb, to compensate 'For Stowey's pleasant winter nights,/ For loves and friendships far away?' and is deeply touched by Lloyd's approach. The poem ends,

> Long, long within my aching heart,
>   The grateful sense shall cherish'd be;
> I'll think less meanly of myself
>   That Lloyd will sometimes think on me.
>
> (M 1, 92–3)

Lloyd stayed at the Bull & Mouth Inn. In him Lamb found a possible close friend ('I do so love him!'[20]). Charles Lloyd introduced Lamb at this time to his brother Robert, but their stay in London was brief and only a respite from Lamb's troubles. Early in February these had come upon him again:

> You & Sara are very good to think so kindly & so favourably of poor Mary. I would to God, all did so too. But I very much fear, she must not think of coming home in my father's lifetime. It is very hard upon her. But our circumstances are peculiar, & we must submit to them. God be praised, she is so well as she is. She bears her situation as one who has no right to complain. My poor old Aunt, whom you have seen, the kindest goodest creature to me when I was at school, who used to toddle there to bring me fag[21] when I school-boy like only despised her for it, & used to be ashamed to see her come & sit herself down on the old coal hole steps as you went into the old grammar school, & opend her apron & brought out her bason, with some nice thing she had caused to be saved for me,—the good old creature is now lying on her death bed,—I cannot bear to think on her deplorable state. To the shock she received on that our evil day, from which she never completely recoverd, I impute her illness. She says, poor thing, she is glad she is come home to die with me. I was always her favourite. (M 1, 96)

And on the thirteenth,

> This afternoon I attend the funeral of my poor old aunt, who died on Thursday. I own I am thankful that the good creature has

ended all her days of suffering and infirmity. She was to me the 'cherisher of infancy,' and one must fall on these occasions into reflections which it would be commonplace to enumerate, concerning death, 'of chance and change, and fate in human life.' Good God, who could have foreseen all this but four months back! I had reckoned, in particular, on my aunt's living many years; she was a very hearty old woman. But she was a mere skeleton before she died, looked more like a corpse that had lain weeks in the grave, than one fresh dead. . . .

He had a message for Lloyd:

Tell Lloyd I have had thoughts of turning Quaker, and have been reading, or am rather just beginning to read, a most capital book, good thoughts in good language, William Penn's 'No Cross, no Crown;' I like it immensely. Unluckily I went to one of his meetings, tell him, in St. John Street, yesterday, and saw a man under all the agitations and workings of a fanatic, who believed himself under the influence of some 'inevitable presence.' This cured me of Quakerism; I love it in the books of Penn and Woolman, but I detest the vanity of a man thinking he speaks by the Spirit, when what he says an ordinary man might say without all that quaking and trembling. In the midst of his inspiration— and the effects of it were most noisy—was handed into the midst of the meeting a most terrible blackguard Wapping sailor; the poor man, I believe, had rather have been in the hottest part of an engagement, for the congregation of broad-brims, together with the ravings of the prophet, were too much for his gravity, though I saw even he had delicacy enough not to laugh out. . . . (M 1, 103)

For Lamb to become interested in John Woolman, the American Quaker who made a life's work of preaching against slavery, and in the *No Cross, No Crown* of William Penn, was to take a step away from Priestley's Necessarianism. Lloyd had lent him Woolman; he was later to say (in 'A Quakers' Meeting'), 'Get the Writings of John Woolman by heart; and love the early Quakers.'[22]

His Quaker anecdote was in part relief from his grief for Aunt Hetty. On the day of this letter he composed the sorrowful 'Written on the Day of My Aunt's Funeral' ('Thou too art dead'), with its reminiscences of her kindness to him as a schoolboy, of his failures of

affection toward his mother, of his 'palsy-smitten' father, now so
changed from the 'merry cheerful man'[23] he had once been. There is
next a long gap in the correspondence with Coleridge. Coleridge
was no longer writing.

Charles Lloyd was already one of Coleridge's problems. In
November of 1796 he had been seriously ill – and recovered. On his
Christmas visit to his family in Birmingham he had managed to get
himself engaged to the charming non-Quaker heiress Sophia
Pemberton. During his absence Coleridge wrote the elder Lloyd
that he could no longer tutor him, though Lloyd might continue to
room and board at his house. He encouraged the father to let his son
marry and perhaps take up gentlemanly farming.[24]

In the earlier illness Coleridge had described one of Lloyd's
attacks:

> He falls all at once into a kind of Night-mair. . . . All his
> voluntary powers are suspended; but he perceives every thing &
> hears every thing, and whatever he perceives & hears he perverts
> into the substance of his delirious Vision. He has had two
> principal fits, and the last has left a feebleness behind &
> occasional flightiness. Dr. Beddoes has been called in.—(Griggs 1,
> 257)

Dr. Beddoes prescribed calm, but also opium.

Between these bouts, Lloyd was restless and very active. He wrote
to his brother Robert – in unhappy apprenticeship to a Quaker
draper–grocer near Cambridge – 'I left Charles Lamb very interested in his favour, and have kept up a regular correspondence ever
since; he is a most interesting young man.'[25] Then Lloyd too stopped
writing for a while: in April Lamb learned from Lloyd that he had
been 'very ill'[26] again.

If Lamb continued to be haunted by death and madness, at least
Mary was better and this buoyed his spirits, as he told Coleridge on
7 April. He had

> taken a room for her at Hackney, and spend my Sundays,
> holidays, &c., with her. She boards herself. In one little half
> year's illness, and in such an illness of such a nature and of such
> consequences! to get her out in the world again, with a prospect of
> her never being so ill again—this is to be ranked not among the
> common blessings of Providence. (M 1, 106)

By mid-April he had sent Coleridge a poem, a true Romantic poem and, like 'Douglas', an objective one, its theme unconnected with his personal life. It concerns a dream, a fountain, a woody dell, and a wanton young woman who has betrayed her brideship to Christ and seeks the cleansing waters to restore herself in His sight from 'sin's foul stains'. He called it 'A Vision of Repentance', some eighty lines, beginning

> I saw a famous fountain in my dream
>   When shady pathways to a Valley led;
> A weeping willow lay upon that stream,
>   And all around the fountain brink were spread
> Wide branching trees, with dark green leaf rich clad,
>   Forming a doubtful twilight—desolate & sad.
>
> (M 1, 106–7)

There are elements of Spenser and of balladry in it – and of Greek myth: the girl is 'Psyche'. Lamb is trying various poetic forms. The first six stanzas have a pleasant, melancholy, flowing cadence as the poet observes the maiden. When she begins to speak the line shortens and the archaisms and inversions (beloved of all the Romantics) are less happy,

> And, night & day, I them augment
> With tears, like a true Penitent,
> Until due expiation made
> And fit atonement fully paid
> The Lord & Bridegroom me present . . .
>
> (M 1, 109)

What is interesting about the ambitious but imperfect piece – a small literary advance for Lamb – is its resemblance to greater poems still unwritten – for example, Keats's 'La Belle Dame Sans Merci' and his 'Eve of St. Agnes' – story ballads in a dreamlike setting. Present are some of the elements of Coleridge's 'Kubla Khan', written this year or the next [27] though Lamb leans on the grandeur of a Christian repentance while Coleridge is freely pagan. The likenesses suggest that the two friends were under the same influences. It is hard to establish that Coleridge was here 'indebted' to Lamb; if so, it was only in the most general way.[28] Coleridge, at any rate, printed Lamb's 'Vision' in the new edition of his poems.

The only other poet friend who might have sought Lamb out in the spring of 1797 apparently did not do so. Robert Southey and his wife Edith migrated to London in March so that Southey, newly blessed with an annuity, could take up his latest, reluctant, thrust at a career – this time in law studies. They saw something of his favourite, Mary Wollstonecraft, and therefore of William Godwin, with whom Southey did not get on. (Mary was now pregnant with the future Mary Shelley, and she and Godwin soon compromised their principles by marrying.) By May the Southeys had fled to Hampshire with his law books for the summer. The news from Lloyd was depressing, as Lamb wrote the silent Coleridge, from whom Lloyd had now departed:

> Poor dear Lloyd, I had a letter from him yesterday—his state of mind is truly alarming—he has, by his own confession, kept a letter of mine unopen'd 3 weeks! afraid, he says, to open it, lest I should speak upbraidingly to him. & yet this very letter of mine was in answer to one, wherein he informed me, that an alarming illness had alone prevented him from writing—. You will pray with me, I know, for his recovery—for Surely, Coleridge, a[n] exquisiteness of feeling like this must border on derangement. But I love him more & more,—& will not give up the hope of his speedy recovery, as he tells me he is under Dr Darwin's regimen——
>
> God bless us all, and shield us from insanity, which is "the sorest malady of all"——(M 1, 109)

Coleridge had decided only in March to add Lloyd's poems to his and Lamb's; the Lloyds' wide and prosperous acquaintance was sure to increase the book's sale.

In June things took a turn for the better. Lamb heard at last from Nether Stowey and the 'little book' of poems was published, by Joseph Cottle of Bristol and the Messrs Robinson in London: *Poems, Second Edition, by S. T. Coleridge, to which are now added Poems by Charles Lamb, and Charles Lloyd.* Southey was delighted:

> Cottle brought with him the new edition of Coleridge's poems. They are dedicated to his brother George in one of the most beautiful poems I ever read. . . . It contains all the poems of Lloyd and Lamb, and I know no volume that can be compared to it. . . .[29]

'All' the poems of Coleridge's two friends it did contain, but there is an amateurish, almost inept, quality about the patchwork it represents, liberally interlarded as the poems are with Coleridgean, explanatory prose.

To begin with, Coleridge *made up* a Latin tag from 'Groscollius' celebrating the eternal friendship of the three, which was to fall into smithereens a year later. Then his tender dedication to his brother, the Reverend George Coleridge, now Rector of Ottery St. Mary, failed to take into account the effect upon George of the little volume's fiercer attacks on the Anglican Church as a blesser of the French war. In Coleridge's 'Religious Musings', for example, came this passage, addressed to 'Britain':

> Thee to defend the Moloch Priest prefers
> The prayer of hate, and bellows to the herd,
> That Deity, Accomplice Deity
> In the fierce jealousy of wakened wrath
> Will go forth with our armies and our fleets
> To scatter the red ruin on their foes!
> O blasphemy! to mingle fiendish deeds
> With blessedness! . . .
>
> (STCP, 56–7)

Coleridge was obliged later to inscribe in at least one copy,

> *N.B.*—If this volume should ever be delivered according to its direction, i.e. to Posterity, let it be known that the Reverend George Coleridge was displeased and thought his character endangered by this Dedication! (STCP, 588)

Coleridge had unjustly accused the banker–poet Samuel Rogers of plagiarism in his 1796 preface. In that of the second edition, at Lamb's urging, he withdraws his allegation at length. He also engages in self-depreciation over the remarks of 'certain Reviewers' in 'detecting my poetic deficiencies',[30] including turgidity. (In fact, three lengthy reviews of the first edition had been favourable.)

More winningly he describes his love of poetry, and accounts for the presence of his friends, Lamb being his 'Friend and old School-fellow'.[31] In an even longer introduction to his own sonnets he derives his 'laws' for the modern form from his old favourite W. L. Bowles and that other influential sonneteer Charlotte Smith. He defines the sonnet as requiring 'lonely feeling' in the passage we have seen.[32] His account of the reasons for its fourteen-line form is marvellously unhistorical and slapdash. A sonnet is brief, he says first, for the sake of unity.

> It is confined to fourteen lines, because as some particular number is necessary, and that particular number must be a small one, it may as well be fourteen as any other number. When no reason can be adduced against a thing, Custom is a sufficient reason for it. (STCP, 543)

Coleridge's poems come first in the book. Lloyd's and Lamb's total output to date follow, including the grannies; each provides fifteen. Lloyd's are facile, expressive of his strong sexuality, and of an almost unrelieved gloom (he was already preoccupied with the fear of madness). 'The Maniac' reads:

> Poor Maniac, I envy thy state
>   When with sorrow and anguish I shrink,
> When shall I *be wise*—and forget!
>   For 'tis *madness* to feel and to think![33]

Charles Lamb's contributions follow the dedication to Mary which we have seen and include the five Anna sonnets, the Margate sonnet, the lines to Mary, 'If from my lips some angry accents fell'. Then come a group of 'Fragments' – 'Childhood', 'The Grandame', 'The Sabbath Bells', 'Fancy, employed on Divine Subjects', 'The Tomb of Douglas' and the 'Lines to Charles Lloyd'.

Coleridge's long, long introductory note to the Supplement at the back ended thus, leaving heaven-knows-what impression with contemporary readers:

> There are some lines too [in addition to Coleridge's] of Lloyd's and Lamb's in this Appendix. They had been omitted in the former part of the volume, partly by accident; but I have reason to believe that the Authors regard them, as of inferior merit, and they are therefore rightly placed, where they will receive some beauty from their vicinity to others much worse. (STCP, 541)

Lamb's only contribution to the Supplement was 'A Vision of Repentance', which deserved a little better.

The book (perhaps because it was a second edition) raised scarcely a critical ripple. Lamb appears not to have been unhappy with it, and Southey's welcome suggests that even such a *mélange* could then seem fresh and rewarding.

Now in June Coleridge again pressed Lamb to come to Nether Stowey. This time his India House superior, Richardson, gave way. Arrangements for leaving old John Lamb and Mary in their separate abodes were quickly made, for Lamb writes at the end of June that he can come! He is dizzy with excitement: 'I can talk as I can think nothing else.'[34]

He took the mail coach to Nether Stowey – a two days' journey into Somerset – and arrived on 7 July.

CHAPTER ELEVEN

To Nether Stowey

Ah! let me then, far from the strifeful scenes
Of public life (where Reason's warning voice
Is heard no longer, and the trump of Truth
Who blows but wakes The Ruffian Crew of Power
To deeds of maddest anarchy and blood).
Ah! let me, far in some sequester'd dell,
Build my low cot; most happy might it prove
My Samuel! near to thine, that I might oft
Share thy sweet converse, best belov'd of friends!
John Thelwall, 1797, to Coleridge.[1]

The records of the Nether Stowey week as it involved Lamb directly
are not copious, but much of it can be reconstructed by what we
know of Coleridge and Wordsworth at the time – and that is much.
Lamb arrived alone[2] on the outside of the coach – the cheaper seats
without protection from wind, sun, cold, or rain, the usual method
of travel for the impecunious. In his scarred and haunted state he
was meeting his old friend on new ground, meeting Mrs Coleridge
for the first time, and feeling somewhat strange if not quite a
stranger.

On taking the Nether Stowey cottage (much later, after he had
left it, he referred to it as a 'hovel'), Coleridge had written to a
friend,

> Our House is better than we expected—there is a comfortable
> bedroom & sitting room for us and C. Lloyd, & another for us—a
> room for Nanny, a kitchen, and out-house. Before our door a
> clear brook runs of very soft water; and in the back yard is a nice
> *Well* of fine spring water. We have a very pretty garden, and large
> enough to find us vegetables & employment. . . . We have
> likewise a sweet Orchard . . . (Griggs 1, 301)

In other reports it was without an oven, damp, dark, with a parlour
chimney that smoked, and mouse-haunted, Coleridge having

scruples about trapping mice. But a number of guests were happy there without complaint, and the 'farm' was an acre and a half, including pigs and poultry. Coleridge's good friend Tom Poole, the reason for his settlement there, had made a gate from it into his own property; Poole's large house and tannery fronted on another street.

With his usual expansiveness, Coleridge had invited no less than *five* visitors to share these tight quarters with his family of three and Nanny: his new friend William Wordsworth and sister Dorothy, Joseph Cottle, his Bristol publisher, and John Thelwall the Jacobin, now a constant Coleridge correspondent. Luckily the last two were not able to come just then, and the group numbered only seven. The family atmosphere was warm, and Sara a miracle of household management – except for one unfortunate mishap. Poetry was the preoccupation of the men and of Dorothy Wordsworth.

They could hardly fail to get to know each other intimately under such circumstances. The household is vividly conveyed in Joseph Cottle's account of his own visit a few weeks later, which coincided with that of Charles Lloyd, now in better health. Cottle learned from Coleridge

> how pleasantly the interview had gone with Charles Lamb. . . . He talked with affection of his old school-fellow . . . who had recently left him; regretted he had not had an opportunity of introducing me to one whom he so highly valued. Mr. C. took peculiar delight in assuring me (at least, at that time) how happy he was; exhibiting successively, his house, his garden, his orchard, laden with fruit; and also the contrivances he had made to unite his two neighbours' domains with his own.
>
> After the grand circuit had been accomplished, by hospitable contrivance, we approached the "Jasmine harbour," when to our gratifying surprise, we found the tripod table laden with delicious bread and cheese, surmounted by a brown mug of true Taunton ale. We instinctively took our seats. . . . While the dappled sunbeams played on our table, through the umbrageous canopy, the very birds seemed to participate in our felicities, and poured forth their selectest anthems. As we sat in our sylvan hall of splendour, a company of the happiest mortals, (T. Poole, C. Lloyd, S. T. Coleridge, and J. C.) the bright blue heavens; the sporting insects; the balmy zephyrs; the feathered choristers; the sympathy of friends, all augmented the pleasurable to the highest point this side the celestial! . . . While thus elevated in the universal

current of our feelings, Mrs. Coleridge approached with her fine Hartley; we all smiled, but the father's eye beamed transcendental joy! (Cottle, 150)

Such a welcome – by Coleridge and the Wordsworths, who had preceded Lamb to Nether Stowey, was no doubt also Lamb's although the host was limping sadly. Coleridge shortly told Southey,

> Charles Lamb has been with me for a week—he left me Friday morning.—/The second day after Wordsworth came to me, dear Sara accidently emptied a skillet of boiling milk on my foot, which confined me during the whole time of C. Lamb's stay & still prevents me from all *walks* longer than a furlong. (Griggs I, 334)

Otherwise Sara seemed then a girl with whom almost any man could be happy. A casual visitor of this period found her 'sensible, affable, and good natured, thrifty, and industrious, and always neat and prettily dressed – indeed a pretty woman'.[3] If she did not much care for rambles in the hills, there were many things to be done in the household and she the only one to do them. As for small Hartley, Coleridge had told Thelwall,

> We are *very* happy—& my little David Hartley grows a sweet boy—& has high health—he laughs at us till he makes us weep for very fondness.—You would smile to see my eye rolling up to the ceiling in a Lyric fury, and on my knee a *Diaper* pinned, to warm. (Griggs I, 308)

Lamb loved children and shared his delight.

Coleridge had been nursing Charles Lloyd, writing the play *Osorio*, preparing *Poems, Second Edition* for the press, preaching regularly in Unitarian chapels, travelling on various projects, and writing a number of reviews for money.

But the momentous development in his career at this point was his growing friendship for 'the Giant Wordsworth—God love him'.[4] Wordsworth had been impressed with Coleridge on brief encounter at Bristol in 1795, and Coleridge was pursuing the acquaintance with ardour. He had read Wordsworth's *Descriptive Sketches* in his last year at Cambridge, where he knew William's brother Christopher. Wordsworth was then rather more obscure than Coleridge, and had published little, but Coleridge never lacked perception. The early-orphaned William had been to Cambridge and to France in crisis, had fathered his illegitimate daughter, and on return to England avoided his relatives' suggestions for a solid profession. Dorothy his sister, his sailor brother John, and his friend Raisley Calvert—who had died, leaving Wordsworth £900—believed in William's destiny as a poet. To these were now added an ardent, disorganized young friend Basil Montagu—and Samuel Taylor Coleridge.

William Hazlitt met Wordsworth at Stowey a year later, and found him much as Lamb must have done:

> I think I see him now . . . gaunt and Don Quixote-like. He was quaintly dressed (according to the *costume* of that unconstrained period) in a brown fustian jacket and striped pantaloons. There was something of a roll, a lounge in his gait, not unlike his own "Peter Bell." There was a severe, worn pressure of thought about his temples, a fire in his eye (as if he saw something in objects more than the outward appearance,) . . . a convulsive inclination to laughter about the mouth, a good deal at variance with the solemn, stately expression of the rest of his face. . . . He sat down and talked very naturally and freely, with a mixture of clear, gushing accents in his voice, a deep guttural intonation, and a strong tincture of the northern *burr*, like the crust on wine. He instantly began to make havoc of the half of a Cheshire cheese on the table, and said triumphantly that "his marriage with experience had not been so productive as Mr. Southey's in teaching him a knowledge of the good things of life."[5]

Dorothy, once they had settled at Racedown and were together for the first time since childhood, had been able to pull him out of a severe depression over his frustrated hopes for the French Revolution. She turned his eyes to the natural world of hill and valley, mountain and stream, insect, bird, and flower, and to a more patient view of man as redeemable by these manifestations of an ordered universe.

In her, William found a marvellous complement to his own gifts, one who could keep house and provide intellectual and emotional companionship. She in turn adored him and welcomed his new friend with enthusiasm. At this time, Dorothy found Coleridge 'thin', pale, and she at first thought plain, with thick lips and 'not very good' teeth,[6] but animation made up for all, once he began to speak. Coleridge was equally taken with Dorothy, as he wrote to the absent Cottle:

Wordsworth and his exquisite Sister are with me.—She is a woman indeed!—in mind, I mean, & heart—for her person is such, that if you expected to see a pretty woman, you would think her ordinary—if you expected to find an ordinary woman, you would think her pretty!—But her manners are simple, ardent, impressive. . . . Her information various—her eye watchful in minutest observation of nature—and her taste a perfect electrometer—it bends, protrudes, and draws in, at subtlest beauties & most recondite faults. (Griggs I, 330–1)

Lamb, then, arrived among his friends at a crucial period in all their lives, when the Coleridges were just coming to know the Wordsworths well. Sometimes the conversation must have turned to the upbringing of children, for the Coleridges were new parents and the Wordsworths had undertaken the care of the motherless small Basil Montagu, son of Wordsworth's disciple.

The Coleridges' social life at Stowey was enjoyed mainly at Tom Poole's and his neighbours the Cruikshanks', both of whom Lamb visited. Thomas Poole the tanner was self-taught and a lover of literature whose home had an interesting and well-stocked book-room with a barrel ceiling. Now entering his thirties, Poole was a native of Stowey who probably first met Coleridge in London, where he had passed some time learning the tanner's trade – and absorbing Jacobin views which on his return caused consternation among his relatives, and among the townspeople as well.[7] One of the steady friends Coleridge so much needed, Poole had soon prospered in his local trade, lent Coleridge money, and was now for the second time raising a fund for him from friends. He too was interested in education and later founded a school at Stowey. For the moment, Coleridge's radical reputation, of which Stowey people were aware, was making life no easier for Poole, who was popular with the labouring classes. In Poole's bachelor household it was Mrs Poole, his sweet-natured, ailing mother, who presided over the teapot in Poole's 'great windy Parlour',[8] where Coleridge felt so at home.

The John Cruikshanks (he was a lawyer) had been married at the same time as the Coleridges and had a baby daughter Hartley's age. Mrs Poole and Mrs Cruikshank provided friendship for Sara. The young Cruikshanks were extravagant and eventually suffered financial reverses, but John made a small literary niche in history for himself by reporting to Coleridge, at about this time, his dream of a 'skeleton ship, with figures on it',[9] which was to turn up in 'The Ancient Mariner'.

It was probably on this visit, too, that Lamb got to know the unfortunate George Burnett, Coleridge's friend and former Pantisocrat, who liked to walk over from Huntspill nearby.[10] He had literary ambitions and some ability, but little patience with hard work, and while staying with the Coleridges at Clevedon had proved incapable of assisting Coleridge on *The Watchman*. He was soon to become another of Lamb's lame ducks in London.

The epochal event of Lamb's stay was, however, the finding of a house – indeed a large mansion – at moderate rental only four miles from Nether Stowey, to which the Wordsworths were delighted to move. The lease was signed on 14 July, the day Lamb left, and the Wordsworths moved in forthwith, the dependable Poole having made the arrangements and recommended the new tenants of Alfoxden to the landlord. 'Our principal inducement was Coleridge's society,'[11] wrote Dorothy.

The Wordsworths, Sara, and Lamb one evening took a walk in the hills by the sea. Coleridge, with his lame foot, was forced to stay at home. Missing his friends, he made a virtue of necessity and celebrated what he imagined of their experience in his finest poem to date, 'This Lime-Tree Bower My Prison', addressed not to the Wordsworths but to Charles Lamb. He sent this first effort to Southey in a letter of 17 July, and a slightly different version to Charles Lloyd.[12] 'This Lime-Tree Bower' (as sent to Southey) conveys the Nether Stowey quality at the moment of Lamb's visit:

. . . While Wordsworth, his Sister, & C. Lamb were out one evening;/sitting in the arbour of T. Poole's garden, which communicates with mine, I wrote these lines, with which I am pleased——

Well—they are gone: and here must I remain,
Lam'd by the scathe of fire, lonely & faint,
This lime-tree bower my prison. They, meantime,

My friends, whom I may never meet again,
On springy heath, along the hill-top edge,
Wander delighted, and look down, perchance,
On that same rifted Dell, where many an Ash
Twists it's wild limbs beside the ferny rock,
Whose plumy ferns for ever nod and drip
Spray'd by the waterfall. But chiefly Thou,
My gentle-hearted CHARLES! thou, who hast pin'd
And hunger'd after Nature many a year
In the great City pent, winning thy way,
With sad yet bowed soul, thro' evil & pain
And strange calamity.—Ah slowly sink
Behind the western ridge; thou glorious Sun!
Shine in the slant beams of the sinking orb,
Ye purple Heath-flowers! Richlier burn, ye Clouds!
Live in the yellow Light, ye distant Groves!
And kindle, thou blue Ocean! So my friend
Struck with joy's deepest calm, and gazing round
On the wide view, may gaze till all doth seem
Less gross than bodily, a living Thing
That acts upon the mind, and with such hues
As cloathe the Almighty Spirit, when he makes
Spirits perceive His presence!
                                        A Delight
Comes sudden on my heart; and I am glad
As I myself were there! Nor in this bower
Want I sweet sounds or pleasing shapes. I watch'd
The sunshine of each broad transparent Leaf
Broke by the shadows of the Leaf or Stem,
Which hung above it: and that Wall-nut Tree
Was richly ting'd: and a deep radiance lay
Full on the ancient ivy which usurps
Those fronting elms, and now with blackest mass
Makes their dark foliage gleam a lighter hue
Thro' the last twilight.—And tho' the rapid bat
Wheels silent by and not a swallow twitters,
Yet still the solitary humble-bee
Sings in the bean flower. Henceforth I shall know
That nature ne'er deserts the wise & pure,
No scene so narrow, but may well employ
Each faculty of sense, and keep the heart

Awake to Love & Beauty: and sometimes
'Tis well to be bereav'd of promis'd good
That we may lift the soul, & contemplate
With lively joy the joys, we cannot share.
My Sister & my Friends! when the last Rook
Beat it's straight path along the dusky air
Homewards, I bless'd it; deeming, it's black wing
Cross'd, like a speck, the blaze of setting day,
While ye stood gazing; or when all was still,
Flew creaking o'er your heads, & had a charm
For you, my Sister & my Friends! to whom
No sound is dissonant, which tells of Life!

(Griggs I, 335–6)

One of the finest of Coleridge's Conversation Poems,[13] 'This Lime-Tree Bower My Prison' has stood the onslaughts of time and remains Coleridge's great testament of his friendship for Charles Lamb. In Coleridge's final, printed version the next-to-last line reads, 'For thee, my gentle-hearted Charles, to whom'.[14] Lamb was to object vehemently to 'gentle-hearted'.

The older poets were aflame with plans and prospects, comparing poetic ideas and reciting verse. Lamb, who already knew *Salisbury Plain* among Wordsworth's earlier work, was no doubt treated both to *Osorio* and *The Borderers* read aloud under the lime trees. *Osorio* was the conventional Shakespearean blank-verse tragedy Coleridge thought Sheridan required, and though it was not then accepted, it was successfully produced some years later as *Remorse*. Wordsworth's battle tragedy (like *Salisbury Plain*) showed a good man driven to crime by circumstances. Its villain, Oswald, represented Godwin's cold intellectualism, and the change of character in its hero was what Wordsworth himself had observed of participants in the French Revolution. From his 1795 sojourn in London[15] he already knew the Joseph Johnson circle of Jacobins – Johnson had published his first poems. Most interestingly, he had pursued a close acquaintance with William Godwin at that time. He had since come to distrust the advocacy of Reason alone as a guide to behaviour, and Godwin's theories in particular. Godwin (and the French Revolution) must have sometimes come into the 1797 country conversations. All three young men were rather fascinated with Godwin himself, while repelled by his doctrines.

Lamb particularly loved Wordsworth's didactic 'Lines Left upon a Seat in a Yew-tree' – about a man whose attempt to live by intellect alone brought him tragedy. And Lamb would soon follow his friends into the effort to write drama.

Until now, the footing of all three as poets was not very disparate: all enjoyed a modest reputation for modest accomplishment. Very soon Wordsworth and Coleridge would enter upon the period of their greatness as poets, leaving Lamb far behind. But he took stimulus from their intensity and their stature as striving artists. It was with regret that Lamb set forth again on the mail coach for smoky London.

He wrote to Coleridge his warm thanks, asking for a copy of Wordsworth's 'Inscription' – the 'Yew Tree' lines – and wondering what had become of the expected 'Patriot':

> I was looking out for John Thelwall all the way from Bridgewater, and had I met him, I think it would have moved almost me to tears. You will oblige me too by sending me my great-coat, which I left behind in the oblivious state the mind is thrown into at parting—is it not ridiculous that I sometimes envy that great-coat lingering so cunningly behind?—at present I have none—so send it me by a Stowey waggon, if there be such a thing, directing for C. L., No. 45, Chapel-Street, Pentonville near London. But above all, *that Inscription!*—it will recall to me the tones of all your voices—and with them many a remembered kindness to one who could and can repay you all only by the silence of a grateful heart. I could not talk much, while I was with you, but my silence was not sullenness, nor I hope from any bad motive; but, in truth, disuse has made me awkward at it. I know I behaved myself, particularly at Tom Poole's and at Cruikshank's, most like a sulky child; but company and converse are strange to me. It was kind in you all to endure me as you did.
>
> Are you and your dear Sara—to me also very dear, because very kind—agreed yet about the management of little Hartley? and how go on the little rogue's teeth? . . .
>
> My love and thanks to you and all of you.
>
> C. L. (M I, 117–18)

The emotion with which Lamb says he would have encountered Thelwall is rather unexpected. It suggests that they must have had at least a conversation or two if not an even closer acquaintance in the course of Lamb's transmission of the letters Coleridge addressed at the expense of the East India Company to Mr 'Lambe', the signal that each so addressed was for another of Coleridge's London friends. Lamb and Thelwall had both poetry and politics in common – Lamb chose to ignore Thelwall's atheism if it came up – and 'politics' in Lamb's case as in Thelwall's arose from sympathy for the poor and detestation for high-living aristocrats.

Lamb's emotion arose in part from the fact that Thelwall's expedition from London to Nether Stowey on foot – a distance of some 150 miles – was part of his 'pedestrian excursion' announced in the February, 1797, issue of the *Monthly Magazine*, of which Lamb was a reader as well as a contributor. The purpose of the walk was to collect 'accurate information as to the progress of the manufacturing system, and particularly with respect to the real and comparative proportions of wages'.[16] It took Thelwall ultimately as far as Wales, and was recounted in a series of articles in the *Monthly* which at length became part of Thelwall's book, *The Rights of Nature* (1796), whose general argument can be gleaned from this excerpt:

> I affirm that *every* man, and *every* woman, and *every* child, ought to obtain something more, in the general distribution of the fruits of labour, than food, and rags, and a wretched hammock with a poor rug to cover it; and that, without working twelve or fourteen hours a day . . . from six to sixty.—They have a claim, a sacred and inviolable claim . . . to some comfort and enjoyment . . . leisure for such discussions, and . . . such information as may lead to an understanding of their rights. . . . (Thompson, 159)

With these sentiments Lamb's strong sense of justice would agree.

Shortly after the notorious John Thelwall's arrival, Tom Poole's cousin Charlotte noted in her diary (23 July):

> We are shocked to hear that Mr. Thelwall has spent some time at Stowey this week with Mr. Coleridge, and consequently with Tom Poole. Alfoxton house is taken by one of the fraternity, and Woodlands by another. To what are we coming? (Hanson, 208)

From all this succeeded a comic-opera situation, amusing since its outcome was harmless, though with the Two Acts in force it skirted serious danger. With the Wordsworths abetting, Coleridge began to do outdoor research for a poem to be called 'The Brook' (eventually abandoned), based on a local stream which the three friends traced to the Bristol Channel. On 11 August a report of one Dr Lysons reached the Duke of Portland, Home Secretary:

> 11th Aug. My Lord Duke—On the 8th instant I took the liberty to acquaint your grace with a very suspicious business concerning an emigrant family, who have contrived to get possession of a Mansion House at Alfoxton, late belonging to the Rev^d Mr. St. Albyn under Quantock Hills. I am since informed that the Master of the house has no wife with him, but only a woman who passes for his Sister. The man has Camp Stools which he and his visitors take with them when they go about the country upon their nocturnal or diurnal excursions and have also a Portfolio in which they enter their observations which they have been heard to say were almost finished. They have been heard to say they should be rewarded for them, and were very attentive to the River near them. . . . These people may *possibly* be under-agents to some principal in Bristol. (Moorman, 329)

A spy was set on them, but the chase was finally abandoned for lack of evidence.[17] No one seems to have worried about the presence of Charles Lamb.

All ignorant of the official excitement they were causing, the Wordsworths settled in happily, their maid Peggy following with little Basil Montagu in August, and began the time of close and fruitful association. (Later in the summer Coleridge was embarrassed to find what a stir Thelwall's visit had made locally. He had urged the Patriot to settle in Nether Stowey and had to withdraw his encouragement rather forcefully, fearing riots – and not without reason. Thelwall retired to Wales.)

The always tolerant Lamb took heart from his friends' new heart and sufficient nourishment from his happy week to buttress him for some time to come.

We note that Lamb gives Coleridge a new (country) address to which to send the coat. Perhaps it was his holiday that provided the impetus to put the bitter associations of Little Queen Street forever behind him and move his father nearer to where Mary could receive her brother's visits. Or perhaps the move came earlier in the year.[18] Both holiday and new surroundings meant a new start in life and Lamb was soon purging his dark thoughts by expressing them in poetry.

CHAPTER TWELVE

Charles Lloyd

I am dearly fond of Charles Lloyd; he is all goodness, and I have too much of the world in my composition to feel myself thoroughly deserving of his friendship. Lamb to Coleridge, June, 1797 (M I, 111)

He is a sad Tattler . . . Lamb to Coleridge, January, 1820 (CL II, 267)

Soon after Lamb's return from his innocent sojourn among the Jacobins, Charles Lloyd descended on him once again out of the blue in mid-August (1797), a good deal recovered in mind after his stay with Dr Darwin. Just now, however, he was agitated about the sudden reversal of his marriage prospects with Sophia Pemberton. Charles Lloyd senior had made his peace with their proposed union, as had Sophia's family, but one or the other had again broached – perhaps as a condition of assent – the elder Lloyd's dearest wish, that Charles should work in the bank, with a view to succeeding him. Matters had progressed so far as the finding of a house in Birmingham, the annual rent to be paid by his father, but all such plans were shelved in consternation as the two resisted the bank most firmly. On all of his problems Lloyd sought Lamb's advice, which Lamb at that moment felt quite helpless to give. Lloyd with his usual disdain of geography (he could pay for good transport) then suggested they seek out Southey in Hampshire, presumably to get his views; Southey always had views. Lamb grasped at the straw and agreed to accompany him to Burton, some seventy miles away – a long day's jolting journey – on Monday, 14 August, returning the next day.

Southey greeted them kindly and listened with sympathy in spite of his private disapproval of Lloyd's marrying at all in his unstable state; he was perhaps flattered by the approach. While they were with him Lloyd composed an 'explicit'[1] letter to Sophia (suggesting they marry secretly at once?) and then decided to stay on with Southey instead of going back to London with Lamb as planned. In London again, deeply worried about his friend's state of mind,

Lamb wrote a poem to Lloyd which marked a new departure both in style and mood. Like Wordsworth's 'Yew-Tree' it is in blank verse, though more Shakespearean than Wordsworthian in diction and tone. Into it creeps the shadow of his own mounting bitterness at a world that drives men mad – Cowper, himself, Mary, and Lloyd. He sent the poem to Coleridge in September.

> A stranger & alone I past those scenes
> We past so late together; & my heart
> Felt something like desertion, as I look'd
> Around me, & the pleasant voice of friend
> Was absent, & the cordial look was there
> No more, to smile on me. I thought on Lloyd
> All he had been to me! And now I go
> Again to mingle with a world impure,
> With men who make a mock of holy things,
> Mistaken, & of man's best hope think scorn.—
> The World does much to warp the heart of Man,
> I may sometimes join its ideot laugh—
> Of this I now complain not.—Deal with me,
> Omniscient father, as thou judgest best;
> And in *thy* season tender thou my heart—
> I pray not for myself. I pray for him
> Whose [soul] is sore perplex'd. Shine thou on him,
> Father of lights, & in the difficult paths
> Make plain his way before him: his own thoughts
> May he not think, his own ends not pursue;
> So shall he best perform thy will on earth.
> Greatest & Best, thy will be ever ours!
>
> (M I, 122)

This was to be the mood of his poetry for the next few months, a sombre thoughtful one, and yet in writing it down, strengthened by his growing religious faith (resistant as it was to the atheists), he was ridding himself of his own particular hell in turning it to creative use.

Lloyd's emotional difficulties, which were to have their effect on Lamb's life, may detain us a moment. Coleridge had described him to Poole as 'assuredly a man of great Genius', who 'for years together met with no congenial minds . . . habitually suppressing his Feelings'.[2] The 'opium eater' Thomas De Quincey, a later friend of both, has provided the most perceptive contemporary analysis. De Quincey thought the source of Lloyd's troubles in part the effect of Quaker stringencies – the suppression of feelings – and of the oddities of the Quaker 'plain' dress, particularly the male dress. The wide-brimmed hat and dark plain suiting, at a time when silks and colour and powdered hair were the hallmarks of a gentleman, were all too apt to cause titters among the servant class when a boy or man in this attire passed them in the streets. Such experiences, De Quincey felt, had increased Charles Lloyd's morbid sensitivity and helped to alienate him from his family's deeply held faith. But there were deeper causes.

'He indeed, of all men,' wrote De Quincey, 'was the least fitted to contend with the world's scorn, for he had no great fortitude of mind. . . . There was something that appeared effeminate about [him] . . . something which conciliated your pity by the feeling it impressed you with, of being part of his disease. His sensibility was eminently *Rousseauish*',[3] and yet there was a 'splendour' about the way Lloyd could analyse human beings. But the splendour 'was quite hidden from himself' and he was – among strangers – preternaturally modest and shy. His discourses on human nature were eloquent 'in proportion to his unhappiness: for unhappiness it was, and the restlessness of internal irritation, that chiefly drove him to exertions of his intellect'. He would talk so 'only before confidential friends, those on whom he could rely for harbouring no shade of ridicule towards himself or the theme. Let but one person enter the room of whose sympathy he did not feel secure, and his powers forsook him as suddenly as the buoyancy of a bird that has received a mortal shot in its wing.'[4]

Lloyd was tall and 'somewhat clumsy'; except for his nose, prominent like his father's, his features 'were not striking but they expressed great goodness of heart'.[5] This quality, as well as his creative and critical gifts, drew to him the loyalty of others similarly sensitive, and for all his shyness he exercised considerable determination to get to know them. (The Romantic generation were interested in human psychology and ready to regard its more aberrant forms with compassion.) But at bottom he suffered from a sense of his own emptiness and the fear that he would disappoint his friends and be rejected by them. In alienating one friend from another, then, he found the kind of power his weakness desperately sought. For he harboured fearful hatreds and resentments, as the pathological always do. When De Quincey, who had known Lloyd well and never ceased to love him, met him on escape from an asylum much later, he was astounded to observe that his friend

> now, for the first time in his life, had dropped his gentle and remarkably quiet demeanor, for a tone, savage and ferocious, towards more than one individual. This tone, however, lurked under a mask . . . (*Lake Poets*, 328)

When his disorder intensified, he suffered from paranoid delusions. He told De Quincey on another occasion

> that his situation internally was always this: it seemed to him as if on some distant road he heard a dull trampling sound, and that he knew it, by a misgiving, to be the sound of some man, or party of men, continually advancing slowly, continually threatening, or continually accusing him; that all the various artifices which he practised for cheating himself into comfort, or beguiling his sad forebodings, were, in fact, but like so many furious attempts, by drum and trumpets, or even by artillery, to drown the distant noise of his enemies; that, every now and then, mere curiosity, or rather breathless anxiety, caused him to hush the artificial din, and to put himself into the attitude of listening again; when, again and again, and so he was sure it would still be, he caught the sullen and accursed sound, trampling and voices of men, or whatever it were, still steadily advancing, though still perhaps at a great distance. (*Lake Poets*, 326)

This, then, was the complex and tortured young man that Lamb regarded with such affection. Modern psychiatry diagnoses the disorder (which came to a crisis in 1815) as paranoid schizophrenia.[6]

Lamb next heard from Lloyd at Bath the news that he was heading *with Southey* for Birmingham (his home and Sophia's) with the purpose of persuading the nineteen-year-old Sophia to a 'Scotch marriage' – both marriage and divorce were more simply and quickly accomplished over the Border. 'I greatly feared,' Lamb wrote to Coleridge, that she would never consent to this, from what Lloyd had told me of her character. But waited most anxiously the result. Since then I have not had one letter—. For God's sake, if you get any intelligence of or from Chas Lloyd, communicate it, for I am much alarmed— (M I, 119)

Only a week or so has elapsed but Lamb's anxiety is such that he has also written the whole story to *George Burnett* (Coleridge's inept assistant on *The Watchman*), begging for news. He feels it necessary to explain to Coleridge why Lloyd has sought out Southey, hitherto little more than an acquaintance, in this most intimate affair, rather than Coleridge himself, so recently Lloyd's dearest friend and idol, not to say nurse and comforter. If Coleridge began to look at Lloyd – and indeed at Southey and Lamb – with a jaundiced eye, it was hardly surprising.

The 'Scotch marriage' proposal, which Southey abetted, in the end proved unsuccessful, Sophia evidently refusing. In September Lloyd was at Stowey again, coinciding with the epochal first visit of the potter's sons Tom and Josiah Wedgwood, which was to ripen into important friendship with Coleridge. A week or so later he was complaining of Coleridge to Lamb and widening the small rift, for Lamb wrote, 'You use Lloyd very ill—never writing to him. I tell you again that his is not a mind with which you should play tricks. He deserves more tenderness from you—.' But the letter is good-natured banter, begging for his 'Great coat—the snow & and the rain season is at hand & I have but a wretched old coat, once my fathers, to keep 'em off— —& that is transitory . . . meek Emblem wilt thou be, old Winter, of a friend's neglect—Cold, cold, cold—'[7]

Between forays afield, Lloyd had decided to stay on with the Southeys, and Southey was allowing it, little as he liked Lloyd's untidiness, 'ficklenesses', 'contemptible frivolities', and want of consistency.[8] Lloyd had given Southey Coleridge's *vices* as his reason for quitting Nether Stowey, in which he had Southey's sympathy. Southey had decided he must be 'of service' to Lloyd, 'therefore I went to Birmingham and now give him a home'.[9]

In October Southey wrote from Bath (where he was visiting), 'Lloyd is here. He has met with a heavy and most unexpected disappointment, and bears the inconstancy of a woman as a man ought to bear it.' Now, said Southey, Lloyd was already 'employed in developing all his feelings and principles in the form of a novel. . . . I never saw a mind so indefatigably active; what he has done pleases very much.'[10] The novel was *Edmund Oliver* and its hero a weak and foolish individual in whose life and proclivities it was all too easy to detect a caricature of Lloyd's erstwhile friend and mentor Samuel Taylor Coleridge. Coleridge's not always favourable comments on *his* friend Southey, purveyed in confidence at Nether Stowey, were now being relayed by Lloyd to Southey. The Southeys returned to London late in November, together with Charles Lloyd.

Lamb had sent his poem on Lloyd – as 'To a Friend', with Lloyd's name deleted from the context – to the *Monthly Magazine*, where it was duly printed in October 1797, his fourth contribution to that periodical, the Cowper sonnet having appeared in December, his poetic letter of disappointment to the Coleridges in January ('Was it so hard a thing?'), and some undistinguished lines to Mary ('Friend of my earliest years') in March. The *Monthly* had been founded only the year before – by Sir Richard Phillips, probably on the initial planning and encouragement of the now-exiled Joseph Priestley. The editor of a rival publication once said that Phillips, 'nursed in the School of Jacobinism, commenced his career as a promulgator of Paine's *Rights of Man*,'[11] and Lamb found himself here in another nest of Radicals. Dr John Aikin, its literary editor, was the centre of a circle of Dissenting liberals, and – besides Coleridge – his contributors then and later included Thelwall, Godwin, Hazlitt, and Southey. (The magazine did very well and continued in relative prosperity until 1824.) Coleridge, it is true, had complained in December that in its pages 'the Infidels have it all hollow'.[12] But religious dissenters like Lamb were represented too and Phillips paid contributors six guineas.

Coleridge was again beset by money worries, as well as Lloyd–Lamb–Southey worries, and Sara worries: she had had a miscarriage earlier, he thought, but by September she was pregnant again.[13] He was now writing popular ballads for cash and had carried his play to Bowles for a first meeting. Bowles was, in person, a disappointment, and the play's fate not decided. Coleridge's general state of irritation and anxiety, as well, no doubt, as the influence of a poet of broader vision than Bowles, led him, almost on impulse, to write three satirical 'Sonnets Attempted in the Manner of "Contemporary Writers"', ridiculing the very kind of poetry he had so ardently defended in *Poems, Second Edition* – the sonnet à la Bowles. He wrote to Cottle the publisher,

I sent three mock Sonnets [to Phillips' *Monthly*] in ridicule of my own & Charles Lloyd's, & Lamb's &c &c—in ridicule of that affectation of unaffectedness, of jumping and misplaced accent on common-place epithets, flat lines forced into poetry by Italics (signifying how well & mouthis[h]ly the Author would read them) puny pathos &c &c—the instances are almost all taken from mine & Lloyd's poems—I signed them Nehemiah Higginbottom. I think they may do good to our young Bards.— (Griggs I, 357–8)[14]

They did little good to anyone, though they were clever and must have amused readers already inclined to scoff at sentimentalities. They did least good to Coleridge's personal relations with Lamb, Lloyd, and *Southey*, for though it is now generally acknowledged that Coleridge was honest in denying Southey as a butt of his lampoons, his three friends, including Lamb, were convinced that Southey was one of those meant. The *Anti-Jacobin, or Weekly Examiner*, a government-inspired organ, was already attacking the 'Jacobin Poets of the New School'[15] with particular reference to Southey, and parodies on him; he was certainly severely sensitized by the time he read 'Higginbottom' and Lloyd no doubt egged on his suspicions. Lamb appears (in extant letters, at any rate) to have taken umbrage only on Southey's behalf. Lloyd was always affected by ridicule, and penned away at *Edmund Oliver* with intensified satirical vigour. The *Anti-Jacobin*'s 'New School' meant precisely Coleridge, Lamb, Lloyd, and Southey, as a later number was to prove. Notoriety is not usually bad for the sale of a book: Coleridge may have had this in mind. He also was much concerned with *self-reform*, and in his eagerness only somewhat conscious of how his parodies would affect the other parties attacked. Whatever else Higginbottom meant, it meant that the poets were becoming known in the small literary world of the time.

Southey's outrage over Higginbottom, now an open quarrel, prompted him a little later to publish a parody directed at Coleridge about one 'Abel Shuffelbottom'. He had also made available to Lloyd his own notes on a Coleridge-like figure in the plot of an abortive novel to be called *Edmund Oliver* which he himself had sketched out in 1796! This ready assistance helps to explain the speed with which Lloyd brought his own *Edmund Oliver* (all unknown to Coleridge) to completion by early January. The role of Southey in this affair suggests that Coleridge was not far wrong when he later spoke of Lloyd as the 'instrument of another man's darker passions'.[16] (Lloyd had done his bit to darken them.) And to whom would Lloyd dedicate *Edmund Oliver*? Why, to his friend Charles Lamb. And so, with Lloyd pulling the strings, the sorry tragicomedy moved forward.

CHAPTER THIRTEEN

The Tragic Poet

Forgive me, O my Maker!
If in a mood of grief I sin almost
In sometimes brooding on the days long past,
And from the grave of time wishing them back . . .
'Written a Year After the Events'

$(P, 21)$

As winter began to come on and Lamb found himself alone with his unrelenting duties, his mood darkened. In September he sent to Coleridge, together with the 'Lloyd' poem, one 'Written a Year After the Events' ('Alas! how I am chang'd'), in which he calls on God to restore him from the 'spiritual death'[1] he has suffered ever since the loss of his mother, hoping that he and Mary will see their mother again beyond the grave, regretting once more the worldliness of the Ann Simmons episode, regretting his lost childhood. Mary is still away from home (he is not, he cries, sufficiently grateful for her recovery), his friends 'gone diverse ways':

> I only am left, with unavailing grief
> To mourn one parent dead, and see one live
> Of all life's joys bereft and desolate . . .
> $(P, 21)$

There remain to him only a few intimates, one especially (probably Mary)

> to bear me on
> To the not unpeaceful evening of a day
> Made black by morning storms!
> $(P, 22)$

The next, 'Written Soon After the Preceding Poem', is addressed to both parents – the dead, whom he wishes he had never made unhappy,[2] and the living, whom nothing can help:

For wounds like his Christ is the only cure,
And gospel promises are his by right,
For these were given to the poor in heart.
Go preach thou to him of a world to come,
Where friends shall meet, and know each other's face.
Say less than this, and say it to the winds.

(*P*, 22)

The darkest of the poems of this time is, however, 'Composed at Midnight', arising from a sleepless night: a man is dying, racked with consumption, on the floor above him, his every struggle for breath audible to Lamb below.

Some few groans more, death comes, and there's an end.
'Tis darkness and conjecture all beyond.

This leads him to ponder on the Established Church, with its 'heaven of gold' for the consciously pious and its devils in hell for sinners. 'Fancy'

Hath o'erstock'd hell with devils, and brought down
By her enormous fablings and mad lies
Discredit on the gospel's serious truths
And salutary fears.

The poem ends,

Blessed be God,
The measure of his judgments is not fixed
By man's erroneous standard. He discerns
No such inordinate difference and vast
Betwixt the sinner and the saint, to doom
Such disproportion'd fates. Compared with him
No man on earth is holy called: they best
Stand in his sight approved, who at his feet
Their little crowns of virtue cast, and yield
To him of his own works the praise, his due.

(*P*, 24–5)

If one can get past Lamb's Shakespearean diction, and the complicated involutions of his thinking, to the desperately lonely man, trying to make sense of all that has happened to him, all that is happening to the man upstairs, the poem is Lamb laid bare. He had written to Coleridge a month after the tragedy,

> God, in the New Testament (*our best guide*) is represented to us in the kind, . . . familiar light of a *parent*. . . . Let us learn to think humbly of ourselves, and rejoice in the appellation of 'dear children,' 'brethren,' and 'co-heirs with Christ of the promises,' seeking to know no further. (M I, 54)

Lamb's uncomplicated but merciful deity is not conventional Christianity. Much as the son would like to offer old John Lamb a future life with friends, he himself cannot be sure of it. His God holds out no promise of an afterlife, only the hope of 'rest':' 'Tis darkness and conjecture all beyond.' But God exists for Lamb, and in these poems sentiment has vanished into the faith that sustains him.

The young poet's need to believe in God is set forth again (though never again so starkly) in 'Living Without God in the World'. This time the cry is against the unbelievers who see Man as lord of himself, the proponents of a mechanistic universe, the Godwins and the Holcrofts:

> Some braver spirits of the modern stamp
> Affect a Godhead nearer: these talk loud
> Of mind, and independent intellect,
> Of energies omnipotent in man,
> And man of his own fate artificer;
> Yea of his own life Lord, and of the days
> Of his abode on earth, when time shall be,
> That life immortal shall become an art,
> Or Death, by chymic practices deceived,
> Forego the scent, which for six thousand years
> Like a good hound he has followed, or at length
> More manners learning, and a decent sense
> And reverence of a philosophic world,
> Relent, and leave to prey on carcasses.
>
> But these are fancies of a few: the rest,
> Atheists, or Deists only in the name,
> By word or deed deny a God. They eat
> Their daily bread, and draw the breath of heaven

Without or thought or thanks; heaven's roof to them
Is but a painted ceiling hung with lamps,
No more, that lights them to their purposes.
They wander "loose about," they nothing see,
Themselves except, and creatures like themselves,
Short-liv'd, short-sighted, impotent to save.
So on their dissolute spirits, soon or late,
Destruction cometh "like an armed man,"
Or like a dream of murder in the night,
Withering their mortal faculties, and breaking
The bones of all their pride.

(*P*, 17–18)

The first section of the excerpt is not easy reading; poetry – the
fusion of sound and sense which elicits a telling response – has been
submerged in philosophic verbal complexities. The argument is
specifically directed at the Godwinites, indeed the second line above
suggests a pun between Godhead and Godwin,[3] and the lines on
Death refer to Godwin's expectation, given voice in *Political Justice*,
that human advance could bring the total conquest of disease and
death. Lamb is grimly sceptical. He resents the lack of humility, lack
of the sense of man's littleness, lack of the ability to wonder and
adore, and resents most of all the overweening pride of mere men
feeling able to *manage* human life that he finds basic to Godwinian
atheistic rationality.

It is ironic, not only that Lamb should later become a close and
sympathetic friend of Godwin in his decline, but that even, perhaps,
as these lines were being written,[4] Death was taking Mary
Wollstonecraft Godwin, soon after the birth of the future Mary
Shelley and as the result of it, to the intense distress of all Lamb's
present and future friends who knew her – particularly Southey,
Basil Montagu, Charles Lloyd, and Coleridge.[5] Godwin provided a
funeral for her and wrote to his friend George Lyman Tuthill – one
day to be the Lambs' doctor – reproving him because Tuthill, of all
Godwin's intimate circle of unbelievers, was, in spite of 'warmest
affection' refusing to attend the religious ceremonies on principle.
Said Godwin:

There is not perhaps an individual in my list whose opinions are
not as adverse to religious ceremonies as your own, and who
might not with equal propriety shrink from, and desert the

remains of the first of women. . . . Think of the subject again.
Consult Holcroft. Act finally upon the genuine decision of your
own judgment.[6]

Even the godless fell back on God when convention demanded it:
how interesting the young Lamb would have found this, had he
known.

The beginning of the poem brings Lamb's religion beyond the
God-as-father concept into the vision of a force mightier than
ourselves, source of the loveliness and grandeur of the natural
world – to which Lamb, for all his love of men in cities, resorted all
his life for holidays and walks and a change of pace. There is a touch
of Wordsworth in the first lines:

> Mystery of God! thou brave and beauteous world,
> Made fair with light and shade and stars and flowers,
> Made fearful and august with woods and rocks,
> Jagg'd precipice, black mountain, sea in storms,
> Sun, over all, that no co-rival owns,
> But thro' Heaven's pavement rides as in despite
> Or mockery of the littleness of man!
> I see a mighty arm, by man unseen,
> Resistless, not to be controul'd, that guides,
> In solitude of unshared energies,
> All these thy ceaseless miracles, O world!
>
> (*P*, 17)

'Composed at Midnight' and 'Living Without God' are fascinating in the revelation of what really bothered Lamb about his world
in his very young manhood. (Years later, from a more tolerant
stance, he would publicly defend his unbeliever friends.[7]) With
'Jacobinism' he felt at home: his own concern was for the weak and
deprived. But as so often happens, it was the faults, as he saw them,
of *allies* in this concern that were most troubling. To these misgivings
he gave vent when writing of his own sorrows. As poetry the
language is too stiff, prosy, imitative of the past, and too immersed in
contemporary argument to have much appeal for modern readers,
yet the two poems are more revealing of Lamb's intellectual and
spiritual progress, and deeper in theme and expression, than the
poem of this period that has best survived – 'The Old Familiar
Faces' of 1798.

CHAPTER FOURTEEN

The Break with Coleridge

. . . As for C. Lloyd, it would be cruel to attribute his conduct to aught but a diseased mind. Thomas Poole to Robert Southey, 8 August 1799[1]

That Charles Lloyd has a bad Heart, I do not even think; but I venture to say . . . that he has not a good one. He is not fit to be any man's Friend, *and to all but a very guarded man he is a perilous acquaintance.* Coleridge to Southey, 15 October 1799 (Griggs 1, 541)

He is a sad Tattler. . . . Twenty years ago he almost alienated you . . . from me, or me from you, I don't know which. Lamb to Coleridge, 10 January 1820 (CL II, 267–8)

A latent irritation with Lamb, Lloyd, and Southey lay behind Coleridge's hastily sending the Higginbottom sonnets to the public press. The new association with the Wordsworths had overnight changed his view of poetry, dispelled his admiration of Bowles, and released powers hardly hinted at in his previous poetry. The shifting allegiances among the friends, fanned by Lloyd's busybodying, affected Lamb as well. Small fissures began to form in the fabric of the Lamb–Coleridge friendship which Lamb's general wretchedness left him ill able to withstand.

Just at this time some of Lamb's earlier correspondence seems to have borne fruit. When Coleridge, William, and Dorothy, now rambling together almost daily, took a walk to Dulverton in November of 1797, Lamb's influence among others may have been at work in the conception of 'The Ancient Mariner'. In the course of the walk was first bruited a plan to write a joint ballad – to raise much-needed funds. As the project proceeded, it took wing in a manner not native to Wordsworth and became Coleridge's own. Did he recall Lamb's exhortation to 'Cultivate simplicity, Coleridge'? Certainly all trace of turgidity vanished in the exquisite short ballad-lines of the new poem, in which the nature of evil is a main theme. The preceding February Lamb had written, 'I have a dim recollection, that when in town you were talking of the Origin of Evil as a most prolific subject for a long Poem—why not adopt it, Coleridge? there would be room for imagination?' Lamb's next sentence, proposing a 'vision or a dream'[2] on another topic (perhaps on the moon), suggests the very essence of the 'Mariner' as it appeared.[3]

But even as the 'Mariner' was born, the poet and his friend were being drawn apart. There is a gap in Lamb's extant letters to Coleridge from September 1797 to January 1798, and Lamb reproved Coleridge in September for not writing.

The Southeys and Lloyd came to London in November and Lloyd at least was soon in contact with Lamb. Lamb's presence may in part account for a letter, now lost but probably of December, in which Lamb wrote a reproof to Coleridge for attacking Southey through the Higginbottom sonnets. We shall come to Coleridge's denial of May 1798. How close Lloyd was to Lamb is indicated in a letter to his brother Robert of September: 'Lamb often talks of you. I wish you would order from London (they are sold at Robinson's, London) a new edition of Coleridge's "Poems"—it contains all mine and his, and is just come out.'[4]

Southey had now had enough of Charles Lloyd as a family attachment – 'Our living together was unpleasant, and we separated, at his proposal,'[5] he wrote to his brother. Lloyd thereupon settled on Lamb's friend Jem White for his London stay. As Southey later recalled, 'No two men could be imagined more unlike each other. Lloyd had no drollery in his nature; White seemed to have nothing else. You will easily understand how Lamb could sympathize with both.'[6] Lloyd wrote a little later to Southey at Bath 'I have here created a sort of settled dependence upon myself for the happiness of one or two individuals—there are no beings in Bath so forlorn as Lamb, nor none to whom I can be of as much moral service as White.'[7] (Moral service? Perhaps to cure him of being Southey's anathema – one who laughed too often.)

Almost immediately Lloyd and Lamb discussed plans for publishing their new verses together – but without Coleridge, who had now a ready collaborator in Wordsworth. Coleridge's enthusiasm for Wordsworth had not escaped the jealous Lloyd in his two summer visits to Stowey, for Coleridge concealed it from no one.

We do not know that Coleridge saw Lamb or Lloyd on any of his three autumn visits to London, but he may have done so. More probably he consciously avoided Lloyd and White (who disliked

Coleridge), and therefore Lamb as well. Or he may have simply forgotten about Lamb again, taken up as he was with projects to earn money.[8]

Ann Simmons was once again in the forefront of Lamb's mind, and he plunged into the writing of *Rosamund Gray*. The work was both a challenge and the exorcizing of a ghost – or so he must have hoped. It was a relief, no doubt, to be celebrating youth and life and love. The first chapters of the novella suggest joy in the writing and escape from the prisonhouse.

The prisonhouse and cribbage with old John Lamb were still very much with him, however, and the next blow struck just before Christmas: Mary reverted to her wild talk and sinister look and had again to be restrained in the Hoxton asylum.

This was a severe setback. Charles had hoped that she might return to her nearly normal state as before the tragedy. Now he could predict with fair certainty that this was not to be – that his life would henceforth consist of a permanent watchful foreboding, punctuated with periods of separation, loneliness, and desperate anxiety. His spirits, just beginning to lift, rapidly plummeted.

Lamb spent several hours of his lonely Christmas writing a poem to Mary. His was a sharp contrast to Coleridge's holiday: Coleridge's fortunes now took a dramatic turn for the better. With Sara again pregnant, he had been seriously negotiating for a paying post as successor to the retiring Unitarian minister at Shrewsbury. But he was already experiencing doubts about Unitarianism and suffering a crisis of conscience when, to his surprise, Tom and Josiah Wedgwood, whom he had met in September at Wordsworth's, sent him £100 at Christmas – say £1000 or $2250 in our day. In January they announced by letter that they so admired his talents that they wished to offer, without conditions, £150 a year for life! Once he had decided to accept this – and with it freedom from the Unitarian ministry – he wrote off to his friends ecstatically, not forgetting Lamb.

Lamb, meanwhile, was subjected to the efforts of White and Lloyd to distract him from his trials. Weary and miserable, he wanted only to be left alone. But the distractions were lifesavers, and it may well be that his friends preserved him from a second serious breakdown.[9]

Rosamund Gray when it appeared was dedicated to his Christ's Hospital friend Marmaduke Thompson. Lamb had maintained a relationship with him that we hear little of until 1799. In the copy of

Blank Verse Lamb gave him Thompson transcribed an excerpt from a letter Lamb wrote him at about this time:

> I spent an evening about a week ago with Lloyd. White, and a miscellaneous company was there. Lloyd had been playing on a pianoforte till my feelings were wrought too high not to require Vent. I left em suddenly & rushed into ye Temple, where I was born, you know—& in ye state of mind that followed [I composed these] stanzas. They pretend to little like Metre, but they will pourtray ye Disorder I was in. (CL i, 121)[10]

The 'disorder' had produced his enduring poem, 'The Old Familiar Faces', in which Lamb managed to transcend the particulars of his situation to express his feelings about it in universal terms. Again he falls into unrhymed stanzas, derived from the Elizabethan dramatist Massinger:

> Where are they gone, the old familiar faces?
>
> I had a mother, but she died, and left me,
> Died prematurely in a day of horrors—
> All, all are gone, the old familiar faces.
>
> I have had playmates, I have had companions,
> In my days of childhood, in my joyful school-days—
> All, all are gone, the old familiar faces.
>
> I have been laughing, I have been carousing,
> Drinking late, sitting late, with my bosom cronies—
> All, all are gone, the old familiar faces.
>
> I loved a love once, fairest among women.
> Closed are her doors on me, I must not see her—
> All, all are gone, the old familiar faces.
>
> I have a friend, a kinder friend has no man.
> Like an ingrate, I left my friend abruptly;
> Left him, to muse on the old familiar faces.
>
> Ghost-like, I paced round the haunts of my childhood.
> Earth seem'd a desert I was bound to traverse,
> Seeking to find the old familiar faces.

Friend of my bosom, thou more than a brother!
Why wert not thou born in my father's dwelling?
So might we talk of the old familiar faces.

For some they have died, and some they have left me,
And some are taken from me; all are departed;
All, all are gone, the old familiar faces.

(M 1, 125)

When he published the poem in *Blank Verse* Lamb included the
first four lines. Thereafter he suppressed them. These were not for
Mary's eyes, nor indeed for anyone else's, when he thought it over.
'The Old Familiar Faces' is easily keyed, and E. V. Lucas's
interpretation is still valid: Ann Simmons is the 'love' of the fourth
full stanza, Lloyd the 'friend' of the fifth, Coleridge of the seventh,
and Mary Lamb the reference in italics of the eighth.[11] Lucas limits
the italics to Mary, but the plural suggests that Ann Simmons is
meant too. The impact is clear, direct, and poignant. The poem is
original; if we are reminded of any other poem at all, we may note
that repetition of one line throughout has somewhat the effect of
François Villon's *Où sont les neiges d'antan?*,[12] probably not even
known to Lamb. We need no special knowledge of the poet's life to
share the emotion which comes to all of us with the passing of time.
Lamb too, at last, has cultivated simplicity.

The poem marked, though Lamb did not know it, the end of the
old, trusting intercourse with his 'more than a brother' Samuel
Taylor Coleridge, who was already well into his *annus mirabilis*,
the wonderful year to which Lamb had helped bring him and in
which Lamb would no longer share, the year of 'The Ancient
Mariner', 'Christabel' and 'Kubla Khan'. Lamb wrote, however,
one more warm letter to Coleridge at the end of January 1798,
responding to the Wedgwood news and to an invitation for Mary to
come to Nether Stowey as soon as she was well enough.

'I rejoyce in your good fortunes— — may God at the last settle
you,' Lamb says. But he no longer feels able to share in Coleridge's
life completely; his own joy is all too detached and measured. Now he
tells Coleridge nothing of his work, nor does he send him 'The Old
Familiar Faces' in spite of its fraternal reference to Coleridge. The
poem must have been ready, for he dated it 'January, 1798' in the
printed version. And yet there is affection and the old readiness to
confide:

[January 28, 1798]

You have writ me Many kind letters, and I have answered none of them—. I do'nt deserve your attentions—an unnatural indifference has been creeping on me, since my last misfortunes, or I should have seized the first opening of a correspondence with *you*—to you I owe much, under God—in my brief acquaintance with you in London your conversations won me to the better cause, and rescued me from the polluting spirit of the world—. I might have been a worthless character without you—as it is, I do possess a certain improveable portion of devotional feelings—tho' when I view myself in the light of divine truth, and not according to the common measures of human judgment, I am altogether corrupt & sinful—this is no cant—I am very sincere————.

. . . I had well nigh quarrelled with Charles Lloyd—& for no other reason, I believe, than that the good creature did all he could to make me happy— —. the truth is, I thought he tried to force my mind from its natural & proper bent, he continually wished me to be from home, he was drawing me *from* the consideration of my poor dear Mary's situation, rather than assisting me to gain a proper view of it, with religious consolations—. I wanted to be left to the tendency of my own mind in a solitary state, which in times past, I knew, had led to quietness & a patient bearing of the yoke—he was hurt, that I was not more constantly with him—but he was living with White, a man to whom I had never been accustomed to impart my *dearest feelings*—tho' from long habits of friendliness, & many a social & good quality, I loved him very much—. I met company there sometimes— ——indiscriminate company, any society almost, when I am in affliction, is sorely painful to me—. . . .

Of his sister he reports,

Mary is recovering . . . . . . [13] but I see no opening yet of a situation for her—your invitation went to my very heart—but you have a power of exciting interest, [o]f leading all hearts captive, too forcible [to] admit of Mary's being with you—. I consider her as perpetually on the brink of madness—. I think, you would almost make her dance within an inch of the precipice—she must be with duller fancies, & cooler intellects . . . [14]I know a young man of this description, who has suited her these twenty years, & may live to do so still—if we are one day restor'd to each other—. . . .(M I, 125–7)

The new poem to Mary, 'Written on Christmas Day, 1797',
maintains the sombre mood of the others we have seen which were
to go into his and Lloyd's *Blank Verse*. It is of great biographical
interest and not readily available to modern readers. It calls again
upon the Christianity which Coleridge had taught him and on
which he endeavoured to lean. We see in these poems the
crystallizing of a certain steadfastness which was never to leave him.
Nor, though he moved away from churches and sectarian creeds,
did his essential Christianity ever leave him. Many years later
Coleridge said as much to his and Lamb's young friend Thomas
Allsop:

> No, no; Lamb's skepticism has not come lightly, nor is he a
> skeptic. The harsh reproof to Godwin for his contemptuous
> allusion to Christ before a well-trained child, proves that he is not
> a skeptic. His mind, never prone to analysis, seems to have been
> disgusted with the hollow pretences, the false reasonings and
> absurdities of the rogues and fools with which all establishments,
> and all creeds seeking to become established, abound.[15] I look
> upon Lamb as one hovering between earth and heaven; neither
> hoping much nor fearing any thing. . . . (Allsop, 60)

And so to Mary:

WRITTEN ON CHRISTMAS DAY, 1797

I am a widow'd thing, now thou art gone!
Now thou art gone, my own familiar friend,
Companion, sister, help-mate, counsellor!
Alas! that honour'd mind, whose sweet reproof
And meekest wisdom in times past have smooth'd
The unfilial harshness of my foolish speech,
And made me loving to my parents old,
(Why is this so, ah God! why is this so?)
That honour'd mind become a fearful blank,
Her senses lock'd up, and herself kept out
From human sight or converse, while so many
Of the foolish sort are left to roam at large,
Doing all acts of folly, and sin, and shame?
Thy paths are mystery!
            Yet I will not think,
Sweet friend, but we shall one day meet, and live

In quietness, and die so, fearing God.
Or if *not*, and these false suggestions be
A fit of the weak nature, loth to part
With what it lov'd so long, and held so dear;
If thou art to be taken, and I left
(More sinning, yet unpunish'd, save in thee),
It is the will of God, and we are clay
In the potter's hands; and, at the worst, are made
From absolute nothing, vessels of disgrace,
Till, his most righteous purpose wrought in us,
Our purified spirits find their perfect rest.

(*P*, 23)

It was a heroic stance in a man not quite twenty-three who wrote to convince himself. He seems at the conclusion to have found a way of coping – with his own weaknesses, with his unhappy lot, and with his sister's. This would be a better poem without what follows 'Or if *not*,' which plunges once more into complexities the poet in Lamb cannot resolve, but its function as comfort and catharsis is clear.

There is again a gap in the Lamb record, though presumably Mary soon recovered as much as she was ever to do, and we know Lamb to have been busy with Lloyd in getting *Blank Verse* ready for a London publisher: it appeared in May from Arch's bookstore. Very soon, too, Lamb was doing the same for *Rosamund Gray*, to be published in the summer by Lee and Hurst of London. Its title appears to have originated in an early poem of Lloyd's whose first stanza concludes,

I'll boast the intuitive feelings of worth—
The virtues of Rosamund Gray.

(WCH, 163)

The story itself, Lamb told Southey in October, came from a bawdy street ballad – 'the first words of that foolish Ballad put me upon scribbling my Rosamund'. The ballad begins,

An old woman cloathed in grey
Whose daughter was charming and young,
And she was deluded away
By Roger's false flattering tongue.

(M 1, 137)

Rosamund's seducer in Lamb's novel – Matravis, a name perhaps taken from an assassin in Marlowe's *Edward II* – sings the street ballad on his deathbed.

Even discerning readers, then and later, fell for *Rosamund*. The poet Percy Bysshe Shelley wrote to Leigh Hunt, 'What a lovely thing is *Rosamund Gray*! How much knowledge of the sweetest, and deepest parts of our nature is in it! When I think of such a mind as Lamb's—when I see how unnoticed remain things of such exquisite and complete perfection—what should I hope for myself, if I had not higher objects in view than fame?'[16] John Scott, celebrated editor of the *London Magazine*, praised it gratuitously, as we have seen. Thomas Noon Talfourd, eminent lawyer, dramatist, and Lamb's first biographer, was enraptured by it.

In the four months between January and May, Lamb's view of Coleridge rapidly deteriorated. Lloyd finished his novel *Edmund Oliver* in January. Southey applied to review *Edmund Oliver* for the *Critical Review* as soon as the manuscript was completed. Ostensibly the book was a refutation of Godwin's views on marriage; Southey disliked Godwin's theories as much as his long nose and found it a pleasure to say so. And Lloyd's novel was in a sense the reviewer's own stepchild. Southey's favourable article did not appear until July.

Dorothy Wordsworth seems to have read *Edmund Oliver* or part of it in manuscript, since she and William were said by Southey to have requested Lloyd to delete a section of it–which he did. They remained firmly on Coleridge's side throughout the quarrels.[17]

In March Lloyd's hostility to Coleridge expressed itself directly when he told his erstwhile friend through Cottle that he wanted his own work omitted from any third edition of Coleridge's *Poems*. Coleridge wrote Cottle that 'it is curious that *I* should be applied to . . . in hope that I might "CONSENT TO GIVE UP" a number of poems which were published at the earnest request of the author. . . . I have no objection to any disposal of C. Lloyd's poems except that of their being republished with mine.'[18]

Lamb's role in all this is unclear. His attempts to shun Lloyd after Mary's setback may have made him less than eager to undertake the kind of criticism he might be expected to give the novel, and Lloyd may not have offered a reading of it to Lamb at that time, knowing that Lamb would recognize the Comberback story and might well resist the entire caricature of Coleridge.

The fact is, however, that *Edmund Oliver* was dedicated to Charles Lamb. Lamb must have read it by publication or very shortly thereafter, by which time his own view of Coleridge had changed so drastically that he may even have approved the portrait. In allowing the dedication he had, by printing-time, now taken sides against his 'more than brother'.

Coleridge by April had written once more to Lamb, as Lloyd tells Cottle on 4 April 1798 (misdating the letter '1797'[19]):

Coleridge has written a very odd letter to Lamb. I don't know what may be his sentiments in regard to our conduct, but I can perceive he is bent on disassociating himself from us—particularly Lamb I think he has used unkindly. (CL I, 104)

Still ignorant of his own role in Lloyd's novel, Coleridge had been composing in a great creative surge nearly all of the poems by which he would be remembered, planning *Lyrical Ballads* with Wordsworth, and meditating an autumn trip to Germany with him. The full measure of Lloyd's treachery burst upon him only when Cottle (whom Coleridge seems to have excused) published *Edmund Oliver* in May. Coleridge was shaken to the core.

What had Lloyd written so to distress him? First, there was the preface: 'The incidents relative to the army were given me by an intimate friend.' One of Coleridge's immediate reactions was an Epigram to Lloyd, 'To one Who Published in Print What Had Been Entrusted to Him by My Fireside':

Two things hast thou made known to half the nation,
My secrets and my want of penetration:
For O! far more than all which thou hast penn'd
It shames me to have called a wretch, like thee, my friend!
(STCP, 448)

Edmund Oliver's description fitted Coleridge – 'large glistening eye', 'dark eyebrows', 'bend in the shoulder', 'dark hair' – and Edmund had a love affair, left college, joined the army. But this was not the worst. Much more degrading were the weaknesses Lloyd chose to dwell upon – Coleridge's growing addiction to opium and his fondness for alcohol. What must have grated most harshly was that opium was a weakness Lloyd himself now shared. Says Edmund, 'I have some laudanum in my pocket. I will quell these mortal upbraidings! I cannot endure them!' Elsewhere: 'My brain phrensied with its own workings—I will again have recourse to my laudanum.'[20] (Dialogue was not Lloyd's strength as a novelist.) Yet elsewhere: 'I have at all times a strange dreaminess about me, which makes me indifferent to the future, if I can by any means fill the present with sensations. With that dreaminess I have gone on here from day to day; if at any time thought troubled, I have swallowed some spirits, or had recourse to my laudanum.'[21]

Though heavily biased, the portrait nailed Coleridge where he was most vulnerable, and Lamb's acquiescence in the malefaction was deeply wounding. Whether Coleridge would be recognized by *Edmund Oliver*'s readers we may wonder, but Coleridge knew that Lloyd's tattling would soon give the game away in literary circles.

Almost immediately Coleridge received a message about Lamb from Lloyd via Dorothy Wordsworth, and this caused him to write to Lamb a long letter, as reasonable as could be expected under the circumstances:

[Early May 1798]

Dear Lamb

Lloyd has informed me through Miss Wordsworth that you intend no longer to correspond with me. This has given me little pain; not that I do not love and esteem you, but on the contrary because I am confident that your intentions are pure. You are performing what you deem a duty, & humanly speaking have that merit which can be derived from the performance of a painful duty.—Painful, for you could not without some struggles abandon me in behalf of a man who wholly ignorant of all but your name became attached to you in consequence of my attachment, caught *his* from *my* enthusiasm, & learnt to love you at my fire-side, when often while I have been sitting & talking of your sorrows & affections [afflictions], I have stopped my conversations & lifted up wet eyes & prayed for you. No! I am confident, that although you do not think as a wise man, you feel as a good man. . . .

. . . When I wrote to you that my sonnet to simplicity was not composed with reference to Southey you answered me (I believe these were the words) 'It was a lie too gross for the grossest ignorance to believe,' & I was not angry with you, because the assertion, which the grossest Ignorance would believe a lie the Omniscient knew to be truth—This however makes me cautious not too hastily to affirm the falsehood of an assertion of Lloyd's that in Edmund Oliver's love-fit, debaucheries, leaving college & going into the army he had no sort of allusion to, or recollection of, my love-fit, debaucheries, leaving college, & going into the army & that he never thought of my person in the description of Edmund Oliver's person in the first letter of the second volume. This cannot appear stranger to me than my assertion did to you; & therefore I will suspend my absolute faith——I write to you not that I wish to hear from you, but that I wish you to write to Lloyd & press upon him the propriety, nay, the necessity of his giving me a meeting either tête à tête or in the presence of all whose esteem I value. . . . Both you & Lloyd became acquainted with me at a season when your minds were far from being in a composed or natural state & you clothed my image with a suit of notions & feelings which could belong to nothing human. *You* are restored to comparative saneness, & are merely wondering what is become of the Coleridge with whom you were so passionately in love. *Charles Lloyd's* mind has only changed its disease. . . . O me! Lamb, 'even in laughter the heart is sad'—My kindness, my affectionateness *he* deems wheedling, but if after reading all my letters to yourself & to him you can suppose him wise in his treatment & correct in his accusations of me, you think worse of human nature than poor human nature, bad as it is, deserves to be thought of.

God bless you & S. T. Coleridge[22]

Dorothy Wordsworth made the copy Coleridge kept. Cottle says Coleridge handed it to him to read with the remark, 'These young visionaries will do each other no good.'[23] Coleridge's analysis of the relationship of the three can only have maddened Lamb by its length, defensiveness, and air of superiority, though Coleridge controlled his phraseology and kept his temper. The obviousness of his effort to do so only compounded the trouble: no one likes to feel that others must strain to be calm, tactful, and generous in dealing with one. Some of the missing letters between the two might change the balance of justification and blame, but quarrelling brings out the best in nobody.

Yet worse was to come. Years later Thomas Allsop learned from Coleridge himself that 'Lloyd in one of his fits had shown to Lamb a letter, in which Coleridge had illustrated the cases of vast genius in proportion to talent and predominance of talent in conjunction with genius in the persons of Lamb and himself. Hence a temporary coolness. . . .'[24] Coleridge (in Allsop) does not deny that this letter was valid, but it is not the sort of thing one friend should pass on to another. Lloyd had no such scruples; he told Lamb next that Coleridge had said, 'Poor Lamb . . . if he wants any *knowledge*, he may apply to me.'[25] It was a long time since Lloyd had received such confidences from Coleridge; he really had to dredge them up. The effect on Lamb was predictable.

Coleridge was writing to others in the fateful month of May, as this of 14 May, to a Unitarian friend, announcing the birth of a second boy, Berkeley Coleridge:

> But I have had many sorrows; and some that bite deep, calumny & ingratitude from men who have been fostered in the bosom of my confidence! — I pray God, that I may sanctify these events; by forgiveness, & a peaceful spirit full of love. (Griggs 1, 407)

Perhaps he was responding to Lamb's May letter (given just below), perhaps merely to earlier events.[26] At any rate, soon after Lloyd had conveyed Coleridge's old 'knowledge' remark, the angry Lamb sat down and wrote to Coleridge:

Theses Quædam Theologicæ.

1. Whether God loves a lying Angel better than a true Man?
2. Whether the Archangel Uriel *could* affirm an untruth? & if he *could* whether he *would*?
3. Whether Honesty be an angelic virtue? or not rather to be reckoned among those qualities which the Schoolmen term *Virtutes minus splendidæ, et terræ et hominis participes?*[27]
4. Whether the higher order of Seraphim Illuminati ever sneer?
5. Whether pure Intelligences can love?
6. Whether the Seraphim Ardentes do not manifest their virtues by the way of vision & theory? & whether practice be not a sub-celestial & merely human virtue?
7. Whether the Vision Beatific be anything more or less than a perpetual representment to each individual Angel of his own present attainments & future capabilities, somehow in the

manner of mortal looking-glasses, reflecting a perpetual complacency & self-satisfaction?

8. & last. Whether an immortal & amenable soul may not come to be damned at last, & the man never suspect it beforehand? Learned Sir, my Friend,

Presuming on our long habits of friendship, & emboldened further by your late liberal permission to avail myself of your correspondence, in case I want any knowledge, (which I intend to do when I have no Encyclopædia, or Lady's Magazine at hand to refer to in any matter of science,) I now submit to your enquiries the above Theological Propositions, to be by you defended, or oppugned, or both, in the Schools of Germany, whither I am told you are departing, to the utter dissatisfaction of your native Devonshire, & regret of universal England; but to my own individual consolation, if thro the channel of your wished return, Learned Sir, my Friend, may be transmitted to this our Island, from those famous Theological Wits of Leipsic & Gottingen, any rays of illumination, in vain to be derived from the home growth of our English Halls and Colleges. Finally, wishing Learned Sir, that you may see Schiller, & swing in a wood (*vide* Poems), & sit upon a Tun, & eat fat hams of Westphalia,

I remain
Your friend and docile Pupil to instruct
Charles Lamb

To S. T. Coleridge   (M I, 128–9)

The sting of the queries, couched in the terms of the 'Schoolmen' (such as Thomas Aquinas, whom Lamb had read), was hardly compensated for by the more jocular tone of the ending – and Coleridge, of course, caught only the sting.

Soon after, probably on 24 May,[28] Coleridge was journeying with Wordsworth to Cheddar. They had heard that Lloyd was at Bristol, and Wordsworth went on there alone to bring him back if possible for the confrontation Coleridge so much desired. Lloyd had, however, left for Birmingham by the time Wordsworth reached Bristol. And he had with him Charles Lamb, whom he had invited home for a fortnight's stay, though of this Coleridge seemed to be unaware.

Coleridge, as usual, had diversion thrust upon him as Cottle arrived at Nether Stowey before May was out and the plan for the

Lyrical Ballads was born. Soon after came the adoring young William Hazlitt to visit, on foot, and then there were the preparations for the German trip to be made. Sara would stay at home with the babe and Hartley – to avoid the germs of travel – under Tom Poole's care.

Meanwhile, as Lamb's and Lloyd's joint *Blank Verse* appeared in London, Lamb arrived in Birmingham (23 May) for his stay with the Quaker Lloyds. He and Coleridge did not correspond again for two long years.

CHAPTER FIFTEEN

The Quaker Lloyds

In feelings and matters not dogmatical, I hope I am half a Quaker. Lamb to Bernard Barton, a Quaker, 1822 (CL II, 333)

Your Society are eminently men of Business. Lamb to Barton, 1823 (CL II, 376)

The truth is, that ninety-nine out of a hundred of them are engaged in trade; and as they all deal and correspond with each other, it is easy to see what advantages they must have as traders, from belonging to so great a corporation. Francis Jeffrey, 1807.[1]

On the surface at least, Lloyd was now reconciled with his parents. The banker had called him home briefly in March 1798, when his younger brother James had been taken with paralysis. Charles must have come to an understanding at home on that occasion – enough to be able to bring Charles Lamb for a visit.

That host and guest arrived in Birmingham on the same day makes it probable that Lamb was with Lloyd in Bristol,[2] especially since from 1798 dates the first known portrait of Charles Lamb, a drawing by Robert Hancock of that city. It was commissioned by Joseph Cottle the publisher, with whom Lloyd no doubt had business to discuss. (Cottle also had the young Coleridge, Wordsworth, and Southey drawn by Hancock for his collection at this period.) Cottle speaks of having got to know Lamb well only in 1802, except for 'one casual visit', probably this one. Lamb's day or two in Bristol may have been taken up in sitting to Hancock. Cottle and Coleridge thought the portrait a good likeness. It has often been ill reproduced from copies, but the original, a profile, suggests all that we read of Lamb's appearance as a young man – handsome, 'Jewish', sober, yet young and vulnerable still.

The business with Cottle completed, they sped north to Birmingham, the city of Dissenters which was still without representation in Parliament, and of the burgeoning smoky mills and factories of new industry. At Bingley House, a mansion on the city's outskirts, Lamb was immersed for the first time in the somewhat alien culture Quakerism was in those days. Much persecuted in the seventeenth century, Quakers had survived as a small but ardent group of the middle class engaged mainly in trade. They had even acquired a certain respectability, particularly as shrewdness, probity, and hard work brought many of them a measure of prosperity.

The Society of Friends was from the beginning unusual in its lack of visible leadership and its feeling that clergymen, formal services, vestments, set prayers and hymns, religious holidays, and 'steeplehouses' (churches) detracted from the personal 'experimental' relationship with God which was the only way to arrive at spiritual truth. George Fox, its seventeenth-century founder, had said that there was an inner light – 'that of God' – in everyone, man and woman alike, and that all men and women were equal in the sight of God, varying only in spiritual progress and power.

Therefore Friends chose temporary leadership for the business of the Society, and organized themselves into Monthly, Quarterly, and Yearly Meetings. They built themselves simple meetinghouses. There they sat, weekly or oftener, in silent worship, though any member who felt moved by God to do so might give to others a message reached in meditation – Friends' substitute for the clerical sermon.

Friends shared with Unitarians the spirit of inquiry. A Friend was, to begin with, a 'seeker' after truth and must find it with God's help, for him- or herself. Jesus Christ 'spoke to' George Fox's 'condition' through His teachings as recounted in Scripture, but Friends believed His gospel of love must constantly be re-examined as it applied to the contemporary world. Was it justifiable that truth was to be enunciated only by *men*, as in the steeplehouses? Friends allowed women an equal part in organization and ministry. Was it Christ's will that some people should make slaves of others? that governments should send some men to kill others? that some should take off their hats to others? Was it moral to spend money on frivolous amusement when there was so much poverty and injustice in the world? (Frivolous amusement in those days included most of the arts.) The Quaker answer to all these questions was no.

Governments were human and fallible and made war, hence the importance of a religion independent of the state. A Friend must be prepared to defy even government when necessary, and to reason with the governors. Calm, rational behaviour, and the search for revelation in silence were central to eighteenth-century English Quakerism, and Friends cared deeply about how men and women treated their fellows. This concern gave the Society a Jacobinical cast, since it actively sought liberty, peace, and relief for the helpless. By some it was greatly respected. Thomas Clarkson, future friend of the Lambs and a graduate of St. John's College, Cambridge, had intended to be an Anglican clergyman. He was diverted from his aim through the writing of his Cambridge prize essay on slavery, and soon found himself devoting his life to the abolition of this evil. It was ultimately he who, by research among ships and harbours throughout England, provided the facts and figures which equipped the Evangelical MP William Wilberforce to sponsor legislation that brought an end to British slavery long before the rest of Europe and America came to it. When Clarkson set out on his crusade in 1785, he found that the Quakers had already assembled a small anti-slavery committee. Like most such committees it included a member of the Lloyd family – young Charles Lloyd's uncle John Lloyd. Travelling to Birmingham in the mid-1780s, Clarkson brought letters of introduction to both Charles Lloyd the elder and his half-brother Sampson Lloyd.[3] Charles Lloyd the banker early became an activist in the abolition campaign together with his brother-in-law David Barclay.

But Quakers were not universally admired, and the other side of the coin may be represented by Francis Jeffrey, who became one of the founders and first editor of the Whig *Edinburgh Review* a few years later. Jeffrey reviewed Clarkson's *Portraiture of Quakerism* somewhat sardonically in 1807, noting that, while 'self-gratification' was forbidden,

> the fruits of [his] industry [the Quaker] is by no means required to bestow in relieving the poor, or for the promotion of piety. He is allowed to employ it for self-gratification in almost every way— but the most social and agreeable! He may keep an excellent table and garden, and be driven about in an easy chariot by a pious coachman and two, or even four, plump horses; but his plate must be without carving, and his carriage and horses . . . of a dusky colour.

Jeffrey found Friends to be killjoys, harsh on the animal spirits of their children, and thought that the pursuit of wealth 'surely holds out a greater temptation to immorality, than the study of music'.[4]

Upon the whole, we are inclined to believe the Quakers to be a tolerably honest, painstaking, and inoffensive set of Christians. Very stupid, dull, and obstinate, we presume, in conversation; and tolerably lumpish and fatiguing in domestic society; active and methodical in their business, and narrow-minded and ill-informed as to most other particulars: beneficent . . . but cold in their affections . . . ; childish and absurd in their religious scruples and peculiar usages . . . ; but exemplary, above all other sects, for the decency of their lives, for their charitable indulgence to all other persuasions, for their care of their poor, and for the liberal participation they have afforded their women in all the duties and honours of the society.[5]

Quaker men wore black, the women white or grey.[6] Jeffrey points out that they did not use 'Mr' or 'Sir', nor bow, nor remove their hats to anyone. All were Friend Lloyd or Friend Lamb. 'Thee' and 'thou', now abandoned even for servants by the rest of the populace, was their form of the second person singular; tribute to pagan gods was avoided in the designation of First Day and First Month for Sunday and January.

The *Anti-Jacobin*, a journal of which we shall hear more, despised particularly their 'pretended Principle against Fighting'. When in August it reviewed *Edmund Oliver* it found Charles Lloyd's supposed repudiation of Godwinism, as announced in the preface, negated by his pacifism and belief in human equality. In it the Lloyd-figure Charles Maurice seeks to turn the Coleridge-figure from the army – as quoted in the review, italics the *Anti-Jacobin*'s:

"But first, Edmund, let me extricate you from this *detestable profession*. You, my friend, disguised in the *badge of slavery and cruelty*! My heart turns sick at the sight."

"You do not mean, Edmund, to enroll yourself among those *who sell themselves to slaughter their fellow men*, to slaughter beings, whom you have never seen, and who have done you no injury! . . ."

"Be merciful, be merciful, Charles," (cried he) "you will drive me to desperation."

"Come then with me, Edmund, and be released from this company of EARTHLY FIENDS."

The *Anti-Jacobin* called this '*declamatory rant*' and pretty seditious.

Indeed, Mr. Charles Lloyd [it continued], you are a very young political arguer; you know very little of the history of mankind, or of the principles of human nature; otherwise you would have perceived, that while human passions continue as they are, *the means of national defence*, as well as of the individual, will be necessary. The feebleness of your arguments prevent[s] us, *who do not think this war an unjust cause*, from being mortified that our opinions are not sanctioned by the authority of your approbation, Mr. Charles Lloyd![7]

Mr Charles Lloyd had not abandoned all of Godwinism or all of his family's Quakerism – as yet.

The Lloyd family of Bingley were, of course, neither saints altogether, nor dull, nor devils. Lamb found them quite delightful and altogether interesting. Bingley had been the home of his friend's granny, Priscilla Farmer, to which the Lloyd children had regularly trekked on Fridays (they were often taken for a school when out walking, said one of the daughters) until her death in 1796 made it their own. There was a library at Bingley from which 'literature' was not excluded: the banker had a taste for the Classics. Mrs Lloyd even allowed herself to be proud of young Charles's poetry. She had sent it on occasion to her good friend Susanna Day, who employed Robert.[8]

Charles Lloyd at twenty-three was the eldest of eleven surviving children. Next in line came the temporarily paralysed James, who was daily carried down to the parlour; over the next two years he gradually recovered his ability to walk. To the family's horror, soon after the outbreak of the French war he had joined the army (at eighteen) and had, like Coleridge, to be willingly rescued. Thereafter he wore a blue coat, and powdered his hair, and indulged his taste for the company of young ladies, going so far as to become engaged to the Quaker Betsey Gurney. He had recently jilted her, but she lived to marry another and become the great worker among women convicts in Newgate Prison, Elizabeth Fry. Later James (in 1802) married the Quaker Sarah Hart, and settled down to his father's bank as partner, in lieu of the defecting Charles.[9]

After James came Robert, already Lamb's friend, then twenty, still fretting in the draper–grocer's shop at Saffron Walden. Loyal to his brother Charles, he had recently told his employers that *Edmund*

Oliver had been published with his parents' approval. His mother reacted firmly, writing to Robert,

> I am sorry thou shouldst have inform'd [Mrs. Day] that "E. Oliver" was published with our "approbation and concurrence." We were never consulted. For my own part I did not comprehend the nature of the Book till I saw it; and tho' I fully allow there are some fine sentiments in it, thou well knowst it was far from having either thy Father's or my indiscriminate approbation—nay, I am sure there was one passage that wounded me to the quick, and thou must frequently have heard me say I hoped Charles would *never* be a Novel writer; I can honestly say that I should rather see him engaged in the most humble occupation that I thought consistent with Christian simplicity. With respect to these writings in general I most sincerely concur in sentiment with S. D[ay], and wish it had been in my power to keep my Family as clear of them as she has done. Till I am convinc'd that the Christian religion is a Fable, I shall never think the imagination can *riot* in the *delicious* luxury of sentiment and warm descriptions of the passions, and the Heart remain pure . . . (LL, 56)

Robert would join the militia for a while (against the threat of French invasion) but give it up before his marriage to James's sister-in-law, Hannah Hart, solemnized under the care of a Friends' meeting.

Thomas, nineteen, worked for a Birmingham merchant and, like the anti-slavery Uncle John before him, was later sent to America for a time before he became a partner in a manufacturing firm. He too married a Quaker.

Another favourite of Lamb's was the seventeen-year-old Plumsted Lloyd, talkative, 'impetuous', and 'Shakespeare-loving' (said Lamb). Apprenticed to a local brewer – alcohol was not then frowned on by English Friends – he never did very well in that trade or in grain, his later pursuit, and married outside of the Quaker fold.

Most of the boys, then were abnormally sensitive and three fond of literature. All flung themselves into forbidden joys for a space: the Quakerism which had seemed so liberating to their forebears assumed the aspect of chains to some of those brought up in it and complicated their normal adolescent rebelliousness.

Then there were the girls – all the six younger children. Priscilla at sixteen was her father's pearl but also independent and headstrong, and she shared to a disturbing degree some of the symptoms of her brother Charles, who took a particular interest in her welfare. Later that year he brought William's brother Christopher Wordsworth home to visit and Christopher lost his heart to Priscilla – 'not slender, not handsome', he wrote, 'but what at times you would, I think, call a fine woman'.[10] Christopher was on his way to becoming an Anglican clergyman, and after their delayed marriage Priscilla produced two Anglican bishops (she grandmothered a third). Lamb encouraged the match and had a warm affection for the fiancée, though Priscilla was privately cool about Lamb, advising Robert not to take up a permanent 'abode' with him: 'He is too much like yourself—he would encourage those feelings which it is certainly your duty to suppress. Your station in life . . . differ[s] widely from his . . .'[11]

Next to Priscilla came Olivia, who charmed Lamb too, and who later married the Quaker banker-poet Paul Moon James, Charles Lloyd senior's comfort in old age. The four young sisters after Olivia included Mary, Caroline, and Anna,[12] still children.

Lamb found the young Lloyds a merry crew and at that moment a happy one. He was later to write to Robert, in illustration of why he did not like collections of Great Excerpts from Great Writers,

Consider a fine family—(if I were not writing to you I might instance your own) of sons & daughters with a respectable father & a handsome mother at their head, all met in one house, & happy round one table—. Earth cannot shew a more lovely & venerable sight, such as the Angels in heaven might lament that in their country there is no marrying or giving in marriage—. Take & split this Body into individuals—shew the separate caprices, vagaries, &c. of Charles, Rob. or Plum. one a quaker, another a churchman.—The eldest daughter seeking a husband out of the pale of parental faith—another warping perhaps—the father a prudent, circumspective, do-me-good sort of man *blest* with children whom no ordinary rules can circumscribe—. I have not room for all particulars—but just as this happy & venerable Body of a family loses by splitting & considering individuals too nicely, so it is when we pick the Best Bits out of a great writer. Tis the *Sum* total of his mind which *affects* us. (M II, 36)

There was also, of course, the elusive Sophia Pemberton, Charles Lloyd's intended. Lamb must have first met her now. Charles Lloyd was on his way to the Church of England, and Sophia was an Anglican, daughter of a Birmingham jeweller. She was handsome, full of figure, red-haired, cultivated, sensible, thoughtful, and – to Thomas De Quincey – 'as a wife and mother not surpassed by anybody I have known in either of those characters'.[13] Her letters show her to have been a faithful friend, loyal wife, and unusually sensitive with children. When John Constable the painter took a tour of the Lakes, where the Lloyds were then living, in 1809, Charles got him to paint the couple's portraits. If Constable's Charles is rather stiff, one supposes he was a self-conscious sitter; Sophia is informal, sensuous, intelligent, and the painter has not missed Charles's unhappiness or Sophia's wistfulness: an air of unease hangs about them both. Lamb became very fond of Sophia.

Over the household presided the elder Charles, descendant of those Lloyds of Dolobran in Wales who had the courage to follow George Fox – even to prison – in rebellion against the worldliness of the Established Church in the seventeenth century. Mr Lloyd's grandfather, Sampson Lloyd the first, had conceived the Birmingham bank as a safeguard for his industrial profits in iron – it was the precursor of the great Lloyds Bank of our day.[14] Charles Lloyd of Bingley, together with his elder half-brother Sampson, was still in iron and banking, though they would gradually phase out the Lloyd industrial interests. David Barclay of another important Quaker banking family had married their sister Rachel and taught the elder Charles the routines of the countinghouse in his youth. All three men were active in Quaker social concerns, founding the Birmingham General Hospital, trying to prevent the American War of Independence through talks with Benjamin Franklin and a petition to the King. Prime Minister Pitt consulted Sampson and Charles on matters affecting the iron industry. Both played an important role in the Quaker Yearly Meeting. When Clarkson founded his larger committee against slavery, including non-Friends such as Priestley and Josiah Wedgwood, their bank handled the anti-slavery funds. Lloyds, Barclays, and their kin were tireless in this cause.

Charles Lloyd the banker, for all his wife's suspicion of literature, in later years devoted himself to Homer and Virgil, seeking advice on his poetic translations from Charles Lamb.

In 1803 Lamb quoted to Coleridge the reconciled Robert's admiring estimate of his father:

Rob. Lloyd has written me a masterly Letter containing a character of his father, see how different from Charles he views the old man "*literatim*—my father smokes, repeats Homer in Greek & Virgil, & is learning when from business with all the vigor of a young man Statian [Statius, a Latin poet]. He is really a wonderful man. He mixes Public & Private business, the intricacies of discording life with his religion & devotion. No one more rationally enjoys the romantic scenes of nature, & the chitchat & little vagaries of his children; & tho' surrounded with an ocean of affairs, the very neatness of his most obscure cupboard in the house passes not unnoticed. I never knew anyone view with such clearness, nor so well satisfied with things as they are; & make such allowance for things which must appear perfect Syriac to him."—by the last he means, the Lloydisms of the younger branches. (M II, 111–12)

The 'old man' was fifty-four at this writing.[15]

Mrs Lloyd, the former Mary Farmer, was weak on the obscure cupboards, but a pious, charming mother to her brood. 'Though quite disposed to perform an act of kindness,' her eldest son later wrote, she 'is most philosophically indifferent to the common affairs of life.' With servants and a careful husband she had little need to be otherwise and could devote herself to her children's moral well-being. She had written to Robert not long ago,

I was grieved to hear of thy appearing in those *fantastical* trousers [rather than knee breeches] in London. I am clear such excentricities of dress would only make thee laugh'd at by the World, whilst thy sincere Friends would be *deeply hurt*. Canst thou love thy Father and yet do things that sink him as well as thyself in the opinion of our best Friends! Thou art, my dear Son, form'd to make an amiable Figure in Society, but for once trust to the judgment of thy Mother, neither thy Person or Mind are form'd for excentricities of dress or conduct.

Father Lloyd added his plea:

Thou wilt please me by observing simplicity in thy dress and manners. Do not let the customs of the world influence thee. (LL, 79–80)

Charles, the eldest child, was chief rebel and chief aid to rebellion among his siblings. Lamb was well aware of how little Charles's private activities would please his mother and father. A month later he wrote to Southey,

> Lloyd is return'd to town from Ipswich, where he has been with his Brother—[Robert]. He has brought home 3 acts of a play, which I have not yet seen——the scene for the most part laid in a Brothel, O tempora O mores!—but as friend Coleridge said, when he was talking bawdy to Miss . . . [16] "to the Pure all things are pure"—(M I, 132)

Charles Lamb among the Lloyds was, then, in a position to observe many elements in the new England hitherto remote from his daily life. His own innate radicalism, for example, could be shown to have a firm moral and religious base, as among these Quakers, and could be courageously defended by men and women of sufficient character and wealth to have the respect of government, if not its approval. At Bingley he found himself at the heart of the rising industrial middle class and could take note that wealth was not always exploitive and that his own yearning for plainness, sincerity, for true godliness, and even for poetry found their counterpart in this Society within English society that was neither aristocratic nor struggling for economic survival. Lamb was perforce a businessman – so were the Lloyds; he loved family life and literature – so did they. His moral and literary biases were upheld even by the Quaker parents. The fact that the strength of friendship the parents conceived for him during his stay continued steady for many years (while that of their children for various reasons did not) is ample demonstration of the affection and respect Lamb inspired. The Birmingham experience, though brief, fortified his own struggle: not all that young Charles Lloyd brought him would turn to dust and ashes.

Lamb absorbed what he found welcome in the faith of Friends. Bingley House confirmed his inclination toward being 'half a Quaker' that remained his state for the rest of his life. What Lamb now began to find admirable in the Quaker approach, he later spelled out in his fine essay 'A Quakers' Meeting'. But he saw paradoxes among them, as had Francis Jeffrey, and could not abandon pipe, strong talk, and theatre or moderate his drinking to join them. (He deals amusingly with certain paradoxes in 'Imperfect Sympathies'.) Restored by his two weeks in the congenial family he turned homeward.

The benefits were permanent, but the sense of tranquility was all too brief. Presently Lamb found himself not only known but notorious, lampooned with his friends in the pages of the *Anti-Jacobin*.

CHAPTER SIXTEEN

Political Lamb

It was a misfortune to any man of talent to be born in the latter end of the last century. Genius stopped the way of Legitimacy, and therefore it was to be abated, crushed, or set aside as a nuisance. The spirit of the monarchy was at variance with the spirit of the age. The flame of liberty, the light of intellect, was to be extinguished with the sword—or with slander, whose edge is sharper than the sword.   William Hazlitt, 'Mr. Coleridge' in *The Spirit of the Age*, 1825[1]

The key to any understanding of the dialogue between Burke and the Revolutionists is that each side was moved by a passion that meant nothing to the other.   H. N. Brailsford, *Shelley, Godwin, and Their Circle* (26–7)

. . . our first boyish heats [were] kindled by the French Revolution, when if we were misled, we erred in the company of some, who are accounted very good men now.   Lamb, 'Newspapers Thirty-five Years Ago' (*Elia*, 225)

That Lamb was not *a*political can no longer be in doubt – nor did he just stop being political after a certain age. At fifty-five, four years before his death, he contributed to William Hone's *Table Book* of 1830 an epigram on the secularization of the monarchy under Victoria's predecessor William IV. Three years earlier he had sent to the same friend a reminiscent one on the very political fate of George IV's nearly divorced Queen Caroline.

When in 1798 the *Anti-Jacobin* saw fit to pillory him together with a select group of radicals, we must assume it had ample cause, according to its lights. Had he not first appeared in print under the wing of the arch-radical Coleridge? Had not he and Charles Lloyd co-published? Was not *Edmund Oliver* dedicated to Lamb? And *Blank Verse* to that other arch-radical Robert Southey? If his own 'sedition' was mild as yet, his willingness to be publicly associated with these Jacobins was sufficiently damning.

Blank Verse had appeared in May. Lloyd was the volume's chief architect – its arranger, dedicator, footnoter, and financial risk-taker, with Lamb again a willing second. Lloyd's dedication to Southey, the *Anti-Jacobin*'s present butt, read:

> In offering these Poems to you I am simply consulting my feelings. The greater part of them were written beneath your roof, and owe their existence to its quiet comforts. They indirectly register to my heart many sentiments of affection and virtue, and must certainly remain unclaimed, if not acknowledged by you.[2]

Though Lloyd was shortly to protest himself an *anti*-Jacobin, he chose at this late date to begin his collection with a warm tribute to the failed Pantisocrats. In its early lines Lloyd saw the world as

> . . . the prisonhouse of man, where Power
> And loathlier Wealth inflict on trembling slaves
> The rackings of despair!
>
> (Pollin, 636)

He went on to the

> noble souls
> Who deemed it wise, e'en in the morn of youth
> To quit this world. . . .
>
> (Pollin, 636)

hoping 'beyond the Atlantic deep' to find virtue. He regretted that he was not one of the Pantisocrats' 'high-soul'd fellowship' but he must chronicle 'their blasted hopes'. A footnote on page 9 identified the group and established the Jacobin nature of their undertaking:

> This alludes to a plan projected by S. T. Coleridge and Robert Southey, together with some common friends, of establishing a society in America, in which all individual property was to be abandoned.[3]

The opportunity has passed, cried the poet, but 'Yes! it shall rise again, your godlike scheme,' and its young hopefuls 'join the elect of Heaven'. Another footnote:

> Wherever the word elect is used in the following pages, the authors by no means intend the arbitrary dogma of Calvinism.

They are both believers in the doctrine of philosophical necessity, and in the final happiness of all mankind. They apply the word elect therefore to those persons whom *secondary causes*, under providence, have fitted for an immediate entrance into the paradisaical state.[4]

There is more than a suggestion of philosopher Godwin's doctrines here, or at the very least Unitarian Priestley's – almost as bad in the eyes of the anti-Jacobins. The poem concludes with a vision of liberty, equality, and fraternity which, however, includes religion, invoking

> that God
> Who destin'd all his creatures *to be good*,
> And who, with sympathies of holiest love,
> Shall teach best fellowship with kindred souls,
> Or loftier breathings of devoutest praise.
>   (Pollin, 637)[5]

Worse from the *Anti-Jacobin*'s point of view were the 'Lines to Mary Wollstonecraft Godwin'. Though no longer on earth to defend herself, she was the particular target of the journal in its (July, 1798) review of Godwin's candid *Memoir* of her. Godwin's own reputation had begun to plummet almost from the very date of her death. He was now widely regarded as the serpent in the national bosom, and with the publication of the *Memoir*, the would-be destroyer not only of the nation but of the British hearth and home. The *Anti-Jacobin* critique of Godwin's memoir asserted that Godwin advocated 'the promiscuous intercourse of the sexes, as one of the highest improvements to result from political justice!' Of Mary it wrote, 'She became the concubine of Mr. Imlay. . . . Her biographer does not mention many of her amours.' Of these, 'Many still remain untold, which if faithfully related would make a book, in comparison with which . . . Moll Flanders would be a model of purity.'[6] In this it overreached itself. Mary had borne a child to Gilbert Imlay, an American, before she knew Godwin well, but she was not in any sense promiscuous.

Even Southey, who admired Mary Wollstonecraft, dissociated himself from Lloyd's apparent purifying of her opinions in his anonymous notice for the October *Critical Review*. Otherwise the review was favourable. He wished only that 'both these authors had paid more attention to harmony', strength of phrasing, and versification. He recommended the little volume 'to those who can derive delight from contemplating "the finest features of the mind," and from seeing the best features of our nature expressed with earnestness and ardour.' Of Lamb he wrote, 'Mr. Lamb describes no longer, as in his first productions, "Vain loves and wanderings with a fair-hair'd maid." His present pieces imply past sufferings and present resignation.' He quotes a section on Lamb's father (from 'Written Soon After the Preceding Poem', addressed to his mother) as not faultless but moving.[7]

Lamb, of course, had written nothing of a political cast in his contributions – the nearest being his complaint against the Established Church in 'Composed at Midnight'. (The anti-Godwin 'Living Without God in the World' was not included.) But Lloyd in his footnotes claimed to speak for both authors. And Lamb had provided 'To Charles Lloyd' for the collection. There was reason to consider both poets well tarred with the Jacobin brush.

One might have expected the *Analytical Review*, of which Mrs Godwin had been editor for Johnson the printer, to welcome *Blank Verse* (reviewed in May) as it did *Edmund Oliver* (in June). But its review was at best equivocal and not at all concerned with politics:

> We may be very deficient in taste: but the whining monotonous melancholy of these pages is to us extremely tiresome. Mr. Lloyd and Mr. Lamb shed a sepulchral gloom over every object, and their poetry is such an unvaried murmur, that, so far from sympathizing in their poetical sorrows, we feel a much stronger propensity to smile, than we do to weep. Mr. Lamb has evinced the warmth of his domestic affections on a former occasion; the same amiable glow is observable in the poems before us. The following extract is a favourable specimen; it is the production of Mr. Lamb.[8]

The anonymous reviewer then quoted 'Composed at Midnight' entire to complete the brief notice.

The *Anti-Jacobin* itself merely dismissed the poems in a footnote to the *Edmund Oliver* review we have quoted:

> This Mr. Charles Lloyd we conceive to be one of the twin-bards who unite their impotent efforts to propagate their principles, which are alike marked by folly and by wickedness, in a kind of baby language which they are pleased to term *blank-verse*.[9]

Were further confirmation of Lamb's 'wickedness' needed, it was already available in the printed work of George Dyer, the bumbling and goodhearted, who had not omitted to include him in his own book of verse, *The Poet's Fate* of 1797, which lauded the prominent radicals among whom he moved and bewailed the poet's difficulties in this controversial age.[10]

In its issue of 9 July, the last as a weekly, the *Anti-Jacobin* came forth with its own verses, probably by George Canning, called 'New Morality', to give the subversive group the come-uppance it deserved, not omitting to mention names, so thinly disguised as to be immediately recognizable to the reading public. And in the first monthly issue of a new series, James Gillray, the devastating political cartoonist, repeated these verses under an oversized fold-out cartoon. This was in fact (also recognizably) an illustration to Burke's *Letter to a Noble Lord* of 1796. The castigated radicals of that sprightly piece (left in the main anonymous by Burke) were here depicted individually, Lamb among them, in a sort of radical zoo.

At this time in Lamb's life – for it was to affect his friends and colour his own writing in the next few years – it is worth asking what 'Jacobinism' really consisted in and why now came the decline of Godwin and the increase in public outcry represented by the *Anti-Jacobin*.

Jacobinism first took its name from the very rational faction of Frenchmen who were in control of the French Revolution from 1792 to 1794, and whose leaders met in the Jacobin monastery by the Place Vendôme in Paris. It was the French National Assembly dominated by this group, the Girondins, which on 27 August 1793 formulated the 'Declaration of the Rights of Man and of the Citizen', a set of radical statements for their time. Its seventeen points, in summary, declared

1. that citizens are born free and equal; social distinctions can be based only on public service;
2. political associations must be based on the rights of liberty, property, security, and resistance to oppression;
3. the origin of sovereignty is in the nation;
4. liberty is the right to do what does not injure others, to be determined by law;
5. law is supreme, and
6. is the expression of the general will determined by every citizen

7 Little Queen Street, where the Lamb tragedy occurred in September 1796

Blenheims, the Ann Simmons cottage at Widford

Plate I   Four places associated with Lamb as drawn by an unknown nineteenth-century artist

Interior of the Salutation and Cat. It apparently represents Lamb talking while Coleridge listens – a reversal of the more likely situation. One wonders why they are seated at separate tables. A reconstruction as 'remembered by a frequenter of the house for over forty years'

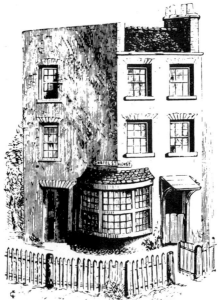

45 Chapel Street, Pentonville, where Lamb lived with his father until old John Lamb's death, and from which he was able to observe Miss Hester Savory living opposite, also on the corner of Chapel (now Chapel Market) and High Streets

William Wordsworth (1798)

Robert Southey (1796)

Samuel Taylor Coleridge (1796)

Charles Lamb (1798)

Plate II The Hancock Portraits (details): Lamb and his poet friends, all drawn between 1796 and 1798 for the publisher Joseph Cottle of Bristol by Robert Hancock, a Bristol artist

National Portrait Gallery

Charles Lloyd the Poet (1775–1839), by John Constable (detail; the present whereabouts of this painting is unknown)

Robert Lloyd (artist unknown)

Sophia Lloyd, Charles's wife, and their child Sophia, by John Constable
Worcester Art Museum, Worcester, Massachusetts

Plate III Young Lloyds: Lamb's close friends among the many children of Charles Lloyd, Quaker banker of Birmingham

Plate IV 'New Morality', cartoon by James Gillray, from the *Anti-Jacobin Magazine and Review* for July 1798, which appeared late: the cartoon is dated 1 August. See text for the verses which appeared below it and for a discussion of its content

Detail from 'New Morality': Charles Lamb and Charles Lloyd, collaborators on *Blank Verse*, as Toad and Frog

Plate V John Thelwall addressing a mass meeting, 26 October 1795, detail from the Gillray cartoon 'Copenhagen House', whose sub-title, derived from a remark about Jack Cade in Shakespeare's *Henry VI, Part II*, reads, '"I tell you, Citizens, we mean to new-dress the Constitution and turn it, and set a new Nap upon it"'. The meeting was held in Copenhagen Fields, Islington, by the Loncon Corresponding Society to win popular support for Parliamentary Reform. The man behind Thelwall holds 'Resolutions' of the Society; the umbrella-holder's collar shows him to be a Dissenting minister. Joseph Priestley, chemist and Unitarian minister, listens to Thelwall with folded arms just behind the fat lady in foreground. Drawn after the French Terror, while the British war with France still continued, the cartoon's clear intent is to show Reformists as French sympathizers ('Citizens') and traitorous agitators. Priestley was one of Lamb's idols, Thelwall soon his friend. (From *The Satirical Etchings of James Gillray*, edited by Draper Hill, New York, Dover Publications, 1976)

Thomas Holcroft (left) and William Godwin at the State Treason Trials, 1794, by Sir Thomas Lawrence
Photo Ashmolean Museum; owned by Kenneth Garlick

Thomas Manning, by an unknown artist (detail)
Royal Asiatic Society

George Dyer in 1795, by J. Cristall
National Portrait Gallery

Plate VI Some of Lamb's close friends who were radicals

Plate VII   Hester Savory (miniature, artist unknown)

through its fairly chosen representatives; citizens are equal before the law;

7. only the law can accuse, arrest, or detain, and citizens owe obedience to the law;

8. laws are to be rational and must exist before the offence;

9. everyone is presumed innocent until proven guilty, and prisoners must be treated humanely according to law;

10. opinion and religion shall be free;

11. freedom of speech is therefore assured;

12. the public force required to maintain the law is accountable to the citizenry;

13. taxation is required to maintain this force and shall be levied on citizens according to their means;

14. the citizenry shall arrange for just taxation;

15. every public official is accountable to the citizenry;

16. no legal government can exist without the separation of powers and guarantee of individual rights;

17. property is sacred and can be taken by government only according to the needs of the nation under law and with just compensation.[11]

Even the rights of property and of religion are respected, we may observe. Small wonder that Lamb's warmhearted, intelligent friends, *their* friends, and even some Whig Lords eager for Parliamentary reform had seized upon many of these notions as new social and political truths whose time had come. Jacobin clubs, however, had sprung up all over France and became a bulwark of the Robespierre group as it overthrew the moderate Girondins. 'Jacobin' now carried connotations of the Terror.

Edmund Burke had continued to the end to fear the French. Dead in 1797, his swan song had been the powerful *Letters on a Regicide Peace*, written at a moment in 1796 when Pitt, bowed down by the French war's vast expense and England's weariness, was considering a peace which he supposed might be had with honour. It did not then transpire. By early 1798 Britain and her allies were increasingly at bay as the result of the strategies of the rising French general Napoleon Bonaparte. The Mediterranean had for a year been a 'French lake'. Switzerland had been invaded. The French had Italy well in hand. When in May Napoleon and his army set out with the French fleet for Egypt instead of England, there was only a moment's relief until it was realized that the adventure was aimed at Britain's crucial India trade. The future Duke of Wellington and his brother were even then defending it in Asia. Now Pitt had the perspicacity to recognize the abilities of a young flag officer, Horatio Nelson, and send him to the Mediterranean to see what could be done. Napoleon for the moment proceeded grandly, seizing Malta on the way. Alarm at home mounted again and anti-Jacobinism swelled.

The inauguration of a monthly *Anti-Jacobin Review and Magazine* to replace the weekly with a 'July' issue (appearing on 1 August, as Nelson won the Battle of the Nile) took cognizance of the Jacobin threat in its prospectus:

> The existence of a Jacobin faction, in the bosom of our country, can no longer be denied. Its members are vigilant, persevering, indefatigable; desperate in their plans and daring in their language. The torrent of licentiousness, incessantly roaring forth from their numerous presses, exceeds, in violence and duration, all former examples . . . (*CLB*, Oct. 1975, 77)

with a good deal more in the same vein.

The *Anti-Jacobin*'s cartoonist Gillray, giant of a new breed, had turned his acidly amusing gift not only against Paine and Priestley but also against Burke himself in 1790 as 'The Knight of the Woeful Countenance' and against the Prince of Wales[12] in 1792 as the bloated 'VOLUPTUARY under the horrors of digestion'. Threatened on another count for prosecution for libel, he had been captured by the brilliant George Canning, Under-Secretary for Foreign Affairs and one of the chief perpetrators of the *Anti-Jacobin*, to use his artistry for the government side; in 1797 Gillray was granted a Treasury pension.

Now he turned his satirical pen to the tribe of – mainly literary – subversives and repeated beneath it Canning's relevant 'New Morality' verses. They were subtitled 'The promis'd installment of the High Priest of the THEOPHILANTHROPES, with the homage of Leviathan and his Suite.'[13] The little-known French 'philosopher' La Reveillère Lepaux was a convenient cord on which to hang English Jacobins. In the poem certain letters of their names were omitted according to the convention of such attacks; it is clear that Lloyd and Lamb had by now achieved sufficient fame for easy recognition. England was, after all, still a very small world: the average number of new publications in Great Britain was, between

1792 and 1802, only 372 annually,[14] and their authors loomed large
in the consciousness of the reading public.

'New Morality' ran:

> —behold! ———————————————————
> The Directorial LAMA, Sovereign Priest—
> LEPAUX—whom Atheists worship—at whose nod
> Bow their meek heads—*the Men without a God!*
> —Ere long perhaps to this astonished Isle
> Fresh from the Shores of subjugated *Nile*
> Shall BUONAPARTE'S victor Fleet protect
> The genuine *Theo-philanthropic* Sect—
> The sect of MARAT, MIRABEAU, VOLTAIRE,
> Led by their Pontiff, good LA-REVEILLERE
> Rejoic'd our CLUBS shall greet him, and Install
> The holy Hunch-back in thy Dome, St. PAUL,
> While countless votaries thronging in his train
> Wave their Red Caps, and hymn this jocund strain:
> "—*Couriers* and *Stars*, Sedition's Evening Host,
> Thou *Morning Chronicle* and *Morning Post*,
> Whether ye make the Rights of Man your theme,
> Your Country libel, and your God blaspheme,
> Or dirt on private worth and virtue throw
> Still blasphemous and blackguard, praise LEPAUX!
> —And ye Five other wandering Bards that move
> In sweet accord of harmony and love
> C-----DGE and S--TH-Y, L---D and L--B and Co.
> Turn all your mystic harps to praise LEPAUX!—[15]

In the verses that follow are mentioned Gilbert Wakefield, the
Unitarian who was shortly to languish in prison for a libel on the
Bishop of Llandaff; Helen Maria Williams the poet and dramatist,
who had like Paine narrowly escaped being guillotined with the
Girondins in Paris; and Samuel Whitbread, Member of Parliament,
as well as others more familiar. The diatribe continued:

> PR---TL-Y and W---F--LD, humble, holy men,
> Give praises to his name with tongue and pen!—
> TH-LW-L, and ye that lecture as ye go,
> And for your pains get Pelted, praise LE PAUX!—
> Praise him, each Jacobin, or Fool, or Knave,

And your cropp'd heads in sign of worship wave!—
All creeping creatures, venomous and low,
PAINE, W-LL--MS, G-DW-N, H-LC--FT, praise LEPAUX!—
And thou, LEVIATHAN! on Ocean's brim,
Hugest of living things that sleep & swim;
Thou in whose nose by BURKE's gigantic hand
The hook was fixed to drag thee to the land
With ----, ----, and ---- in thy train
And W---- wallowing in the Yeasty main,
Still as ye sport, and puff, and spout, and blow,
In puffing and in spouting, praise LEPAUX!

Here we come upon the whale, focal figure of the cartoon, representing Francis Russell, fifth Duke of Bedford, the close friend of Charles James Fox. Why Bedford?

The clue lies in Edmund Burke's hook, firmly stuck in Bedford's Leviathan nose. In actual fact, not many of the literati depicted had much to do with Bedford, but he was known as a friend of radicals and the cartoon also included politicians. Bedford's crime, the immediate occasion of the *Letter to a Noble Lord* (addressed to Lord Grenville), was that the Duke, together with the Earl of Lauderdale, had publicly questioned Burke's right to the State pension he sorely needed on his retirement from Parliament. Bedford, a wealthy devotee of scientific farming, had become a major Whig debater in the House of Lords and opposed the Tory clamp on radicals.[16] Burke in his *Letter* had set out to convince the world that Bedford was the mere tool of Paine, Priestley, Thelwall, Godwin, and their ilk. When these took over the country, said Burke, they would carve Bedford's whale's carcass into tidy morsels.[17] (His biting prose was rife with the animal images Gillray had seized upon.)

The cartoon itself is equal to its sources. Lepaux the hunchback looms tall to the right of the group, behind him three sorry Madame Defarges labelled 'Justice', 'Philanthropy' and 'Sensibility' (sensitivity, or the capacity to feel).

Prominent among the worshippers central to the picture are Lloyd and Lamb as a large toad and frog, clutching *Blank Verse*, and Godwin as an ass, with *Political Justice*. His *Enquirer* and *The Wrongs of Women*, representing his dead wife, are among the books and pamphlets castigated. 'Colridge' and Southey, two more asses, hold respectively 'Dactylics' and 'Saphics' (so spelled); *Joan of Arc* is in

Southey's pocket. Holcroft, a sort of devil, inscribes with the handle of his pitchfork, 'Letter from an Acquitted Felon'. Thelwall sits ahead of Fox on the whale's head in his French cap, holding 'Thelwall Lectures'. Paine is a crocodile, Miss Williams a snake. Wakefield's 'answer to the Bishop of Llandaff' obscures his face; Priestley holds 'Political Sermons'. The 'seditious' papers and periodicals are present, some in the form of seedy *sans-culottes* – the *Courier*, *Morning Chronicle*, *Morning Post*, and the *Analytical* and *Critical Reviews*. All were exactly those to which Coleridge and the others had been contributing. On the extreme right, a large sack labelled 'Philanthropic Requisition' holds Communion plate and an Archbishop's hat, while the Bible and Prayerbook are tied up, destined for the toilet.

We do not know what Lamb thought on the immediate occasion. Southey was amused but concerned in a letter to a close friend:

I have seen myself Bedfordized, and it has been a subject of much amusement. Holcrofts likeness is admirably preserved. I know not what poor Lamb has done to be croaking there. What I think the worst part of the anti-Jacobin abuse is the lumping together of men of such opposite principles:[18] this was stupid. We should all have been welcoming the Director, not the Theophilanthrope. The conductors of the Anti-Jacobin will have much to answer for in thus inflaming the animosities of the country. . . . The old systems of government I think must fall; but in this country, the immediate danger is on the other hand—from an unconstitutional and unlimited power. Burleigh saw how a Parliament might be employed against the people, and Montesquieu prophesied the fall of English liberty when the Legislature should become corrupt. You will not agree with me in thinking his prophecy fulfilled. (C. C. Southey, 106)

To another correspondent he added, 'The fellow has not, however, libeled my likeness, because he did not know it; so he clapped an ass's head on my shoulders.' The same principle applied, no doubt, to the Toad and Frog.

In September there was another onslaught from the same quarter in a poem called 'The Anarchists', which mispelled Lamb ('their mighty dam' is Anarchy):

> See! faithful to their mighty dam,
> C-----DGE, S--TH-Y, L---D, and L--BE,

In splay-foot madrigals of love,
Soft moaning like the widow'd dove,
Pour, side by side, their sympathetic notes;
    Of equal rights, and civic feasts,
    And tyrant Kings, and knavish priests,
Swift through the land the tuneful mischief floats.
And now to softer strains they struck the lyre,
    They sung the beetle, or the mole,
    The dying kid, or ass's foal,
By cruel man permitted to expire.

                                        (*Life*, 166)

What did the *Anti-Jacobin* crusade signify? Not a great deal in the lives of Lamb and his closest friends in and of itself. In the long run it proved only the convulsive contortions of the England-that-had-been in her death throes.[19] The enemies of the attackers were the new men and women, the direction which the future was to take, and Lamb had a legitimate place among them. But as true subversives, this nonviolent crew offered little physical danger to the English monarchy. In a very few years the same Noble Lord to whom Burke's letter had been addressed included in the Grenville cabinet Charles Fox as Foreign Secretary and Thomas Erskine – defender of Paine, Thelwall, and Holcroft – as Lord Chancellor.

The assaults had, however, the effect of making vivid to *Anti-Jacobin* readers what the journal had already propounded in its very first issue as a weekly (20 November 1797) – the presence in England of a 'school' of Jacobin *poets* with Southey as ringleader. In parodying Southey, *The Anti-Jacobin and Weekly Review* had been carrying out its professed intention to

> select from time to time, from among those effusions of the *Jacobin* Muse which happen to fall our way, such pieces as may serve to illustrate some one of the principles on which the poetical, as well as the political, doctrine of the *New School* is established. (Haller, 231)

After a December–July hiatus, 'New Morality' named for the first time the other members of the dangerous new school. So to the *Anti-Jacobin* must be accorded the honour of being the first to record and ridicule the arrival of what we now call the Romantics on the poetic scene, though it had as yet no reason to fasten upon Wordsworth.[20]

Once the political tumult had subsided, the *Monthly Magazine* and *Critical Review* would forget politics and begin to chide the new poetic school for its 'vulgar' language, its scenes from humble ('low') life, and its 'enthusiasm'. These taunts were taken up by editor Francis Jeffrey in the earliest issue of the great Whig *Edinburgh Review* in 1802. Jeffrey's taste in poetry leaned on the past. In the course of his remarks he did pay tribute to 'all the sweetness of Lambe and all the magnificence of Coleridge', while deploring their faults.[21]

A number of writers and journalists went to prison in the next few years, when 'sedition' or 'blasphemy' could be proved against them in the courts – among them Wakefield, the publisher Johnson, and editors James Perry and Benjamin Flower. George Dyer took fright and for an 1802 edition of *The Poet's Fate* purified his verses to omit Pantisocrats and benighted poets, including Lamb, altogether. A second thought about the new edition's preface, too – perhaps one phrase was dangerous – caused him greater expense after printing than he could reasonably bear.[22]

Charles Lloyd took fright as well. A letter of Coleridge's testifies to the fact that when he entered Caius College, Cambridge, as he did in August, 1798, and Christopher Wordsworth wrote to his uncle Mr Cookson that he was to tutor Lloyd in Greek, Cookson recommended caution and wondered 'whether or no an intimacy with so marked a character might not be prejudicial to his academical Interests'.[23] Christopher used a quotation from *Edmund Oliver* to reassure his uncle that Lloyd was not at all a Democrat. Lamb too must have been a marked character, especially since there was a tendency, at least once recorded, for readers not to remember which of the Lamb-and-Lloyd 'twin-bards' was which at this period.

Worrying about the attacks, particularly the *Anti-Jacobin*'s footnote about his and Lamb's 'folly and wickedness', Lloyd, soon after, busied himself composing the 'Letter to the Anti-Jacobin Reviewers' (a thirty-eight-page pamphlet) in which he presented himself as blameless while neatly straddling the fence: 'I disapprove of all war; . . . but while I do this, I doubt not . . . of the relative expediency and necessity of the "war with the regicides" '.[24] He defended himself as the author of *Edmund Oliver*, so opposed to Godwinian philosophy, as he pointed out. He defended Lamb:

The person you have thus leagued in a partnership of infamy with me is Mr. Charles Lamb, a man who, so far from being a

democrat, would be the first person to assent to the opinions
contained in the foregoing pages: he is a man too much occupied
with real and painful duties—duties of high personal self-
denial—to trouble himself about speculative matters. Whenever
he has thrown his ideas together, it has been from the irresistible
impulse of the moment, never from any intention to propagate a
system, much less any of "folly and wickedness."[25]

When the *Anti-Jacobin* declared Lloyd absolved, it did not comment
on Lamb.

Lloyd also wrote a *poem* in pamphlet form for the 'State Fast' of 27
February 1799, a special national holiday devoted to prayer for the
British war cause, including in a footnote 'the following striking
extract, from some lines intended as a satire on the Godwinian
jargon'[26] – by Charles Lamb, whom Lloyd named. It was the anti-
Godwin section from the as yet unpublished 'Living Without God in
the World'. Lloyd's own anti-Godwin lines were much harsher and
won the April, 1799, approval of the *Anti-Jacobin*, which had also
received assurances from a correspondent unnamed,

> who professes to have *a most intimate knowledge of him*, "that
> Mr. Lloyd is an honest and real friend to his country, an actual
> and sincere Christian, a determined Anti-Jacobin, and, as far as
> he at all concerns himself in temporary and particular politics, a
> *friend* to the *present war* and the *present Ministry*."[27]

Lloyd's anxious jumping into the bandwagon with the aid of
Lamb's poem must have given Lamb and Southey some cynical
amusement, especially as Lamb remained more 'Jacobin' privately
than Lloyd allowed. The *Anti-Jacobin* continued intermittently to
comment favourably on the new Lloyd; the *Analytical* and *Critical*
Reviews were now very sharp about his political shift.

Lamb did not scare so easily. He continued to befriend radicals,
expressing in his own life what he says of John Tipp in the "South-
Sea House' essay – 'neither was it recorded of him, that for lucre, or
for intimidation, he ever forsook friend or principle'.[28] Much later
he defended his radical and free-thinking friends by name in his
open 'Letter of Elia to Robert Southey' – Poet Laureate Southey,
who had chided Elia in a review for want of sufficient religion in his
essays. Here Lamb made his own philosophy of 'association'
explicit:

It is an error more particularly incident to persons of the correctest principles and habits, to seclude themselves from the rest of mankind, as from another species; and form into knots and clubs. The best people, herding thus exclusively, are in danger of contracting a narrowness . . . Instead of mixing with the infidel and the freethinker—in the room of opening a negociation, to try at least to find out at which gate the error entered—they huddle close together, in a weak fear of infection, like that pusillanimous underling in Spenser . . . (*Misc.*, 230)

But Lamb too had reacted to the attacks – and George Canning's part in them. In 1820, at the height of the controversy between George IV and Queen Caroline he would do a broadside relating to it for John Thelwall's *Champion*, with this on Canning:

> Bid him leave off his shallow Eton wit
>   More fit to soothe the superficial ear
>   Of drunken PITT, and that pickpocket Peer
> When at their sottish orgies they did sit,
> Hatching mad counsels from inflated vein,
> Till England, and the nations, reeled with pain.
>   (*P*, 106)

Pitt, of course, had died long before, and Lamb is recalling his own feelings in youth. (Lord Melville, the 'pickpocket Peer', was acquitted when impeached as First Lord of the Admiralty for embezzling from it, but doubts had lingered.) Lamb's 'The Unbeloved', of the same year and periodical, begins

>   Not a woman, child or man in
> All this isle that loves thee, C-----g.
>   (*P*, 106)

The verses are heavy with contemporary political allusion, but the drift of the concluding lines is plain:

>   . . . thou unamiable object,—
> Dear to neither prince, nor subject;—
> Veriest, meanest scab, for pelf
> Fast'ning on the skin of Guelph,

Place-and-heiress-hunting elf,
Thou, thou must, surely, *loathe thyself*.

(*P*, 107, 338)

Lamb could give as good as he got, and these fierce stanzas are well within the conventions of the time; they may surprise those who have thought Lamb primarily a purveyor of sweetness and light.

Lloyd now powdered his hair and required that his letters be addressed to 'Mr.', thus confirming his departure from the radical fold. In October 1799 Southey reported him to have been christened, so 'that he might not be unlike other people! . . . he was sick of antisocial speculations . . . ceasd to expect virtue in this world'.[29] Southey fully expected him to take orders in the Church next – but, though Lloyd himself had the intention, this did not transpire. Lloyd by this time had married (in church) the now acquiescent Sophia, who brought with her £10,000. Lamb continued friendly with him.

To return to the summer of 1798, *Rosamund Gray* next appeared, and though little noticed in the press, enjoyed a moderate success. It was 'inscribed in friendship to Marmaduke Thompson of Pembroke Hall, Cambridge', to whom Lamb must have felt close at the time, though beyond the letter about 'The Old Familiar Faces' and mysterious reference to an escapade in which Lamb and Thompson and Robert Lloyd had a part, little evidence survives.

So Lamb was now a literary figure, and a Jacobin literary figure at that. Yet his last publisher – and friend – Edward Moxon, wrote that he was 'no politician, though in his youth he had once assisted to draw through the streets Charles James Fox!'[30] Daniel Stuart, the *Morning Post* editor for whom he wrote briefly, thought Lamb had no head for politics, as Lamb acknowledged to Thomas Manning in 1800:

Public affairs—except as they touch upon me, & so turn into private—I cannot whip my mind up to feel any interest in.— —I grieve indeed that War and Nature & Mr. Pitt that hangs up in Lloyd's best parlour, should have conspired to call up three necessaries, simple commoners as our fathers knew them, into the upper house of Luxuries— —. Bread, and Beer, and Coals, Manning.—But as to France and Frenchmen, And the Abbe

Sieyes & his constitutions, I cannot make these present times
present to me. I read histories of the past, and I live in them;
altho' to abstract senses they are far less momentous, than the
noises which keep Europe awake. . . . (M 1, 187)

Later he maddened Thomas De Quincey by not joining in the
public excitement at the fall of Paris in 1814, when Napoleon
seemed to be finally defeated:

> I rejoiced . . . : Lamb did not. Then I was vexed. . . . One
> might have thought that, if he manifested no sympathy in a direct
> shape with the primary cause of the public emotion, still he would
> have sympathized, in a secondary way, with the delirious joy
> which every street, every alley, then manifested, to the ear as well
> as to the eye. But no! Still, like Diogenes, he threw upon us all a
> scoffing air, as of one who stands upon a pedestal of eternity,
> looking down upon those who share in the transitory feelings of
> their own age. How he felt in the following year, when the mighty
> drama was consummated by Waterloo, I cannot say, for I was not
> then in London.[31]

Lamb does not mention Waterloo in extant letters, but he does
allow himself, writing to Hazlitt, to have been 'cut up about' the
(1805) death of Nelson – 'He was the only pretence of a Great Man
we had.'[32] Yet he is not very serious, throughout *three* letters on
Nelson to Hazlitt, and we become aware that he is pulling the leg of
a Napoleon worshipper. Similarly, a letter to George Dyer that
appears somewhat harsh on rick-burners is aimed at Dyer's
sympathy with the poor and oppressed: Lamb is gently teasing his
friends' preoccupations. Otherwise he is mostly silent on these
matters.

In fact he did not care about day-to-day politics except when
forced to as a journalist or when deeply stirred at injustice or
wickedness in high places. De Quincey, always astute, throws light
upon Lamb the political lampooner, jabbing at hypocrisy:

> The case of insincerity, above all others, which moved his bile,
> was where, out of some pretended homage to public decorum, an
> individual was run down on account of any moral infirmities,
> such as we all have. . . . In such a case, and in this only, almost,
> Lamb could be savage in his manner.[33]

and

> so far from welcoming wicked, profligate, or dissolute people by
> preference, if they happened to be clever—he bore with numer-
> ous dull people, stupid people, asinine people, for no other reason
> upon earth than because he . . . believed them to have been ill-
> used or oppressed by some clever but dissolute man. . . . without
> further question, they had 'their place allowed' at Lamb's
> fireside. . . . Refuse anybody, reject anybody, tell him to begone,
> he could not, no more than he could have danced upon his
> mother's grave.[34]

Lamb's politics was a politics of the heart and reason in
compassionate collaboration, answerable only to his own
convictions. It is significant that all his life he wrote nearly always
for liberal, Reformist publishers and editors: John Fenwick of the
Albion; Dan Stuart of the *Morning Post*; Leigh Hunt of the *Examiner* –
long *the* English radical weekly; William Hone of the *Table Book* and
Every-Day Book; John Thelwall of the *Champion*; William Godwin of
the Juvenile Library; John Scott and John Taylor of the *London
Magazine*.[35] Where Wordsworth, Coleridge, and Southey loved
Mankind and Womankind, Lamb came to love many men and
women, with the kind of near-total understanding that the theorists,
full-time poets, philosophers, and politicians rarely had time for.
This, perhaps is the chief difference between him and them, and the
backbone of *Essays of Elia*.

CHAPTER SEVENTEEN

New Friends: Dyer
and Southey

I have never made an acquaintance . . . that lasted; or a friendship, that answered, with any that had not some tincture of the absurd in their characters. . . . The more laughable blunders a man shall commit in your company, the more tests he giveth you, that he will not betray or overreach you . . . he who hath not a dram of folly in his mixture, hath pounds of much worse matter in his composition. Lamb, 'All Fools' Day' (*Elia*, 44)

He was as simple as the daisy, which we think we admire, and daily tread under foot. Bryan Waller Procter ('Barry Cornwall') on George Dyer[1]

He hangs like a film and cobweb upon letters . . . he would not hurt a fly. William Hazlitt, 'On the Conversation of Authors', also on Dyer[2]

Are you intimate with Southey?—what poems is he about to publish—he hath a most prolific brain, & is indeed a most sweet poet. Lamb to Coleridge, 10 January 1797 (M I, 90)

It was time, in 1798, that Lamb had something to laugh about, and life had recently sent him George Dyer, the Cambridge Classics scholar. Soon it would send him Robert Southey, as well turned out, earnest, and sure of himself as Dyer was shabby, earnest, and absent-minded. Both were poets and radicals. Lamb had been much acted upon; now he began to mould and direct the currents of his own life, within the limits set, drawing to himself the friends who appealed to him. These became, gradually, a regiment of intimates and near intimates. More than most of us Lamb was driven to live through his friends and to make of those like George literary and epistolary capital; Southey, *not* written about except to friends, would now be his confidant in place of Coleridge. Mary was

Charles's central concern as his father failed, but Lamb would not write about her until later. We barely hear of the elder John now, or even (in letters still extant) of his death in the spring of 1799.

We hear of Dyer increasingly. Lamb probably first met him around 1796, through Coleridge. It is then that he first appears in Lamb's letters. Dyer as a comic figure is almost too good to be true – but the testimony of many witnesses suggests that most of the stories about him are true ones. Because he was so absent-minded – and hence often ridiculous – his contemporaries, including Lamb, were apt to underestimate him.

In fact, Dyer was something more than Lamb allowed. Modern scholars[3] take him seriously as the activist and reformer (if a minor one) whose published prose was influential and who acted as informal coordinator and catalyst for many of his radical generation. He was taken seriously by *some* of his contemporaries: the *Literary Chronicle* (1824) described him as a 'gentleman as amiable and as much esteemed in private life, as he is respected on account of his classical attainments, or his moral and political integrity'. Lord ('Citizen') Stanhope thought so highly of Dyer that he made him tutor to his sons and in his will named him an executor of the Stanhope estate. (George refused the executorship but benefited by an annuity from the Stanhope heirs.)

His generosity was proverbial: he had already come to Coleridge's financial rescue after the failure of *The Watchman* – and been warmly thanked for it – though his own bachelor purse was hardly thicker than Coleridge's.[4] 'It was *literally* the case with him,' said Henry Crabb Robinson, 'that he would give away his last guinea.'[5] He was without guile and without much humour: this it was that made him Lamb's butt – partly from exasperation that someone so gifted could be at the same time so absurd.

George took his own poetry very seriously, and rather over-estimated his place in the poetic firmament, which Lamb found funny. Others found it so too. His friend John Rickman asked, 'Could any body but Dyer have been so simple as to inscribe a poem, The Padlocked Lady?'[6] and another acquaintance wrote,

> The world all say, my gentle Dyer,
> The Odes do very much want fire.
> Repair that fault, my gentle Dyer,
> And throw thy Odes into the fire.[7]

But Dyer went on publishing his undersubscribed expensive verses with elaborate footnotes and making immense corrections in the final proofs, having to sweat away at his drudgery tasks to repair his losses. An editing chore that finally deprived him of his poor eyesight altogether was Dr James Valpy's edition of the Greek and Latin Classics in 141 volumes (1819–30), in which Dyer wrote 'all that is original' out of his vast erudition.

Much time, unpaid for, he spent in helping people – as Coleridge and Southey with the distribution of their joint play *Robespierre*. He gave Mary Hays a copy of Wollstonecraft's *Vindication of the Rights of Woman*, which led to their friendship and to Wollstonecraft's introduction through Miss Hays to William Godwin. He would soon start John Rickman, whom Southey had met in Hampshire, on his London career by getting him a literary job there. He introduced Rickman to Lamb; they became lifelong friends.

Ten years older than Lamb, Dyer was born of an impecunious family in Bridewell, where his father was a shipwright. Two elderly ladies arranged for his admission to Christ's Hospital, where he attracted more friends and patrons, emerging as a Grecian twelve years later, to enter Emmanuel College, Cambridge. There he met William Frend. Through Frend Dyer became a Nonconformist, thus sacrificing a University career. Frend, ejected from the University after his trial over the pamphlet, went to London and became a prosperous actuary of the Rock Life Insurance Company. In London he knew Lamb, who wrote,

> Friend of the friendless, friend of all mankind,
> To thy wide friendships I have not been blind;
> But looking at them nearly, in the end
> I love thee most that thou art Dyer's Frend.[8]

After Cambridge Dyer became for a while an 'usher' or under-teacher in two schools. Then, through Frend, he met Robert Robinson, a fine man and a Baptist (later Unitarian) preacher of considerable reputation. For ten years Dyer was tutor to Robinson's many children and on their father's death edited two of his theological works and wrote his life, a work much admired by Wordsworth.

In 1792 he moved to London for a literary career and settled for life at Clifford's Inn. Besides writing for periodicals and working for publishers he managed to produce almost a book a year for the next ten years and others after that – *Complaints of the Poor People of England*, books on convicts, on the libel laws, on Benevolence, on the history and practices of Cambridge University – some sixteen in all.

He was also, of course, more than a little mad – an Ichabod Crane, a Don Quixote, a Cyrano de Bergerac – who might be seen

> with a classical volume in his hand, and another in his pocket, walking slowly along Fleet Street or its neighborhood, unconscious of gazers, cogitating over some sentence, the correctness of which it was his duty to determine. You might meet him murmuring to himself in a low voice, and apparently tasting the flavor of the words. (Cornwall, 90)

Another observer saw his

> gaunt, awkward form, set off by trowsers too short . . . and a rusty coat much too large . . . his long head silvered over with short yet straggling hair, and his dark eyes glistening with faith and wonder (Talfourd, 166),

while a third listened to him:

> 'You have met with a curious and rare book, you say? Indeed, sir; abd—abd—abd—I should like to see it, sir; abd—abd—abd— perhaps you would allow me to look at it; abd—abd—abd—well, sir; but however—' (Cameron 1, 416).

John Rickman, arriving in London at the turn of the century, visited his lodging:

> G. Dyer is a great curiosity; his room more so; and I was witness to the regular apologies he makes to every visitor on its usual disorder. Their answers are as regular, that they never saw it otherwise. He is busy printing some poetry. (Williams, 27)

After an evening visit to Leigh Hunt he is said to have left behind one of his shoes. There are three classic Dyer stories relating to Lamb, the first probably by Lamb himself, concerning Walter Scott's anonymous novels:

Such was that silly joke of L---[Lamb], who, at the time the question of the Scotch novels was first agitated, gravely assured our friend—who as gravely, went about repeating it in all companies—that Lord Castlereagh had acknowledged himself to be the author of Waverly! (*Elia*, 313)

Lamb's first biographer, Talfourd, recalls:

Or shall I endeavour to revive the bewildered look with which, just after he had been announced as one of Lord Stanhope's executors and residuary legatees, he received Lamb's grave inquiry, "Whether it was true, as commonly reported, that he was to be made a Lord?" "O dear no! Mr. Lamb," responded he with earnest seriousness, but not without a moment's quivering vanity, "I could not think of such a thing; it is not true, I assure you." "I thought not," said Lamb, "and I contradict it wherever I go; but the Government will not ask your consent; they may raise you to the peerage without your even knowing it." "I hope not, Mr. Lamb; indeed, indeed, I hope not; it would not suit me at all," responded Dyer, and went his way, musing on the possibility of a strange honour descending on his reluctant brow. Or shall I recall the visible presentment of his bland unconsciousness of evil when his sportive friend taxed it to the utmost, by suddenly asking what he thought of the murderer Williams, who, after destroying two families in Ratcliffe Highway, had broken prison by suicide, and whose body had just before been conveyed, in shocking procession, to its cross-road grave! The desperate attempt to compel the gentle optimist to speak ill of a mortal creature produced no happier success than the answer, "Why I should think, Mr. Lamb, he must have been rather an eccentric character." (Talfourd, 166–7)

Though dim of eye, George was not blind to the charms of women and the hope of love. But his concentration on the life of the mind kept him very untidy and not often bathed. The clean intellectual women and pleasant widows who caught his eye would have none of him, until he was fifty-nine, when a kindly, motherly neighbour (not a laundress as has been said, and not an intellectual either, but the widow of a solicitor in comfortable circumstances) took him in hand and, with Frend's approval, married him, cleaned him up, and made his old age a happy one. Lamb wrote then, 'Everybody says how clean he is now. That is all the idea Frend seems to have of his old college crony. Beasts! not to have discovered G. D. but by the courtesy of a Little Soap.'[9]

But this lay far in the future. Lamb longed to write a novel about George, and of course used him anyway – in his second Elia essay, of 1820, 'Oxford in the Vacation', meaning Cambridge. With a few minor alterations George in this essay could just as well have been George at the turn of the century. ('Amicus Redevivus', about George's rescue from drowning, came out of an actual episode much later in the lives of both.)

George, of course, read the 'Oxford' piece in the *London Magazine*, recognized himself, threw caution to the winds, and took public umbrage at two paragraphs about his alleged mistreatment at the hands of exploiters. These, he declared to the *London*'s editor, were grossly inaccurate, and Lamb was obliged to retract them – though only as 'Elia', whose identity the innocent George may not yet have penetrated. George was not really a daisy to be trodden on, but his ire appeared to have been mainly in behalf of those said to have mistreated him, unidentified though they were.[10] The matter left no lasting bitterness, though George occasionally offered mild complaint at being made fun of, whereupon Lamb would assure him once again of his respect and love.

The rest of 'G. D.' at 'Oxford' George allowed to stand. Lamb wrote of him affectionately in this essay:

> I found [G. D.] busy as a moth over some rotten archive, rummaged out of some seldom-explored press, in a nook at Oriel. With long poring, he is grown almost into a book. . . . D. is assiduous in his visits to these seats of learning. No inconsiderable portion of his moderate fortune, I apprehend, is consumed in journeys between them and Clifford's Inn————where, like a dove on the asp's nest, he has long taken up his unconscious abode, amid an incongruous assembly of attorneys, attorneys' clerks, apparitors, promoters, vermin of the law, among whom he sits, "in calm and sinless peace." (*Elia*, 10)

After recounting some of George's vagaries he ends with a tribute,

> On the Muses' hill he is happy, and good, as one of the Shepherds on the Delectable Mountains; and when he goes about with you

to show you the halls and colleges, you think you have with you the Interpreter at the House Beautiful. (*Elia*, 11–12)

George Dyer was creeping up on Lamb, but the acquaintance ripened only gradually. More important to him in the late summer of 1798 – as Wordsworth and Coleridge prepared to go to Germany in September – was Robert Southey, who was also now cool on Coleridge. Lamb craved intimacy more than ever and Southey shared most of Lamb's interests. He had too a steadiness of character – and in youth an appealing exuberance – which offered welcome contrast to Lamb's previous intimates.

So for the next few months many of Lamb's letters were addressed to Southey, who was, among other projects, compiling his first *Annual Anthology*. This was to be modelled on the European 'Almanac', then popular, and to provide a poem for every day in the year. To this first *Anthology* Lamb contributed 'Living Without God in the World'.

Lamb was an ardent reader of Southey's revolutionary poems, as we have seen. Southey liked to experiment with meters from the Greek and Latin. One such effort, subtitled 'Dactylics', was called 'The Soldier's Wife' and had a third stanza by Coleridge. Its theme was anti-war – the widow left wandering with her baby – and its last line ended 'God help thee, widow'd one'. Charles Lamb had damned it pleasantly to Coleridge two years earlier, with his own parody, ending, 'God help ye, rhyming Ones'. (Coleridge had been sore about the parody.)

The *Anti-Jacobin* had also damned the poem, with its own parody:

Come, little Drummer Boy, lay down your knapsack here;
I am the Soldier's Friend—here are some Books for you;
Nice clever Books by Tom Paine the Philanthropist.
Here's Half-a-crown for you—here are some Hand-bills too—
Go to the Barracks and give all the soldiers some:
Tell them the Sailors are all in a Mutiny . . .

(Simmons, 70)

As practical reformer, though he had given up Pantisocratic exodus, Southey continued to be busy with humanitarian schemes.

Even when he later retreated from his revolutionary principles,[11] he remained compassionate and concerned about the social causes of revolution. Just now he was moving about nervously from place to place – for his health, for his wife Edith's, for other reasons. He was busy on a Welsh epic called *Madoc*, and a second edition of *Joan of Arc*.

He learned on 28 July that *Joan of Arc* 'delighted' Lamb, whose major message was to provide Southey with the Theses letter sent to Coleridge and the comment, 'Samuel Taylor hath not deign'd an answer—was it impertinent in me to avail myself of that offer'd source of knowledge?'[12]

In August Mary was ill again, involving her brother in a sober, lonely few weeks, but by mid-October he was deep in the seventeenth century poets both he and Southey loved.[13] He sent his fastidious friend a volume of George Wither's *Emblems* 'that "old book and quaint," as the brief author of *Ros Gray* hath it . . . in a most detestable state of preservation. . . . Some child, the curse of antiquaries . . . hath been dabbling in some of [the woodcuts] with its paint and dirty fingers . . .' This was the sort of thing Lamb collected for his own library from street stalls; he was the despair of proper bibliophiles: 'I have pickt up too another copy of Quarles[14] for ninepence!!!' In his next to Southey he copies out some Marlowe, from *The Jew of Malta*, revealing with what attention he devoted himself to Elizabethans in spare time. He has had a letter from Charles Lloyd at Cambridge, 'busy recanting the new heresy, metaphysics,—for the old dogma, Greek', an oblique jibe at Lloyd's recent political switch, and adds that 'his Brother Robert, the flower of their family, has left his ugly situation in Saffron Wald[e]n'. Mary is still in health, though she has had a 'slight' attack, 'which frighten'd me a good deal, but it went off unaccountably'.[15]

As the autumn moves into November he criticizes one of Southey's poems with the frankness and effort to be helpful he had earlier bestowed on Coleridge, ending, 'I cut my letter short, because I am call'd off to business—.'[16] Much thoughtful literary work has been tucked between bills of lading.

There was other contemporary poetry to occupy the friends – and to drive the smallest of wedges between them. The first *Lyrical Ballads* of Wordsworth and Coleridge – anonymous because of Coleridge's radical reputation – appeared in October. Southey had got a copy in advance from Cottle, by request, and published in the October *Critical Review* the first critique to appear anywhere. The book began with the 'antique' early version of 'The Ancient Mariner' and ended with Wordsworth's 'Tintern Abbey'. There were many interesting poems in between, some of them controversial as to poetic merit from that day to this. (Wordsworth provided most of the volume.) Southey knew quite well who were the poets, though he had to pretend not to, and while he was above being malicious if he truly admired a work,[17] he did *not* admire 'The Ancient Mariner', a circumstance which did not help his future reputation. Otherwise the review was lukewarm; Southey found a few poems to praise, among them 'Tintern Abbey'. The secret of the critic's identity was soon out: Lamb guessed it at once.

Of the 'Mariner', Southey had said, 'This piece appears to us perfectly original in style as well as in story. Many of the stanzas are laboriously beautiful, but in connection they are absurd or unintelligible. . . . We do not sufficiently understand the story to analyse it. It is a Dutch attempt at German sublimity. Genius has here been employed in producing a poem of little merit.'[18]

On 8 November 1798, Lamb leaped to its defence:

. . . If you wrote that review in 'Crit. Rev.,' I am sorry you are so sparing of praise to the 'Ancient Marinere;'—so far from calling it, as you do, with some wit, but more severity, 'A Dutch Attempt,' &c., I call it a right English attempt, and a successful one, to dethrone German sublimity. You have selected a passage fertile in unmeaning miracles, but have passed by fifty passages as miraculous as the miracles they celebrate. I never so deeply felt the pathos as in that part,

> A spring of love gush'd from my heart,
> And I bless'd them unaware—

It stung me into high pleasure through sufferings. Lloyd does not like it; his head is too metaphysical, and your taste is too correct; at least I must allege something against you both, to excuse my own dotage—

> So lonely 'twas, that God himself
> Scarce seemèd there to be!—&c., &c.

But you allow some elaborate beauties—you should have extracted 'em. 'The Ancient Marinere' plays more tricks with the mind than that last poem, which is yet one of the finest written. But I am getting too dogmatical; and before I degenerate into abuse, I will conclude with assuring you that I am

Sincerely yours,
C. Lamb
(M I, 141–3)

Lamb was then almost alone among his contemporaries – many of whom shared Southey's dim view of the work as a whole – in seeing Coleridge's masterpiece for what it was, nor did his present quarrel with Coleridge affect his judgment.

Meanwhile the first *Annual Anthology* under Southey's editorship proceeded apace. The volume was published in 1799, and a sequel in 1800. Some of its authors, like Charles Lamb, wrote under their own names, others under pen names,[19] particularly Southey, who found himself, not perhaps unwillingly, obliged to fill up half the volume with his own verses, many reprinted from the daily press. (The total of all contributions numbered about a hundred, the 'Almanac' plan having fallen short.) Though poets like Charles Lloyd here mingled with the poetasters among Southey's old school friends, the *Anthology* contributors were generally an interesting group, including William Taylor of Norwich, known for his translation of Bürger's 'Lenore', a German poem which impressed Lamb and other Romantics; Southey's dead brother-in-law the Quaker Pantisocrat Robert Lovell; Joseph Cottle, poet as well as publisher; the ubiquitous Charles Lloyd; and George Dyer – on the 'River Cam'. The sole female contributor was the attractive Amelia Alderson Opie, who had just spurned the widowed William Godwin for the portrait painter John Opie, to whom her 'To Mr. Opie' was a tribute. Thomas Beddoes and Humphrey Davy exemplified the cross-fertilization between science and the arts. Beddoes, Lloyd's Bristol doctor, had recently employed Davy, a young chemist, in his experimental Pneumatic Institution at Bristol, where Davy had purified laughing gas and got to know Southey and Coleridge. Beddoes would father a future poet of note, and Davy – later President of the Royal Society and inventor of the miner's safety lamp – would shortly be entrusted by Wordsworth with proofreading the second edition of *Lyrical Ballads*! Lamb would meet him before long in London.

The 1799 volume was also tinged with radical politics, though an item by Southey called 'War Poem' was removed at the last minute – already in bound pages – as being 'unpatriotic'. Like 'The Soldier's Wife' it concerned the wartime fate of an innocent family and innocent babe. One of Southey's contributors, a close friend and a civil servant, complained of the *Anthology* that, invited to dine on roast beef, he had been given a French hash. Southey replied that there was something in it for everyone; and Charles Lloyd found it possible to sign his name in both volumes. Southey's own contributions included fare as various as 'Love Elegies by Abel Shuffelbottom', his reply to Coleridge's Higginbottom sonnets, the anti-war 'Battle of Blenheim', still to be found in anthologies, and 'Ode to a Pig, while his nose was being bored'.

The 1800 volume (to anticipate a little) included no Lamb – 'Lamb is lazy and will give me nothing,' wrote Southey.[20] He was not without mention, however. Coleridge, returned from abroad and restored to Southey's friendship, provided more than a dozen items (some of them, like Southey's, reprinted from newspapers), including 'This Lime-Tree Bower', addressed openly 'to Charles Lamb, of the India House'. 'To a Friend, who had declared his intention of writing no more poetry', also to Lamb, was less obvious. 'Fire, Famine, and Slaughter' was Coleridge's vigorous attack on Prime Minister Pitt. A second woman poet, brought in by Coleridge, was Mrs Mary 'Perdita' Robinson, discarded mistress of the Prince of Wales, a beauty painted in her heyday by Gainsborough and Reynolds. Her acting career was ruined by the scandal, and she had later become paralysed and confined to a wheelchair. She now pursued a literary career in the radical ranks with vigour and courage. She was a good friend of Godwin's.

In publishing with Southey, as with Coleridge and Lloyd, Lamb had again gravitated quite naturally to the radical fold. The government's alternative stringency and tolerance – for the *Anthology* got off relatively unscathed – the casualness of public association and risk on the part of those poets who had had second thoughts, and even the principles by which an editor suppressed one poem and printed another must puzzle the modern reader. England was still of two minds, and English 'Liberty!' – so hard won in 1688 – was still untarnished in its appeal for many English men and women. Even Canning of the *Anti-Jacobin* was within a few years obliged to call off the dogs of Gillray.[21]

In November of 1798 Lamb wrote to Southey that he was taking Charles Lloyd briefly to the country haunts of his childhood and youth, to Ware – and Blakesware. The Blakesware wilderness would come into a play he was writing. Lamb let nothing go that had once been part of him.

CHAPTER EIGHTEEN

Robert Lloyd and *John Woodvil*

I am in love with this green earth; the face of town and country; the unspeakable rural solitudes, and the sweet security of streets. 'New Year's Eve' (*Elia*, 29)

My Tragedy will be a medley (or I intend it to be a medley) of laughter & tears, prose & verse & in some places rhime, songs, wit, pathos, humour, & if possible sublimity,—at least, tis not a fault in my intention, if it does not comprehend most of these discordant atoms,—Heaven send th[e] y dance not the dance of Death! Lamb to Southey, 28 November 1798 (M 1, 152).

Charles Lloyd's brother Robert, who had met Lamb in London (and possibly in Birmingham as well) became in the summer of 1798 a new correspondent. Now it was Lamb's turn to encourage an unhappy boy, as Coleridge had done for him. In searching out ways of coping for Robert before and after that young friend left Saffron Walden, Lamb had to present himself as mature, hopeful, and cheering. As he thought things through, he concluded that at the root of his own depressions and of Robert's lay the sin of pride, or selfishness, which had tragic implications for the proud but was redeemable through penitence, humility, and courage. One must look outward to find strength in religion and human friendship or, if friendship fails, strength in God alone. It struck him, in the course of the summer, that this theme would make a fine play. He would call it *Pride's Cure*, and he started work on it without delay.

Robert was miserable in his grocer–draper apprenticeship in Saffron Walden and seized upon Lamb as a sort of surrogate elder brother unconnected with his family in whom he could safely confide. The elder Lloyds must have felt that their Charles's problems lay in part in their not having kept his nose to the grindstone. Robert must not be allowed to moon about so aimlessly as Charles had done: the apprentice contract would oblige him to live a steady, productive, disciplined life for several years. The

cultured Robert, however, was much more like his brother Charles
than like his parents. Today he would have been thought of as
University material, but there was the serious Quaker scruple about
subscribing to the official Church's Thirty-nine Articles, then
required for a degree. (Brother Charles, at Cambridge from 31
August, now found no difficulty about this stricture, but he was
about to leave the Quaker fold and beyond rescue.)

So Robert had fretted and chafed under his three-year commercial apprenticeship and written to Lamb of his woes. He did not
know what he wanted to do in life any more than had Charles Lloyd
at the same age. Lamb tried to help him without being subversive of
the parents:

> I wish, Robert, *you* could find an object, I know the painfulness of
> vacuity, all its achings, & inexplicable longings—. I wish to God
> I could recommend any plan to you—stock your mind well with
> religious knowledge; discipline it to wait with patience for duties,
> that may be your lot in life; prepare yourself not to expect too
> much out of yourself; *read* & *think* . . . (M 1, 134)

But Lamb had troubles too. In August Mary was ill again – a
'calamity', he told Robert. His next letter finds her better. He tries
once more to guide Robert: one can get along without even a friend,
if one must. At some length he expresses his own philosophy of
friendship and the traps it may set for the unwary. Robert must not
overestimate Lamb as a friend: 'I say it before God, and I do not lie,
you are mistaken in me. I could not bear to lay open all my failings
to you, for the sentiment of shame would be too pungent.'[1] His
preoccupation with friendship was to be strong in *Pride's Cure* (he
later changed its name to *John Woodvil*).

By mid-November Robert, now back in Birmingham with his
family, was complaining again. Lamb responded with humour,
then with his own perception of life's sweetness:

> My dear Robert,
>   one passage in your Letter a little displeas'd me.—The rest was
> nothing but kindness, which Roberts' letters are ever brimful of—
> —. You say that "this World to you seems drain'd of all its
> sweets!"——At first I had hoped you only meant to insinuate the
> high price of Sugar! but I am afraid you meant more—. O
> Robert, I do'nt know what you call sweet,—— Honey & the

honey comb, roses & violets, are yet in the earth. The sun & moon yet reign in Heaven, & the lesser lights keep up their pretty twinklings——meats & drinks, sweet sights & sweet smells, a country walk, spring & autumn, follies & repe[ntan]ce, quarrels & reconcilements, have all a sweetness by turns—. . . good humor & good nature, friends at home that love you, & friends abroad that miss you, you possess all these things, & more innumerable, & these are all sweet things————. You may extract honey from every thing; do not go a gathering after gall—. the bees are wiser in their generation than the race of sonnet writers & complainers. . . . (M I, 144)

Also in November, he sent Southey an extract from *Pride's Cure* involving another autobiographical element – about a youth who pined away after attending his Anna's wedding to another. 'Anna' once more! By 1801 Lamb managed to shake this juvenile effusion off too and wrote to John Rickman,

Moreover, I have excluded . . . the Gentleman who died for Love, having since discovered by searching the parish register of St. Mary Ottery, that his disorder was a stranguary, tho' some rimes upon his grave-stone did a little lean to my hypothesis. (MII, 37)

With 'The Dying Lover' the lovesick boy in Lamb (had he been at Ann's wedding?) makes his exit once and for all, though the Ann of his interior landscape will endure.

The play as it evolved was Shakespearean in style and tone. Very weak as drama, it nonetheless marks an advance in Lamb's literary powers. The final version shows an aptitude for Elizabethan verse, and the autobiographical elements – they are many – are now set at a slight *remove*, though Lamb is again wrestling with a personal problem, or set of problems. He certainly had the Coleridge quarrel in mind and the troubles of Robert Lloyd: the friendship motif looms large. So does the evil effect of too much drink. Woodvil himself is conscious of weakness;

> I want some seasonings of adversity,
> Some strokes of the old mortifier Calamity,
> To take these swellings down, divines call Vanity.
> (P, 158)

Woodvil's downfall results from his corruption by dissolute friends in the court of Charles II. His noble father, Sir Walter Woodvil, is being sought on suspicion of Cromwellian treason and is now hiding in Sherwood Forest with his decent son Simon, with Margaret, John's erstwhile fiancée, and other companions, as John knows. John yearns, like Lamb, for a friend. In a drunken moment John betrays his father to the friend he has lit upon unwisely, one Lovel. Lovel seeks out Sir Walter and is about to arrest him when Sir Walter, sensing John's complicity, falls dead, apparently of a heart attack.

Overcome by remorse and despised by all, John is in a sorry state when the unsullied Margaret, her heart touched by his misery, seeks him out. She devotes herself to restoring his confidence and calming his horror at what he has done. *He* devotes himself to religion. The former cynic is thus restored to virtue by calamity, his pride cured. *Finis*.

The abrupt halt to the action, which has proceeded in lively fashion up to Sir Walter's death, effectively kills the play as well, though Lamb, concerned with the poetry and interesting philosophic undercurrents, resisted all comments to this effect until long after, spending four years in revision before he published the play at his own expense. Southey declared that in *John Woodvil* Lamb 'will please you by the exquisite beauty of his poetry and provoke you by the execrable silliness of his story'. Lamb wrote to Rickman in November 1801 about some drastic reductions in the script, 'The whole ends with Margaret's Consolation, where it *should* end, without any pert incident of surprise and trick to make a catastrophe.'[2] Herein lay his mistake, of course. Surprise was necessary, if not trick. Motivation, development of character, and plot must rise to a convincing climax of somewhat more exciting dimensions than sudden reform. But by now he was wedded to his personal theme and solutions.

The character of Woodvil, with his abrupt shifts, is reminiscent of both Coleridge and Lloyd, though Lamb shows him flat and unbelievable. The father is a stock figure of wronged nobility, as is Lovel of villainy. Margaret, however, comes to life and is more or less demonstrated to be strong, pure, and compassionate, a true Shakespearean heroine. She is a kind of Sophia Pemberton Lloyd, who after her marriage became a rescuing angel for Charles Lloyd. She is also the prototype of the woman Lamb was to fall in love with twenty years later, the actress Fanny Kelly. She represents what Lamb considered his own best self; Woodvil, with his drinking and folly, his worst.

There are other intriguing autobiographical elements in *John Woodvil*. Margaret is blonde like Ann Simmons, and her lover plays with her hair as had Lamb with Ann's, in his early sonnets. Blakesware is recalled in the words of Margaret the consoler:

> Dost yet remember the green arbour, John,
> In the south gardens of my father's house,
> Where we have seen the summer sun go down,
> Exchanging true love's vows without restraint?
> And that old wood, you call'd your wilderness. . . .
>   (*P*, 171)

Coleridge's birthplace comes into a dozen or so attractive lines when going to church plays a part in John's redemption and he hears the bells of Ottery St. Mary, his 'native village'. There is a witch with a curse, whom Lamb extracted from the finished play but kept as subject of a detached poem.

There had also been a rumination by the repentant Woodvil that recalls Lamb's poem 'Composed at Midnight' with its complaint about the heaven and hell of the Established Church. Woodvil begins his complex argument, ' "Infinite torment for finite offences." I will never believe it. How divines can reconcile this monstrous tenet with the spirit of their Theology!'[3] In drastic cutting Lamb later slashed through the soliloquy (as 'German puerilities') and substituted a servant's *account* of his master's distraught state offstage. When his Cambridge friend Thomas Manning objected in 1802, Lamb countered,

> *A pro pos*, I think you wrong about *my* Play. All the omissions are *right*. And the supplementary Scene in which Sandford *narrates* the manner in which his master is affected, is the Best in the Book. It stands, where a Hodge podge of German puerilities used to stand. I insist upon it, that you like that Scene. Love me, love that scene. (M ɪɪ, 55–6)

Manning had shown the play to Thomas Holcroft, the actor-playwright, 'who had taste enough to discover', Manning wrote, 'that 'tis full of poetry—but the plot he condemns in toto. . . . I think you were ill advised to retrench so much.'[4]

Lamb had described his severe cuts[5] to Rickman:

—Moreover, I have gone thro' and cut out all the Ahs! & Ohs! and sundry weak parts, which I thought so fine three or four years ago. . . . I have been so particular, because you have shewn more liking to my Margaret, than most people, and my alterations were *in part* the offspring of your suggestions; not wholly, for I have long smelt a jumble. I hope you will find it now nearly all of a piece. (M ɪɪ, 37)

Rickman, who liked the play and offered to help pay for its publication, had said he would fall in love with Margaret if he ever met her counterpart in real life. (John Clare the poet was also to praise 'Woodvil'[6] in a sonnet to Lamb of 1831.)

But for all his cuts, Lamb had not touched the gravest trouble – *John Woodvil*'s lack of dramatic form. The scene containing the play's best-known passage remained.[7] First it argues a point of philosophic concern to the playwright:

[SIMON]
'Tis now nine months almost,
Since I saw home. What new friends has John made?
Or keeps he his first love?—I did suspect
Some foul disloyalty. Now do I know,
John has prov'd false to her, for Margaret weeps.
It is a scurvy brother.
　　　　　　　[SIR WALTER]
Fie upon it.
All men are false, I think. The date of love
Is out, expired, its stories all grown stale,
O'erpast, forgotten, like an antique tale
Of Hero and Leander.
　　　　　　　[SIMON]
I have known some men that are too general-contemplative for
the narrow passion. I am in some sort a *general* lover.
　　　　　　　[MARGARET]
In the name of the boy God, who plays at hood-man-blind with
the Muses, and cares not whom he catches: what is it *you* love?
　　　　　　　[SIMON]
Simply, all things that live,
From the crook'd worm to man's imperial form,
And God-resembling likeness. The poor fly,
That makes short holyday in the sun beam,

And dies by some child's hand. The feeble bird
With little wings, yet greatly venturous
In the upper sky. The fish in th' other element,
That knows no touch of eloquence. What else?
Yon tall and elegant stag,
Who paints a dancing shadow of his horns
In the water, where he drinks.

[MARGARET]

I myself love all these things, yet so as with a difference:—for
example, some animals better than others, some men rather than
other men; the nightingale before the cuckoo, the swift and
graceful palfrey before the slow and asinine mule. Your humour
goes to confound all qualities. (*P*, 152–3)

Young John Lamb's views are those of Simon. Margaret's opposing
conviction will be that of Charles Lamb in the Elia essay 'Imperfect
Sympathies'.

A speech of Simon's won praise from Lamb's friends. Margaret
asks, directly after the scene above, 'What sports do you use in the
forest?'

[SIMON]

Not many; some few, as thus:—
To see the sun to bed, and to arise,
Like some hot amourist with glowing eyes,
Bursting the lazy bands of sleep that bound him,
With all his fires and travelling glories round him.
Sometimes the moon on soft night clouds to rest,
Like beauty nestling in a young man's breast,
And all the winking stars, her handmaids, keep
Admiring silence, while those lovers sleep.
Sometimes outstretcht, in very idleness,
Nought doing, saying little, thinking less,
To view the leaves, thin dancers upon air,
Go eddying round; and small birds, how they fare,
When mother Autumn fills their beaks with corn,
Filch'd from the careless Amalthea's horn;
And how the woods berries and worms provide
Without their pains, when earth has nought beside
To answer their small wants.

> To view the graceful deer come tripping by,
> Then stop, and gaze, then turn, they know not why,
> Like bashful younkers in society.
> To mark the structure of a plant or tree,
> And all fair things of earth, how fair they be.
>   [MARGARET] (*smiling*)
> And, afterwards them paint in simile.
>
> <div align="right">(<i>P</i>, 153)</div>

William Godwin is said by William Hazlitt to have sought the 'hot amourist' passage among the Elizabethans, forgetting where he had read it, and to have inquired about it everywhere until at length he asked Charles Lamb.

Other isolated lines are graceful:

> Green clinging tendrils round a trunk decay'd
>   (*P*, 151)

> Better the dead were gather'd to the dead,
> Than death and life in disproportion meet.—
>   (*P*, 151)

> A bird let loose, a secret out of hand
> Returns not back.
>   (*P*, 164)

> These black thoughts, and dull melancholy,
> That stick like burrs to the brain, will they ne'er leave me?
>   (*P*, 165)

> Now, no more
> Must I grow proud upon our house's pride.
>   (*P*, 170)

The play's 'beauties', as these excerpts show, were largely in elements that did not advance the drama, such as it was. John Woodvil's close resemblance to the Shakespeare of 'As You Like It' was admired by loyal friends, but there is nothing worse than the imitation of a great dramatist that does not come off. Plot and subplot are so thin as to be almost nonexistent. The elements leading to the sudden and pointless 'catastrophe' do not have their origins either in developing character or the force of inevitable events.

Lamb's central figure is all fatal weakness without redeeming qualities – in short, a bore. With the possible exception of Margaret, *John Woodvil* is composed of stick figures. They move not by their own power but by the manipulation of the inexperienced playwright – one who yet had the critical ability to detect such faults in plays he saw and was soon expert in dramatic analysis. The difference between knowing abstractly, as audience, what succeeds on the stage and making a play succeed as creator are profound. These gifts may occur in the same individual; very often they do not – certainly not in Lamb's first venture into writing for the theatre. John Kemble of the Drury Lane (and possibly George Colman, another producer, as well) knew what he was about in rejecting *John Woodvil.*

On publication in 1802 contemporary critics damned the play,[8] yet *John Woodvil* was more precious to Lamb than any of his previous writings, because he had discovered through it something crucial to his own future. The optimism of its ending – that through Calamity one may come to one's own best self – is his own emergence from the struggle, his determination to leave bitterness to others. That he failed as dramatist was less important to his life in the long run than that he had attempted much and arrived at a sustaining philosophy through the effort itself. Failure for the strong is challenge. Had Lamb's imitations – of Burton, of Shakespeare – been successful, he would (as has been said) perhaps have persisted in them, and we would not have had *Essays of Elia.*

From 1798 to 1802 the play is often mentioned in his letters to his friends. Even twenty years after, the attachment of the father for the crippled child is evident in the letter dedicating to Coleridge the first volume of Lamb's collected *Works* of 1818:

One piece, Coleridge, I have ventured to publish in its original form, though I have heard you complain of a certain over-imitation of the antique in the style. If I could see any way of getting rid of the objection, without rewriting it entirely, I would make some sacrifices. But when I wrote John Woodvil, I never proposed to myself any distinct deviation from common English. I had been newly initiated in the writings of our elder dramatists; Beaumont and Fletcher, and Massinger, were then a *first love*; and from what I was so freshly conversant in, what wonder if my language inperceptibly took a tinge? The very *time*, which I had chosen for my story, that which immediately followed the

Restoration, seemed to require, in an English play, that the English should be of rather an older cast, than that of the precise year in which it happened to be written. I wish it had not some faults, which I can less vindicate than the language.

I remain,

My dear Coleridge,

Your's,

With unabated esteem,

C. LAMB.[9]

CHAPTER NINETEEN

Cheerfulness Breaks In

*When a poor creature . . . comes before thee, do not stay to inquire whether the
'seven small children' . . . have a veritable existence. . . . It is good to believe
him.* 'A Complaint of the Decay of Beggars in the Metropolis'
(*Elia*, 120)

*I know that if my parents were to live again, I would do more things to please
them, than merely sitting still six hours a week.* Lamb to Robert Lloyd,
23 April 1799 (M I, 169)

> *When maidens such as Hester die,*
> *Their place ye may not well supply,*
> *Though ye among a thousand try,*
> *With vain endeavor.*
> Lamb's 'Hester' (M II, 107)

By some of the means we have seen, Lamb was gradually adjusting
to his difficult life, sublimating his India House discontent, keeping
interested in his friends' affairs, carrying on as an enthusiastic critic
and writer of poetry, and being almost light-hearted as he studied
George Dyer. He had even enjoyed a mute love passage (quite one-
sided, we may suppose) inspired by a girl who lived opposite in
Pentonville. When old John Lamb's death occurred, it was as
though he had already come to terms with that too, so long as Mary
made progress. His letters to Southey over the next few months
begin to show intimations of Elia as he practises his growing comic
gift.

He has been trying bits of *Pride's Cure* on his oddest friend:

. . . I shew'd my Witch & Dying Lover to Dyer last night, but
George could not comprehend how that could be poetry, which
did not go upon ten feet, as George & his predecessors had taught
it to do; so George read me some lectures of the distinguishing
qualities of the Ode, the Epigram, & the Epic, & went home to

illustrate his doctrine by correcting a proof sheet of his own Lyrics. . . . (M I, 151)

Southey's serious nature did not always respond to Lamb's humour, as in his remark to Edith already quoted: 'Lamb loves to laugh at every thing—he speaks of every body in a joke except Bishop [Jeremy] Taylor.' Lamb laughed at Wordsworth and Coleridge in Germany, not quite accurately: 'I hear that the Two Noble Englishmen have parted no sooner than they set foot on german Earth, but I have not heard the reason—Possibly to give Moralists an handle to exclaim, "Ah! me! what things are perfect?"'[1] The suspected friction did not, in fact, exist. Coleridge had serious designs on German philosophy and literature; Wordsworth and Dorothy gave up on both and used the time for a working holiday.[2]

Late in December, Lamb pressed Southey to help him get a place as 'extra clerk' in the East India House for a destitute, nameless young man, through Southey's friend John May, who knew one of the directors.[3] Some five months later Southey reported to his Edith that the protégé had turned out 'a thorough and compleat rascal. Lamb says he did not think any man could have behaved so villainously!'[4] But at this time Lamb described himself as 'tormented with anxiety'[5] about the man and urged Southey to apply to May with haste. Southey complied. The quick response of all suggests an attractive network of Benevolence among the friends.

An interesting paragraph concludes Lamb's letter: 'I suppose you have somehow heard, that poor Mary Dollin has poisoned herself, after some interviews with John Reid, the ci-devant Alphonso of her days of hope.'[6] The only other information on Mary Dollin is contained in a letter from Charles Lloyd (who knew Reid's mother), to Thomas Manning, his Cambridge maths tutor, some ten days after Lamb's comment, in a passage concerning Southey. 'I find now,' Lloyd continues, 'alas too late! that he had "day dreams" of marrying me to Miss Dollin—& why forsooth?—because the poor girl had passions & fell on Lambs knees—the fellow will make me vain, if all damsels that he may hear of that lack "daily bread" excite in him "dreams" about me.'[7]

Lamb must have met the girl through Lloyd or Dyer or Mary Hays, and lent a sympathetic ear to the tale of her unrequited passion for Reid – or so his detachment about her demise seems to indicate. But the incident puts him squarely, again, in touch with the Godwinite group, for Reid, a physician with an interest in nervous disorders, was a friend of the same Mary Hays, the feminist, who had introduced Godwin to Mary Wollstonecraft. Dr Reid is said to have been indignant about Charles Lloyd's attack on Miss Hays in *Edmund Oliver*, that unfortunate novel. It was generally assumed that Lloyd had portrayed her as Gertrude Sinclair, who breaks off her engagement to Oliver, lives with a married man (as the actual Miss Hays did not), bears his child and dies ignominiously, destroyed by Godwinism. The Mary Dollin episode is a sad little footnote on the radical circle.

Lamb's correspondence with Southey continued into 1799. January brought veiled references to Charles Lloyd's 'most distressful family perplexities', probably those again delaying his marriage, among others, including his sister Priscilla's illness and the announcement that

> His brother Robert (the flower of his family) hath eloped from the persecutions of his father and has taken shelter with us. What the issue of his adventure will be, I know not. He hath the sweetness of an angel in his heart, combined with admirable firmness of purpose: an uncultivated, but very original, and, I think, superior genius. But this step of his is but a small part of their family troubles. (M 1, 156)

He thanks Southey for John May's intercession on behalf of the desperate young man, whom May 'has liberally supplied . . . with money',[8] and sends him a section of *Pride's Cure* (later expunged) on John Woodvil's early valour in battle.

A little later he wrote again, telling Southey that Priscilla was recovering, and that

> Robert still continues here with me, his father has proposed nothing, but would willingly lure him back with fair professions. But Robert is endowed with a wise fortitude; and in this business has acted quite from himself, and wisely acted. His parent must compound[9] in the End. . . . I like reducing parents to a sense of undutifulness. I like confounding the relations of life. . . . (M 1, 159)

Rosamund Gray, he noted, was selling well in London in spite of the 'non-reviewal of it'[10] and, more important, 'my sister Mary was never in better health or spirits than now'.[11]

. Charles Lloyd came – by 5 February – to join Robert at Lamb's; by 18 February they had moved to another friend, whence Charles wrote that he had 'happily brought Robert & my father to a better understanding'[12] – the brothers are returning to Birmingham at once by night coach. Robert had been in London a month, Charles some two weeks, busybodying in his usual style, this time at the expense of Mary Hays, with whom he had got Lamb somewhat embroiled too, though we hear of this only later from Lamb.

Southey was regularly sending Lamb his poems for Lamb's criticism, usually acute:

> I think you are too apt to conclude faintly, with some cold moral. . . . A Moral should be wrought into the body and soul, the matter and tendency, of a Poem, not taggd to the end, like . . . "God send the good ship into harbour" at the conclusion of our bills of Lading. . . .
>
> These remarks, I know, are crude & unwrought, but I do not lay claim to much accurate thinking—I never judge system-wise of things, but fasten upon particulars—(M 1, 163)

This last observation has been much quoted. It sets Lamb at the large end of the telescope and light-years from Coleridge, who liked to view whole galaxies through the small end in the attempt to see wholes.

He dashed off another letter to Southey five days later, taking off from the idea of the spider as a subject for poetry. His flight of rather tough, ironic fantasy suggests that John Lamb may have been visiting his father's sickbed, for it is very much in the vein of John's cruelty-to-animals pamphlet. His last comment concerns his old Christ's Hospital friend Sam Le Grice, who could confound old Boyer with a quip:

> Poor Sam. Le Grice! I am afraid the world, and the camp, and the university, have spoilt him among them. 'Tis certain he had at one time a strong capacity of turning out something better. I knew him, and that not long since, when he had a most warm heart. I am ashamed of the indifference I have sometimes felt

towards him. I think the devil is in one's heart. . . . He was at one time, and in the worst of times, my own familiar friend. . . . I have known him to play at cards with my father, meal-times excepted, literally all day long . . . to save me from being teased by the old man, when I was not able to bear it.

God bless him for it, and God bless you, Southey. (M 1, 166–7)

Before the next letter could be written, old John Lamb was dead. For a third time Charles undertook the summoning of relatives and friends to a funeral, including his brother John but probably not his sister Mary.

Sober citizens in black for the occasion, they would cluster in candlelight toward the front of St. Andrew's, Holborn, cluster round the open pit just outside, next to the graves of Elizabeth Lamb and queer Aunt Hetty, attending to the Anglican finality of the service – ashes to ashes, dust to dust – spoken sonorously by the unfamiliar preacher from whose flock Charles Lamb had fallen away – and shivering a little in the spring damp. After the event, the muffled conversation, the two-mile city journey to Chapel Street in funereal conveyances, then a warming glass or two, loosening the tongue. Voices becoming more normal; news exchanged; kindly hands on the young shoulders; the clan gathered and dispersed. Tall young John, genuinely moved but not quite managing to say the right thing: Charles's relief to see his broad back disappearing through the doorway. Charles Lamb alone once more – but Mary could be brought home, a new life begun.

Lamb had, of course, kept in touch with Mary through visits to her lodgings and long walks together on fine days. She had been shielded, no doubt, from her father's dying. Now his first business was to move from the sad rooms to a rented flat of their own. The search led him no further than No. 36 Chapel Street, only a few doors across the road from the corner house, No. 45, where father and son had stayed. There cannot have been much of a garden, but the neighbourhood was tidy and respectable, its dwellings suburban and neat, with the open countryside a step away. Charles would spare Mary the moving, too, and the further disposition of his father's few belongings. The books he kept – John Lamb's verses in *Poetical Pieces on Several Occasions*, his *Hudibras*, his bound volume of *The Guardian*.

Was it in this period of upheaval in April – 'last month', rather than 'last week' as Southey reported in mid-May – that Charles encountered Ann Simmons Bartram by chance, brought her up to date on his situation and was invited twice to dinner? Or had Mary too been invited to the Bartrams'? For by mid-April Mary had joined him. Southey came to London on a long-delayed visit and was staying with the brilliant, somewhat older surgeon, Anthony Carlisle, one of Mary Wollstonecraft's doctors as she lay dying. Though scientific and strong-minded, having to amputate before the days of anesthesia, Carlisle had imagination as well as compassion and his conversation was to charm Lamb always. Southey shared a meal or two with Lamb and perhaps introduced him to Carlisle then.

Lamb had been alone with his ill father for a long time (except for the maid Hetty) and had been cheated, therefore, of much social life. This is surely the explanation of a silent 'love affair' of this period, which seems to have existed only in Lamb's fancy but gave rise to one of his best-known poems. It was probably in his very early days at Pentonville that Charles first encountered, walking by the neat picket fences of Chapel Street, the demure Quaker girl in dove colour or white – Miss Hester Savory. She lived directly opposite Lamb and his father at the T-shaped junction of Chapel and Islington High streets, some two miles north of Blackfriars Bridge and the Strand, where Hester's father Joseph kept a silver-and-goldsmith's shop. She may have been nineteen, Lamb twenty-one, when each first noticed the other.

The eldest child of her family, Hester had two younger sisters and a brother. The four of them lived on their own, no doubt under the eye of a watchful servant or two. Their mother was long dead, and in 1786 Joseph Savory had been married again to Mary Pryor, an ardent plain Quaker like himself. Mary soon bore him three more daughters. Perhaps because the couple wanted to keep open house for travelling Friends and a large family made this difficult, perhaps also because of family strains, the father established his first set of children in Pentonville and lived with his new family in Finsbury, not far away to the northeast.

The period of Lamb's nodding acquaintance with Hester was an interesting one for all the Savorys. Lamb may have known something of them through the Lloyds; Hester was probably, too, a relative of the Savory who entered the East India House the same day as Lamb, whom he mentions casually in a letter of 1797.

In the middle 1790s Joseph Savory's second cousin William Savery, a Quaker tanner of Philadelphia (the Americans spelled the name differently), went to the Continent via England to give encouragement to pockets of Quakers in France, Germany, and Holland isolated by the war. His reputation was such that George III invited Savery to report to him personally on the general state of affairs in Europe, at an informal interview when the Queen was also present. (Afterwards the King was overheard to say, 'Charlotte, how satisfactory this has been',[13] in spite of Savery's emphasis on the hardships war was causing everywhere.) In London, where he started and finished his travels, Savery made Joseph's Finsbury home his headquarters and from it journeyed over England as well; he was a charismatic speaker to Quaker meetings. Betsey Gurney, recovering from her jilting at the hands of James Lloyd, fell a little in love with him, and through his influence began to take her family's faith seriously: he was in a sense the inspirer of her impressive work at Newgate Prison after she had married Joseph Fry.

Savery was soon on terms of warm affection with his new-found cousins, and it is from his diary we learn something more of Hester than we have known before. He took a particular fancy to Hester's sister Nancy, who accompanied him on some of his English trips. On at least one occasion this office fell to Hester, when she went with Savery and a companion to Bristol.

William Savery often visited Pentonville with Joseph, and his description of a walk after tea at Hester's house suggests the sort of outing Lamb too would have taken, with mention of landmarks of the neighbourhood:

> a long walk afterwards through the fields, over steples [stiles?] &c, where a vast many people walk; passed by White's Conduit House and garden, which are public for every decent person to walk in, also by Copenhagen House, a tea drinking place & to Highberry, a pretty village, mostly inhabited by Londoners, among whom are some Friends. (Taylor, 396)

Savery's diary as it touches the Pentonville Savorys is described by his biographer:

> In the accounts of this home in Pentonville, whether "to visit my young cousins," or "with J. Savery, to drink tea at his

daughters'," or "with the girls," there is an atmosphere of radiant and enthusiastic youth. It was not confined to sociability alone. After dining with them, in company with their father, at one time, William Savery "had a solid opportunity, in which I was favored to relieve my mind of something which had lain on it for some time, on account of these dear young people." Hester, Nancy and their brother, Ady Bellamy Savory, were then at home, and they "left them in much tenderness." (Taylor, 407)

The sight of Hester, though he says they never exchanged a word, made a deep impression on the lonely Charles Lamb opposite, enhanced, no doubt, by what he saw and knew of her family. As late as 1832 he was chided about her as 'the white witch' – an allusion to her costume, for she was dark and dainty, with a triangular face, soft-curling fringe visible beneath her plain bonnet, and large, luminous eyes, their lurking humour shielded by Quaker modesty. 'No,' said Lamb, punning to the end, 'if a witch at all, as she lived at the *last* house in our street, she must be the Witch of End-door.'[14]

Hester is said to have been the subject of a vignette in Lamb's essay 'Valentine's Day'. To her 'E. B.' sent an unsigned Valentine from across the street, and

from his watchful stand, the next morning, he saw the cheerful messenger knock, and by and by the precious charge delivered. He saw, unseen, the happy girl unfold the Valentine, dance about, clap her hands, as one after one the pretty emblems unfolded themselves. She danced about, not with light love, or foolish expectations, for she had no lover; or, if she had, none she knew that could have created those bright images which delighted her. . . . (*Elia*, 57)

Though 'E. B.' was identified by Lamb as Edward Burney, of the family of Fanny the novelist, several of whose members he later knew well, he may very well have twisted the facts as he so often did, and thus disguised a Pentonville experiment of his own. A sure reference to Hester occurs in one of his 1800 London rhapsodies, written to Manning: 'Authors in the street with spectacles, George Dyers (you may know them by their gait), Lamps lit at night, Pastry cook and Silver smith shops, Beautiful Quakers of Pentonville . . . [15]

By this time Charles and Mary had just left Pentonville, and Lamb is regretting her. In July, 1802, Hester married Charles Dudley, a merchant of Lambeth, and – after seven short months – died of a fever at twenty-five, as happened with awful frequency in those days. On 23 March 1803, Lamb wrote:

> dear Manning,
>   I send you some verses I made on the death of a young Quaker (you may have heard me speak of as being in love with for some years, while I lived at Pentonville, tho' I had never spoken to her in my life). She died about a month since. . . . (M ii, 107)

He enclosed one of his happiest poetic efforts: a graceful tribute in a meter favoured by Robert Burns. It strikes exactly the right note for Hester and achieves the rare distinction of being a cheerful, radiant memorial for one recently dead. Hester shall be remembered *happily*, Lamb seems to say, and so she has been, in anthologies, ever since. 'The Old Familiar Faces' and 'Hester' are the two gems, perhaps the only two, from all Lamb's earnest years of trying to be a poet.

> Hester Savory.—
> When maidens such as Hester die,
> Their place ye may not well supply,
> Though ye among a thousand try,
>   With vain endeavor.
>
> A month or more hath she been dead,
> Yet cannot I by force be led
> To think upon the wormy bed,
>   And her together.
>
> A springy motion in her gait,
> A rising step, did indicate
> Of pride and joy no common rate,
>   That flush'd her spirit.
>
> I know not by what name beside
> I shall it call; if twas not pride,
> It was a joy to *that* allied,
>   She did inherit.

Her parents held the Quaker rule,
Which doth the human feeling cool;
But she was train'd in Nature's school;
    Nature had blest her.—

A waking eye, a prying mind,
A heart that stirs, is hard to bind;
A hawk's keen sight ye cannot blind;
    Ye could not Hester's!

My sprightly neighbour! gone before
To that unknown and silent shore,
Shall we not meet? as heretofore,
    Some summer morning,

When from thy chearful eyes a ray
Hath struck a bliss upon the day,
A bliss that would not go away;
    A sweet forewarning!
                    (M II, 107)

When Lamb published his two-volume *Works* in 1818, 'Hester'
led off Volume I.

A charming miniature of Hester survives – no wonder he flirted
with her, teasing a little with his own handsome twinkle, as they
passed in the street over so many months and as he watched her
sometimes from his window. Such unexpressed 'relationships' are
not unusual in the lives of the young and shy, and it was a diversion
for him in the melancholy years of 1796 to 1799, the more delightful,
perhaps, for requiring nothing of either but a smile, a half-
acknowledged glance: quite safe.

CHAPTER TWENTY

Mary Lamb – and Coleridge – Come Home

Bridget Elia has been my housekeeper for many a long year. 'Mackery End in Hertfordshire' (*Elia*, 75)

I have great affection for Lamb/but I have likewise a perfect Lloyd-and-Lambophobia! Coleridge to Southey, 15 October 1799. (Griggs 1, 542)

Within ten days of their father's death, by 23 April (1799) Mary had joined her brother in the new household – neat, uncluttered, and spare, as Lamb liked a place to be.

The details of the arrangements by which he managed to keep her out of State confinement, once she had recovered from the fearful attack of 1796, were not recorded by Lamb in any surviving document, but his contemporary biographer Talfourd tells us as much as anyone knew (only old friends knew the full story). Charles, he says,

was passionately desirous of obtaining her liberty. The surviving members of the family, especially his brother John, who enjoyed a fair income in the South Sea House, opposed her discharge;—and painful doubts were suggested by the authorities of the parish, where the terrible occurrence happened, whether they were not bound to institute proceedings, which must have placed her for life at the disposition of the Crown, especially as no medical assurance could be given against the probable recurrence of dangerous frenzy. But Charles came to her deliverance; he satisfied all the parties who had power to oppose her release, by his solemn engagement that he would take her under his care for life; and he kept his word. Whether any communication with the Home Secretary occurred before her release, I have been unable to ascertain; it was the impression of Mr. Lloyd, from whom my own knowledge of the circumstances, which the letters do not ascertain, was derived, that a communication took place, on which a similar pledge was given; at all events . . . she left the asylum and took up her abode for life with her brother Charles. . . . ¹

Had the tragedy occurred three years later, Mary would have had no option. Only in 1799 was passed the 'Act of 39 and 40 George III' requiring 'an insane person charged with a criminal offence' to be 'kept in custody during His Majesty's pleasure'. Before that time, and still operative at the time of Mrs Lamb's death in September 1796, an act was in effect allowing that such a person could be 'liberated on security being given that he should properly be taken care of as a lunatic'.²

Modern psychiatry, as we have seen, diagnoses Mary's case as manic depressive. Such a disability is not usually violent, since in depression the will to act is all but paralysed, and in mania the victim exhibits a hysterical happiness in which the motivation for violence is absent.³ Mary's matricide came about from the combination of emotional instability with unbearable external pressures. But who could tell when such a combination might not arise again? Charles at twenty-two, with an income of a hundred pounds a year (about £1000 or $2250 today) must have been highly spoken of to the authorities, and strings perhaps pulled through some of the lawyers to whom the family was known in the Temple, to make the miracle possible. It would be known, of course, that her elder brother earned considerably more than Charles.

The anxiety that Mary might again commit a crime and be lost to him forever under the new law was from 1796 ever present in Lamb's mind. In 1818 Sara Hutchinson, Wordsworth's sister-in-law and Coleridge's youthful flame, said when she was seeking a friend to stay with in London, 'At Miss Lambs I *durst* not sleep.'⁴ Within the next few years it fell once to Coleridge to get Mary to hospital with all speed: he too kept a wary eye. Young John Lamb clearly feared her. Charles chose to love her and take his chances, knowing full well that the obverse side of even the strongest love – Mary's for him – is hatred, in the demented as in those less troubled.

So Mary, free of serious illness for many months, now came home, Charles carrying her few bags and bundles into the new surroundings at No. 36 Chapel Street. There must have been great joy on the occasion for both, for Mary was still only thirty-five and as susceptible to rapture as her brother. With the maid Hetty's help Charles would have made the few rooms fresh and gleaming and bright, sweet spring scents blowing from the nearby fields and gardens through the open windows. Little would be new among their furnishings. Aside from the question of money, their tastes were not luxurious and both were happiest with things known and familiar – the bookcase containing Lamb's 'ragged veterans' and newer books for Mary, the old grandfather clock, the green baize card table, the family dining table and chairs. On the walls a few black-and-white engravings from Renaissance painters, or homely modern scenes; perhaps already a Hogarth. Beds – even a spare – for sleeping, chairs for sitting: they were, after all, heirs to a long-established family. Dinner, then cards, perhaps, with the candles brought; excited conversation with the maid Hetty joining in, Lamb dancing attendance to make Mary quite comfortable: the happiest evening of all their lives.

The casual friend could now drop in to call – White or Dyer or Gutch or Randal Norris. The circle was still a small one and Lamb had time to himself – for *Pride's Cure* (*John Woodvil*) – and soon for his Burton imitations. He could read to his heart's content. Now for the first time it was the main task of two women to keep *him* happy. Inevitably, he began to settle down a little, to feel the satisfaction of being master in his own house. His pleasure in domesticity is recorded in his essays, notably 'Old China', which begins with the Chinese scene on a teacup bought many years later. He considers, with his 'cousin Bridget' how delightful it is – in 1820 – to be able to buy what they want when they want it. But at this remark 'a passing sentiment seemed to overcloud the brow of my companion. I am quick at detecting these summer clouds in Bridget.' Bridget responds, capturing the essence of the life that began for both around the century's turn:

"I wish the good old times would come again," she said, "when we were not quite so rich. I do not mean, that I want to be poor; but there was a middle state;"—so she was pleased to ramble on,—"in which I am sure we were a great deal happier. A purchase is but a purchase, now that you have money enough and to spare. Formerly it used to be a triumph. When we coveted a cheap luxury (and, O! how much ado I had to get you to consent in those times!) we were used to have a debate two or three days before, and to weigh the *for* and *against*, and think what we might spare it out of, and what saving we could hit upon, that should be an equivalent. A thing was worth buying then, when we felt the money that we paid for it.

"Do you remember the brown suit, which you made to hang upon you, till all your friends cried shame upon you, it grew so thread-bare—and all because of that folio Beaumont and Fletcher, which you dragged home late at night from Barker's in Covent-garden? Do you remember how we eyed it for weeks before we could make up our minds to the purchase, and had not come to a determination till it was near ten o'clock of the Saturday night, when you set off from Islington, fearing you should be too late—and when the old bookseller with some grumbling opened his shop, and by the twinkling taper (for he was setting bedwards) lighted out the relic from his dusty treasures—and when you lugged it home, wishing it were twice as cumbersome—and when you presented it to me—and when we were exploring the perfectness of it (*collating* you called it)—and while I was repairing some of the loose leaves with paste, which your impatience would not suffer to be left till day-break—was there no pleasure in being a poor man? or can those neat black clothes which you wear now, and are so careful to keep brushed, since we have become rich and finical, give you half the honest vanity, with which you flaunted it about in that over-worn suit . . . ?"

They went out for picnics:

" . . . do you remember our pleasant walks to Enfield, and Potter's Bar, and Waltham, when we had a holyday—holydays, and all other fun, are gone, now we are rich—and the little hand-basket in which I used to deposit our day's fare of savory cold lamb and salad—and how you would pry about at noon-tide for some decent house, where we might go in, and produce our store—only paying for the ale that you must call for—and speculate upon the looks of the landlady, and whether she was likely to allow us a table-cloth. . . . Now, when we go out a day's pleasuring, which is seldom moreover, we *ride* part of the way. . . . "(*Elia*, 248–50)

She recalls their trips to the theatre:

> "You are too proud to see a play anywhere now but in the pit. Do you remember where it was we used to sit, when we saw the battle of Hexham, and the surrender of Calais, and Bannister and Mrs. Bland in the Children in the Wood . . . three or four times in a season in the one-shilling gallery . . . and when the curtain drew up, what cared we for our place in the house . . . when our thoughts were with Rosalind in Arden, or with Viola at the Court of Illyria? . . .
>
> "There was pleasure in eating strawberries, before they became quite common—in the first dish of peas, while they were yet dear—to have them for a nice supper, a treat. . . . It is the very little more that we allow ourselves beyond what the actual poor can get at, that makes what I call a treat. . . . None but the poor can do it. I do not mean the veriest poor of all, but persons as we were, just above poverty. . . . "(*Elia*, 250)

He regrets those stringent times:

> " . . . but could you and I at this moment, instead of this quiet argument, by our well-carpeted fire-side, sitting on this luxurious sofa—be once more struggling up those inconvenient stair-cases, pushed about, and squeezed, and elbowed by the poorest rabble of poor gallery scramblers—could I once more hear those anxious shrieks of yours—and the delicious *Thank God, we are safe*, which always followed when the topmost stair, conquered, let in the first light of the whole cheerful theatre down beneath us—I know not the fathom line that ever touched a descent so deep as I would be willing to bury more wealth in than Crœsus had, . . . to purchase it. And now do just look at that merry little Chinese waiter holding an umbrella, big enough for a bed-tester, over the head of that pretty insipid half-Madona-ish chit of a lady in that very blue summer-house." (*Elia*, 251–2)

This near-peace became, then, the fabric of their lives, with the occasional visit from Brother John, the buyer of pictures, the lover of animals, as seen in 'My Relations':

He is courageous as Charles of Sweden, upon instinct; chary of his person, upon principle, as a travelling Quaker.—He has been preaching up to me, all my life, the doctrine of bowing to the great—the necessity of forms, and manner, to a man's getting on in the world. He himself never aims at either, that I can discover,—and has a spirit, that would stand upright in the presence of the Cham of Tartary. It is pleasant to hear him discourse of patience—extolling it as the truest wisdom—and to see him during the last seven minutes that his dinner is getting ready. . . . He has some speculative notions against laughter, and will maintain that laughing is not natural to *him*—when peradventure the next moment his lungs shall crow like Chanticleer. He says some of the best things in the world—and declareth that wit is his aversion. (*Elia*, 72–3)

In 'Mackery End' Mary is introduced to *London Magazine* readers:

Bridget Elia has been my housekeeper for many a long year. I have obligations to Bridget, extending beyond the period of memory. We house together, old bachelor and maid, in a sort of double singleness; with such tolerable comfort, upon the whole, that I, for one, find in myself no sort of disposition to go out upon the mountains, with the rash king's offspring, to bewail my celibacy. We agree pretty well in our tastes and habits—yet so, as "with a difference." We are generally in harmony, with occasional bickerings—as it should be among near relations. Our sympathies are rather understood, than expressed; and once, upon my dissembling a tone in my voice more kind than ordinary, my cousin burst into tears, and complained that I was altered. We are both great readers in different directions. While I am hanging over (for the thousandth time) some passage in old Burton, or one of his strange contemporaries, she is abstracted in some modern tale, or adventure, whereof our common reading-table is daily fed with assiduously fresh supplies. . . .

It has been the lot of my cousin, oftener perhaps than I could have wished, to have had for her associates and mine, free-thinkers—leaders, and disciples, of novel philosophies and systems; but she neither wrangles with, nor accepts, their opinions. That which was good and venerable to her, when a child, retains its authority over her mind still. She never juggles or plays tricks with her understanding.

We are both of us inclined to be a little too positive; and I have

observed the result of our disputes to be almost uniformly this—
that in matters of fact, dates, and circumstances, it turns out, that
I was in the right, and my cousin in the wrong. But where we have
differed upon moral points; upon something proper to be done, or
let alone; whatever heat of opposition, or steadiness of conviction,
I set out with, I am sure always, in the long run, to be brought
over to her way of thinking.

I must touch upon the foibles of my kinswoman with a gentle
hand, for Bridget does not like to be told of her faults. . . . (*Elia*
75–6)

So they began their life of 'double singleness'.

The other development of the year 1799 important to the Lambs
was Coleridge's return from Germany in July and the patching up
of his quarrels with both Southey and Lamb – now generally
acknowledged to have been the fault of Charles Lloyd. Lamb, with
his consistent compassion for weakness, took the revelations in his
stride and continued to be Lloyd's friend. Since his marriage to the
patient Sophia Pemberton, Lloyd had become a somewhat easier
man to know.

Coleridge arrived in England, then, his head full of Lessing,
Kant, and the other German thinkers. Again he spawned projects
and carried only some of them through, and again he made do with
domesticity in the person of Sara. Since his children were so precious
to him, it seems extraordinary that he had not come home on the
death of little Berkeley in February: it was Sara's bereavement he
could not face. Poole and Southey had got her through the
immediate impact; she had stayed with the Southeys. But she had
run out of money and yearned for his return: his failure to come to
her was one of the cruelties to which his weaknesses so often led him
at this period. Opium, too, was exacting its toll, and beyond Sara's–
perhaps any wife's – power to overcome or accept.

Coleridge now came upon Southey's *Lyrical Ballads* review, but
he did not let it stand in the way of his determination to make things
up with his brother-in-law. And in a very short time the Southeys
and Coleridges were travelling together, reconciled by Tom Poole,
who had confirmed to Southey Lloyd's role in the quarrel. Though
there is no record of the reconciliation with Lamb, we may assume it
took a similar course. By autumn, as if to make up for lost time,

Lamb was writing a good many letters to Coleridge which have disappeared. Charles Lloyd was writing to Coleridge too, as eagerly as if nothing had ever happened between them, but Coleridge could not so easily forget *Edmund Oliver*.

Lamb referred to the break in his and Coleridge's friendship only much later, in 1820 when he wrote to Coleridge, 'He is a sad Tattler, but this is under the rose. Twenty years ago he estranged one friend from me quite, whom I have been regretting, but could never regain since.'[5] This friend's identity is lost in the mists of time.[6] Lamb goes on: 'he almost alienated you (also) from me, or me from you, I don't know which. But that breach is closed. The dreary sea is filled up.' There is an oblique reference, too, in tender jest, in the dedication to Coleridge of the poetry volume of the 1818 *Works*:

> My friend Lloyd and myself came into our first battle (authorship is a sort of warfare) under cover of the greater Ajax. How this association, which shall always be a dear and proud recollection to *me*, came to be broken,—who snapped the three-fold cord,—whether yourself (but I know that was not the case) grew ashamed of your former companions,—or whether (which is by much the more probable) some ungracious bookseller was author of the separation,—I cannot tell;—but wanting the support of your friendly elm, (I speak for myself,) my vine has, since that time, put forth few or no fruits; the sap (if ever it had any) has become, in a manner, dried up and extinct; and you will find your old associate, in his second volume, dwindled into prose and *criticism*. (I, vi)

On Coleridge's death in 1834 Lamb wrote, 'He was my fifty years old friend without a dissension.'[7]

Having restored two of the more important relations of his life – even Sara was somewhat mollified – Coleridge now had more uncertainties to contend with. The Wordsworths, whom he had not yet seen, had returned from Germany in April and Wordsworth was in poor health. William and Dorothy had at length determined to settle in the Lake District, from which they had sprung. Tom Poole wanted the Coleridges to stay at Nether Stowey; Coleridge wavered. Little Hartley was thought to have scabies. Coleridge came down with rheumatism; he had been ridiculed by an enemy in coffee-houses; he was still sore at Lloyd and worried about money. To his general feeling of victimization we may lay the following, addressed in October to Southey:

> I have great affection for Lamb/but I have likewise a perfect Lloyd-and-Lambophobia!—Independent of the irritation attending an epistolary Controversy with them, their *Prose* comes so damn'd dear! Lloyd especially writes with a woman's fluency in a large rambling hand—most dull tho' profuse of Feeling—/I received from them in the last Quarter letters so many, that with the postage I might have bought Birch's Milton. (Griggs I, 542)

As if to escape all this, he almost immediately dashed with Joseph Cottle to where Wordsworth was staying, at Sockburn in Yorkshire with the Hutchinson clan of orphaned young people – where Coleridge met Sara Hutchinson for the first time. He and Wordsworth (not so ailing after all) then walked to the Lakes with Wordsworth's sailor brother John, and he fell in love with that marvellous country.

Happily unaware that he was giving Coleridge pain by his letters in that direction, Lamb had in September–October an irritation of his own. Marmaduke Thompson, the Christ's Hospital friend to whom he had dedicated *Rosamund Gray*, would not be greatly missed when he disappeared – as, not very long after, he did – to India. Lamb told Robert Lloyd,

> Thomson remains with me. He is pe[r]petually getting into mental vagaries. He is in Love! and tosses and tumbles about in his bed, like a man in a barrel of spikes. He is more sociable; but I am heartily sick of his domesticating with me; he wants so many sympathies of mine, and I want his, that we are daily declining into *civility* . . .[7] I shall be truly glad when he is gone . . .[8] I find tis a dangerous experiment to grow too familiar. Some natures cannot bear it without converting into indifference—I know but one Being that I could ever consent to live perpetually with, and that is Robert. . . . (M I, 170)

The first *Annual Anthology* was published in September. Lamb 'passed a few red-letter days with much pleasure'[9] in Hertfordshire in October, revisiting Blakesware, probably without Mary. Early in December Coleridge came to London – where Sara Coleridge and Hartley soon joined him – to work for Daniel Stuart, editor of the *Morning Post*: he was good at journalism though he hated it. He waxed indignant on the publication of *Beauties of the Anti-Jacobin*, a volume of excerpts including 'New Morality'. A footnote from *Beauties* elicited the following mention in his 1817 *Biographia Literaria*:

> I subjoin part of a note from *The Beauties of the Anti-Jacobin*, in which, having previously informed the public that I had been dishonor'd at Cambridge for preaching Deism . . . , the writer concludes with these words: 'Since this time he has left his native country, commenced citizen of the world, *left his poor children fatherless, and his wife destitute. Ex his disce, his friends* Lamb *and* Southey.' With severest truth it may be asserted that it would not be easy to select two men more exemplary in their domestic affections than those whose names were thus printed at full length as in the same rank of morals with a denounced infidel and fugitive, who had left his children *fatherless and his wife destitute*! (BL, 40)

Lamb did not mention the attack[10] in extant letters.

Before the Coleridges' arrival, however, Lamb had heeded the pleas of the seven-months-married Charles and Sophia Lloyd to visit them in Cambridge. Mary Lamb's health continued good, though she was not yet ready to risk the cold winter stage journey. The ancient maid, Hetty, was on hand to look after her, and Charles Lamb was ready for a change of air.

CHAPTER TWENTY ONE

Thomas Manning

I believe I told you I have been to see Manning.—*He is a dainty chiel.—A man of great Power.—An enchanter almost.—Far beyond Coleridge or any man in power of impressing—when he gets you alone, he can act the wonders of Egypt.—Only he is Lazy & does not always put forth all his strength—; if he did, I know no man of genius at all comparable to him—* Lamb to Robert Lloyd, 7 February 1801 (M 1, 271)

I am glad you esteem Manning, though you see but his husk or his shrine. He discloses not, save to select worshippers, and will leave the world without any one hardly but me knowing how stupendous a creature he is. Lamb to Coleridge, 22 March 1826 (CL III, 39)

After their long honeymoon in the Lakes, Charles Lloyd had recently settled with his bride in Jesus Lane, Cambridge, at the lodging house of a Mr Styles. Here Lamb duly arrived to spend the first week of December, 1799.

He was later to record himself as supremely happy in a University town. How he must have marvelled at the august colleges – sheltering so many books! – with the winter gardens of their 'Backs' touching the banks of the mild Cam, a scene particularly lovely when the sun threw long afternoon shadows, catching the four elegant turrets of King's College Chapel, glinting on its ancient stained glass. There he walked 'gowned', fancying himself a Cambridge scholar. The college to which Lloyd was attached, Gonville and Caius, would please the Elizabethan in Lamb. Named for two of its founders, it was usually called 'Keys', as Queen Elizabeth's physician no doubt pronounced his name. Its three fine Renaissance gateways, designed by Dr Caius himself, were named for the ideal stages of studentship – Humility, Virtue, and Honour.

Cambridge meant, too, a warm welcome from Lloyd and the now pregnant Sophia. But it was of particular significance for Lamb because in the course of the week he first met Lloyd's mathematics tutor, Thomas Manning. Tall, dark like Lamb, sturdy though not an athlete, Manning was cool and steady, blessed with a fey sense of humour, great independence of mind and manner, and a sparkling eccentricity. He combined originality and depth of spirit with an extraordinary kindness, and his '*fine dogmatical, sceptical, face*'[1] won Lamb on first sight. Then twenty-seven, he wrote a little poetry and read widely, but cherished no literary ambition.

Though characterized as often 'lazy', by Lamb, Lloyd, and others who knew him, his enduring claim to fame is as the first Englishman to enter Lhasa, the remote capital of Tibet, in 1812 (no other followed till 1877), and the first European since 1745. He was even now eager to travel in China, a venture doomed to failure. The effort he underwent to get to the East in the next decade was hardly that of a lazy man. On his death in 1840 he received one of the longer obituaries in the *Gentleman's Magazine* – longer than those of most bishops, earls, and major-generals. The *Gentleman's* described him as 'the celebrated linguist' (he knew fifteen languages), 'one of the best Sinese scholars in the world',[2] and did not overlook his Lhasa exploit.

What troubled his critics was his unwillingness – or emotional inability – to *record* much of his knowledge and experience, though he did keep a fascinating journal of his Lhasa trip (published long after his death) in spare, concise prose. Indeed he, of all Lamb's correspondents, strikes one as the most modern in feeling and expression. He was, no doubt, indolent in fits – and Southey thought him a disappointed man in age, where W. S. Landor noted only the 'beauty of his face'.[3] His greatest gift was to be the stimulus and catalyst which brought out the best in those lucky enough to be his friends. Sir John Davis met him in Canton:

I knew Manning well, and liked him much. His eccentricities were quite harmless, and concerned only himself personally. . . . He was seldom serious, and did not often argue any matter gravely, but in a tone of banter in which he humourously maintained the most monstrous paradoxes, his illustrations being often highly laughable. . . . Being one day roused by a strange shouting, I went out and discovered it was Manning, who, wishing to cross [a river], and finding nobody who would attend to him, commenced a series of howls like a dog, supplemented by execrations derived from the Chinese vernacular. This led our attendant mandarins very naturally to infer that he was mad, and they lost no time in conveying him over the river to the other side, which was all he wanted. I was sorry to part with him in 1817 . . . when he returned home.[4]

Thomas Allsop, young friend of Lamb and Coleridge, describes the occasion, around 1820, on which Manning gave Lamb the idea for 'Roast Pig' – for Manning was instrumental as early as 1801 in encouraging Lamb to write essays:

> I retain a very vivid recollection of Manning. . . . I think few persons had so great a share of Lamb's admiration, for to few did he vouchsafe manifestations of his *very* extraordinary powers. Once, and only once, did I witness an outburst of his *unimbodied* spirit, when such was the effect of his more than magnetic, his magic power, . . . that we were all rapt and carried aloft into the seventh heaven. He seemed to see and to convey to us clearly . . . what was passing in the presence of the Great Disimbodied ONE, rather by an intuition or the creation of a new sense than by words. Verily there are *more things on earth* than are dreamed of in our philosophy. I am unwilling to admit the influence this wonderful man had over his auditors, as I cannot at all convey an adequate notion or even image of his extraordinary and very peculiar powers. Passing from a state which was only not of the highest excitement, because the power was *felt*, not shown, he, by an easy, a graceful, and, as it seemed at the time, a natural transition, entered upon the discussion, or, as it rather seemed, the solution of some of the most interesting questions connected with the early pursuits of men. Among other matters, the origin of cooking . . . (Allsop, 126)

Manning shared Lamb's interest in good cooking; he could play the flute; he loved making odd faces and was a master of mimic. Like Lamb he punned. He enjoyed congenial company, drinking, and merriment of an evening, and was frequent host to lively gatherings in his Cambridge rooms, above Mr Crisp the barber at No. 3 St. Mary's Passage.

Thomas Manning was born in the Anglican parsonage of Broome, Norfolk, son of the Reverend William Manning of Diss and Broome and his wife Elizabeth Adams. He was the third in a family of three boys and four girls,[5] his elder brother William succeeding their

father as Rector of Diss; his younger sister Frances surviving
Thomas to transcribe the Lhasa diary. His father educated the
promising boy himself, except for a year Thomas spent at the Bury
St. Edmund's grammar school. Young Manning's health was said
to be delicate. He entered Caius College at eighteen and did
brilliantly. 'Affecting, however, the plain dress of Quakers, and with
it adopting their strong repugnance to all oaths and tests,' says the
Gentleman's obituary, 'he felt himself disbarred from all academic
honours and preferments.'6 Manning could not, therefore, take a
degree. He stayed on for a while as lecturer and tutor and published,
in two volumes, a work on arithmetic and algebra (1796–8).

When Charles Lloyd belatedly entered Caius in the summer of
1798, he at once fastened on Manning and Christopher
Wordsworth as his closest friends, particularly Manning, who soon
drew Lloyd into his own circle – a group who were to bring Caius
and indeed Cambridge itself significant scholastic revival after the
turn of the century. Among Manning's friends were future officials
of the college like William Gimingham and John Drew Borton, later
its President; and Martin Davy, most responsible for Caius's revival
as its Master from 1803 to 1839. Christopher Wordsworth was to
become Master of Trinity College, Cambridge. Here again Lamb
moved among the constructive shapers of the near future.

It was a pleasure for him to be with the Lloyds. Sophia was 'very
highly spoken of by everybody',7 as Dorothy Wordsworth soon after
wrote; Lamb later told Robert Lloyd, 'No husband & wife can be
happier, than Sophia & your Brother appear to be in each other's
company.—Robert must marry next—I look to see him get the start
of Wordsworth & Priscilla, whom yet I wish to see united—.'8 Even
Charles Lloyd had written to Manning on his honeymoon, 'Sophia
is everything to me that I could ask—& possessed of more goodness
than I believed fell to the share of any human being—.'9 Lloyd's
'dearest Manning' was soon beloved of Sophia too.

Manning shared Lamb's latent Radicalism. A vivid section of his
Lhasa diary, written when, after being useful to Lhasa's Chinese
rulers as a doctor, he came under their suspicion, describes how his
earlier 'sight of the despotic pomp of the Mandarins at Canton,
where I was perfectly secure, has turned me almost sick'. As he
writes he envisions his own possible execution at their hands:

I put myself in imagination in the situation of the prisoner
accused; I suppose myself innocent; I look around; I have no

resource, no refuge; instruments of torture . . . of execution are brought by florid, high-cheeked, busy, grinning, dull-hearted men . . . no kind judge to take my part, as in England, but on the contrary, because I am accused (and perhaps by my judge) I am presumed guilty. . . . This friendlessness, this nothingness of the prisoner is what sickens me to think of.

He does not know if he could 'submit to execution with firmness and manliness'.[10]

Manning's imaginative sympathy with the oppressed existed, of course, before this real fear was stirred in him – as did his religious scepticism. He wrote in his Lhasa diary,

All religions as they are established have a mixture in them of good and evil, and upon the whole they all perhaps tend to civilise and ameliorate mankind; as such I respect them. As for the common idea that the founders of all religions except our own were impostors, I consider it a vulgar error. (Markham, 291)

He was not therefore quite the atheist Lamb chided him for being in the letters each was soon writing to the other.

The meeting with the mathematics tutor acted like a sunburst on Lamb's hitherto constricted life: here at last was an end to loneliness. Lamb's side of the exchange was fuller than Manning's, who did not care so much for letter-writing. Lamb, for once, kept all his friend's letters till the day of his death. The tone of the exchange was affectionate, the manner bantering, awful-punning, serious, and thoughtful by turns. In considering it from the twentieth century we must remember that letter-writing, as everything else in Lamb's time, had undergone a sea change. The revolt against eighteenth-century formality and detachment, against its deprecation of 'enthusiasm', had come full circle. Young men, and young women too, told each other what 'sensibility', or feeling, dictated, and told it warmly without (in most cases) homosexual overtones, or if so only marginally and most innocently. Not until the style of the Duke of Wellington, hero of Waterloo, caught on after 1815 would the pendulum be set swinging again toward reticence and the stiff upper lip. The passionate friendships of Rousseau and of Goethe, even the ready tear for 'affecting' circumstances, were the Romantic model. The exchange of uninhibited letters was the popular form for the novel of sensibility (Lamb had used it for the latter part of

Rosamund Gray). Formality was a barrier between human beings; 'manliness' meant the ability to survive (or to die) gracefully, not the suppression of emotion; friendship as well as love was taken most seriously.

Lamb wrote to Manning almost immediately upon returning home:

[Mid-]Decemr 99

Dear Manning,

    the particular kindness, even up to a degree of attachment, which I have experienced from you, seems to claim some distinct acknowledgment on my part. I could not content myself with a bare remembrance to you, conveyed in some letter to Lloyd—

    Will it be agreeable to you, if I occasionally recruit your memory of me, which must else soon fade, if you consider the brief intercourse we have had? I am not likely to prove a troublesome correspondent. My scribbling days are past. I shall have no sentiments to communicate, but as they spring up from some living and worthy occasion. . .[11]—

    I look forwards with great pleasure to the performance of your promise, that we should meet in London early in the ensuing year—. The century must needs commence auspiciously for me, that brings with it Manning's friendship, as an earnest of its after gifts.———

    I should have written before, but for a troublesome inflammation in one of my eyes, brought on by night travelling with the coach windows sometimes up—

    What more I have to say shall be reserved for a letter to Lloyd.—I must not prove tedious to you in my first outside, lest I should affright you by my ill judg'd loquacity.

I am
Yours most sincerely
C Lamb
(M I, 173)

Meanwhile Father Lloyd had sought Lamb at the India House and found him gone to Cambridge. Mr Lloyd looked him up again at mid-month and wrote home that 'C. Lamb dined here a few days ago and is to breakfast here on fifth day'[12] – Quaker parlance for Thursday. He charmed Lamb with reminiscences of his London countinghouse, to which he took his young visitor for a chat, as

Lamb told Robert. Manning too was engaged in correspondence with Robert, sharing with Lamb the bolstering of his confidence. Manning now answered Lamb's first letter:

Cambridge,
Dec. 15. [1799]

Dear Lamb,

You must not suppose that my slowness in answering your letter proceeds from an indifference to your correspondence. I *have* been, & *still am*, harrass'd by business—I have obtained another Pupil; & the hour of Examination draweth nigh—and really when my occupation for the day is over, I find myself so dispirited & cold, that I am unfitted for writing—At this very time I feel frozen. I *would* express my thankfulness for your letter, & the satisfaction I experience (not at this instant, but when I am myself) in the prospect of our future correspondence, & inter-course—but I hate to have recourse to memory on these occasions—so I must beg of you, my dear Friend, to take cheerfully in payment all I have to give, & allow me credit for the rest.

I rejoice exceedingly in the hope of spending some time with you, when I come to Town, w^h I believe will be in about 5 weeks.

I had some conversation the other day with Sophia concerning your Tragedy; & she made some very sensible observations (as I thought) with respect to the unfitness of its title. The Folly, whose consequences humble the Pride & ambition of John's heart, does not originate in the workings of *those* passions, but from an underpart in his character, & as it were accidentally, viz from the ebullitions of a drunken mind & from a rash confidence. You will understand what I mean, without my explaining myself any further. God bless You,—& keep you from all evil things, that walk upon the face of the Earth—I mean Night-mares, Hobgoblins, & Spectres.

I shall expect a letter from you very soon. I am

Your affectionate Friend
Thomas Manning.

Postscript.—(*Here is a page of drawings of queer beasts.*) I wish I could draw. It will not do.   (**ML**, 21)

The 'queer beasts' establish at once the sense of escaping into foolishness indulged in by both serious men. *Pride's Cure* was discussed in Lamb's answer, after a 'decent interval', of December 28.

> Do your night parties still flourish? & do you continue to bewilder your company, with your thousand faces, running down thro' all the Keys of Ideotism, (like Lloyd over his perpetual harpsichord,) . . . ?
>
> But, seriously, I long to see your own honest Manning-face again—I did not mean a pun,—your *man's* face, you will be apt to say, I know your wicked will to pun—. . . .(M 1, 176–7)

Lamb had now sent *Pride's Cure* to John Philip Kemble of Drury Lane, who acknowledged it warmly, as Lamb told Charles Lloyd at the end of December.

The Coleridge family meanwhile arrived in London and on 23 January 1800, Lamb wrote congratulating Coleridge on his attack in the *Morning Post* on the Tory Ministry. He adds, 'I expect Manning of Cambridge in town tonight—will you fulfill your promise of meeting him at my house? He is a man of a thousand. . . .'[13] We know that Coleridge on this occasion discussed an earlier falling out between Charles Lloyd and Mary Hays: he despised both and made no secret of it. Manning defended Lloyd. He wrote to Sophia that he was 'dazzled' by Coleridge and she professed lightly to be jealous. Coleridge, on his side, had 'conceived a most high . . . opinion of you, most illustrious Archimedes,'[14] as Lamb soon told him. Manning stayed for three days with the Lambs and spent the rest of the week at 25 Cecil Street.

Robert Lloyd wrote to Manning in February,

> I find you have been in London. I doubt not but you spent your time very happily at Lamb's. He sometimes, indeed often, writes to me. I prize his letters as I do yours. . . . I value them more than books, or any other writings—I quite nurse them up. (LL, 109–10)

Manning replied that he had been

> indeed very happy at Lamb's; I abode there but three days. He is very good. I wish you and He and myself were now sitting over a bowl of punch or a tankard of porter. We often talked of You, and

were perfectly agreed; but I won't tell you what we agreed to about you, lest you should hold up your head too high. You will be sufficiently vain, I doubt not, Master Robert, at having been made the subject of conversation between such great men as *Lamb* and *I* (*are likely to be*). I was introduced to Coleridge, which was a great satisfaction to me. I think him a man of very splendid abilities and animated *feelings*. (LL, 110–12)

Off to a strong start in friendship, before very long Manning and Lamb were deeply involved in trying to make sense out of what had taken place between Charles Lloyd and Mary Hays the writer over some months, part of it when Lloyd had dashed to London to see his brother Robert at Lamb's. Though he was to marry Sophia Pemberton on 24 April (1799), Lloyd had written to Manning as late as 25 March, 'I never see Miss Pemberton.'[15] In February of 1799, then, he still felt bachelor-free, or at any rate behaved so. The English mails – between Southey and Coleridge, Coleridge and Southey, and now Manning and Lamb – sizzled fitfully with the affair over some nine months. Southey, writing to his wife Edith in May, told the story most coherently, though it is hard to establish the truth in the accounts of the two very emotional people he had to depend on:

I called on Mary Hays. She appeared glad to see me, and the conversation of course turned upon Lloyd. She told me Lloyd had behaved very ill to her. The circumstances were these. One evening when her spirits were very much oppressed by some grief, she went on a visit somewhere with Lloyd and Stephen Weever Browne: a man who you know talks most mightily. From the effort which persons often make when they are depressed, she had talked with a degree of gaiety, so as to exhaust herself. They went home with her. Stephen Browne's talking fatigued her still more. He left her first, and when she came into her lodgings and sat down she burst into tears. Lloyd was full of expressions of friendship—had she anything on her mind? etc. etc. etc. The following day wrote her a letter full of professions and sentiment and feelings. But Lloyd tells this story in company with these alterations—that Mary Hays was in love with him—that she contrived to send away St. Brown that she might be left alone with Lloyd, and burst into tears because Lloyd would not understand her. This was repeated to her, and she wrote to Lloyd, rather rallying him for his ridiculous vanity than reproaching him, because it was so contemptible and because she did not fully understand the whole abuse till his reply. He answered by confessing that he had traduced her character—and apologizing most humbly for it, alledging that her principles were so very bad that he had suspected her conduct—yet saying that no one who knew her could doubt her excellence unless he were a fool or a villain. . . . he evidently has said that she would have prostituted herself to him if he had pleased—and now comes out with a canting repentance. It has sadly sunk him in my opinion. She told me these circumstances because she thought I might hear something of them from him. She spoke with temper and great good sense. You know I like Mary Hays. About his marriage she blamed him for telling every body that he had no affection for Sophia. (NL, 187–8)

Mary Hays was then aged thirty-nine to Lloyd's twenty-four. Before she had introduced Wollstonecraft to Godwin she was said to have nourished a passion for Godwin herself, following upon her previous attachments to a fiancé who had died and to William Frend, the Cambridge radical. She was in any case still an enthusiastic Godwinian. Her own long, long letters to Godwin and to Frend figured, or so her friends and enemies believed, in her autobiographical novel *The Memoirs of Emma Courtney* (1796), which had enjoyed a certain success. She was at present a contributor to the *Analytical Review* on feminist topics and the butt of some of the *Anti-Jacobin*'s nastier attacks. Her current effort, which took her several years, was *Female Biography, or Memoirs of Illustrious and Celebrated Women*. Though Southey and Crabb Robinson the diarist liked her, she was too brash for Lamb. Lamb later wrote a jingle –

> G-- forbid I should
> pass my days
> with Miss H-ys.
> (CL II, 117)

Yet he must have known her well enough to have been entrusted by her with the so-called letter of apology she had had from Lloyd, who had dictated it to his younger sister Olivia. In this he suggested she had thrown herself indecently at him as previously to Godwin and Frend. Lamb, who had till now been willing to excuse Lloyd all his transgressions, perhaps on the ground that he was mad at times, was appalled. It was a letter, he told Manning in February, 'I could not have sent to my Enemy's Bitch':

> . . . My whole moral sense is up in arms against the Letter. To my apprehension, it is shockingly & nauseously indelicate, and I perceive an aggravation or multiplication of the Indelicacy, in Lloyd's getting his sister Olivia to transcribe it. An ignorant Quaker girl, I mean ignorant in the best sense, who ought not to know, that such a thing was possible or in rerum naturæ, that a woman should court a man . . .[16] And a dear sister, who least of all should apprehend such an omen! realiz'd in her o[wn] Brother. . . . I will sum up the controversy in the words of Coleridge, all he has since said to me, "Miss Hays has acted like a fool, & Charles Lloyd not very wisely."——(M 1, 181–2)

What did Manning think?

Probably not wanting to exacerbate matters further, perhaps pitying Lloyd's 'madness' – the only charitable explanation of his behaviour – Manning remained loyal to Lloyd and mild in his behalf:

> I do lay my hand upon my heart & say that Lds conduct . . . (tho erroneous I *think*) has been such as to produce in me towards him no diminution of respect of honour or of Love. That you may entertain similar sentiments is the wish of / Your very affectionate Friend/T.M. (ML, 26)

Lamb clearly admired this attitude even when he could not himself share it. The affair occupied a half dozen letters between them and Lamb took his new friend's lead in determining 'to live a merry Life in the midst of Sinners',[17] having just noted that he could 'not but smile at Lloyd's beginning to find out that Col. can tell lyes'. In Manning Lamb now had a friendly barometer against which to measure the events of his trying life.

By 8 February 1800, Manning had sent him a turkey, just in time for a dinner Lamb was giving for Coleridge – and William Godwin! The Arch-devil, Lamb learned on first meeting him the day before, was as small in stature as himself. To Manning he jested,

I begin to think you Atheists not quite so tall a species! . . . When we die, you & I must part, the sheep you know take the right hand signpost, & the goats the Left——. Stript of its allegory, you must know the sheep are *I*, and the apostles, and the martyrs, & the Popes, & Bishop Taylor, . . . & Coleridge &c &c—the goats are the Atheists & adulterers & fornicators & dumb dogs & Godwin & M-----g[18] & that . . . crew—yaw! how my saintship sickens at the idea— (M 1, 186)

There is a note of real alarm in Manning's response, for letters *were* opened, or confiscated by government, quite regularly in the case of John Thelwall, and who knew if not also the letters of friends of Coleridge and Southey and William Godwin? Manning recalls the Smithfield martyrs:[19]

—One thing, tho, I must beg of you—that is, not to call me Atheist in your letters—for tho it be mere raillery in *you*, & not meant as a serious imputation on my Faith, yet, if the Catholic or any other intolerant religion should . . . become established in England . . . & if the Post-people should happen to open & read your letters (which, considering the sometimes quaintness of their form, they may possibly be incited to do) such names might send me to Smithfield on a hurdle,—& nothing, *upon earth*, is more discordant to my wishes, than to become one of the Smithfield Illuminati. (ML, 32)

So the correspondence proceeds, the most relaxing Lamb has known. They discuss White's *Falstaff's Letters*, into which he urges Manning to 'dig, dig, dig,' if they are to be properly understood. Jonathan Swift's friend Bishop Burnet (*History of His Own Times*) brings Lamb's statement that Burnet's revolution was real to him because Lamb lived in the past. 'The French Revolution, by a converse perversity in my nature, I fling as far *from* me—.'[20] This proved not altogether true when he shortly took up the profession of journalism.

Early in March Mrs Lloyd senior and the sinned-against Olivia invited him to breakfast in London. Since he mightn't fall in love with the 'charming' daughter, he told Manning, he was half in love with the mother—'so fine & graceful a complete Matron-Lady-Quaker'. (The parents were quite unaware of the storms their Charles had recently set rocking.) Mrs Lloyd presented him with 'two little Books'.[21] And soon Robert and Priscilla Lloyd were paying Lamb brief visits – Priscilla to see the popular Sheridan musical play *Pizzarro* and thus evading her Quaker uncle, who would not approve.

Then Lamb fell silent, as Manning complained; Lamb's explanatory letter crossed Manning's:

Dear Manning,

I am living in a continuous feast. Coleridge has been with me now for nigh three weeks, and the more I see of him in the quotidian undress and relaxation of his mind, the more cause I see to love him and believe him a *very good man*, and all those foolish impressions to the contrary fly off like morning slumbers—. He is engaged in Translations, which I hope will keep him this month to come. .—

He is uncommonly kind & friendly to me—. He ferrets me day and night to *do something*. He tends me, amidst all his own worrying and heart oppressing occupations, as a gardiner tends his young *tulip*—. Marry come up, what a pretty similitude, & how like your humble servant! !— He has lugg'd me to the brink of engaging to a Newspaper, & has suggested to me for a 1st plan the forgery of a supposed Manuscript of Burton the Anatomist of Melancholy—I have even written the introductory Letter—and if I can pick up a few guineas this way, I feel they will be most *refreshing*—bread being so dear—. (M 1, 189–90)

Among his exuberant postscripts he notes, 'flour has just fallen nine shillings a sack! we shall all be too rich! . . . Mary . . . keeps in fine health! . . . Huzza Boys! and down with the Atheists— —.'

Even when he told Manning (on 5 April) that his hopes of journalism to expand his income were for the present dashed, he was hardly downcast: 'Coleridge has left us, to go into the North, on a visit to his God, Wordsworth.— With him have flown all my splendid prospects of engagement with the Morning Post, all my visionary guineas, the deceitful wages of Unborn Scandal.' Instead he worked away at his Burton imitations and sent two of these to Daniel Stuart of the *Post* hoping to interest that editor anyway, but to no avail: 'I'm afraid they wont do for a Paper. Burton is a scarce gentleman, not much known. Else I had done 'em pretty well'.[22] And he had dashed off what he called some 'Burton verses' on melancholy for Manning, which begin, 'By myself walking,/To myself talking,' and carry on through 'Black thoughts continually/ Crouding my privacy,' to a *melange* of terrors akin to Manning's Beasts:

> Fierce Anthropophagi
> Spectra, Diaboli,
> What scared St. Anthony,
> Shapes undefined,
> With my fears twined,
> Hobgoblins, Lemures . . .
> (M I, 194)

The lightweight verses are a spoof on melancholy, and on Burton. More seriously, he makes a heavily Romantic verse translation out of a part of Schiller's *Wallenstein* which Coleridge has turned into prose. Also for Manning's delectation he copies out the old ballad 'Edward, Edward' – 'the very first dramatic poem in the English language—. If you deny that, I'll make you eat your words.'[23]

By August, 1800, Manning was pressing him to come to Cambridge again in terms Lamb would find it hard to resist:

> If you wish to see my honest face (& tis a very honest face, but I may be a damned rogue for all that for as the learned Author of the Latin Grammar judiciously observeth 'fronti nulla fides'[24]) you must come to Cambridge—if you wish to give me a particular satisfaction, you must come to Cambridge—if you wish to give me no cause of dissatisfaction, you must come to Cambridge. . . . The very thoughts of your coming makes my keg of Rum *wobble* about like a porpoise & the liquor (how fine it smells!) goes *Gultch squlluck* against the sides for joy. (ML, 37)

For the moment Lamb had to say no: he was having to do 'double Duty (this hot weather!)'[25] for a fellow clerk on holiday.

Thomas Manning was now firmly chained in Lamb's affections and the feeling was mutual. The Cambridge scholar would become, too, a 'darling of Miss Lamb's'. Except for his negligence in writing from great distances, Manning was never to cause either of them a moment's pain.[26]

CHAPTER TWENTY TWO

Godwin

Why sleep the Watchman's answers to that Godwin?   Lamb to
Coleridge, 7 July 1796 (M 1, 40)

*Godwin I am a good deal pleased with—. He is a well-behaved decent
man . . .*   Lamb to Manning, 18 February 1800 (M 1, 185–6)

> *Nor will I not thy holy guidance bless,*
> *And hymn thee,* GODWIN! *with an ardent lay . . .*
> Coleridge, 'To William Godwin' 1795 (STCP, 41)

Scott *told me some shocking stories of Godwin. . . . His base, & anonymous
attack on you is enough for me . . .*   Coleridge to Thelwall, 13 May
1796 (Griggs 1, 214)

*I shall be in a beautiful country—& have house-room and heart-room for you /
and you must come & write your next work at my house—My dear
Godwin!*   Coleridge to Godwin, 21 May 1800 (Griggs 1, 588)

*Tho' I did it only in the zenith of his reputation, yet I feel remorse ever to have
spoken unkindly of such a man.*   Coleridge (*c*.1800?) (Smith, 55)

*The four principal oral instructors to whom I feel my mind indebted for
improvement were Joseph Fawcet, Thomas Holcroft, George Dyson, and
Samuel Taylor Coleridge.*   William Godwin (Paul 1, 17)

By December, 1799, the month in which Lamb first met Manning,
Samuel Taylor Coleridge's view of William Godwin had undergone
its second dramatic reversal. Coleridge wrote to Southey from
London on Christmas Eve:

> To morrow Sara & I dine at Mister Gobwin's as Hartley calls
> him—who gave the philosopher such a Rap on the shins with a

ninepin that Godwin in huge pain *lectured* Sara on his
boisterousness. I was not at home. . . . [Hartley] is somewhat
too rough & noisy/but the cadaverous silence of Godwin's
children is to me quite catacomb-ish:& thinking of Mary
Wolstencroft [*sic*] I was oppressed by it the day [Humphry] Davy
& I dined there. (Griggs I, 553)

Christmas with the Atheist! How times had changed. The three-
year-old Hartley in cracking Godwin over the shins was merely
expressing a little of Coleridge's own ambivalence. Bad-mannered
or not, Hartley played with Godwin's little girls, the five-year-old
Fanny Imlay and the two-year-old future Mary Shelley. He
favoured Mary.

Godwin was fond of children: even Southey found him 'brimfull
of benevolence—as kind hearted as a child would wish. It should be
known to his credit that he is a father to Imlay's child'[1]–Imlay,
who had deserted Mary Wollstonecraft and caused her near suicide.
Godwin soon gave the child his name. The children's meekness was
bought at a price: Godwin lacked a saving sense of humour.

He was struggling along with his motherless household rather
manfully just now. There was a maid, of course, and his good friend
and general helper James Marshal, who acted as amanuensis,
agent, secretary, and at the moment household superintendent.
They all lived in one of a group of houses called the Polygon, in
Somers Town on the outskirts of London. Godwin needed a wife,
and he knew it.

He had recently published a new novel, *St. Leon*, which Byron,
Shelley, and Keats were to admire. Its heroine was modelled on dead
Mary. To Coleridge's wonder, the book immediately brought
Godwin £400 (£4000 or $9000 today) and went rapidly into a
second edition, in spite of the author's growing unpopularity.
Among his *Anti-Jacobin* attackers of the previous year had been, of
course, Charles Lloyd. In Lloyd's 'Lines Suggested by the Fast'
Godwin was a 'spirit evil and foul'.[2]

The defection of Godwin's erstwhile friend James Mackintosh,
author of one of the most effective answers to Edmund Burke's
Reflections on the French Revolution, had been a more serious blow.
Shortly before Burke died, he had invited Mackintosh to his home
for three days of earnest conversation from which Mackintosh had
emerged a convert to Burke's own views. Not sparing Godwin from
personal attack, Mackintosh had made his conversion known in a

series of lectures given in the spring of 1799. The radicals had cried 'Judas!', one and all – a cry Lamb himself was to take up in 1801. Though ostensibly Mackintosh's friend, Coleridge ran him down privately and constantly.

Despising both Lloyd and 'the great Dung-fly'[3] Mackintosh, Coleridge was now Godwin's champion, partly because Godwin was now an underdog, but chiefly because Godwin, met again in London, had made it clear at once that *he* valued Coleridge, and because the philosopher's atheism presented the kind of challenge Coleridge relished.

Son of a Dissenting minister, Godwin had for a while followed this profession too, but pondering the French philosophers had made him an atheist at twenty-seven. (France herself briefly abolished God in 1793.) He could recall no childhood such as others knew, and 'when I was a very little boy' wondered how he could read 'all the books that there are in the world?'[4] By 1800, approaching forty-four, he had read vastly and accomplished much. He was, as we have seen, somewhat overbalanced on the side of Reason as guide to behaviour, to the detriment of domestic affection. The most discussed passage of *Political Justice* had been the recommendation that if one could save the life of but one person when several were at stake, one should rescue the socially most valuable, leaving one's relative, if need be, to perish. He was to reproach his daughter Mary Shelley for her grief at a baby's loss.

The doggedness with which he attempted to reason his way through life did not, however, prevent Godwin in middle age from changing his opinions when he met an impressive person who caused him to rethink his premises:

In my forty-fourth year I ceased to regard the name of Atheist with the same complacency I had done for several preceding years. . . . My theism, if such I may be permitted to call it, consists in a reverent and soothing contemplation of all that is beautiful, grand, or mysterious in the system of the universe. . . . —into this train of thinking I was first led by the conversations of S.T. Coleridge. (Paul, 357–8)

Godwin's finest hour – helping to rescue Holcroft and others from the hangman – was receding: as widowed father and public target he was harried and unhappy. He wrote a long and pathetic analysis of himself at this period, facing his faults squarely, the better (he thought) to overcome them:

> . . . I am bold and adventurous in opinions, not in life; it is impossible that a man with my diffidence and embarrassment should be. This, and perhaps only this, renders me often cold, uninviting, and unconciliating in society. . . . My nervous character . . . often deprives me of self-possession. . . . I am feeble of tact. . . . (Brown, 196–7)

This unusual apologia was all too true. Feeling himself inadequate, he was inclined to despise others for inadequacy. Crabb Robinson in 1810 noted that Godwin 'made me feel my inferiority unpleasantly'. But Robinson also observed, 'I now and then saw interesting persons at his house; indeed, I saw none but remarkable persons there.'[5] Godwin was not unprepossessing in spite of his short stature, large head, and prominent nose, and for one so rational placed a high value on friendship. He won young disciples still. If he had little conversation unless spoken to, the lovely women he knew found it not difficult to engage him in intelligent talk. Unfortunately, searching for a wife, he tried to argue some of them into marriage in extraordinarily obtuse, self-righteous letters which seem to belie his advanced views on sexual equality. Only the dead Mary had met this challenge, and her bruised heart had sorely needed rescuing.

Godwin's diary consists almost entirely of names – the works he wrote, the books he read daily, with page numbers, but above all the people he encountered, set down day after day in the present tense, linked only with 'dine', 'sup', 'call on' and the like. Easily hurt, he trained himself to seek out and reason with the nearer enemies and deprecators, appearing to bear no grudges. That he did bear grudges, evade certain issues, and fall compulsively into an irrational pattern of life became apparent in his decline, which began, more or less, as Lamb first met him. 'Démêlé' is his diary euphemism for 'quarrel'. His borrowing, begun on the 'logical' theory that those who have should share with those who are valuable, became pathological. Callousness was then his only defence for incorrigible weakness – or perversity. And yet the Irish statesman John Philpot Curran, six years his senior, loved and lent to him unstintingly.

On Friday, 7 February 1800, he and Lamb were invited to the Coleridges' lodgings in Buckingham Street, Adelphi. Godwin says he met Lamb (it was for the first time) at 'tea' there on that day. Dinner was an afternoon meal; tea was taken anywhere from five-thirty to eight or nine. Supper was a late-evening repast, preceded as a rule by strong drink; so 'tea' could well extend to supper if guests arrived a little after eight to spend the evening. Lamb had written to Manning on Friday, 'I am to sup with Coleridge tonight—Godwin will be there, whom I am rather curious to see—& Col. to partake with me of Manning's Bounty tomorrow—.' Manning's bounty was the promised turkey. Next morning at the top Lamb added, 'Saturday.⁶ The Turkey is just come—the Largest I ever saw—.' At the bottom of the letter, he added, 'Philosopher Godwin! dines with me on your Turkey this day. . . . I expect the roof to fall and crush the Atheist. I have been drunk two nights running at Coleridge's—how my Head burns!'⁷

The Friday meeting was a red-letter one for both. Godwin entered on some blank pages of his 1796 diary a list of most of his friends under the years he met them, from 1773 to 1802. Those whom he particularly valued – for some special quality of mind, talent, or character – he underlined. Coleridge and Lamb (but not Southey) share this honour with 'Wolstencraft', Davy, Carlisle, Holcroft, Sheridan, Opie, Horne Tooke and a number of others.

Coleridge had been either a little wicked or over-optimistically conciliatory in his mix that Friday night, for one of his invited guests (duly recorded in Godwin's diary) was the twenty-nine-year-old Basil Montagu, illegitimate son of the dissolute erstwhile Lord of the Admiralty Lord Sandwich and the actress Martha Ray, shot to death by her clergyman lover. Montagu, lately widowed, with a small son, had been the intimate successively of Wordsworth, Godwin – and now Mackintosh! – in his search for a father figure. He had recently renounced Godwin and all his works, as Coleridge well knew. (Godwin may have learned of Montagu's defection only that night, since he had commended him warmly to his friend Dr Samuel Parr as late as January.)

Montagu was an attractive young man. Crabb Robinson found his 'feeling face and gentle tones'⁸ appealing, and Fanny Kemble the actress was impressed by his 'ability, eccentricity, and personal beauty. . . . His conversation was extremely vivid and sparkling, and the quaint eccentricity of his manner added to the impression of originality which he produced upon one.'⁹ He had managed to be both wild and diligent at Cambridge, where he had achieved the status of sixth wrangler, a mathematics distinction. Wordsworth had directed him to a serious view of life at the time when the poet was advising young men (says Hazlitt) to 'read Godwin on Necessity'. Montagu had next pursued Godwin, rambled with him through England, and attended him as Mary Wollstonecraft lay dying: the two could hardly have been closer. Married, soon widowed, and financially adrift after a break with his father, he had entrusted the small Basil to the willing Wordsworths while he sought a profession. Wordsworth had even lent him the greater part of the Calvert legacy that was supposed to make William and Dorothy independent. Under Mackintosh's guidance Montagu was now studying law.

With Montagu came two other young men. One was Montagu's former pupil the wealthy John Frederick Pinney, whose father owned the sugar island of Nevis in the West Indies and whose own enthusiasm for Wordsworth had provided William and Dorothy with Racedown, his family's little-used country estate, rent-free. The second, a Tobin, was most likely the nearly blind Jem, Wordsworth's friend,[10] who was soon to die on Nevis.

Wordsworth at this moment was hard up and trying, through Pinney, to press Montagu for a repayment on which he had defaulted. Montagu's Godwinian theory, conveniently retained, was that Pinney should lend him the money for Wordsworth, but Pinney, to whom Montagu was already in debt, had declined the suggestion. Coleridge, the preceding Tuesday, had described to one of the Wedgwoods[11] the tangled relationships between three of the Friday group. It included Montagu's withholding of a letter from Wordsworth to Pinney, to whom Montagu refused to yield it.[12]

Lamb, Godwin, Pinney, Montagu, Tobin, the Coleridges – this was the party, and the air as they gathered must have fairly bristled with the various antagonisms, including Lamb's for Godwin. It is not surprising that the drinks flowed freely between tea and supper, nor that Godwin and Lamb concentrated upon each other while Coleridge was occupied with the defecter from Godwin and his friends. Godwin would note Montagu's new coolness with hurt; and Lamb, so often belligerent with new people, was perhaps the more so with one who had been his Arch-devil. But with drink they talked; Godwin was at once attracted to Lamb. Southey wrote after Lamb's death,

Coleridge introduced him to Godwin, shortly after the first number of the *Anti-Jacobin Magazine and Review* was published, with a caricature of Gillray's in which Coleridge and I were introduced with asses' heads, and Lloyd and Lamb as toad and frog. Lamb got warmed up with whatever was on the table, became disputatious, and said things to Godwin which made him quietly say, "Pray Mr. Lamb, are you toad or frog?" Mrs Coleridge will remember the scene, which was to her sufficiently uncomfortable. But the next morning Coleridge called on Lamb, and found Godwin breakfasting with him, from which time their intimacy began.[13]

Entranced by the question, no doubt, Lamb mellowed; very soon he asked Godwin to dine with him and the Coleridges at Pentonville next day. (We may guess that it was at Saturday's dinner, not breakfast, that Coleridge was surprised to find Godwin, who makes no mention of breakfast in his journal: he seldom took that meal out.)

Lamb remained long enough to get 'drunk' before stumbling out into the cold – drunk enough to give him a head, but not to prevent him going to the India Office (after the early-morning arrival of the Manning turkey) for half a day of work before the hosting of his dinner.

The Pentonville dinner *à cinq* – Sara Coleridge was present and presumably Mary – must have been a more wholehearted occasion than that of the night before: all seem to have enjoyed one another. Godwin went home with a book: on Sunday morning he read *Rosamund Gray* from cover to cover. A little later (18 February) Lamb wrote to Manning,

> Godwin I am a good deal pleased with—. He is a well-behaved decent man, nothing very brilliant about him or imposing as you might suppose; quite another Guess sort of Gentleman from what your Anti Jacobins Christians imagine him—. I was well pleased to find he has neither horns nor claws, quite a tame creature I assure you. A middle-sized man both in stature & in under-standing—whereas from his noisy fame, you would expect to find . . . a Tityus tall enough to pull Jupiter from his Heavens! (M 1, 185)

Atheist or not, Godwin was a bookworm, a symbol for radicals – and like Lamb he was writing a play. It was called *Antonio*, and it proceeded at a snail's pace, sometimes as little as eight lines a day, polished, for this was the philosopher's method.

On the evening of 2 March, Sara Coleridge was leaving the city with Hartley to stay with friends while Coleridge moved to the Lambs'. That afternoon Godwin had the Lambs and Coleridges to dine. Now it was Coleridge's turn to be tipsy, and he found it necessary next day – settled at Lamb's – to write Godwin an apology, which concluded, 'The Agnus Dei and the Virgin Mary desire their kind respects to *you*, you sad Atheist—!'[14] Godwin forgave the 'irrationality' Coleridge had acknowledged; his journal for March shows him in constant contact with 'Coleridge' and 'Lamb'. In the course of the month he read the latest version of *Pride's Cure*.

On Sunday the twenty-ninth Coleridge was preparing to 'go into the North, on a visit to his God, Wordsworth',[15] as Lamb put it to Manning – Coleridge's first stay at the Grasmere cottage. Godwin, his 'conversion' completed, had Coleridge to breakfast, dine, and sleep before departure. On Monday Godwin went 'to the West End w. Coleridge' to see him off. The Lambs, who presumably saw him off too, went to dinner with Godwin at the Polygon once more.

In April the meetings with Godwin were fewer: Lamb was kept busy in his free hours seeing Coleridge's translations of plays from Schiller's *Wallenstein* through the press, keeping in touch with Manning, entertaining young Lloyds, doing errands for Coleridge, and wrapping up the loose ends Coleridge had left behind him – a number of these were 'authoresses' of Coleridge's acquaintance. One, a Miss Elizabeth Ogilvy Benger, bluestocking and aspiring writer of twenty-two, invited the Lambs to tea (with macaroons, 'a kind of cake I much love,' said Charles). She talked so much about intellectual matters Lamb knew little of – declaring 'that no good poetry had appeared since Dr. Johnson's time'[16] – that she left him irritated and exhausted. She became the subject of one of his most amusing letters, to Coleridge, at the end of which he noted,

> Godwin has called upon us. He spent one evening here. Was very friendly. Kept us up till midnight. Drank punch, and talked about you. He seems, above all men, mortified at your going away. Suppose you were to write to that good-natured heathen— . . . ? (M 1, 200)

The evening was 12 April. Three days later, on Easter Sunday, Godwin was again the subject of public attack, this time by his old friend Dr Samuel Parr, a Whig clergyman who had once been one of his strongest advocates, in the Spital Sermon Lamb had so often attended as a pupil of Christ's Hospital. In it Parr took harsh issue with Godwin, perhaps himself now climbing on the safer bandwagon, perhaps from a sincere change in view. Thereafter Godwin tried, somewhat too lengthily, to reason with him; ultimately Parr requested the philosopher to spare himself the trouble. Godwin's public rebuttal, a pamphlet called *Thoughts Occasioned by . . . Dr. Parr's Spital Sermon* showed a wiser, more humane Godwin than ever before, but it was his swan song as a reformer. From now on he would leave public affairs alone and endure in silence the conservative climate from which England would not rally for a generation. Thenceforth he usually wrote under names less damning than his true one.

Later in April Lamb supped at Godwin's, and Godwin must have been particularly interested in the substance of their conversation – alone at the Polygon – since he noted in his diary, 'talk of Rousseau, Milton, Brown, &c.'[17] 'Brown' was Sir Thomas Browne, seventeenth-century author of *Religio Medici* and *Urn Burial*, whose originality and autobiographical mode had a special appeal for Lamb (and other Romantics). By May his intimacy with the Archdevil was flowering rapidly.

The meeting with Godwin was again the beginning of a lifetime association, which was to have its ups and downs. The little man interested Lamb much, and he was soon helping Godwin with *Antonio*.

CHAPTER TWENTY THREE

The Move to London

I almost wish that Mary were dead. . . .   Lamb to Coleridge, 12 May 1800 (**M** 1, 203)

. . . give me a ramble by night, in the winter nights in London—the Lamps lit . . . the shops all brilliant . . . —give me the old Bookstalls of London—a walk in the bright Piazzas of Covent Garden.—I defy a man to be dull in such places. . . . —I . . . have cried with fullness of joy at the multitudinous scenes of Life in the crouded streets of ever dear London.   Lamb to Robert Lloyd, 7 February 1801 (**M** 1, 270)

April, 1800, except for the intrusion of Coleridge's odd acquaintances and the welcome glimpses of Robert and Priscilla Lloyd, was a tranquil one for the Lambs. But it saw the distancing of old friends – the removal of the Charles Lloyds from Cambridge to Olton Green near Birmingham in search of quiet during Sophia's pregnancy, Coleridge's Lake District preoccupation (now he seriously thought of taking his family there) and the Southeys' departure for Lisbon. Robert Southey's ills had not abated; they hoped the climate of Portugal would restore his health.

One of the more interesting acquaintances Southey made in Portugal was John Hookham Frere, another Caius man, who had met George Canning at Eton, been associated with him in Parliament and in government office – and on the *Anti-Jacobin*. He had just been appointed British Ambassador at Lisbon. When Southey, as an English resident, left the customary calling card at the Embassy, Frere paid him a visit, remembering all too well his own and Canning's attacks on Southey and on Southey's friends Lamb and Coleridge. So that Frere met Southey (Southey wrote)

not without considerable embarrassment on his part even to a faltering of the voice—perhaps in recollection of the rascally note about Coleridge—of which I shall not be slow in speaking my opinion to him if I can find an opportunity. He is a man whose manners would be very pleasant if they were not somewhat over courteous. (NL 1, 236)

Southey certainly enjoyed the embarrassment. But their common interest in Portuguese history and Frere's abilities as an amateur writer before long made Frere and Southey friends for life! If the literary age was harsh, its reversals were often astonishing.

In one of Lamb's Elia essays he describes how John Lamb the younger, in a moment of unconscious humour, 'upon seeing the Eton boys at play in their grounds', exclaimed, 'What a pity to think, that these fine ingenuous lads in a few years will be changed to frivolous members of Parliament!'[1] This remark may have inspired Lamb's *Morning Post* attack on Canning and Frere two years later:

> At Eton School brought up with dull boys,
> We shone like *men* among the *school-boys*;
> But since we in the world have been,
> We are but *school-boys* among men.
>
> (*P*, 102)[2]

By the end of April the Lambs' aged servant Hetty was seriously ill, and a few days later she died, the nursing and shock reviving old horrors in Mary's mind. Charles was forced once more to put her under restraint nearby. Lamb's later friend and biographer 'Barry Cornwall'[3] has described the melancholy departures repeated to the end of Charles's life:

> Whenever the approach of one of her fits of insanity was announced by some irritability or change of manner, he would take her, under his arm, to Hoxton Asylum. It was very afflicting to encounter the younger brother and his sister walking together (weeping together) on this painful errand; Mary herself, although sad, very conscious of the necessity for temporary separation from her only friend. They used to carry a strait jacket with them. ('Cornwall', 52)

Their neighbours in the small village of Pentonville were now gossiping about Mary with alarm: the time of peace and hope, not threatened so severely since 1796, was at an end, and Lamb himself was shattered. On 12 May he wrote:

My dear Coleridge,
    I dont know why I write except from the propensity misery has to tell her griefs.—Hetty died on Friday night, about 11 o Clock, after 8 days illness. . Mary in consequence of fatigue and anxiety is fallen ill again, and I was obliged to remove her yesterday.— I am left alone in a house with nothing but Hetty's dead body to keep me company. . . . Tomorrow I bury her, and then I shall be quite alone, with nothing but a cat, to remind me that the house has been full of living beings like myself.— My heart is quite sunk, and I dont know where to look for relief—. Mary will get better again, but her constantly being liable to such relapses is dreadful,—nor is it the least of our Evils, that her case & all our story is so well known around us. . We are in a manner *marked*.— Excuse my troubling you, but I have nobody by me to speak to me.
    I slept out last night, not being able to endure the change and the stillness.—But I did not sleep well, and I must come back to my own bed—I am going to try to get a friend to come & be with me tomorrow—
    I am completely shipwreck'd.—My head is quite bad. . . . I almost wish that Mary were dead. . . . [4]

God bless you
Love to Sara & Hartly
C Lamb
(M 1, 202–3)

So he buried yet another member of the household, with the moral support of James White, now a clerk in the treasurer's office at Christ's Hospital, and their schoolmate James Matthew Gutch, law stationer in Chancery Lane. Lamb made one new friend on 15 May, when he dropped in on Godwin and found with him Ralph Fell, a young writer. After Mary's collapse he had stayed overnight at White's; he decided after all to remain with him until he could find fresh quarters. He said to Manning, 'I expect Mary will get better, before many weeks are gone—but at present I feel my daily & hourly prop has fallen from me..[5] I totter and stagger with weakness, for nobody can supply her place to me—. White has *all kindness*, but not *sympathy* . . . '[6]

Two sad letters to the Lloyds relieved him further. Coleridge commented to Godwin on 21 May,

> My poor Lamb!—how cruelly afflictions crowd upon him! I am glad, that you think of him as I think—he has an affectionate heart, a mind sui generis, his taste acts so as to appear like the unmechanic simplicity of an Instinct—in brief, he is worth an hundred men of *mere* Talents. Conversation with the latter tribe is like the use of leaden Bells—one warms by *exercise*—Lamb every now & then *eradiates*, & the beam, tho' single & fine as a hair, yet is rich with colours, & I both see & feel it. (Griggs 1, 588)

Gutch it was who now proved Lamb's rescuer, as he informed Manning:

> I am in much better spirits than when I wrote last. I have had a very eligible offer to Lodge with a friend in Town. He will have rooms to let at Midsummer, by which time I hope my sister will be well enough to join me. . It is a great object to me to live in town, where we shall be much more *private*, and to quit a house & a neighborhood where poor Mary's disorder, so frequently recurring, has made us a sort of marked people. .[5] We can be no where private except in the midst of London—. We shall be in a family where we visit very frequently. . . . .[5] Only my Landlord and I have not yet come to a conclusion. He has a partner to consult.— I am still on the tremble. For I do not know where we could go into Lodgings, that would not be in many respects highly exceptionable. Only God send Mary well again, and I hope all will be well.— The prospect, such as it is, has made me quite happy—. (M 1, 207)

His friends old and new did what they could to help. On 28 May Lamb and Fell supped at Godwin's together and on Friday the thirtieth he was invited to dine at Fells' with Godwin and Godwin's housemate James Marshal. Fell is a shadowy figure – a lively drinking companion who told long stories, by Lamb's account, and one whom Godwin underlined in his diary as a special person. Fell published a travel book (rather dull) and would later do a life of Charles James Fox, the Whig leader, and edit or write a 'Naval Chronicle'. Lamb regarded Fell ultimately as one who had encouraged his own drinking and joking propensities to no very good end, but Fell's good cheer seems to have been a welcome antidote just now to the gloom of both Lamb and Godwin.

Lamb may still have been living with White when Godwin had tea at White's with Lamb and Gutch on the twenty-ninth of May, but (with Gutch's partner Anderson approving) he probably moved soon afterward to Chancery Lane, a stone's throw from the Temple. He – and after the fifteenth, Mary – may have had temporary quarters at or near Gutch's until Midsummer (21 June), when the apartment became vacant.[7]

At Whitsun – 1 June in 1800 – Lamb took a long weekend to get away to his haven at Widford, writing to Manning from an inn on the Ware road,

> Poor Mary is very bad yet. I went yesterday hoping I should see her getting well, then I might have gone into the country more chearful, but I could not get to see her. This has been a sad.[8] damp. Indeed I never in my life have been more wretched than I was all day yesterday. I am glad I am going away from business for a little while, for my head has been hot & ill—. I shall be very much alone where I am going, which always revives me. (M 1, 208)

In Hertfordshire all was lovely at that season – the time of bluebells and Queen Anne's lace in woods and fields, of yellow mustard, blue speedwell, and red campion. May trees still bloomed; laburnum, lilac, rhododendron, and the first roses scented cottage gardens. Lamb diverted himself by writing a poem on a social theme, 'The Old and the Young Courtier', on the pathos of old age. It was inspired by the antique manner of a song out of Percy's *Reliques*, source of old ballads. He sent it to Coleridge.

Meanwhile he had restored his equilibrium at Blakesware, returning home to find Mary, as he tells Manning on Sunday 8 June, 'perfectly recover'd. She is to join me next Sunday.' The trip has done his own spirits 'a world of good'.[9]

Now the task of moving had to be undergone again – to No. 27 Southampton Buildings. They shared the house with Gutch and his business and the Lambs had 'three rooms (including servant) under £34 a year'. Gutch knew 'all our story'.

I am afraid we are not placed out of the reach of future interruptions..[10] But I am determined to take what snatches of pleasure, we can, between the acts of our distressful drama . . . (M I, 215)

He apparently collected Mary on Sunday 15 June as planned. By Sunday the twenty-second the Lambs were themselves entertaining again – Godwin, Marshal, Fell, and Gutch the dinner guests in their new home.

Early in July, Godwin departed for a six-week restorative trip to Ireland, accepting the invitation of his friend John Philpot Curran. 'Before he went,' said Lamb to Coleridge, 'I past much time with him, and he has shew'd me particular attentions..N.B. A thing I much like.'[11] Godwin was still a hero to the rebellious Irish. (Marshal held the fort in Somers Town.)

Lamb, meanwhile, heartily cheered by Mary's recovery, played a joke on Gutch in a letter to him while Gutch was away in Birmingham courting the coachmaker's daughter he later married. Lamb described Gutch's partner Anderson as having decamped, and a young clerk as having run off with Gutch's money. 'For Gods sake set out by the first coach. Mary has been crying all day about it, and I am now just going to some law stationer in the neighborhood . . . to get him to come and be in the house for a day or so, to manage. . . . 'All calculated to make Gutch frantic until he turned the page, where Lamb wrote,

A Bite ! ! !

Anderson is come home, and the wheels of thy business are going on *as ever*

The boy is honest, and I am thy friend.—

And how does the coach maker's daughter.—Thou art her Phaeton, her Gig, and her sociable.[12]—Commend me to Rob.—

C Lamb   (M I, 211–12)

Childish perhaps; Lamb began to be more of a prankster than he had been hitherto and to call more readily upon humour – sometimes, to be sure, out of desperation, but oftener because it offered constructive aid and mental balance in meeting life's more dreadful onslaughts.

Ralph Fell got married on 5 July (with the Lambs in attendance?), an event that the girl Lamb called 'his pretty Spousa',[13] who soon bore four children, may later have rued. Her impecunious husband was to pine in Newgate while some of them were still toddlers.

Early in July, too, he tells Coleridge, he passed

> two days at Oxford on a visit, which I have long put off, to Gutch's family.—The sight of the Bodleian Library and above all a fine Bust of Bishop *Taylor* at All Soul's, were particularly gratifying to me. .[10] Unluckily it was not a family, where I could take Mary with me, and I am afraid there is something of dishonesty in any pleasures I take without *her*. She never goes anywhere. (M 1, 215)

By late July Coleridge had moved with his family into Greta Hall, at Keswick in the Lake District. To him early in August Lamb reported his care of all the odds and ends his friend had left him to do, sending north Coleridge's dictionaries and German books and a 'dressing-gown (value, fivepence) in which you used to sit and look like a conjuror, when you were translating "Wallenstein." A case of two razors and a shaving box and strap. This it has caused me a severe struggle to part with.' Lamb has – perhaps in revenge for this and much other labour (described in detail) – 'torn up' 'Buonaparte's letters, Arthur Young's Treatise on Corn, and one or two more light-armed infantry, which I thought better suited the flippancy of London discussion than the dignity of Keswick thinking. . . . Mary says you will be in a damned passion about them . . . but you must study philosophy . . . and then be angry with an absent friend if you can.' He chides Coleridge for 'gentle-hearted Charles' in 'This Lime-Tree Bower' just printed in Southey's 1800 *Anthology*: 'the meaning of gentle is equivocal at best, and almost always means poor-spirited, the very quality of gentleness is abhorrent to such vile trumpetings'.[14] Coleridge is to order the new, 1800 edition of *Lyrical Ballads* for him as soon as possible.

Sophia Lloyd's child, Charles Grosvenor, has appeared at last on 31 July – Lamb writes his blessings on the baby to Manning on 9 August, though 'I could *curse* the sheet full; so much stronger is Corruption than Grace in the Natural man!' He yearns to see Manning and notes that

Coleridge is settled with his Wife (with a child in her Guts) and the young philosopher [Hartley] at Keswick . . . George Dyer too—that goodnatur'd Heathen—is more than 9 months' gone with his Twin volumes of Ode, pastoral, sonnet, . . . well, God put it into the hearts of the English Gentry to come in shoals & subscribe to his Poems, for He never put a kinder heart into flesh of man than George Dyer's!—(M 1, 221–2)

E. V. Lucas inserts in his 1935 edition of the Lambs' letters at this point a description by Southey of Lamb and Manning carousing while Sophia Lloyd was in childbed above them, but there seems never to have been a time when this could have taken place. Lamb has clearly not seen Manning as recently as 31 July or he would have conveyed the news of Coleridge and Dyer personally.[15] We may guess that Southey's account is from the time of Lamb's Cambridge visit in December, 1799, when Sophia was newly pregnant and above-stairs, while Lamb, Manning, and Lloyd remained below. Manning was now (August 1800) begging Lamb to come to Cambridge for another visit–his rum going gultch squlluck in anticipation. The Southey description suggests the gaieties envisaged; he says the two were

drinking punch in the room below till three in the morning— Manning acting Le Brun's passions (punchified at the time), and Charles Lamb (punchified also) roaring aloud and swearing, while the tears ran down his cheeks . . . ; Charles Lloyd the while (not punchified) praying and entreating them to go to bed, and not disturb his wife by the uproar they were making. (CL 1, 201)

Lamb could not go to Cambridge in August,

But for You to come to London in stead!——muse upon it, revolve it, cast it about in your mind—. I have a Bed at your command—. You shall drink Rum, Brandy, Gin, Aquavitae, Usquebagh, or Whiskey a nights— —& for the after-dinner-Trick I have 8 Bottles of genuine Port which mathematically divided gives 1 1/7 for every day you stay, provided you stay a week. Hear John Milton sing,

"Let Euclid rest & Archimedes pause."

21st Sonnet—(M 1, 223)

The scholarly touch was the humble clerk's reminder to his university-trained friends that he too had read a good deal, but it also pleased him to turn a joke that way, quoting or misquoting. What is extraordinary is the extent to which the books and poems he had read – like Milton's sonnet – stuck with him. He retained most of what his eye and mind once lit on with astonishing ease, and was able to dredge up at will what had impressed or amused him.

His 14 August letter to Coleridge attacks his friend once more for calling him 'gentle-hearted'.

My head is playing all the tunes in the world, ringing such peals! it has just finished the "merry Xt. Church Bells" and absolutely is beginning "Turn again Whittington." Buz, buz, buz, bum, bum, bum, wheeze, wheeze, wheeze, feu, feu, feu, tinky, tinky, tinky, *craunch*. . . . I have been getting drunk two days running . . . I have sat down to read over again your Satire upon me in the Anthology—. . . . In the next edition . . . please to blot out *gentle hearted*, and substitute drunken dog, ragged-head, seld-shaven, odd-eye'd, stuttering, or any other epithet which truly and properly belongs to the Gentleman in question. And for Charles read Tom, or Bob, or Richard, *for more delicacy.*—Damn you, I was beginning to forgive you, & believe in earnest that the lugging in of my Proper name was purely unintentional on your part, when looking back for further conviction, stares me in the face Charles Lamb of the *India House*. *Now* I am convinced it was all done in Malice, heaped, sack-upon-sack, congregated, studied Malice. You Dog!— (M 1, 224)

In a drinking age, it took very little alcohol to make Lamb 'drunk', perhaps because of some weakness of the liver.[16] His letter to Coleridge anticipates the 1813 essay 'Confessions of a Drunkard', in which one suspects Lamb to be perpetrating one of his jokes. It was first contributed to the *Philanthropist*, a very moral journal.[17] The joke boomeranged, however, as his authorship came to be known, and more than one critic took the 'Confessions' seriously in print. Lamb had some trouble living it down, the more so as he was not one to retire from late-night opportunities such as Manning and Fell offered. These released the inhibitions caused by his shyness and stammer, for in liquor he could *talk*. Lamb did now begin to think of drinking as one of his problems, though it seems to have been a damaging one only toward the end of his life when his problems multiplied. But it probably contributed to the ailments which allowed his early retirement from the East India Company.[18] Mary disapproved strongly, of course, and one of Lamb's amiable weaknesses was his inability to reform, try as he might, recording the ups and downs as he went. Pipe-smoking accompanied alcohol: Lamb saw it too as a solvent for speech. Godwin's Dr Parr is said to have once asked Lamb how he got to smoking so fiercely. Lamb answered, 'I toiled after it, sir, as some men toil after virtue.'[19] His attractive light verses, 'A Farewell to Tobacco', proved only an *au revoir*.

Drink, with tobacco, was one way of escaping permanent pain.

CHAPTER TWENTY FOUR

Lamb Among the Lions

I do not think there is anything deserving the name of society to be found out of
London. . . . First, there is neighbourhood *elsewhere, accidental or*
unavoidable acquaintance . . . ; you can pick your society nowhere but in
London. The very persons that of all others you would wish to associate with in
almost every line of . . . intellectual pursuit, are to be met with there.
Secondly, London is the only place in which each individual in company is
treated according to his value in company, and to that only . . . it is not
inquired whether he is rich or poor . . . but whether . . . he is a man of
understanding or a blockhead. . . . William Hazlitt, 'On Coffee-
House Politicians'[1]

Among the most remarkable [of Godwin's friends] *was the great Irish*
orator, Curran—a man extremely ugly . . . ; his talk rich in its idiom and its
imagery; and in the warmth of his feelings, he was all passion . . . Henry
Crabb Robinson. (Morley, 14)

No man of liberal tendencies could have talked in 1788 with Horne Tooke, then
in the thick of his fight for Parliamentary reform, without having his heart
moved as by a trumpet. M. Ray Adams, *Studies in the Literary*
Background of English Radicalism (p. 30).

The move to Southampton Buildings – a group of houses at the
Holborn end of Chancery Lane – was happy for Charles in putting
him immediately in touch with his London friends and soon into the
much wider world of the famous and near-famous. He was now
close to the Southampton Coffee House, and the taverns of Fleet
Street where a man could drink beer of an evening with his male
friends. Plain speech was the order of these evenings – as Lamb's
description of Sara Coleridge 'with a child in her Guts' – and Lamb
enjoyed it as much as anyone. (E. V. Lucas, in editing Lamb's
letters, suppressed a few expressions he considered vulgar: Marrs
has restored them.) Not far was the red light district around Covent
Garden; by twenty-five such activity normally repelled him. Failing
the happy marriage he would have preferred, celibacy appears to

have been his choice, and his relation to his sister that of younger brother, companion, and protector.[2]

His balance once again restored, Lamb sharpened his gift for comic portraiture in ebullient letters. On 21 August he inquires of Manning,

> . . . have you a Copy of your Algebra to give away? . . . Poet George Dyer made me a visit yesternight on purpose to borrow one, supposing, rationally enough I must say, that you had made me a present of one before this . . . I could lend him no assistance. . . . (M 1, 228)

George had been diverted by a mathematical dispute.

Two days later Lamb is rapturous; Manning is coming to town:

> George Dyer is an Archimedes, and an Archimagus, and a Tycho Brahe, and a Copernicus, and thou art the darling of the nine [Muses], and midwife to their wandring babe also! We take Tea with that learned Poet & Critic on Tuesday night at half past five, in his neat Library, the repast will be light and Attic, with Criticism—if thou couldst contrive to wheel up thy dear carcase on the Monday, and after dining with us on Tripe . . . might we not adjourn together to the Heathen's?—thou with thy Black Backs and I with some innocent volume of . . . Shenstone or the like— —it would make him wash his old flannel gown, (that has not been washed to my knowledg[e] since it has been *his*—O the long Time!) . . . (M 1, 230)

Lamb's poetry (he told Manning) had now attracted the attention of Dr James Anderson, whom Dyer had brought to see him – 'an old Gentleman who ties his breeches knees with packthread'.[3] Anderson was editor of a monthly called *Recreations in Agriculture, Natural History, Art, and Miscellaneous Literature*. He had already reprinted a section from Lamb's 'Living Without God' in his November 1799 issue. *Recreations* for November 1800 contained the extracts from *John Woodvil* – 'The Dying Lover',[4] the delicate 'Description of a Forest Life' and 'The General Lover'. The arrangements for publication were made, no doubt, on a return visit with Dyer in September to the Doctor's home at Isleworth where the 'agreable old Gent.', nearly as eccentric as Dyer, gave them a hot leg of mutton and grape pie.

On Monday 25 August Manning arrived, Tuesday they had tea with Dyer and gave him Manning's maths books. On Wednesday Godwin, who had returned from Ireland on the nineteenth, took Marshal to dine at the Lambs' with Manning.

To Coleridge on 26 August Lamb proudly sent Mary Lamb's first poem, based on the Blakesware Plumer portrait Lamb particularly loved. In 'Helen repentant too late' Mary imagines that the blonde girl has repulsed a suitor into old age:

> High-born Helen!
> Round your dwelling
> These twenty years I've pac'd in vain;
> Haughty Beauty,
> Your Lover's duty
> Has been to glory in his pain.
>   (M I, 233)

At length the old lady acknowledges, 'You to all men I prefer.' It was pleasant amateur verse-making, and an indication that Mary was feeling normal again. The poem is happily uninhibited in conception. Since Mary with Charles's encouragement was to go down in history as the co-author of the Lambs' *Tales from Shakespear* (never out of print from that day to this), 'Helen' marked a certain milestone.

The letter concludes with a humorous account of Joseph Cottle's epic, *Alfred*, just received from the author; it was heavy with Gothic horrors. Cottle's brother Amos died in London in October (1800). Joseph came down from Bristol and Lamb attended the wake. He was, as usual at solemn gatherings, on the edge of hysterical laughter. George Dyer soon managed to divert the grieving brother by mentioning *Alfred*. Lamb picked up the lead with relief and proceeded out of kindness to 'beslabber' *Alfred* 'with most unqualified praise', or only a little qualified. 'At that moment I could perceive that Cottle had forgot his brother was so lately become a blessed spirit. In the language of Mathematicians the Author was as 9 the brother as 1.'[5] Lamb's description to Coleridge is a comic gem on an unlikely subject.

We hear no more of the Manning visit; on 3 September Lamb dined at Godwin's without him. By 22 September Manning had sent his usual gourmet's tribute from Cambridge – 'fine birds' and a hare – eliciting from Lamb one of his culinary appreciations.

Now Godwin began to introduce Lamb to others of his circle besides Ralph Fell. Among his closest intimates – and Fell's – were the John Fenwicks. Eliza Fenwick, who dressed in grey from poverty and had been a faithful nurse to Mary Godwin at the last, was author of one novel, called *Secrecy*, and future author of children's books published by Godwin. She was spirited and resourceful, though sometimes a complainer, and had just about given up on her hard-drinking husband, the lordly borrower who became 'Ralph Bigod' in Lamb's 'The Two Races of Men'. But the Fenwicks went out together still, often with their daughter and small son. John was editor of a Jacobin evening paper called the *Albion*, subsidized by wealthy Radicals. Lamb took to Fenwick at once, and Fenwick to him. As borrower, 'Bigod had an *undeniable* way with him. He had a cheerful, open exterior, a quick jovial eye, a bald forehead, just touched with grey. . . . He anticipated no excuse, and found none.'[6]

It was the preposterous ne'er-do-wells that became grist to Lamb's pen. He barely mentioned in letters or elsewhere the better-known figures he soon came to meet as well. But we know from Godwin's diary[7] that he began to move among the lions at this time, if not to invite them home.

On 3 September, 1800, John Philpot Curran, the Irish politico and Godwin's recent host, was staying with Godwin, and Lamb was invited to meet him at dinner. Curran had trained at the Middle Temple in London and, as the advocate with the greatest reputation in all of Ireland, soon entered Irish politics. A Protestant member of the Dublin Parliament – no Catholic could serve there – he took up the cause of Catholic Emancipation. In the Irish state trials (1794–1803), result of abortive rebellion, he was a fearless defender of rebel leaders. At his own trial he was acquitted and later granted the post of Master of the Rolls. Irish nationalism, to Curran's distress, had recently sustained its severest defeat in Pitt's Act of Union, abolishing the Irish Parliament[8] and bringing the 'United Kingdom' to birth, a move spurred by Irish traffic with the French and the fear of French invasion from Ireland.

Among the English, Curran[9] seemed startlingly uninhibited. When an Englishman he didn't know made fun of him from the top of a coach, Curran responded, 'May God almighty never humanise your countenance, you odious baboon!' – one of many stories about him. He was Godwin's unstinting friend – 'the sincerest friend I ever had'.[10]

Also present at dinner was Frederick Reynolds, who saw produced in his lifetime a hundred of his plays to full houses. They bore titles such as *Better Late Than Never, Folly As It Flies*, and *The Dramatist*, with which he made his name in 1793; all are forgotten today except by the social historian. His comedies were broad and full of action – as they had to be in the enormous theatres of the time. Crabb Robinson dismisses him loftily: 'He talks with the ease and assurance of one who goes much in company, but I suspect him to be an ordinary person.'[11] Lamb, however, trying to be a dramatist himself, must have looked at Reynolds with some awe. The other member of the party was Godwin's friend William Nicholson, later the compiler of a chemical dictionary and an encyclopedia, and editor of a literary review.[12]

The lion Lamb already knew – Samuel Taylor Coleridge – and with whom he was again in correspondence, had a second surviving son, Derwent,[13] in September for whom he asked Godwin to be godfather. (Godwin refused, his conversion not extending to approval of christening.) Coleridge was now a constant companion of the Wordsworths at the Lakes, where Dorothy was continuing her famous journal. On 4 October she wrote,

> Read a part of Lamb's play. The language is often very beautiful, but too imitative in particular phrases, words, etc. The characters, except Margaret's, unintelligible, and, except Margaret's, do not show themselves in action. Coleridge came in while we were at dinner, very wet . . .[14]

(The Charles Lloyds, not altogether to the Wordsworths' delight, though they soon loved Sophia, were also now near Grasmere at Ambleside, and soon constant visitors at the Wordsworth cottage. Coleridge was regularly whisked away by William and Dorothy whenever the Lloyds were about to call: he saw them never.)

Coleridge wrote to Godwin in response to a piece of happy news about *Antonio* at the hands of Sheridan and Kemble, 'Your Tragedy to be exhibited at Christmas!'[15] About this time Godwin conceived the notion of having Charles Lamb write its prologue and epilogue, a flattering tribute to their friendship.

Godwin supped twice at Lamb's in September, once when 'Le Grice' was present, probably Sam, the younger brother, since Lamb and Sam Le Grice that autumn attended a Christ's Hospital Old Boys' dinner, where Sam (said Charles) 'attracted the notice of all by the singular foppishness of his dress'.[16] He was at present a commissioned officer in the Sixtieth Foot. In two years he would die of typhoid fever in the West Indies. Lamb probably never saw him again.

On 18 October Lamb and Godwin went to one of the select dinners given by James Perry, editor of the great Whig paper the *Morning Chronicle*. Among Lamb's fellow guests that Saturday was Richard Porson, Regius Professor of Greek at Cambridge from the age of thirty-three (already long acquainted with Coleridge and Manning), and John Horne Tooke, another 'acquitted felon' of the 1794 Treason Trials.[17] Also on hand were Robin Adair, later British Ambassador to Turkey, and two others, one of whom ('C.' in Godwin's diary) was probably Curran again, who was constantly in Godwin's company just then: he and Porson would sleep next night at the Polygon. Lamb of course knew *of* Perry, Tooke, and Porson – a glittering trio for one of Lamb's political sympathies. He had commented on Coleridge's verse tribute to Tooke in 1797 and carried newspaper copy from Coleridge to Perry.

Porson of Cambridge[18] was a man of commanding height and thoughtful countenance. His good looks, somewhat marred by devotion to drink, consisted in a Roman nose, sensitive mouth, and sharp eye framed by curling lashes in a well-shaped head. There his elegance ended. He was uncombed, unclean, and careless of his dress as George Dyer: servants were known to have rebuffed him at the door of great houses to which he was invited. By fits hard-working and lazy, he was an exuberant companion by night in familiar company; his mornings were proverbially hung over. Known for his intellectual pride, political integrity, and disdain of money, he spent most of his Cambridge Professorship in London, living in the Temple and editing the plays of Euripides. He had married Perry's sister and briefly reformed, but she soon died. He and Perry continued close friends, and Porson wrote so often on current affairs for the *Chronicle* that he was upbraided for 'giving up to Perry what was meant for mankind'.[19] One of his radical tracts was *A New Catechism for the Use of the Swinish Multitude: Necessary to be Had in All Sties*. 'Swinish multitude', we recall, was the phrasing of Edmund Burke. Drink was to bring on Porson's early decline and death.

Though Lamb knew no Greek his respect for the Classics was

strong, and he could follow Porson into Latin. In his surviving
Commonplace Book Lamb copied down 'Porson's Gerundial Pun':

> When Dido found, Eneas would not come,
> She mourned in silence, and was Di do dum.[20]

In November he encountered Porson once more at John Rickman's.

Coleridge, we recall, had observed that Porson could '*crush*
Godwin, Holcroft &c—They absolutely tremble before him!' and
even Horne Tooke was careful in his presence.'A keen, iron man,'
said Coleridge, Tooke was 'always making a butt of Mr.Godwin.'[21]
Godwin's air of 'Come, kick me,' which Southey had noted, was
most in evidence in this sort of quick-witted, brilliant company,
which Godwin clung to nevertheless.

Tooke, however, had kissed Godwin's hand, publicly if
sardonically, for saving his life in 1794. Born John Horne, he
attended Westminster, Eton, and Cambridge. An able lieutenant of
John Wilkes in the days of 'Wilkes and Liberty!' Horne earned,
through his brilliant espousal of a legal case for one William Tooke,
that gentleman's gratitude and an income for life. Later Horne
added Tooke's name to his own. He had in the late 1770s signed an
advertisement seeking funds for the families of 'our beloved
American fellow-subjects, who, faithful to the character of *Englishmen*, preferring death to slavery, were for that reason only,
inhumanely murdered, by the King's troops at or near Lexington
and Concord'.[22] For this he was fined heavily and committed to
King's Bench Prison for a year. In 1786 he produced his much-
admired *Diversions of Purley*, Purley being the home of William
Tooke where he had spent many happy hours. The book was really
a grammar in which Horne Tooke expounded his new philological
theories. (These proved, alas, short-lived.)

Tooke at this Perry dinner was sixty-four, of middling height,
sturdy, handsome, and keen of eye. He took some care over his
grooming and attire. Lamb dubbed Hazlitt's later sketch of him 'a
matchless portrait':[23] it affords an insight into the evening at
Perry's. Cool, sardonic, and merciless, Tooke

> was without a rival (almost) in private conversation. . . . his
> intellect was like a bow of polished steel, from which he shot
> sharp-pointed poisoned arrows at his friends in private, at his
> enemies in public. . . . He threw others off their guard by

thwarting their favourite theories . . . to chafe them into madness. . . . He took up any topic by chance and played with it at will, like a juggler with his cups and balls. . . . Once at Godwin's he defended Pitt from a charge of verbiage, and endeavoured to prove him superior to Fox. . . . Porson was the only person of whom he stood in some degree of awe, on account of his prodigious memory and knowledge of his favourite subject, Languages.

Manning already knew Tooke and was on occasion invited to Tooke's 'public dinners'. By early 1802 he mentions Lamb as sometimes dining in Tooke's company as well.[24]

James Perry, their host, for whom Lamb later worked as a part-time journalist – was at fifty-four a little stooped and nearsighted from long hours and steady pressures. Attractive, lively, attentive to women, and a regular host to lions, he had the reputation of being the most charming talker at his own table. Perry was a Scot whose well-to-do family fell upon evil days, causing his early withdrawal from Aberdeen University and requiring him to make his own way. After several false starts he accomplished this brilliantly, rising from humble London reporter to editor–owner of the most powerful Whig daily, for whose present large circulation Perry himself was responsible. Perry's three months in Newgate had resulted from a slur on the House of Lords, whose function the *Chronicle* suggested was purely decorative: 'the dresses of the opera-dancers are regulated there'.[25] On his release there was a great party at the London Tavern, and thereafter Perry took care to avoid recapture, though not by toning down his politics. His enemies said he kotowed to the Whig leaders, who were happy to dine with him, but journalistic ability was what interested him, and he employed at one time or another Hazlitt, Sheridan, Mackintosh, and Charles Dickens to enliven the *Morning Chronicle*'s pages. Lamb describes him as a pleasant man, 'with a dash, no slight one, either, of the courtier,'[26] and Perry's daughter recalled Lamb as one of her especial friends in her childhood.

We have no word beyond Godwin's terse outline on the evening at Perry's, but it must have given the young student of human oddities plenty to chew upon and set him thinking again about journalism and politics. Though Lamb was never a name-dropper and is mostly silent on his more eminent London contacts, casual comments by Manning, Miss Perry, and – rarely – Lamb himself indicate that these three friends of Godwin were men he continued to see. It must have pleased him that Porson came of humble origins in Norfolk, Tooke's father had been a poulterer, and Perry had once assisted in a draper's shop.

In November, through Dyer, he was introduced to Southey's Hampshire friend John Rickman. He had recently come to London from Burton on foot: only his luggage was transported. Southey had made him his agent in literary matters. An Oxford graduate, he was a humorous, 'seditious' young man of nearly twenty-nine, with an unfailing sense of duty and an interest in facts as well as literature, one whom any shrewd employer would immediately entrust with a job. No sooner had Rickman settled at 33 Southampton Buildings than he became, through the kindly Dyer, editor of a commercial and agricultural magazine. He did not think that writing poetry was a worthy full-time occupation for a grown man. Lamb told Manning,

> I have made an acquisition latterly of a *pleasant hand*, one Rickman, to whom I was introduced by George Dyer!!! Not the most flattering auspices under which one man can be introduced to another—. . . . This Rickman lives in our Buildings immediately opposite our house—the finest fellow to drop in a nights about nine or ten oClock, cold bread & cheese time, just in the *wishing* time of the night, when you *wish* for somebody to come in, without a distinct idea of a probable anybody—. Just in the Nick, neither too early to be tedious, nor too late to sit a reasonable time—. . . . a fine *rattling* fellow, has gone through Life laughing at solemn apes; himself hugely literate, oppressively full of information . . . from matter of fact to Zenophon and Plato—can talk Greek with Porson, politics with Thelwall, conjecture with George Dyer, nonsense with me, & any thing with anybody—. A great farmer: somewhat concerned in an agricultural magazine—. Reads no Poetry but Shakspeare . . . very intimate with Southey, . . . relishes George Dyer— thoroughly penetrates into the ridiculous wherever found — understands the *first time* . . . you need never twice speak to him. Does not want explanations, translations, limitations, as Professor Godwin does when you make an assertion. . . . You must see Rickman to know him, for he is a Species in one. A new Class. An

exotic, any slip of which I am proud to put in my garden pot—(M I, 243–4)

Rickman was equally pleased, and, what was more, enthusiastic about *John Woodvil*. He wrote to Southey (still in Lisbon) in December,

> I have a very pleasant neighbour opposite, C. Lamb. He laughs as much as I wish, and makes even *puns*, without remorse of conscience. He has lately completed a dramatic piece, rather tragic (without murder). The language entirely of the last century, and farther back: From Shakespeare, Beaumont, and Fletcher. He demurs on printing it. I wish him to *set it forth* under some fictitious name of that age—Shirley (perhaps) who was burnt out at the great fire of London. Lamb is peculiarly happy in his heroine, and altogether I have not seen a play with so much humour, moral feeling and correct sentiment, since the world was young.(Williams, 39)

All was not well with *Woodvil*, alas, as Lamb had told Manning:

> At last I have written to Kemble to know the event of my Play, which was presented last Christmas— —. As I suspected came an answer back, that the Copy was lost & could not be found, no hint that any body had to this day ever looked into it—with a courteous (reasonable!) request of another Copy (if I had one by me) and a promise of a definitive answer in a week. I could not resist so facile & moderate demand, so scribbled out another, omitting Sundry things, . . . in one day & a half!— — I sent it last night, and am in weekly expectation of the Tolling Bell—& death warrant—(M I, 244)

(In time the death warrant came. Manning said loyally, 'I wonder what fool it was that read it!'[27])

On 16 November, Lamb and Mary played host to Godwin, the Fenwicks, Gutch – and John Stoddart. Lamb had known Stoddart slightly as long ago as June, 1796, when he wrote to Coleridge of Bob Allen's atheism, 'Stodart or Stothard a cold hearted well bred conceited disciple of Godwin does him no good.'[28] But, as so often, his opinion changed on close firsthand acquaintance. A lawyer–journalist two years Lamb's senior, John Stoddart had taken his

Oxford bachelor's degree in civil law in 1798, published one translation from the French and two from Schiller, and was shortly to write *Remarks on Local Scenery & Manners in Scotland* . . . (1801). In Edinburgh he had met Walter Scott, who had not yet published even his *Minstrelsy of the Scottish Border*. Stoddart was enthralled by Scott's knowledge of local history and folklore. From 22 October to 4 November, on his way home, Stoddart had been one of the first guests of the Coleridges at Greta Hall and had spent a day conversing with the Wordsworths. Stoddart thus became a link between Scott and the Wordsworths, and would shortly make them acquainted. He brought a letter to Lamb from one of his Lake District friends[29] and Lamb forthwith invited him to dinner.

Not everyone liked Stoddart; Southey took, perhaps unfairly, a jaundiced view of his Scottish journey when the *Edinburgh Review* damned *John Woodvil* in 1803. Southey rose valiantly to *Woodvil*'s defence, telling Rickman,

> That rascally Scotch Review of *John Woodville* provoked me bitterly by its dishonesty in exaggerating every fault and overlooking every beauty. The last lines of that play are some of the finest that ever I remember and the whole is full of beauty. The story indeed is very defective, and that from a love of imitation. Lamb loves the Old Plays and thinks he loves them for their whole composition when in fact it is only for particular excellencies which outweigh their defects. Coleridge thinks that the reason why those Scotchmen hate him as they evidently do, is because Stoddart once went to Edinburgh and fell in company with these men and his praise—God knows would be motive enough to make honester men a priori dislike the object. Exempli gratia if you and I had never seen or known Lamb or Coleridge and heard this unhappy Spider-brained metaphysician speak of them as the greatest men in the world and his most particular friends—should not we be apt to think that Birds of a feather flock together, and put down his friends for a couple of Jack Daws? (NL I, 315–16)

Lamb, however, remained a loyal friend to Stoddart throughout his somewhat chequered career, and Stoddart's later account of Lamb to Barron Field, on reading ('Serjeant') Talfourd's Lamb biography, shows that the friendship was returned and that not all Lamb's evenings in 1800–3 were spent smoking and drinking:

The time of my closest intimacy with Charles was so long previous to the Serjeant's knowledge of him that few traces of it could be expected to appear in the Book . . . I had [spent some time] in Scotland, & returning . . . through Westmoreland and Cumberland, paid a short visit to Wordworth & Coleridge, one of whom charged me with a letter to Lamb. I then lived in Lincoln's Inn, and Lamb, I think, in Southampton Buildings just by. . . . In that period, he had few friends of tastes similar to his own, who lived at hand. My personal intimacy with Coleridge, Wordsworth & R. Allen, my taste for Shakspeare, Chaucer, Chapman, Burns, Jeremy Taylor, & other gods of his idolatry, and my freedom from the professional avocations to which a few years after I became bound, occasioned our being much together, not only on evenings, but Sundays, or holidays, when he was able to ramble abroad. Nor did our change of lodgings remove us far from each other, for he only moved to the Temple, and I to a small set of chambers in Bell Yard Doctors Commons. Narrow as my space there was I continued to fit up a few Shelves, which Lamb & I between us filled with old books, picked up chiefly on the Stalls. In this way, I got most of Jeremy Taylor's folios, as well as Burton, Chapman, Ben Jonson &c, all in folio, and mostly in their ancient binding. As I neither drank nor smoked, our time (at my rooms at least) was chiefly passed in reading or discussing passages of our favorite authors, or compositions of our own. Mary Lamb was always of the party, and joined in the criticisms, in her mild, unpretending way. She, too, occasionally wrote short copies of verses, which Charles had great pleasure in repeating. I have still by me a copy of John Woodvil, on the blank leaf of which he transcribed her sweet, quiet lines. . . .

In 1803 I married, & shortly afterward went out as King's Advocate to Malta. I however first introduced my Wife to the Lambs, and she still retains a warm affection for Mary[who survives]. It has often struck me that Charles Lamb's bantering way with strangers was often employed by him as a mode of trying their powers of mind. The first time that he was in company with my Wife & Mother, I happened to retire, on account of a headache, when Charles gravely turned to my Wife & said "I suppose you know he is subject to fits." My poor Mother who took him literally, made some very indignant answer, when he replied, with the utmost coolness "O Madam I did not mean it for you; it was intended for the young Wife."

Fortunately the young Wife knew enough of me to be satisfied, that if I had been subject to any sort of illness I should have told her so myself; and her taking the joke so quietly served to raise her in Charles's estimation, as well as that of Mary, who was present. . . .

The interval between my first & second residence at Malta, was filled up with too much business, on my part, to allow of my devoting much time to Lamb's society; nor had he much need of a companion. His kind feelings towards me, however, were always the same.[30]

In 1801 Stoddart became a Doctor of Civil Law and was thenceforth known as 'Dr.' Stoddart. In the course of his government service he underwent the common transformation from Godwinian radical to flaming conservative. In Malta (1803–7) he proved helpful as Coleridge's host and sponsor. From 1813 to 1816 he was editor of *The Times*, writing 'those fierce declamations which caused Stoddart to get the name of *Doctor Slop*'– among Radicals – 'and the paper the title of *The Thunderer*'.[31] These were not popular and in 1816 he was dismissed in favour of Lamb's friend Thomas Barnes, another Christ's Hospital old boy and *The Times*'s first great editor, a liberal. Stoddart started his own *New Times*, to which Lamb occasionally contributed during its short life. William Hone (another Lamb friend) pilloried him in *A Slap at Slop* . . . in 1820. In 1826 Stoddart returned to Malta as a magistrate and in 1827 was knighted by a grateful monarch.

Stoddart was soon to be uneasy brother-in-law to the permanently radical William Hazlitt, whose marriage did not last. Lamb's close friendship with Hazlitt no doubt had something to do with the 'business' that interfered with later intimacy between himself and Stoddart. But Sarah Stoddart (Hazlitt), his sister, became one of Mary Lamb's few close intimates.

Just now Stoddart, Lamb, and Godwin got on well.

The Times: Theatrical Interlude

A mob of men is better than a flock of sheep—— —and a crowd of happy faces justling into the playhouse at the hour of six is a more beautiful spectacle to man than the shepherd driving his 'silly' sheep to fold——Come to London & learn to sympathize with my unrural notions. Lamb to Robert Lloyd, 7 February 1801 (M 1, 271)

The most supernatural of actors. Lord Byron on John Philip Kemble[1]

Mrs. Siddons in her visit to me behaved with great propriety and modesty. . . . Neither praise nor money, the two powerful corrupters of mankind, seem to have depraved her. Dr Samuel Johnson[2]

If there was anything Charles Lamb loved as much as poetry, human justice, and his battered library, it was the theatre. (He would soon write theatre criticism.[3]) Now in December, 1800, he was for the first time to be intimately connected with an actual theatrical production as author of the prologue and epilogue of Godwin's *Antonio*. The play was to be put on at the Drury Lane, one of the only two theatres, (Covent Garden was the other) licensed for serious drama and straight comedy.

The impressions of some of Lamb's contemporaries throw interesting light on Lamb's enthusiasm. Just now the Wordsworths' sea-captain brother John had left them after a visit to the Lakes and gone to London to await the departure of his East India Company ship. He went to see the current rage, *Pizarro*, adapted – with music – from the German of Kotzebue by Richard Brinsley Sheridan, and wrote to Mary Hutchinson (the future Mrs William Wordsworth),

I have been several times to the play since I came to London— the houses are so large that you can hear nothing & I think we

shall never see another play well acted upon the London stage—
  the favorite Pizarro is beatiful in the scenery but the noise rant
and flare acting is excessively disgusting   Shakespears plays are
not liked by the town   the reason I conceive to be is that many of
the beatiful passages are not heard and understood   the houses
being so large and I think too a great deal must be lost in the
acting the characters being many of them more imagination than
reality—[4]

Young Leigh Hunt, soon after he left Christ's Hospital at fifteen
in 1799, began the theatregoing which led to his becoming a
professional drama critic at an early age. Hunt writes of the theatre
of 1800 in his *Autobiography* of 1850:

. . . forty or fifty years ago people of all times of life were much
greater playgoers than they are now. They dined earlier, they
had not so many newspapers, clubs, and pianofortes; the French
Revolution only tended at first to endear the nation to its own
habits; it had not yet opened a thousand new channels of thought
and interest; nor had railroads conspired to carry people, bodily
as well as mentally, into as many analogous directions. Everything was more concentrated, and the various classes of
society felt a greater concern in the same amusements. Nobility,
gentry, citizens, princes,—all were frequenters of theatres, and
even more or less acquainted personally with the performers.
Nobility intermarried with them; gentry, and citizens too, wrote
for them; princes conversed and lived with them. Sheridan,
and other Members of Parliament, were managers as well as
dramatists.

Of the reigning theatrical family he says,

The Kembles, indeed, as Garrick had been, were received
everywhere among the truly best circles; that is to say, where
intelligence was combined with high breeding; and they deserved
it: for whatever difference of opinion may be entertained as to the
amount of genius in the family, nobody who recollects them will
dispute that they were a remarkable race, dignified and elegant
in manners, with intellectual tendencies, and in point of aspect
very like what has been called "God Almighty's nobility".
(Hunt, 136–7)

(Lamb speaks of 'the collective majesty of the whole Kemble family'.[5])

The Kembles – John Philip (now forty), Mrs Sarah Siddons his sister (now forty-five), with their younger brother Charles (still cast in lesser roles) had led the field as tragedians for many years and were to do so for many more. Kemble had just been restored to the managership of Drury Lane. As actor he was not without critics, Leigh Hunt among them, who found him often too deliberate, cold, tame, or even flat. Sir Walter Scott thought him good as Coriolanus, Brutus and Hotspur, but added, 'I think his *Macbeth, Lear,* and especially his *Richard III* inferior in spirit and truth.'

Kemble's effectiveness was somewhat at the mercy of his mood. When he was in fine fettle the word would go round, 'Black Jack is in power tonight.' He was not without humour; one of the best anecdotes about him is Tom Moore's:

> One night, when John Kemble was performing at some country theatre one of his most favorite parts, he was much interrupted . . . by the squalling of a young child. . . . At length . . . Kemble walked with solemn step to the front of the stage, and addressing the audience in tragic tones, said, "Ladies and Gentlemen, unless the play is stopped, the child cannot possibly go on." The effect on the audience of this earnest interference on behalf of the child may be conceived.[6]

(Anecdotes have a way of changing in the telling and retelling, but they show what a public finds it easy to believe about a popular figure.)

Sarah Siddons had failed dismally and been dismissed from Drury Lane in 1775 on her first London appearance, but after further experience in the provinces had been summoned to return by Sheridan. She was a dazzling success this time, in Southerne's *Isabella, or The Fatal Marriage*, which Lamb later saw, as he indicates in 'My First Play'. The *Morning Post* next day proclaimed her the first tragic actress of the English stage. From then on she had no rival. As Lady Macbeth in the sleepwalking scene her audiences adored her. When one thinks of Lady Macbeth, Lamb says, it is really Mrs Siddons one pictures. We recall the 'exquisite' pleasure he enjoyed when 'Mrs. Siddons has been the Lady Randolph' in

Douglas.[7] The young Crabb Robinson was once reduced to hysteria by her performance and at her death in 1818 called her 'the most glorious female I ever beheld'.[8]

Their younger brother Charles Kemble was the last of twelve children in the legendary family. In Charles's heyday somewhat later, Leigh Hunt preferred him to John. Charles's 'ideal face and figure' were 'the nearest approach I ever saw to Shakespeare's gentlemen and to heroes of romance'.[9] (He was to father actress Fanny Kemble.)

John Kemble and Sarah Siddons, after some years of wearing 'modern' dress in all their parts – as had David Garrick – decided that these were ill adapted to the playing of tragedy, which demanded great freedom of movement. They then sought costumes more appropriate to the times depicted, be these Greek, Roman, or Elizabethan. Mrs Siddons dispensed with hoop skirt and piled hair for the looser garments soon to become English fashion generally. Thomas Gainsborough painted her magnificently in the old style, Sir Thomas Lawrence in the new, and Sir Joshua Reynolds, who had portrayed her earlier as 'The Tragic Muse', applauded her reforms.

In spite of the praise Sarah Siddons had received, the new respect she had gained for the profession of actress, and the general feeling that she was the star of her family, only her brother John was lavishly fêted at a retirement banquet, some years after her own more modest departure from the stage. Samuel Rogers, the banker–poet, saw her at this time, and she said to him wistfully, 'Well, perhaps in the next world women will be more valued than they are in this.' Rogers felt the justice of her complaint, for 'doubtless,' said he, 'she was a far, far greater performer than John Kemble'.[10]

One of her triumphs was in Shakespeare's *Richard III*. Richard's victims, the little princes in the Tower, were played at the Drury Lane sometimes by small girls, and the extraordinary fact – which would have interested Lamb deeply had he been prescient in December, 1800 – was that the young actress with whom he was to fall in love in his forties, Fanny Kelly, was acting one of these parts in repertory just then. She had reached her tenth birthday in October.

Fanny was the niece of Michael Kelly, the florid, genial Drury Lane musical director and opera composer, who had known Mozart well in Vienna and sung in the first performance of *The Marriage of Figaro*. Stringent family circumstances dictated her early training for the stage – and she was a natural actress. She became a small member of the chorus in Michael's profitable opera *Bluebeard* at seven. She soon caught John Kemble's attention as he found her one day following *Hamlet* from the wings. He spoke to her kindly, she says:

"And what is your little name?"
"Fanny, sir. Mr. Kelly's niece." . . .
"And what can Mike Kelly's niece do, I wonder?"

Having determined she could read but not write, he asked,

"Do you think you could learn a small part?"
"Oh yes, sir, I know ever so many."
"And what may they be, Mike's niece?"
"*Rolla*, sir." (This the male lead in *Pizarro*.)
"Oh! But that is my part!"
"And *Cora*, sir."
"But that's Mrs. Jordan's!" . . .

Finally Kemble said, 'If you come to my room, Mr. Banks shall measure you for a pair of black satin breeches.'[11] Thus she captured her first speaking role, the young Duke of York to Kemble's Richard III.

This period in Fanny's life was the subject, twenty-five years later, of Lamb's Elia essay 'Barbara S----'. Godwin's *Antonio* was to make its debut on 13 December; on 11 December Fanny had her second speaking part as Prince Arthur in Shakespeare's *King John*, to Mrs Siddons's Queen Constance.

Lamb in his essay disguises little Fanny, Mrs Siddons, and the play. Frances Maria Kelly, when she told Lamb the story, was no more than thirty-five; in the essay Elia has it from the 'aged actress' Barbara S----, who soon thereafter died.

Not long before she died I had been discoursing with her on the quantity of real present emotion which a great tragic performer experiences during acting. I ventured to think, that though in the first instance such players must have possessed the feelings which they so powerfully called up in others, yet by frequent repetition those feelings must become deadened in great measure, and the performer trust to the memory of past emotion, rather than express a present one. She indignantly repelled the notion, that with a truly great tragedian the operation, by which such effects were produced upon an audience, could ever degrade itself into what was purely mechanical. With much delicacy, avoiding to instance in her *self*-experience, she told me, that so long ago as when she used to play the part of the Little Son to Mrs. Porter's Isabella, (I think it was) when that impressive actress has been bending over her in some heart-rending colloquy, she has felt real hot tears come trickling from her, which (to use her powerful expression) have perfectly scalded her back.

I am not quite so sure that it was Mrs. Porter; but it was some great actress of that day. The name is indifferent; but the fact of the scalding tears I most distinctly remember. (*Elia*, 203-4)

Miss Kelly has left her own version for Lamb's public, providing interesting light on Lamb's matter-of-lie method. She tells how Lamb and other friends of theirs had been 'warmly engaged' to prove that 'acting was itself so artificial as to preclude any performer— even the most celebrated—from feeling the passion of a character or scene during the acting'. Miss Kelly then 'crushed the cold theory':

When I was a child I stood up, straight, yet trembling, in curls and white silk hose—the *Prince Arthur* to the *Queen Constance* of Mrs. Siddons. I stood awestruck in her grasp, as though the clutch of an eagle was upon me. Her energy was appalling: it seems to strain me now. But when she leant over me in love-lost and passionate yet majestic sorrow, the light of those large, deep dark eyes fell on me like a sad glory and charmed me to the spot. Then I felt that she was indeed Queen Constance, and when her grand forehead was torn from my little shoulder the small white collar on my neck was wetted through and through with her scalding tears. (Holman, 13)

Michael Kelly tells the sequel of Fanny's own performance in his *Reminiscences*:

Mr. Sheridan called upon me one day, and said, "Last night I was at Brookes's [Club]; Charles Fox came there with Lord Robert Spencer,—they had both been at Drury Lane to see 'King John.' I asked him if he was pleased with the performance." He replied, "that he was particularly with Mrs. Siddons. But," he added, "there was a little girl who acted Prince Arthur, with whom I was greatly struck; her speaking was so perfectly natural; take my word for it, Sheridan, that girl in time will be at the head of her profession."[12]

Fanny fulfilled her promise, grew up to be an outstanding comedienne and in time the founder of the first English dramatic school, who sometimes lent her theatre to Charles Dickens—Fanny of the 'divine plain face' (said Lamb), to whom 'Barbara S----' is affectionate tribute. Though disguised, its story is in essence a true one – of how little Fanny on pay day was owed a half-sovereign for her work as an actress but accidentally given a full sovereign by the Drury Lane treasurer. After dreadful qualms of conscience she returned the extra allotment which her struggling mother could have used and which the careless treasurer would not have missed.

The attraction of Drury Lane for the London public of all classes is not complete without mention of its owner–manager 'our late incomparable Brinsley',[13] as Lamb calls him, though the two seem never to have met. Sheridan was as colourful as his crew – Whig Parliamentarian, successful playwright, author of *The Rivals* and *The School for Scandal*, and in 1800 doing very well at the Drury Lane with the musical *Pizarro*. The stories about him are legion; one must suffice. When he learned in 1809 that the Drury Lane was burning down he stuck to his important Parliamentary debate. In the evening he is said to have watched it burn at a nearby tavern with the quip 'And where may a man smoke his pipe if not by his own fireside?'[14]

Both Drury Lane and Covent Garden burned down regularly, hundreds of candles and oil lamps providing the only illumination until well into the nineteenth century, when gas came in. The Drury Lane in which *Antonio* would be shown had been rebuilt in 1792 to its present huge proportions. It had five tiers of galleries encircling the pit, with its benches for critics and walking space for 'Fops' Alley'. Audiences were noisy and inclined to hurl oranges.

Every fool in England was writing a play, it was said, and among the Romantics this was certainly true. The reason, of course – besides the glamour, the glory, and the availability of fine actors – was money. The playwright's average take for a successful piece was not less than £300 (£3000 or about $6750 in 1979). Between 1803 and 1810 Frederick Reynolds sometimes made £700. *Pizarro's* long-term profits ran into the thousands. (By 1820 the rewards were less, and by mid-century it was novelists such as Dickens and Thackeray who prospered most.)

Godwin, needing money desperately for his little family, and Lamb in support of him, now hoped earnestly for the success of *Antonio, or the Soldier's Return*, in which all three Kembles were to appear.

CHAPTER TWENTY FIVE

Antonio

The play is the man's you wot of—, but for God's sake (who would Not like to have so pious a professor's work damned)—do not mention it——it is to come out in a feign'd name, as one Tobins— Lamb to Manning, 13 December, 1800 (M 1, 251)

A new tragedy, entitled Antonio, or The Soldier's Return, was performed here on Saturday night, in presence of a crowded and brilliant circle. The Morning Post, 15 December, 1800 (CL 1, 226)

As writer of the Prologue and Epilogue to *Antonio* and frequent adviser to its author, Lamb was feeling particularly optimistic as the day of its first presentation neared. His refusals of invitations from both Manning and the Charles Lloyds (now homeowners at Old Brathay, Ambleside) were light-hearted. He even composed a joking letter to Godwin in excusing Mary from the dinner he and Marshal shared with Godwin at the Polygon on 7 December.

Thursday morning [December 4, 1800]

Dear Sir

I send this speedily after the Heels of Cooper[1] (O! the dainty expression!) to say that Mary is obliged to stay at home on Su[n]day to receive a female friend, from whom I am equally glad to escape. So that we shall be by ourselves. I write, because it *may* make *some* diffrence in your marketting &c—

CL

I am sorry to put you to the expence of Two Pence Poste. But I calculate thus; if Mary comes she will

eat Beef	2 plates	4d
Batter Pudding	1 do. _____	2
Beer	a pint _____	2
Wine	3 glasses _____	11 I drink no wine!
chestnuts after dinner _____		2
Tea and Supper at moderate calcn—		9
		2.6

from which deduct _____ 2 postage

You are clear gainer by her not coming— 2.4——(M 1, 249–50)

Antonio had already had a long and stormy passage at the Drury Lane, one extremely well documented. Godwin had begun this, his first play, some two years ago in sanguine confidence. He had succeeded at everything else – why should he not at drama? – especially since the younger George Colman's adaptation of *Caleb Williams*, Godwin's novel, as *The Iron Chest* had been such a success. Godwin had reaped from it (he complained) not a penny.

Fashionable tragedy called for Shakespearean blank verse, and in blank verse Godwin wrote *Antonio*. Its plot is summarized by his biographer Kegan Paul:

> Helena was betrothed, with her father's consent, to her brother Antonio's friend, Roderigo. While Antonio and Roderigo were at the wars, Helena fell in love with, and married, Don Gusman. She was the king's ward, who set aside the pre-contract. Antonio, returning, leaves his friend behind; he has had great sorrows, but all will be well when he comes to claim his bride. When Antonio finds his sister is married, the rage he exhibits is ferocious. He carries his sister off from her husband's house, and demands that the king shall annul the marriage with Gusman. There is then talk of Helena's entrance into a convent. At last the king, losing patience, gives judgment, as he had done before, that the pre-contract with Roderigo was invalid, and the marriage to Gusman valid. Whereupon Antonio bursts through the guards and kills his sister. (Paul II, 37)

Godwin worked intensively, revising a good deal. In the spring of 1799 he had an offer from Sheridan to put the play on in September. The playwright declined – and continued to revise. By June of 1800 he offered *Antonio* to Colman instead, who briefly and firmly turned it down. Godwin revised again and by September got Sheridan to accept the play for December showing. Kemble suggested further revisions. Godwin baulked; Coleridge advised him tactfully that the professionals probably knew their business. He continued to revise, perhaps accepting some of Kemble's suggestions. In delivering part of the play to Kemble he withheld the ending for further revision, and Kemble besought him to send it. The upshot of a conference between the two on 31 October was that Kemble declined to play Antonio and proposed another prominent actor, Mr Barrymore, for the part.[2]

Godwin forthwith (1 November) wrote one of his long, clear,

irritating screeds to Kemble, urging him to reconsider. A few days later he appealed to Sheridan, again at great length:

> Whether, sir, it is in your power to remove his objections I know not, but the consequence is little less than fatal to me. My story is not complicated; my incidents are not multifarious; the whole interest of the piece turns upon the energies & dignity of one character. Upon that character I have endeavoured to lay out my whole strength. . . . Had my character been of an ordinary stamp an inferior actor might have represented it. [As things are] it should be in the hands of an actor whom the public is accustomed to respect. . . .
>
> Mr. Kemble professes to have a disadvantageous opinion of the piece: I do not affect to entertain much deference for Mr. Kemble's judgment. . . . (Cameron 1, 236–8)

'I am sure, sir,' he concludes, 'you will be disposed to relieve me, if you can in this unmerited distress.'

Answering his own letter from Godwin, Kemble pointed out that 'you asked me my sincere opinion of your Tragedy, and I sincerely told you I thought it would not succeed. I am of that opinion still.'[3] But he was now bound to put it on: he begged Godwin again for the completed manuscript.

By 15 November Sheridan had exerted his pressure and Kemble wrote, 'I will undertake Antonio. I fear the event, but you shall not want the Assistance you are so good as to say I might render you.'[4]

Godwin continued to correspond: he wanted his own hated name kept out of the affair, and got the playwright John Tobin[5] to come to rehearsals that *Antonio* might be thought his.

Godwin revised and kept writing to Kemble, so frequently that Kemble once forgot what he himself had written in reply. On 2 December he said, 'I intend to advertise Antonio for Saturday se'-night, and I hope nothing will happen to prevent its being acted on that evening; though this is but a sickly season with us. . . . '[6] 'Sickly season?': Godwin became alarmed and wrote of his alarm to Kemble. Kemble responded on 9 December, 'as to next week's being *eminently* unfavourable to the Theatre, whoever told you so was eminently ignorant of what he pretended to know' – and proceeded to give examples of the successes he had had in seasons said to be sickly, ending, 'There is no time unfavourable to a work of real merit, with Judges so good, so unbiassed, and considerately

kind, as generally compose the Audiences in London.'[7] On the
brink of production Kemble noted that Godwin's latest 'Alterations
and Additions are too late; for the copy is sent to the Lord
Chamberlain; – nor do I think them material for the Stage.'[8]

Absent as he was from rehearsals in the interests of secrecy,
Godwin (while Kemble sweated) continued to see his many friends,
Lamb not least. But Lamb was forced to beg off once in the week
preceding the fateful opening on the thirteenth. He had caught
cold – the cold even kept him from the office for several days. He
recovered just in time for office and play on the Saturday. At the
East India House he picked up a letter from Manning, and in reply
hastily sent him the Epilogue. Most of it has little to do with *Antonio*,
'which is' (he told Manning) 'about promise-breaking'.[9]

It was an odd epilogue for a tragedy and Lamb had written it in
too offhand a manner – perhaps there had never, in the Godwin–
Kemble struggle, been a proper copy of *Antonio* for him to read. So
he had fallen back on his old resource, humour, producing a
pleasant enough piece of light verse which conveys something of his
own delight in the theatre but is hardly what was required even by
the relaxed standards of the day:

> Ladies, ye've seen how Guzman's consort died,
> Poor victim of a Spaniard Brother's pride,
> When Spanish honor thro' the world was blown,
> And Spanish Beauty for the Best was know[n].
> In that romantic, unenlighten'd time,
> A *breach* of *promise* was a sort of crime—
> Which of y[ou] handsome English ladies here,
> But deems the penance bloody & severe?—
> A whimsical old Saragossa fashion,
> That a dead father's dying inclination
> Should *live*, to thwart a *living* daughter's passion‖
> Unjustly on the sex *we* men exclaim,
> Rail at *your* vices & commit the same—
> Man is a promise-breaker from the Womb,
> And goes a promise breaker to the tomb— —
> What need we instance here the lover's vow,
> The sick man's purpose, or the great man's bow?—
> The Truth by few examples best is shewn—
> Instead of many, which are better known,
> Take poor Jack *Incident* that's dead & gone——

Jack, of dramatic genius justly vain,
Purchas'd a renter's share at Drury Lane,
A prudent man in every other matter,
Known at his Club room for an honest hatter;
Humane & courteous, led a civil life,
And has been seldom known to beat his wife;
But Jack is now grown quite another man,
Frequents the Green room, knows the plot & plan of each new
    piece,
And has been seen to talk with Sheridan!
In at the play house just at 6 he pops,
And never quits it till the curtain drops,
Is never absent on the *Author's night,*
Knows Actresses & actors too—by sight;
So humble, that with Suett he'll confer,
Or take a pipe with plain Jack Banister.—
Nay with an Author has been known so free,
He once suggested a Catastrophe—
In short, John dabbled till his head was turnd;
His wife remonstrated, his neighbours mourn'd,
His customers were dropping off apace,
And Jack's Affairs began to wear a piteous face.
One night his wife began a curtain lecture;
"My dearest Johnny, husband, spouse, protector,
"Take pity on your helpless babes & me,
"Save us from ruin, you from bankruptcy—
"Look to your business, leave these cursed plays,
"And try again your old industrious ways—"—

Jack, who was always scar'd at the Gazettee,
And had some bits of scull uninjur'd yet,
Promis'd amendment, vow'd his wife spake reason,
"He would not see another play that season"—
Three stubborn fortnights Jack his promise kept,
Was late & early in his shop, eat, slept,
And walk'd & talk'd, like ordinary men,—
No *wit*; but John the hatter once again—
Visits his Club:—When lo! one *fatal night*
His wife with horror view'd the wellknown sight,
John's *hat, wig, snuffbox*; well she knew his tricks—
And Jack decamping at the hour of six—

Just at the counter's edge a playbill lay,
Announcing that Pizarro was the play.—
"O Johnny, Johnny, this is your old doing."—
Quoth Jack "Why, what the devil storm's a brewing?
"About a harmless play why all this *fright*?
"I'll go & see it, if it's but for spite—
"Zounds woman! *Nelson's* to be there tonight"—(M 1, 251–4)

Charles Kemble was to speak the Prologue.[10] Lamb told
Manning that the Epilogue 'was intended for Jack Banister to
speak; but the stage managers have chosen Miss *Heard*, except Miss
Tidwell the worst actress Ever seen or *heard*— — — . . .

'I must go and dress for the Boxes! 1st night—'[11]

Godwin too was hopeful – and the most nervously hopeful of all
was the faithful James Marshal. In the grandeur and glitter of
Drury Lane all three sat together.

Did *Antonio* have any virtues at all? Coleridge thought so, but his
off-the-cuff opinions were often affected by friendship. Lamb hoped
so. Kegan Paul, Godwin's biographer, thought not:

> It will be seen that here is no human interest. We cannot at all
> sympathize with Antonio, or with the neglected lover, for whom
> we have only Antonio's word that he was an excellent man; and
> since there is no poetry in the blank verse, the effect of the whole is
> dull beyond measure or belief. (Paul II, 38)

When at last he took the stage as Antonio, Kemble, not surprisingly,
was just going through his lines. The evening was a total disaster –
not only for Godwin but for Lamb, since his contributions shared in
the derisive newspaper comment. As disaster it afforded Lamb the
writer with one of those comic opportunities which were the only
way he knew of beating the devil at his work. Many years later he
appended his vivid account of the evening to the essay 'The Old
Actors'[12] in the *London Magazine* of April 1822, after his reminiscences of Kemble:

> . . . I remember it was the fashion to cry down John Kemble
> . . . but, I thought, very unjustly. No man could deliver brilliant
> dialogue—the dialogue of Congreve or of Wycherley—because
> none understood it—half so well as John Kemble. . . . But,

indeed, John had the art of diffusing a complacent equable
dulness (which you knew not where to quarrel with) over a piece
which he did not like. . . . I remember, too acutely for my peace,
the deadly extinguisher which he put upon my friend
G.'s"Antonio." . . .

John, who was in familiar habits with the philosopher, had
undertaken to play Antonio. Great expectations were formed. A
philosopher's first play was a new era. The night arrived. I was
favoured with a seat in an advantageous box, between the author
and his friend M[arshal]. G. sate cheerful and confident. In his
friend M.'s looks, who had perused the manuscript, I read some
terror. Antonio in the person of John Philip Kemble at length
appeared, starched out in a ruff which no one could dispute, and
in most irreproachable mustachios. . . . The first act swept by,
solemn and silent. . . . The second act (as in duty bound) rose a
little in interest; but still John kept his forces under—in policy, as
G. would have it—and the audience were most complacently
attentive. . . . M. wiped his cheek, flushed with a friendly
perspiration. . . . He had once or twice during this act joined his
palms in a feeble endeavour to elicit a sound—they emitted a
solitary noise without an echo—there was no deep to answer to
his deep. G. repeatedly begged him to be quiet. The third act at
length brought on the scene which was to warm the piece
progressively to the final flaming forth of the catastrophe. A
philosophic calm settled upon the clear brow of G. as it
approached. The lips of M. quivered.

The interest failed to warm: in the third act the audience began to
cough – even the actors coughed; Kemble was frigid:

—then G. "first knew fear;" and mildly turning to M., intimated
that he had not been aware that Mr. K. laboured under a
cold; . . . from the onset [Kemble] had planted himself, as upon
a terrace, on an eminence vastly above the audience, and he kept
that sublime level to the end. He looked from his throne of
elevated sentiment upon the under-world of spectators with a
most sovran and becoming contempt.

When Antonio killed the heroine

with an irrelevancy that seemed to stagger Elvira herself—for she
had been coolly arguing the point of honour with him— . . . the

whole house rose up in clamorous indignation demanding justice.
The feeling rose far above hisses. I believe at that instant if they
could have got him, they would have torn the unfortunate author
to pieces. . . . (*Elia*, 290–4)

Lamb wrote on his playbill, 'by Godwin' and 'Damned with
Universal Consent'[13] in his best East India hand.
On Monday Lamb told Manning, 'We are damned!—'

not the facetious Epilogue itself—could save us.—For, as the
Editor of the Morning Post, quicksighted Gentleman, hath this
morning truly observed (I beg pardon if I falsify his *words*, their
profound *sense* I am sure I retain) both prologue & epilogue were
worthy of accompanying such a piece, and indeed (mark the
profundity, Mister Manning) were receivd with proper indignation by such of the audience only, as thought either worth
attending to.— —Professor, thy glories wax dim— —. Again the
incomparable Author of the True Briton declareth in *his* paper,
(bearing same date) that the Epilogue was an indifferent attempt
at humour and character, & failed in both.—I forbear to mention
the other papers, because I have not read them— —. (M I, 258–
9)[14]

Lamb had called on the Professor next day, he said, found him out
but in his study observed evidences of Godwin's hopes for success.

—the Professor has won my heart by this *his* mournful
catastrophe—
You remember Marshall, who dined with him at my house!—I
met him in the lobby immediately after the damnation of the
Professor's play, and he looked to me like an angel; his face was
lengthen'd and all over sweat; I never saw such a care-fraught
visage. I could have hug'd him, I loved him so intensely . . . the
professor's poor nerves trembling with the recent shock, he
hurried him away to my house to supper, and there we comforted
him as well as we could. He came to consult me about a change of
catastrophe— — but alas the piece was condemned long before
that crisis. I . . . have since joind his true friends in advising him
to give it up. He did it with a pang; and is to print it as *his*. (M I,
259)

Coleridge wrote to Godwin on 17 December, 'I received the [*Morning Post*] with a beating heart & laid it down with a heavy one. But cheerily, Friend! it is worth something to have learnt what will not please.'[15]

Holcroft, writing from abroad, was sure the play was doomed because Godwin's name had got out as author. He worried about Godwin's family and finances. The lovely Mrs Inchbald, actress and successful playwright, had less mercy, remembering a quarrel between herself and Godwin on his wife's death. When he sent her the play in book form she wrote,

I most sincerely wish you joy of having produced a work which will protect you from being classed with the successful dramatists of the present day, but which will hand you down to posterity among the honoured few who, during the present century, have totally failed in writing for the stage. (Paul II, 77)

Lamb made a number of notes and tentative revisions aimed at a second edition of the *Antonio* text, which was first published (with astonishing speed) by 22 December under Godwin's name. Two letters of consultation from Lamb to Godwin and a copy of the play annotated by Lamb survive – evidence of the hours he put in trying to reclaim something from the wreckage – but a second edition of *Antonio* was never called for, though Godwin continued to regard it as a masterpiece.

The two saw each other as frequently after the disaster as before; Lamb's compassion was infinite. On Christmas Day Lamb came by and took Godwin home to Southampton Buildings for dinner with Mary and the two other singletons, George Dyer and John Rickman.

There was yet another reason for the Lambs' concern. Godwin's close friend Mary Robinson, contributor to Southey's *Annual Anthology* and the Prince of Wales's abandoned 'Perdita', whom Godwin had visited constantly in the summer and autumn, lay mortally ill, and on Boxing Day (26 December) she succumbed.

Godwin recorded on 28 December in the red ink he used for events of importance, 'M. Robinson dies'. On the 27th, with his customary calm, he went to the theatre to see a frivolous piece, not allowing himself to give way to grief. On the 28th he dined at Marshal's lodgings, together with the Fells and the Lambs. On the 30th he proceeded to the funeral at Englefield Green. Among the few mourners there on 31 December only Godwin and 'Peter Pindar' the satirical poet[16] were present from the great world beyond the little village.

And so the year ended for William Godwin. Lamb, close as he was to Godwin then, would have known Perdita's story, and have heard it afresh between her death and her funeral. The fate of that gallant lady surely lent venom to the pen with which Lamb wrote his satirical verses on the 'Prince of Whales' for Leigh Hunt's *Examiner* in 1812.

CHAPTER TWENTY SIX

The Journalist: 1801–2

. . . Mister Perry, in common with the great body of the Whigs! ! thinks the
Albion very low. I find I must rise a peg or so, be a little more decent and less
abusive: for to confess the truth, I had arrived to an abominable pitch. I spared
neither age nor sex, when my cue was given me.   Lamb to Manning, 31
August 1801 (M II, 16)

I heard *that you were going to China, with a commission from the*
Wedgewoods to collect hints for their pottery, and to teach the Chinese
perspective. . . . I shall trouble you with a small present for the Emperor of
Usbeck Tartary . . . it is the fragment of a dissertation on the "state of
political parties in England at the end of the 18th Century," . . . written
originally in English for the use of the two *and* twenty *readers of the*
Albion . . . but becoming of no use, when the albion stopt, I got it translated
into Usbeck Tartar by my good friend Tibet Kulm, who is come to London
with a civil *invitation from the Cham to the English nation to go over to the*
worship of the Lama.   Lamb to Manning, same letter (M II, 15)

Lamb now had a time of relative tranquility as Mary enjoyed nearly
three years of uninterrupted sanity (June 1800 to March 1803), the
longest relief she would ever know. On 25 March 1801 – after a hint
from Gutch – they moved from Southampton Buildings back to
their beloved Temple, to the top floor of No. 16 Mitre Court
Buildings on King's Bench Walk. Here Lamb expected to find more
privacy, 'for my present lodgings', he wrote to Manning before the
move, 'resemble a minister's levee, I have so encreased my
acquaintance (as they call 'em) since I have resided in Town'.[1] It is
evident from Godwin's diary that the number of Lamb's callers
decreased little if at all, but he had two purposes requiring privacy –
the endless work on *John Woodvil* and, very soon, the stab at
journalism he had long had in mind to help make ends meet. The
expenses of moving had forced them to sell their guest bed, and the
new rent may well have been higher. Even at this time he was
lending to Coleridge and in the course of the year expecting
repayment of a £50 loan to a borrower unnamed.

He describes some of his journalistic experiences in the pleasant essay of 1831, 'Newspapers Thirty-five Years Ago' (actually thirty), though not with more than usual accuracy. He suggests that he started out on the *Morning Post* with Dan Stuart, when in fact his first regular journalism was for Fenwick's *Albion, or Evening Advertiser*. He calls the former owner of the *Albion* 'Lovell' – not his name.[2] He suggests that his own work at the India House was from eight to five when we know it was officially ten to four. He claims to have provided jokes to Stuart for a 'twelvemonth'; in a sense he did almost this, but not consecutively and not all for Stuart, so we must tread warily. 'In those days,' he says,

every Morning Paper, as an essential retainer to its establishment, kept an author, who was bound to furnish daily a quantum of witty paragraphs. Sixpence a joke—and it was thought pretty high too—was Dan Stuart's settled remuneration in these cases. The chat of the day, scandal, but, above all, *dress*, furnished the material. The length of no paragraph was to exceed seven lines. Shorter they might be, but they must be poignant. . . .

Somebody has said, that to swallow six cross-buns daily consecutively for a fortnight would surfeit the stoutest digestion. But to have to furnish as many jokes daily, and that not for a fortnight, but for a long twelvemonth, as we were constrained to do, was a little harder execution. "Man goeth forth to his work until the evening"—from a reasonable hour in the morning, we presume it was meant. Now as our main occupation took us up from eight till five every day in the City; and as our evening hours, at that time of life, had generally to do with any thing rather than business, it follows, that the only time we could spare for this manufactory of jokes—our supplementary livelihood, that supplied us in every want beyond mere bread and cheese—was exactly that part of the day which (as we have heard of No Man's Land) may be fitly denominated No Man's Time; that is, no time in which a man ought to be up, and awake, in. To speak more plainly, it is that time, of an hour, or an hour and a half's duration, in which a man, whose occasions call him up so preposterously, has to wait for his breakfast.

O those headaches at dawn of day, when at five, or half-past-five in summer, and not much later in the dark seasons, we were compelled to rise, having been perhaps not above four hours in bed—(for we were no go-to-beds with the lamb, though we anticipated the lark ofttimes in her rising—we liked a parting cup at midnight, as all young men did before these effeminate times, and to have our friends about us— . . .)

Reader, try it for once, only for one short twelvemonth. (*Elia*, 221–3)

For over a hundred and fifty years no scholar had traced remaining copies of the *Albion* until the 1960s, when ten nearly consecutive issues of June–July 1801, the time of Lamb's employment, turned up in a library at Bath, England.[3] New information has enabled us to trace its history.

In common with other outspoken radical papers, the *Albion* was subject to government prosecution in the person of its owner, the usual charges being libel, blasphemy, or sedition. As often as not the owner went to jail, selling his paper to another entrepreneur who then combined its readership with his own. On release from prison the former owner would often found a new radical paper, with a different name, as soon as financial support could be reassembled.

It has now been established[4] that the *Albion* was founded, probably by one George Ross, in September, 1799. He sold it to Allen or Allan MacLeod, in September of 1800. By November MacLeod was in jail for a libel against the Prince of Wales in his earlier paper the *Gazetteer*. (Lamb in 'Newspapers' refers to this term as that of 'Lovell' in the 'pillory'.) But we know MacLeod owned the *Albion* as late as 14 April 1801, since the following year he began a three-year sentence in Newgate for *Albion* libels on the Earl of Clare including that date. By June, 1801, Fenwick had bought the *Albion* from MacLeod and was employing Lamb. The necessary funds for purchase and support came in part from Lord Stanhope, the Duke of Northumberland, the Earl of Lauderdale, and probably Lord Petre, a leading Roman Catholic peer who welcomed the *Albion's* support of Catholic Emancipation.

Newspapers at the turn of the century were very often in someone's pay, an aspect kept as dark as possible by their owners. Stuart's *Morning Post*, before he bought it in 1795, had been the creature first of the Treasury, then of the Prince of Wales. By the time of Gillray's 'toad and frog' cartoon it was an *Anti-Jacobin* target. As a relatively independent organ, the *Albion* and its fellows were important in the development of a free press, a British–American achievement by the mid-nineteenth century which is still a rarity in the rest of the world.

The *Albion* office was at 197 Fleet Street, and Lamb may have gone there for an hour or two daily on his way to work, to assist his editor, for

> Here in murky closet, inadequate from its square contents to the receipt of the two bodies of Editor, and humble paragraph-maker, together at one time, sat in the discharge of his new Editorial functions (the "Bigod" of Elia) the redoubted John Fenwick.
>
> F., without a guinea in his pocket, and having left not many in the pockets of his friends whom he might command, had purchased (on tick doubtless) the whole and sole Editorship, Proprietorship, with all the rights and titles (such as they were worth) of the Albion, from one Lovell; of whom we know nothing, save that he had stood in the pillory for a libel on the Prince of Wales. With this hopeless concern—for it had been sinking ever since its commencement, and could now reckon upon not more than a hundred subscribers—F. resolutely determined upon pulling down the Government in the first instance, and making both our fortunes by way of corollary. For seven weeks and more did this infatuated Democrat go about borrowing seven shilling pieces, and lesser coin, to meet the daily demands of the Stamp Office, which allowed no credit to publications of that side in politics. An outcast from politer bread, we attached our small talents to the forlorn fortunes of our friend. Our occupation now was to write treason.
>
> Recollections of feelings—which were all that now remained from our first boyish heats kindled by the French Revolution, when if we were misled, we erred in the company of some, who are accounted very good men now—rather than any tendency at this time to Republican doctrines—assisted us in assuming a style of writing, while the paper lasted, consonant in no very under-tone to the right earnest fanaticism of F. Our cue was now to insinuate, rather than recommend, possible abdications. Blocks, axes, Whitehall tribunals, were covered with flowers of so cunning a periphrasis . . . that the keen eye of an Attorney General was insufficient to detect the lurking snake among them. (*Elia*, 224–5)

This must indeed have been the atmosphere and pressure under which Lamb wrote, whatever his trifling with details. He seems to have had the treason department (opinion, as opposed to straight reporting) pretty much to himself, with one or two columns of the *Albion*'s sixteen to fill up regularly, and not only with 'paragraphs': he did serious articles as well. Through the happy accident that he had been deep in the imitations of Robert Burton, and the observable fact that newspapers normally employed as few italics then as they do now, it has been possible to identify almost certainly a good many of Lamb's earliest published essays by his extravagant use of italics – à la Burton. That this was his habit is evident from the newspaper versions of articles we know to have been his, as 'The Londoner' (*Morning Post*, 1802).

Attack on government was buried in the *Albion* among columns of war news and rumour, with datelines from everywhere. Britain and France were even then negotiating in talks which were to result in the short-lived Peace of Amiens within the year, but war went on on all fronts, from India to the West Indies. The doings of Nelson, Lord Elgin, the First Consul of France Napoleon Bonaparte, Toussaint Louverture, and Alexander I (liberal new Czar of all the Russias) enlivened the *Albion*'s pages. The French journals, excerpted or summarized, provided interesting communiqués in which the British became 'the enemy', against whom in their island an expedition was contemplated. Also from Paris came news of ribbons and laces, and what Frenchwomen were wearing.

Prime Minister Pitt had resigned in February, after a disagreement with George III over the issue of Catholic Emancipation, which Pitt was anxious to pursue after the Act of Union; the King opposed relaxation. Pitt's friend the ineffectual Tory Henry Addington had taken over the nation's leadership, but the *Albion* continued to harp on Pitt's misdeeds, chiefly those concerned with national finance. Otherwise Catholic Emancipation, the ever-mounting National Debt, the wheat shortage caused by blockade, land enclosure, Ireland after the Act of Union, and non-residence of the clergy were among the Parliamentary issues stressed. Scandalous court cases were lent dignity by the comments of the brilliant advocate Thomas Erskine, and Lord Kenyon as King's Bench judge. One of the most shocking concerned the diabolical abortion pill sold by a Mr White of St. Paul's Churchyard to an adulterous Quaker, Mr F*y. A black man was seen to turn white; lightning caused freak fatalities. There were experiments with steam engines, and factory accidents to children. The gentle rambles of the (half-mad) King and his family at Weymouth were reported in loyal detail. There was something for everyone in the *Albion*, and a good deal of ground covered in ten days.

For the first time Lamb had the heady sensation of seeing whatever he wished to write printed and distributed immediately: 'In the old Albion the seal of my wellknown hand-writing was enough to drive any nonsense current.'[5] A few other writers were no doubt drawn in from time to time – Fell perhaps, Rickman, even Manning (a report from Cambridge is signed 'M.'); probably not Godwin.[6]

Lamb's very personal use of italics allows us, then, to take a leisurely look at some of his probable contributions, offering as they do new perspectives on his involvement with current events. Of his satirical 'paragraphs' the following are fair samples[7], one including a favourite poet:

> The wretched and illiberal *nationalities*, which the Ministerial Journals indulge in, against the French, as if, because we are at war with France, we must not allow a Frenchman to be a *man*, sadly bring to our mind some beautiful lines of Andrew Marvell, in a far different strain of nobleness and candor. They occur in a poem, written to discountenance the bitter animosities which subsisted in his time between the north and south inhabitants of this island.

> > The world in all does but *two nations* bear,
> > The *bad*, the *good*, and these *mix'd every where;*—
> > Under the *poles* place either of these *two*,
> > The *bad* will *basely*, *good* will *bravely* do. (1 July p. 3)[8]

Here the 'Greek professor' is Porson of Cambridge:

> The splendid political sophisms of Mr. Burke are daily served up, disfigured by ill-cookery, in the Ministerial Journals. These men, when they get a good thing into their hands, give it a *twist* by their aukward handling; like the *crooked man*, of whom a facetious Greek Professor relates this comical story, that he swallowed a *tenpenny nail*, and voided it out a cork-screw! (1 July p. 3)

A good many depend on puns, of which this is probably the worst:

> *Origin of the name of Vansittart:*—Dean Swift being at a dinner party where there was a Gentleman with a very *sour* countenance, the Dean said to him, in his punning way; "Sir, I believe you *Fancy a tart.*" The name was immediately fastened on the Gentleman, and has been continued to his descendants, who have also preserved the *characteristic features* by which it was acquired. (2 July, p. 3)

(Nicholas Vansittart, Tory MP, was later, as Baron Bexley, Chancellor of the Exchequer.)

There are many more.

We know that Lamb was an admirer of Joseph Priestley, who fled to America and there suffered the attacks of William Cobbett (author of *Rural Rides*). Cobbett had returned from America a Tory, only to turn as sharply radical a few years later. In a short, harsh article studied with italics and entitled 'Emigration to America', it is Lamb, apparently, who takes a stab at Cobbett in the *Albion* of 29 June 1801.

A longer and better piece, one that can be proved to be Lamb's, was 'What Is Jacobinism?' in the *Albion* of 30 June (page 3).[9] It contains references to people we know to be his friends, those he admired, or his literary favourites; it expresses his sympathy with the poor. Most significantly it dwells, in the last paragraph, on Lamb's quite original concern with 'general lovers' and 'general haters', which is an element in the forest scene of *John Woodvil* and later the theme of his Elia essay 'Imperfect Sympathies'.

'What Is Jacobinism?' begins humorously, with a parrot which cries 'Jacobin!' to passers-by. The subject is the wholesale labelling of political opponents with an unpopular name. (Today the parrot would have cried 'Communist!') The writer soon gets into his theme: 'After all, *what is Jacobinism*? These men have set up an universal *idol*, or *idea*, under that name, to which they find it convenient to refer *all evil . . .*' He goes on to defend certain 'Jacobins' – Opposition leader Charles James Fox and William Godwin, naming their accusers including 'Dr. P---' and 'Mr. M---h'. He defends Methodist Meetings, Sunday newspapers (then being attacked as 'atheist' – the *Albion* itself did not publish on Sunday), Whigs in general, even 'Milton, Sydney, Harrington, and Locke,' who suffered retroactive besmirching. The style is curiously laboured, intricate, and unlike Elia: a glance at *The Anatomy of Melancholy* reveals that the author has picked up not only Burton's italics but his antique style as well. What *Albion* readers made of the convoluted sentences we can only guess. ('What Is Jacobinism?' can be read in full in Appendix B.)

Another piece (of 1 July) one suspects to be Lamb's appears to be a straight news item until one thinks it over. Perhaps for this reason it lacks italics:

> We some months since mentioned the arrest, &c. of the Chinese Prime Minister Ho-xeno.— The following are the heads of the principal charges, preferred and published by order of the Emperor:—
>
> "That being in the late Emperor's life-time summoned to his country seat at Yuen-Ming-Yuen, he had entered the left door of the hall on horseback, behaving like a man who did not acknowledge the authority of his Sovereign; that he had divulged the secrets of the empire; that he had retained in his hands, or destroyed some important letters, respecting military operations in the Northern districts; that he had concealed some of the decrees of the deceased Emperor, and fabricated others in their stead; that he had encouraged vagabonds and robbers; that he had caused himself to be carried out, and brought into the Imperial Palace through the door Xin-U: that he had not reported the inability of some of the Mandarins to perform their functions; that he had in his palace many apartments built of the wood Nam Mu, a material sacred to the Royal habitation; that he had imitated the Emperor's country house in the style of his apartments, gardens, &c.; that he had in his possession 200 strings of pearls, a number far exceeding that possessed by his Royal Master; and among other jewels, a ball of coral, of wonderful magnitude and incalculable value."
>
> The gold and silver already discovered and confiscated belonging to Ho-xeno, amounts to about 1,000,000 l. (p. 4)

It is a spoof, as we learn a day or two later. Ho-xeno is really Hoax-enow, shortly to be used for editorial purposes in one of a series of attacks on Pitt's fiscal policies, most of which are signed 'R.' These do not carry heavy italics and are generally serious, with much statistical information in the final articles. Did Lamb compose the

China material for the statistical Rickman, a possible 'R.'?[10] The evidence points strongly in this direction. By late June, 1801, China was very much on Lamb's mind, since Thomas Manning had just announced his intention of going there. China-ribbing had already been a feature of some of Lamb's letters to Manning. China remained Lamb's Never-never-land, where anything might happen, for years thereafter – to the 'Dissertation on Roast Pig', best known of the Elia essays. Lamb was a confirmed hoaxer; none of his other writing friends was addicted to this kind of joke.

The next long article apparently his is the entirely serious obituary of 'The Late Lord Petre', 'the whole tenor' of whose life had been 'devoted to the cause of religious and political freedom'.[11] Petre had been an ardent fighter for the Catholic minority and was thought so well of that he had once played host for several days to George III. He had even sent a regiment to help in the King's war of 1793, asking that his son be made its commanding officer – but Catholics were ineligible for officership. Petre had to take his son's consignment to the ranks with good grace. Lord Petre's last battle was with the Post Office, as he sued to be allowed, like other members of the Lords, to frank his mail. The legal challenge met with defeat: Catholic Peers were not allowed even to take their seats in Parliament. Lamb sings his praises.

On 8 July appeared a long piece, with italics, on John Horne Tooke, whom Lamb had met in company with Godwin at dinner. Tooke had succeeded after a number of tries in being elected to Parliament, where he proved an effective opponent to Addington's government. Like so many university men, Tooke had once been ordained (indelibly) in the Anglican Church at his father's behest, though he did not pursue the clerical profession. Addington seized on the fact of his ordination and put through a bill, directed at Tooke alone, which made it illegal for clergymen to be MPs. The bill passed: Tooke was allowed only to finish his brief term. This was the kind of political behaviour which enraged Lamb, and he made the most of its injustice in 'John Horne Tooke', which begins,

A more signal testimony was never afforded, than has been in the case of Mr. John Horne Tooke, of that personal dignity, that individual importance, and that *single superiority*, claiming immediately from nature, with which the character of an incorrupt and strenuous citizen is invested, in the eyes of corrupt and time-serving politicians. (p. 2)

He makes a good case for Tooke's integrity in straightforward, effective style.

In the same issue occurs a review, entitled 'Love Letters!', of a pamphlet by a Mr Sturt vindicating himself from complicity in his cuckolding by the Marquis of Blandford. Attributable to Lamb, it is quite funny, and scurrilous enough to help the *Albion*'s sagging circulation. A second and final instalment followed a few days later.

Next day, 9 July, appears a long notice of John Stoddart's *Remarks on Local Scenery and Manners in Scotland, During the Years 1799 and 1800*. This occupies most of the *Albion's* front page. The reviewer (Lamb again, I presume) is enthusiastic, and cannot forbear quoting large chunks. An examination of the book itself indicates that the reviewer, not the author, has peppered the quoted material with italics to indicate some of its beauties. The notice finishes with a quotation Wordsworthian in feeling and grandeur, about a country Lamb himself was soon to explore from the same heights. Says Stoddart,

> "A feeling of this kind, which once absorbed my whole mind, on a mountain in Cumberland, will never be blotted from my memory. It was a bright, warm day, and I stood contemplating with admiration on a beautiful vale, with its glittering lake, rich woods, and numerous buildings. Gradually a thick mist rolled like a *curtain* before it, and took away every object from my view. I was left *alone*, on the mountain top, the *sun* shining full upon my *head*; it seemed, that I was suddenly transported into a new state of existence, cut off from every meaner association, and *invisibly united with the surrounding purity and brightness*." . . .
>
> Mr. Stoddart [says the critic] every where unites the Gentleman, the Scholar, and the Man of Taste. . . . We cannot dismiss this volume without expressing, that we have been particularly pleased with the spirit of gratitude and honest warmth, with which the author never fails to speak of Scottish kindness, and the hospitalities which he received from strangers in Scotland, as well as from those numerous friends—
>> "Who freely told to him their hearts,
>> As he did his to them." (p. 1)

This was Lamb's *Albion* writing at its best and freest, a worthy office for a deserving friend.

In this next-to-last issue of the Bath *Albion* run is the note (9 July),

MARRIED.

Yesterday, at St. Bride's Church. Randal Norris, Sub-Treasurer
to the Honourable Society of the Inner Temple, to Miss Faint, of
the Temple. (p. 4)

We know that Mary Lamb was a bridesmaid at this wedding and
enjoyed the rest of the day in Richmond with bride and groom; it
brings us very close to the Lambs. Randal Norris, their father's old
friend, later in life the only one remaining to call Lamb Charley,
was the subject of his essay 'A Death-Bed' in 1827, and Lamb kept in
touch with the former Miss Faint and her daughters to the end of his
life.

But wicked Lamb could not help being, and he did not resist
sharp thrusts at the Godwin-attacker James Mackintosh. In the
Albion of 29 June 1801, had appeared Lamb's 'paragraph',

> So, after all, it is not certain that Mr. Lecturer M--------- *has* got
> the splendid appointment to India, which was mentioned. We
> heartily wish that every man, whose honesty is *problematical*, may
> be rewarded with appointments *as problematical*. (p. 3)

By mid-August Mackintosh's fortunes had revived, or so Lamb
believed (the India appointment did not materialize until 1803),
and he thought to squash Mackintosh once and for all, at least
verbally. Did he know that Mackintosh had defended Allen
MacLeod (unsuccessfully) in the Prince of Wales libel case?[12] Had
he known, would it have made any difference? He wrote to
Manning on 31 August, 'The Albion is dead, dead as nail in door,
and my revenues have died with it.'[13] He had already given
Manning the reason:

> I will close my letter [perhaps of date 22 August] . . . with an
> Epigram on Mackintosh . . . who has got a place at last; one of
> the last I *did* for the Albion.—
> > Tho thou'rt like Judas an apostate black,
> > In the resemblance one thing thou dost lack;
> > When he had gotten his ill-purchas'd pelf,
> > He went away & wisely hang'd himself;
> > This thou may do at last; yet much I doubt,
> > If thou hast any Bowels to gush out!—(M II, 13)

Lamb says in 'Newspapers Thirty-Five Years Ago',

> Already one paragraph, and another, as we learned afterwards
> from a gentleman at the Treasury, had begun to be marked at
> that office, with a view of its being submitted at least to the
> attention of the proper Law Officers—when an unlucky, or
> rather lucky epigram from our pen, aimed at Sir J——s M——h,
> who was on the eve of departing for India to reap the fruits of his
> apostacy, as F. pronounced it, (it is hardly worth particularising),
> happening to offend the nice sense of Lord, or, as he then
> delighted to be called, Citizen Stanhope, deprived F. at once of
> the last hopes of a guinea from the last patron that had stuck by
> us; and breaking up our establishment, left us to the safe, but
> somewhat mortifying, neglect of the Crown Lawyers. (*Elia*, 225)

Before the year was out, Fenwick went on to start a new daily, *The
Plough*, with funds provided by the Duke of Northumberland; the
editor, said Lamb, gave a ball and bought new hats for his women-
folk. It too failed. In time Fenwick left his wife and children
permanently – or they left him. The Lambs continued to see her
rather more often than her easygoing husband.

Lamb told Manning on 31 August, 'I am not as a man without
hope. I have got a sort of an opening to the Morning Chronicle!!!
Mr. Manning, by means of that Common Lyar of Benevolence
Mister Dyer. I have not seen Perry the Editor yet, but I am
preparing a specimen.'[14] Perry, he said, thought the *Albion* very low.

By early September he was working for Perry; by mid-September
the *Chronicle* stint was over. 'I did something for them, but I soon
found it was a different thing writing for the Lordly Editor of the
Great Whig Paper to what it was scribbling for the poor Albion.
More than 3.4ths of what I did was superciliously rejected . . .'[15]

He thought of quitting journalism, but after return from a
holiday and a few weeks' rest he went after Dan Stuart of the
Morning Post, hoping to get theatrical reviews ('Kemble's chief
characters and Cooke's'[16]) as well as paragraphs. By late December
Stuart had hired him at two guineas a week and on 4 January
appeared his first theatrical review, based on an earlier sight of
G. F. Cooke as Richard III. He told Rickman that it was 'but an
unfinished affair at first, and by the *intelligent artifice* of the Editor was
made more chaotic still. . . . But it is most probably the last
theatrical morceau I shall do: for they want 'em done the same

night, and I tried it once, & found myself non compos. I ca'nt *do* a thing against time.'[17] He was deeply interested in Cooke as Richard, and in analysing Cooke's strengths and faults as an actor, though the critic's manner is almost as laboured as in the 'Jacobinism' article:

> The hypocrisy is too glaring and visible. It resembles more the shallow cunning of a mind which is its own dupe, than the profound and practised art of so powerful an intellect as *Richard's*. It is too obstreperous and loud, breaking out into *triumphs* and *plaudits* at its own success, like an unexercised *noviciate* in *tricks*. It has none of the silent confidence, and steady self-command of the *experienced politician*; it possesses none of that *fine address*, which was necessary to have betrayed the heart of *Lady Anne*, or even to have imposed upon the duller wits of the *Lord Mayor* and *Citizens*. . . . (*Misc.* 37–8)

Lamb told Rickman that he had also 'made the Lord Mayor's Bed' in the *Post* of 4 January, 'which you are welcome to rumple as much as you please'. This was a very short piece on an elaborate bed, by Lamb's account 'sufficiently capacious to receive two well-fed people'.[18]

'Dick Strype', another Lamb piece in the *Post*, had political undertones ('And never shall P-TT leave his juggling tricks'); it was capable light verse about a man who loved a pipe and his wife who hated it. She made him stop smoking. When she died he disappeared for a little.

> At last they found him—reader, guess you where—
> 'Twill make you stare—
> Perch'd on REBECCA's *Coffin*, at his rest,
> SMOKING A PIPE OF KIRKMAN'S BEST.
>
> (CL I, 297)

Lamb had recently said to Rickman, 'I still keep my attachment to Brandy & Tobacco, which "grow with my decay & strengthen with my weakness",'[19] at twenty-seven.

Not discouraged by the Mackintosh experience, but keeping within bounds, he tried further epigrams, two of which were published – that of Frere and Canning as schoolboys and one on Addington's sudden access to glory:

I put my night-cap on my head,
And went, as usual, to my bed:
And, most surprising to relate,
I woke—a Minister of State!

(*P*, 102)

His best piece for the *Post*, which he hoped to make a series, was 'The Londoner', which appeared on 1 February 1802. This has already been worked up in letters extolling the virtues of city as against country life to Wordsworth, Robert Lloyd, and Manning. It is a happy inspiration, and vintage Lamb. He copied it out entire for Manning's delectation; Manning admired it and urged him to write more such essays, thereby assisting the genesis of Elia.

But this success did not satisfy Stuart. 'My Editor uniformly rejects all that I do considerable in length,' he had told Rickman, and 'my poor paragraphs do only get in, when there are none of anybody's else. Most of them are rejected; all, almost, that are *personal*, where my forte lies. And I cannot get at once out of the delightful regions of scurrility, the "Delectable Mountains" of *Albion*, where whilom I fed my sheep, into the Rickshaws of fashionable tittle tattle, which I *must learn*.'[20] By mid-February, he reported that

I am no longer Paragraph spinner. The fact is, that Stuart was wonderfully polite and civil at first, I suppose because Coleridge recommend[ed] me, from whose assistance in the Paper he expected great things, but Coleridge from ill health & unsettlement having hung an Arse, as the saying is, I gradually got out of favor, and Stuart has at last twice told me, that I must take more pains about my paragraphs, for he has not been able to draw above one in five from what I have sent him. This in connection with his altered behavior was hint quite enough for me, who do not require hints as big as St. Paul's Church to make me understand a coldness, excited my magnanimous Spirit to endite a Valorous Letter of Resignation, which I did with some qualms, when I remembe[re]d what I gave up: but to tell truth, the Little I have done has been very irksome, and rendered ten times more so from a sense of my employer not being fully satisfied: and that little has subtracted from my pleasures of walking, reading, idling, &c. which are as necessary to me as the "golden vapour" of Life itself. My health (silly as it seems to relate) has suffered bitterly. The Routine has been drinking one night in noisy Company, & writing the next upon a head ach. My Spirits absolutely require freedom & leisure, & I think I shall never engage to do task work any more, for I am sick.—I must cut closer. . . . (M II, 51–2)

Dan Stuart was by now a tough newspaperman, not above some of the corrupt practices of the time such as 'stock-jobbing' – printing false reports to affect the stock market. Perhaps he did not get on well with Lamb, for Lamb's paragraphs seem up to others of the day, and when Stuart sold the *Post* in 1803 Lamb was able to return to that paper again as chief paragrapher.

Lamb speaks warmly of Stuart in the 'Newspapers' essay as 'one of the finest-tempered of Editors,' if indifferent to the fine arts, and contrasts the *Post's* 'handsome apartment', rosewood desks and silver inkstands with *Albion's* shabby quarters.[21] He finds an even less successful paragrapher in the person of his old school friend Bob Allen and makes the most of his journalistic misadventures.

Stuart wrote after Lamb's death,

[As] for good Charles Lamb, I never could make any thing of his writings. Coleridge often and repeatedly pressed me to settle him on a salary, and often and repeatedly did I try, but it would not do. Of politics he knew nothing; they were out of his line of reading and thought; and his drollery was vapid, when given in short paragraphs fit for a newspaper: yet he has produced some agreeable books, possessing a tone of humour and kind feeling, in a quaint style, which is amusing to read, and cheering to remember. (M II, 53)

Lamb continued, at intervals, to supply political commentary to other editors – as Leigh Hunt of the *Examiner*, very popular in the second decade of the nineteenth century – Stuart notwithstanding.

CHAPTER TWENTY SEVEN

Lamb and Co.: Life and Letters, 1801–2

I am never C. L. but always C. L. and Co. To Mary Hutchinson Wordworth, 1818 (CL II, 226)

He chose his companions for some individuality of character which they manifested. . . . They were, for the most part, persons of an uncertain fortune. . . . His intimados, *to confess a truth, were in the world's eyes a ragged regiment. He found them floating on the surface of society; and the colour, or something else, in the weed pleased him. The burrs stuck to him— but they were good and loving burrs for all that.* Lamb on Lamb, Preface to *The Last Essays of Elia* (*Elia*, 152).

Journalism was not all of Lamb's life in 1801 and 1802. The *Albion* took up perhaps two months, mid-June to mid-August, 1801; the *Morning Chronicle* two weeks in September, and the *Morning Post* some six weeks from early January 1801, to mid-February 1802. Around and even during these periods he was much occupied with friendship. Only some thirty-five letters survive from these two busy years,[1] something less than two a month, but from Godwin's diary we know that Lamb was at home most of this time and learn a good deal about his social life. New on the London scene was that feckless companion of Pantisocrats George Burnett, not to mention someone called the Goul, another ne'er-do-well, sometimes assistant to Rickman.

Lamb's next move after the *Antonio* fiasco was to take up an invitation from Manning, to whom he went in early January. He first pretended to have rejected it in favour of a summons to the Lakes from Charles and Sophia Lloyd, but over the page told Manning, 'Hills, woods, Lakes and mountains, to the Eternal Devil. I will eat snipes with thee, Thomas Manning. Only confess, confess a *Bite.*—'[2] Before leaving home he wrote to Manning of George Dyer's dancing about in dirty 'Nankeen Pantaloons four times too big for him', put on to impress a lady who was 'nice about these things'. Dyer

> must go to the Printer's immediately—the most unlucky ac-
> cident—he had struck off five hundred impressions of his Poems,
> which were ready for delivery to subscribers—and the Preface
> must all be expunged—there were 80 Pages of Preface, and not
> till that morning he had discovered that in the very first page of
> said preface he had set out with a principle of criticism
> fundamentally wrong, which vitiated all his following
> reasoning—the preface must be expunged, altho' it cost him
> £30——the lowest calculation taking in paper & printing—. In
> vain have his real friends remonstrated against this
> . . Midsummer madness—. George is as obstinate as a primitive
> Xtian—and wards and parrys off all our thrusts with one
> unanswerable fence—"Sir, its of great consequence that the *world*
> is not *mislead*"—. (M 1, 262–3)

Lamb thereupon dubbed George 'Cancellarius Magnus'.
The 'other Professor' (Godwin) was deep in books on Persian travel for his *new* play, but

> Vanish from my mind, Professors one and all——. I have
> metal more attractive on foot— —
> Man of many snipes,
>   I will sup with thee, Deo volente, et diabolo nolente,[3] on
> Monday night the fifth of January in the new year, and crush a
> cup to the Infant Century—(M 1, 263)

Lamb had a good time and returned to praise Manning ('a dainty chiel . . . an enchanter almost') to Robert Lloyd. By the summer of 1801 Manning – who came to London occasionally in these years – was seriously planning to go to China. Manning too was a Romantic in his way, and the lure of the unknown, the obstacles to be overcome, the ancient culture to be explored soon had him in thrall. There was a good teacher of Chinese in Paris. By the Peace of Amiens in 1802 it became possible to *go* to Paris; to Paris Manning went. Lamb's dismay at his removal is evident in the joking letters – about Napoleon, of whom Manning caught a glimpse, about the possible cannibals in 'Tartary', and the like. But Manning's will was strong and his London friend knew better than to attempt outright dissuasion.

Coleridge in Keswick and occasionally in London was often ill and increasingly disenchanted with his marriage, though not sufficiently to avoid the birth of the child Sara in 1802. To Wordsworth had fallen most of the work (and the famous Preface) of the second edition of the *Lyrical Ballads*. Lamb received a copy in January and thanked Wordsworth in a friendly letter, with his usual frank critique. This was to regret, first, that Coleridge had 'christened his Ancient Marinere "a poet's Reverie"—it is as bad as Bottom the Weaver's declaration that he is not a Lion but only the scenical representation of a Lion'. Wordsworth had included in this edition rather belittling comment on the *Mariner*, which roused Lamb to its defence. 'For me,' said Lamb, 'I was never so affected with any human Tale. After reading it, I was totally possessed with it for many days.'⁴ The long letter, praising London as against mountain regions, ended with a postscript exclamation, for he had sent *John Woodvil* to Grasmere long ago: 'Thank you for Liking my Play!!—'⁵

His letter brought forth immediate response. On 15 February he tells Manning,

> I had need be cautious henceforward what opinion I give of the Lyrical Balads.—All the north of England are in a turmoil. Cumberland and Westmorland have already declared a state of war.—I lately received from Wordsw. a copy of the second volume, accompanied by an acknowledgment of having received from me many months since a copy of a certain Tragedy, with excuses for not having made any acknowledgment sooner, it being owing to an "almost insurmountable aversion from Letter writing."— This letter I answered in due form and time, and enumerated several of the p[ass]ages which had most affected me, adding, unfortunately, that no single piece had moved me so forcibly as the Ancient Marinere, the Mad Mother, or the Lines at Tintern Abbey. The Post did not sleep a moment. I received almost instantaneously a long letter of four sweating pages from my reluctant Letterwriter, the purport of which was, that he was sorry his 2d vol. had not given me more pleasure (Devil a hint did I give that it had *not pleased me*) and "was compelled to wish that my range of Sensibility was more extended, being obliged to

believe that I should receive large influxes of happiness & happy
Thoughts" (I suppose from the L.B.—) With a deal of stuff about
a certain "Union of Tenderness & Imagination, which in the
sense he used Imag. was not the characteristic of Shakesp. but
which Milton possessed in a degree far exceeding other Poets:
which Union, as the highest species of Poetry, and chiefly
deserving that name, He was most proud to aspire
to". . . . Coleridge, who had not written to me some months
before, starts up from his bed of sickness, to reprove me for my
hardy presumption: four long pages, equally sweaty, and more
tedious, came from him: assuring me, that, when the works of a
man of true Genius, such as W. undoubtedly was, do not please
me at first sight, I should suspect the fault to lie "in me & not in
them"—&c. &c. &c &c. &c.— —What am I to do with such
people?—I certainly shall write them a very merry Letter.(M I,
272–3)

The 'merry letter' has disappeared, if it was written, but for
Manning he copied out 'She dwelt among the untrodden ways', as
the 'best Piece' in the new second volume. He was elated by the
move to the Inner Temple. In April, from his new home, he urges
Manning to

bring your glass, and I will shew you the Surrey Hills. My bed
faces the river, so as by perking up upon my haunches, and
supporting my carcase with my elbows, without much wrying my
neck, I can see the white sails gliding by the bottom of the King's
Bench walks as I lie in my bed. An excellent tiptoe prospect in the
best room: casement windows with small panes, to look more like
a cottage. (M II, 3)

He had been ill for more than a month with a bad cold – 'I am afraid
I must leave off drinking'.

In 1801 he was much with Godwin, as we learn from that Professor's
diary, seeing him five or six times a month. He reports having fallen
down in February on his way home from supper with 'new Rum' at
Godwin's 'and broke my nose'. There were many meals taken, and
evenings spent, with Fell and Fenwick; Mary was often of the party.
On 16 February 1801, he met a new group of distinguished

Londoners at Godwin's, among them Humphry Davy the chemist, who had now abandoned Bristol for the Royal Institution in Albemarle Street, where he was to give popular lectures on Galvanism. With him were James Northcote, the well-known painter, and Anthony Carlisle the surgeon. The first and last remained Lamb's friends, Carlisle sometimes his doctor.

Godwin's Persian play was soon abandoned for one called *Faulkener*, on which Lamb tried to help him in thoughtful letters. (The play, doctored by Holcroft, was produced with a prologue by Lamb in 1807.) Godwin's need for money soon became acute – and his borrowing chronic – as he found an intelligent but prickly widow, Mary Jane Clairmont, who was willing to become the second Mrs Godwin. She was a neighbour at the Polygon; she had called to him one day from her window, 'Is it possible that I behold the immortal Godwin?'[6] She was plump, pleasant to look at, and resourceful; she could cook. Very soon 'C^t' became frequent in his diary, the occasions including the Lambs as often as not. She brought with her two children of her own, Claire and Charles. Lamb described the Philosopher's happy state to Rickman in September 1801:

> the Professor (Godwin) is *Courting*. The Lady is a Widow* with green spectacles & one child,[7] and the Professor is grown quite juvenile. He bows when he is spoke to, and smiles without occasion, and wriggles as fantastically as Malvolio, and has more affectation than a canary bird pluming his feathers when he thinks somebody looks at him. He lays down his spectacles, as if in scorn, & takes 'em up again from necessity, and winks that she may'nt see he gets sleepy about eleven oClock. You never saw such a philosophic coxcomb, nor any one play the Romeo so unnaturally. (M II, 22)

Lamb's star after 'Widow' referred to his footnote, 'a very disgusting woman.—,' and this remained his attitude for life.

Godwin and Mary Jane were married in December 1801. She proved a trial to his friends, Godwin himself sometimes complaining of her temper and her 'baby sullenness for every trifle',[8] but strictly between themselves. She was nosy, often deceitful, and a gossip, three faults Lamb could not forgive; he later satirized her as 'Mrs Pry'. She caused many quarrels and coolnesses between Godwin and his old friends: with Holcroft the break ended on his

(Holcroft's) deathbed in 1809. Only Aaron Burr, the American, who knew the Godwins well in 1812, found her a 'sensible, amiable woman'.[9] Lamb complained of her in February, 1802, and things were no better by September: 'That Bitch has detached Marshall from his house: Marshall, the man who went to sleep when the Ancient Mariner was reading, the old steady, unalterable, friend of the Professor——.'[10] The frequency of Lamb–Godwin encounters did decline in 1802, but Lamb abused Mary Jane only in private, to vent his spleen. Outwardly he kept up appearances – a wise adjustment in the event, for it was Mrs Godwin who thought of turning publisher, and Lamb's and Mary's works for children would one day appear under the couple's joint imprint.

A small contretemps which took place at about the time of the *Albion*'s demise in mid-August, 1801, is revealing. It was perhaps not unconnected with the anxieties Lamb experienced just then, particularly over capsizing the *Albion* and with it John Fenwick, a family man.

Walter Wilson had been a fellow clerk of Lamb's at the India House since 1798. He was a cultured Dissenter, relative of John Walter, an owner of *The Times*, and later himself one of its owners, after a stint at bookselling and publishing.[11] Wilson tells of going on a Thames pleasure trip with Lamb and some other companions. They had a happy country afternoon, dining out, or stopping at a tavern. Lamb had a drink or two. On the way home, says Wilson,

> those in the boat found the utmost difficulty in restraining [Lamb] from the performance of some of his accustomed gambols. . . . The consequence was that the boat was within a hair's-breadth of being upset; and if none of us had received any other injury than a ducking I believe he was the only one who would have viewed it in the nature of a sport. He had placed us all, however, in imminent peril . . . (M II, 12)

Wilson wrote Lamb a protesting letter, mentioning too his distress that Lamb 'could not restrain his wit, even upon the most solemn subjects. This I considered offensive, and expressed myself accordingly.' Lamb responded with one of the few altogether sober letters of this smoky-drinky period:

August 14, 1801

Dear Wilson,

I am extremely sorry that any serious difference should subsist between us on account of some foolish behaviour of mine at Richmond; you knew me well enough before—that a very little liquor will cause a considerable alteration in me.

I beg you to impute my conduct solely to that, and not to any deliberate intention of offending you, from whom I have received so many friendly attentions. I know that you think a very important difference in opinion with respect to some more serious subjects between us makes me a dangerous companion; but do not rashly infer, from some slight and light expressions which I may have made use of in a moment of levity in your presence, without sufficient regard to your feelings—do not conclude that I am an inveterate enemy to all religion. I have had a time of seriousness, and I have known the importance and reality of a religious belief. Latterly, I acknowledge, much of my seriousness has gone off, whether from new company or some other new associations; but I still retain at bottom a conviction of the truth, and a certainty of the usefulness of religion. I will not pretend to more gravity or feeling than I at present possess; my intention is not to persuade you that any great alteration is probable in me; sudden converts are superficial and transitory; I only want you to believe that I have *stamina* of seriousness within me, and that I desire nothing more than a return of that friendly intercourse which used to subsist between us, but which my folly has suspended.

Believe me, very affectionately yours,
C. Lamb
(M II, 10–11)

Wilson could hardly fail to be mollified; he forgave Lamb at once.

The hard-working John Rickman was fashioning a career for himself with lightning speed. While still in Hampshire he had written a paper on a proposed method of taking a British census. This caught the attention of Charles Abbot, MP, and within a year of Rickman's arrival in London his proposal had been made law. By March 1801, his editorial work gave place to the superintending of Britain's first systematic population count. Soon after, Abbot became Chief Secretary for Ireland and Rickman departed for Dublin Castle as his secretary—in September, 1801.

The Southeys returned from Portugal that summer. Rickman procured a post for Southey as secretary to another official in Dublin, but Southey soon tired of bureaucracy and returned to England. He began to think seriously, at Coleridge's suggestion, of sharing the Keswick house, Greta Hall, and devoting himself to his writing. Southey in Ireland reported that Rickman was a great man in Dublin. But within six months Rickman returned with Abbot to London, glad to be home; he was courting an English girl. On Abbot's election as Speaker of the House of Commons in 1802, Rickman became Secretary to the Speaker – a secure position in which he continued for many years as he married and raised a family.

Charles Lamb came often into his Dublin correspondence. He followed Lamb's journalistic fortunes and wrote to Southey, 'When daily papers run against one another in peace, in times of no intelligence, where can such an aid be found as Lamb? I have heard wit from him in an evening to feed a paper for a week.'[12] Rickman was also concerned to help Lamb print *John Woodvil*, as Lamb now threatened to do out of his own pocket.

Again to Southey:

Tell Lamb I want to hear from him, and of his play. I shall receive money enough (from the Population business) soon, and he may draw largely on that projected publication. Though as a *play* (in the abstract) it is not good, there is much too good to be lost in it, besides I wish to give the world one more chance of shewing taste. (Williams, 64–5)

In early 1802 it came out, together with a poem or two, the Burton imitations, and Mary's poem 'Helen'. Lamb himself spent £25 or more on the printing, but refused Rickman's offer until the *Morning Post* money ended, when he granted that 'Your Guineas (which let me tell you are too much)'[13] would be useful – and allowed the subsidy.

Rickman was for a long time very patient with George Burnett, whom Lamb soon christened George II, George I being Dyer.

Burnett was the constant worry of all from the time (1801) he abandoned a Unitarian country ministry to come to London, where for brief intervals he tried every form of job his friends could devise or obtain for him – as editorial hack, writer, statistical assistant, clerk, copy boy. All were beneath him or presented unusual difficulties (a Lion is in his footpath, said Lamb[14]). He was said to be brilliant – he published two books – and even lovable. But he had a tiresome way of blaming his friends for his troubles. He exhausted Rickman's patience and Southey's; Lamb was baffled; even kindly George Dyer declared to Rickman, 'I *must* give up *Burnett*, for, I fear, his will prove [a] case of distress, unless you can find some snug berth for him in Ireland; you know the man.'[15]

Rickman knew, and did not pursue the suggestion. Then – probably through the resurgent Dyer – Burnett suddenly fell upon the ideal employment, that of tutor to Lord Stanhope's two sons, who by an earlier plan unrelated to Burnett immediately ran away from home.[16] Says Lamb to Rickman:

> George declares, that he is only sorry on Lord Stanhope's account, who is much agitated, but on his own he dont care at all: nay I have no doubt he is ready to leap at his heart, for Lord S. desires he will stay in his house, & he will try to get him something. So George has got his old desirable prospect of food & clothing with no Duty to perform for it. I could fill vols. with a History of his absurdities since the date of my Last——. Take one or 2. Imprimis he overstay'd his 3 weeks—then he wrote to Lord S from town to write to him, but forgot to mention his own address—then he was forced to write again to say he forgot, & begg'd his Lordship to tell him the Exact situation where his Lordships House stood, that he might have no trouble in finding it!!! to write to a Peer of the Realm to tell the Number of his house! Then he determines to set off for Chevening[17] next morng. & writes that he will come down by the 8 oClock stage—then he comes to us the Night before at 11 & complains bitterly of the difficulty of getting up so early—then he goes away & White & I lay wagers that he wont go at all. Next Morning 11 oClock— Enter Geo. the 2d. in a dirty neckcloth—he could not go, because he had no Linen, & he had not time to go to Southey to borrow it, & inadvertently slips out that to be sure there was a Coach went at $\frac{1}{2}$ pas 10—then my Tutor gapes & stares, & borrows a neckcloth & sets off with all proper humility to My Lord's in a Post

Chaise—drives up to the Door in Style—& there I leave him bowing and gaping to see the fine Pictures— (M II, 49–50)

For nearly a year Burnett ran minor errands for His Lordship and enjoyed his idle life, until Stanhope let him go with £200 – to fall back on his London friends once more.

Yet another of the burrs who stuck to Lamb may have been 'Captain Jackson', subject of an Elia essay. 'Jackson' was poverty-stricken but incurably hospitable, with the expansive manners of the well-to-do and much gratitude for his poor pickings. There have been several conjectures as to his identity, but it remains obscure.

The most interesting of the fey friends, George Dyer, continued to provide Lamb with merriment and concern. First George published his *Poems* early in 1801, *sans* Preface, as Lamb told Manning:

At length George Dyer's 1st vol. is come to birth.—One volume of three. . . . I paid two guineas for you and myself, which entitle us to the whole.— I will send you your copy, if you are in a *great hurry*. Meantime you owe me a Guinea. George skipped about like a pea with its arse scorched, at the receipt of so much Cash.— To give you one specimen of the beautiful absurdity of the Notes, which defys imitation, take one. "Discrimination is not the *aim* of the present volume. It will be more strictly attended to in the next."—One of the Sonnets . . . is entitled the Madman, "being collected by the author from several madhouses"; it begins, Yes, yes, tis He.— (M I, 274)

In late October, 1801, George was in a parlous state. Lamb to Rickman:

A letter from G. Dyer will probably accompany this. I wish I could convey to you any notion of the whimsical scenes I have been witness to in this fortnight past. Twas on Tuesday week the poor heathen scrambled up to my door about breakfast time. He came thro' a violent rain with no neckcloth on & a *beard* that made him a spectacle to men & angels and tap'd at the door. Mary open'd it & he stood stark still & held a paper in his hand importing that he had been ill with a fever. He either wouldn't or couldn't speak except by signs. When you went to comfort him he put his hand upon his heart & shook his head & told us his complaint lay where no medicines could reach it. I was dispatch'd for Dr. Dale, Mr. Phillips of St. Paul's Church yard & Mr. Frend who is to be his executor. George solemnly delivered into Mr. Frend's hands & mine an old burnt preface that had been in the fire with injunctions which we solemnly vow'd to obey that it should be printed after his death with his last corrections & that some account should be given to the world why he had not fulfill'd his engagement with subscribers. Having done this & borrow'd two guineas of his bookseller . . . he laid himself down on my bed in a mood of complacent resignation. By the aid of meat & drink put into him (for I all along suspected a vacuum) he was enabled to sit up in the evening, but he had not got the better of his intolerable fear of dying; he expressed such philosophic indifference in his speech & such frightened apprehensions in his physiognomy that if he had truly been dying and I had known it I could not have kept my countenance. . . .

The doctor came and prescribed powders.

The fact was he had not had a good meal for some days & his little dirty Neice (whom he sent for with a still dirtier Nephew & hugg'd him; & bid them farewell) told us that unless he dines out he subsists on tea & gruels. And he corroborated this tale by ever & anon complaining of sensations of gnawing which he felt about his *heart* which he mistook his stomach to be & sure enough these gnawings were dissipated after a meal or two & he surely thinks that he has been rescued from the jaws of death by Dr. Dale's white powders.

Lamb saw what was needed.

I have proposed to him to dine with me. . . . I will take his money beforehand & he shall eat it out. If I don't it will go all over the world. Some worthless relations of which the dirty little devil that looks after him & a still more dirty nephew are component particles, I have reason to think divide all his gains with some lazy worthless authors that are his constant satellites. The literary Fund has voted him seasonably £20 & if I can help it he shall spend it on his own carcase. (M II, 28–30)

Mary Lamb had nursed him and Charles wrote letters from Dyer's dictation. Southey saw Dyer soon after and reported that 'Lamb has made a perfect cure'.[18]

In January of 1802 Lamb described his own life to Rickman, with a touch of G. D. and another of his noble friends:

> I have delayed to write (I believe I am telling a Lye) until I should get a book ready to send (but I believe this has been all along a pretext . . . rather than the true cause, which was mixed up of busy days & riotous nights, doing the Company's business in the morning, straining for Jokes in the afternoon, and retailing them (not being yet published) over punch at night). The Lungs of Stentor could not long sustain the Life I have led. I get into parties, or treat them with Pope Joan [a card game] four times in a week—. You have dropt in eer now when Norris was courting at such a Party, and you know the game. I stick to it like any *Papist*. Tis better than Poetry, Mechanics, Politics, or Metaphysics—. That's a stop—there's pope—you did not take your ace—what a magic charm it sounds— —. . . .
>
> Dyer has at last met with a madman more mad than himself— the Earl of Buchan . . . this old man of near eighty is come to London on his way to France, & George & he go about every where—. George brought the mad Lord up to see me—I wa'nt at home but Mary was washing—a pretty pickle to receive an Earl in! Lord have mercy upon us a Lord in my Garratt! my utmost ambition was at some time or other to receive a Secretary! well, I am to breakfast with this mad Lord on Sunday. I am studying manners. . . . George is as proud as a Turkey Cock & can talk of nothing else; always taking care to hedge in at the end, that he don't value Lords, & that the Earl has nothing of the Lord about him. O human nature! human Nature! for my part I have told every Body, how I had an Earl come to see me— —.
> (M II, 42-3)

(Buchan was brother to Thomas Erskine, defence counsel at the 1794 Treason Trials.)

After reporting Burnett 'happy as the Great Mogul' with Stanhope, Rickman was critical (to Southey) of the next George Dyer development, in February 1802:

Of the other George I have more doleful tidings. Mary Lamb and her brother have succeeded in talking him into love with Miss Benjay or Bungey or Bungay; but they have got him into a quagmire and cannot get him out again, for they have failed in the attempt to talk Miss Bungey or Benjey into love with him. This is a cruel business, for he has taken the injection, and it may probably soon break out in sonnets and elegies. (Williams, 75–6)

The lady was of course the bluestocking Elizabeth Ogilvie Benger; we hear of the affair only from Rickman. George survived the experience as he had survived much else. Shortly a committee of his friends was set up to provide him with an annuity: Lord Stanhope sent £50.

A few days later Lamb wrote to Rickman:

Frend was here yesterday. He desires me to set down every day Dyer dines with me, & the Committee will pay me, as George is to have no money of his own. George contrives constantly to dine here. . . . Now he is got well, he is freakish as King David at Gath. Nothing can be done with him; save that the Committee will preserve him from felo de se, that he shant starve himself. (M II, 53)

So much for the extraordinary assortment of London friends. Lamb had one holiday in 1801, just after the collapse of his *Chronicle* engagement – in September he and Mary went for two weeks to the seaside at Ramsgate. By August of 1802 he had a month's holiday coming, and, yearning for a sight of Coleridge,[19] arrived unexpectedly at Greta Hall in Keswick, again with Mary.

Coleridge had had an uncomfortable year as opium made inroads on his health. In March 1801 he had told Godwin that the poet was dead in him. Sara Coleridge was growing plump with the coming baby Sara, but their domestic life was no longer the happy one of Nether Stowey and the Lambs observed them quarrelling. Coleridge was now pursuing his interest in Sara Hutchinson, whose sister Mary would marry William Wordsworth in October. At the time of the Lambs' visit to the Lakes Dorothy and William were in France, sorting out the matter of his illegitimate daughter by Annette Vallon and preparing the latter for his English marriage.

Coleridge was often alone on the mountains of his beautiful district, and he wrote to Sara Hutchinson some lively accounts of his energetic rambles, on one of which the Lambs were with him. But the holiday (10 August to 5 September) is for Lamb to describe, as he told it to Manning on 24 September 1802.

> I set out with Mary to Keswick, without giving Coleridge any notice, for my time being precious did not admit of it; he received us with all the hospitality in the world, and gave up his time to shew us all the wonders of the country. He dwells upon a small hill by the side of Keswick, in a comfortable house, quite enveloped on all sides by a net of mountains: great floundering bears & monsters they seem'd, all couchant & asleep. We got in in the evening, travelling in a Post Chaise from Pe[n]rith, in the midst of a gorgeous sun shine, which transmuted all the mountains into colours, purple &c. &c. We thought we had got into Fairy Land. But that went off (as it never came again, while we stayed, we had no more fine sun sets) and we entered Coleridge's comfortable study just in the dusk, when the mountains were all dark with clouds upon their heads. Such an impression I never received from objects of sight before, nor do I suppose that I can ever again. . . . Coleridge had got a blazing fire in his study, which is a large antique ill-shaped room, with an old fashioned organ, never play'd upon, big enough for a church, Shelves of scattered folios, an Eolian Harp, & an old sofa, half bed &c. And all looking out upon the last fading view of Skiddaw & his broad-breasted brethren: What a night!— . . .

There they stayed three weeks, visited the Clarksons[20] – 'good people and most hospitable' – for a day or two and saw Lloyd. (Clarkson had damaged his health pursuing his slavery research and had retired to the Lakes to regain it.) Lamb reported that the

> Wordsworths were gone to Calais. They have since been in London, & past much time with us: he is now gone into Yorkshire to be married, to a girl of small fortune. . . . So we have seen Keswick, Grasmere, Ambleside, Ulswater (where the Clarksons live) and a place at the other end of Ulswater, I forget the name, to which we travelled on a very sultry day over the middle of Helvellyn.— We h[a]ve clambered up to the top of Skiddaw, & I

have waded up the bed of Lodore. In fine I have satisfied myself, that there is such a thing as that, which tourists call *romantic*. . . .

Mary had been very tired on Skiddaw, but they 'came to a cold rill' and 'with the reinforcemt. of a draught of cold water, she surmounted it most manfully'.

> It was a day that will stand out, like a mountain, I am sure, in my life.—But I am returned (I have now been come home near 3 weeks (I was a month out)) & you cannot conceive the degradation I felt at first, from being accustommed to wander free as air among mountains, & bathe in rivers without being controuled by any one, to come home & *work:* I felt very *little*. I had been dreaming I was a very great man. . . . My habits are changing, I think; i.e. from drunk to sober: whether I shall be happier or no, remains to be proved. . . . O Manning, if I should have formed a diabolical resolution, by the time you come to England, of not admitting any spirituous liquors into my house, will you be my guest on such shame worthy terms? Is life, with such limitations, worth trying.—The truth is that my liquors bring a nest of friendly harpies about my house, who consume me.— (M II, 68–70)

Lamb had thanked Coleridge, indicating that he saw little of the Charles Lloyds in this visit, though they were living nearby. The Wordsworths while in London had stayed, Lamb said, with Basil Montagu near the Temple: 'They dined with us yesterday, & I was their guide to Bartlemy Fair!'[21] – Bartholomew Fair, the annual event, was Lamb's delight but not Wordsworth's. *He* found it a vulgar 'Parliament of Monsters', microcosm of London itself, and so described it in his *Prelude*.[22] (Lamb's innocent enthusiasm, as he led the sensitive Lake Poet and his sister through the deafening fairground tumult proved his unwitting revenge for Wordsworth's scolding over the second *Lyrical Ballads*.)

In Keswick Lamb had, as usual, fallen for a child. He finishes his letter to Coleridge with a question about two-year-old Derwent, whose pronunciation of flying opossum had won him a new nickname:

> Particularly tell me about little *Pi-Pos* (or flying Opossum) the only child (but one) I ever had an inclination to steal from its

parents. That one was a Beggar's brat, that I might have had cheap. I hope his little Rash is gone. (M ii, 66)

They had had a happy time, Coleridge's misery (and the misty weather) not withstanding, for Coleridge could rouse himself to hospitality and forget his misery. With Coleridge Lamb began his friendships and with the visit to Coleridge we shall end.

One more intimate remains to be heard from. The closest friend of all wrote to Sarah Stoddart in December (Miss Stoddart was then in Salisbury) a letter which brings herself, Charles, John Stoddart, and his sister into full view as Mary Lamb saw them:

Decr 1 [1802]

My dear Miss Stoddart

I am truly and heartily ashamed of myself, I have been so very long without writing to you. I have nothing to offer in excuse. I have been very ill but that has been only these few weeks past: . . .

I have been to the Lakes,—in a long jou[r]ney of three hundred miles, and a month passed in scenes so new and strange to me, I ought to have picked up something worth telling you about, but my dull head, cannot just now recollect a single circumstance I think will entertain you. My poor head is just now full of the memory of our walks together—driving along the Strand so fast (lest the scotch broth should be spoiled in our absence) we were ashamed of shewing of red faces at your friend's in westminster, or bustling down Fleet-Market-in-all-its-glory of a saturday night, admiring the stale peas and co'lly flowers and cheap'ning small bits of mutton and veal for our sunday's dinner's, returning home in all haste, to be scolded for not laying the cloth in time for supper (albeit it being nine o'clock) and then chidden for laughing in an unseemly manner. I have never half liked being at your brothers rooms since you left them:—they[23] sit and preach about learned matters, while I turn over an old book, and when I am weary look in the window in the corner where you and your work-bag used to be, and wish for you to rout them up and make us all alive.

Your brother promises you shall be in town again after christmas, I look forward to the time with very great pleasure. . . . I have seen the famous Dr Stoddart in his fine scarlet robes,[24] unfortunately the wig was at the barbers, so that I saw but half the show: we will have another grand exhibition when you come, if you will promise not to laugh.

If you will forgive my ill usage and be a good natured girl and write to me directly I will promise always to answer your letters immediately, and I will try to be less-dull another time, but I am not yet half well, my head ach's, and my spirits are very indifferent.

God bless you, Charles sends his love

I am your most affectionate friend

M Lamb

(M ii, 89–90)

If Charles Lamb had suffered much, and failed at much, by 1802 he had served his apprenticeship as a writer, especially in the marvellous letters, and built a life from unpromising materials with exemplary courage. He was not quite twenty-eight; he would publish no more of consequence for several years. Meanwhile his philosophy, his politics, and his social pattern were set, Mary Lamb's well-being as secure as he could make it, his early acquaintance changing. Coleridge, ever more restless and opium-addicted, would leave his family and eventually join John Stoddart in the more healthful climate of Malta, where Stoddart by 1804 was married and King's Advocate. The Lloyds, cooling perhaps, were far away. Southey, installed in Greta Hall, Keswick, would soon find himself in permanent charge of all three Fricker sisters and their offspring. Godwin, married, was less accessible. Manning, in Paris, would return to England for a while before setting sail for the Far East. Only a few of the old friends remained in London. By 1803 the Lambs began to meet a new circle, always including the burrs and those others (such as Thomas Holcroft, home from the Continent) whose conversation so impressed young William Hazlitt as he became one of them. Before very long – through the emotional ups and downs attendant on Mary's recurrent madness – many of the Romantic writers who made the literary history of their time would be found, on established 'evenings', before the warm and cheerful if often-changing hearths of Charles and Mary Lamb.

But that is another story.

Appendix A

The three Nehemiah Higginbottom sonnets contributed by Coleridge to the *Monthly Magazine* for November 1797 (from BL, 14–15):

SONNET I

Pensive at eve, on the *hard* world I mused,
And *my poor* heart was sad; so at the Moon
I gazed, and sighed, and sighed: for ah how soon
Eve saddens into night! mine eyes perused
With tearful vacancy the *dampy* grass
That wept and glittered in the *paly* ray:
And I *did pause me* on my lonely way
And *mused me* on the *wretched ones* that pass
O'er the bleak heath of sorrow. But alas!
Most of *myself* I thought! when it befel,
That the *soothe* spirit of the *breezy* wood
Breath'd in mine ear: 'All this is very well,
But much of *one* thing is for *no* thing good.'
Oh *my poor heart's* Inexplicable Swell!

SONNET II

Oh I do love thee, meek Simplicity!
For of thy lays the lulling simpleness
Goes to my heart and soothes each small distress,
Distress tho' small, yet haply great to me.
'Tis true on Lady Fortune's gentlest pad
I amble on; and yet I know not why
So sad I am! but should a friend and I
Frown, pout and part, then I am *very* sad,
And then with sonnets and with sympathy
My dreamy bosom's mystic woes I pall;
Now of my false friend plaining plaintively,
Now raving at mankind in general;

341

But whether sad or fierce, 'tis simple all,
All very simple, meek Simplicity!

Sonnet III

And this reft house is that, the which he built,
Lamented Jack! and here his malt he piled,
Cautious in vain! these rats that squeak so wild,
Squeak not unconscious of their father's guilt.
Did he not see her gleaming thro' the glade!
Belike 'twas she, the maiden all forlorn.
What though she milk no cow with crumpled horn,
Yet, *aye* she haunts the dale where *erst* she strayed:
And *aye* beside her stalks her amorous knight!
Still on his thighs their wonted brogues are worn,
And thro' those brogues, still tattered and betorn,
His hindward charms gleam an unearthly white.
Ah! thus thro' broken clouds at night's high Noon
Peeps in fair fragments forth the full-orb'd harvest-moon!

Appendix B

Lamb's earliest known published essay first appeared in my article 'New Lamb Texts from *The Albion?* Part 1', in *CLB*, Jan. 1977, pp. 6–9, which see for my arguments in proof of authorship (pp. 9–11). The complete Lamb text:

WHAT IS JACOBINISM?

We were led into the train of thoughts which follow, by the circumstance of having been amused with a *parrot*, which a bookseller in Pall-Mall has taught to cry *Jacobin* to the passers by. We suddenly found *ourselves* accosted with this opprobrious epithet, and not perceiving at first the source from which it came, were inclined to be angry, and resent the injury; but we laughed heartily, when we discovered, that the voice proceeded from this *green goose*, which the ingenious bookseller had instructed to become the vehicle of his own party spleen. It brought us to reflect, what were the common grounds and motives, upon which *men*, not more discriminating than this *parrot*, were led to bestow the uncivil language of party, and brand better men than themselves with Jacobinism. After all, *what is Jacobinism?* These men have set up an universal *idol*, or *idea*, under that name, to which they find it convenient to refer *all evil*, something like the *Manichean principle*. To define the boundaries and the natures of human action, to analyse the complexity of motives, to settle the precise line where *innovation* ceases to be *pernicious*, and *prejudice* is no longer *salutary*, is a task which requires some thought, and more candour. It is an easier occupation, more profitable, and more fitted to the malignant dispositions of these men, violently to force into *one class*, modes and actions, and principles *essentially various*, and to disgrace that *class* with one ugly name: for *names* are observed to cost the memory and application much less trouble than *things*. *Jacobinism* originally designated a faction of men, who from France newly republicanized, desired to introduce their own improvements, as they thought, among the surrounding nations, at the expence of rooting up of ancient usages,

343

prejudices, and the forms *politic* of old and hoary prescription. Among those who entertained sad apprehensions of the motives, the energies, and the probability of success, of these men, *Jacobinism* naturally became a word of reproach: at least, the propriety of the bare and confined application of it none could deny.—In fact, the *Jacobin Club* had been its own godfather, and christened itself with the name, which it could not blame its adversaries for *adopting* with some degree of asperity. *Names* often associated with hostile and unpleasant feelings, in turn engender and augment those feelings, and the *thing* Jacobinism began to be disliked for the *name* of *Jacobin*. All this was natural, and in the every day course of allowable political warfare. But a *name* was an advantage, not so easily to be exhausted, or so confinedly to be limited. It became, like *John* or *Peter*, general appellatives of vast classes of men, differing *in toto* in all else but the appellation. Was a man of penetrating and almost *prophetic* reach of mind, gifted like Mr. Fox, with a correspondent kindness of soul, desirous to put a stop to the idle waste of blood, in the mad attempt to thrust a code of distasteful principles down the reluctant throat of a Great Nation; the hireling writers of the day had their cue given them, and the exalted name of Mr. Fox was unnaturally and basely leagued with the invidious opprobrium of Jacobinism. Did a man, like Mr. Godwin, of long views, and an ardent thirst for the amelioration of his species, who in exulting visions of the *possible future* sought repose for his mind, wearied and fatigated with the consideration of the *actual state* of mundane affairs, did such a man, in an amiable enthusiasm of speculation, trace in the accelerating operation of a grand principle, a *time*, when vice, and error, and misery, "with all their disgustful circumstances, as they now exist in the world, shall be ultimately thrown off, of [*sic:* or?] the burden greatly diminished; when man shall cease to *walk in a vain show and to disquiet himself in vain;*" did he seek to hasten the progress of these "days of greater virtue and more ample justice," which, as he believes, are to "descend upon the earth," by no violence, by nothing but the silent operation of principle, and trusting to the unarmed and naked truth? *he* too came under the convenient name of *Jacobin*. The author of *The Pursuits of Literature* tuned the *pitch pipe;* the yelping *treble,* and the growling *bass,* of Porcupines, True Britons, and Anti-Jacobin Reviewers, took up the note, and the respectable name of Dr. P---, and the *once* respectable name of Mr. M---h, were not ashamed to be found *hallooing* and encouraging the pack. But the instances we have chosen were distinguished characters, *nomina memorabilia*, intellectual *Goliahs* [*sic*] against whom these dextrous *Davids* might be allowed to hurl the sharpest stones in their artillery [:] had large views, and ample theories of benevolent purpose to mankind, which these men had neither the mind to *grasp*, nor the soul to *embrace*; their only alternative was to *depreciate*. But what shall we say to their malign attacks upon persons and objects most *foreign* to politics? upon *Methodist meetings*, where the religion or superstition of devout men resort to have their fires *kindled*, and their imaginations *entertained*, and their passions *fed*, with more intense fires, with more earnest appeals, and more highly seasoned food of rhetoric, than they can find in the *cold manner*, and *colder matter*, of established preachers? upon *Sunday schools*, where the children of poor people receive the alms of a little more knowledge, and a little more morality (for is it not a *little*?) than they could otherwise attain, as society is sadly constituted? upon the Unitarian Christian, who believes a little *less*, and the zealous Calvinist, who believes a little *more*, than themselves? upon *Sunday newspapers*, which disseminate among the lower orders of men some knowledge (not to be otherwise attained) of the state of public affairs, of the conduct of men in office, in which they are so deeply concerned; and, *what is more valuable*, by representing the daily occurrences of domestic events, births, and deaths, and marriages, and benefits, and calamities, and sad accidents of individuals or families, with all the multitudinous "goings-on of life," teach their readers to be *men*, by the link of human interest, and human passion, to human affairs; transferring their rude and partial domestic feelings over a wide range of sympathy with *strangers* and persons *unknown*, which is reflected back with accumulated intenseness upon that charity which they are to manifest in relationships *which they do know:* add, that the poor man finds his *consequence* increased, and himself to be *something* in the "list of men," when the power of judging, and reasoning, and censuring public measures, and private actions, is put into his hands. And who would grudge to the poor a consequence so *imaginary*, and an importance so *harmless*, which in some sort repays him for what he is liable to suffer by the insolence of wealth, and assumptions of men in office? But he who *reads*, and he who *vends*, Sunday Prints, is alike branded with the calumniating name of *Jacobin*, and *profane*, and *Atheist*; by scurrilous

Ministerial Papers, and abusive sermons. What is religion? is it grimace, and talk, and a solemn face of *abstraction*, which enters not into human interests? or, rather, does not a great part of it *consist* entirely of human interests, the *nil humani alienum* so beautifully expressed by *Terence*? — and what promotes this generous feeling more strongly, than that *humane* and *virtuous curiosity*, which *accounts* of public and private *accidents* in *histories* and *newspapers* (the *poor* man's *history books*), both excite and satisfy? Are the duties of prayer and attendance upon sermons at all slackened or weakened by the man's having access in the intervals to a newspaper? Ridiculous! as if the assertors themselves of this idle calumny absolutely confined themselves on the sabbath to praying, preaching, and psalm-singing! as if *they* never employed themselves in the profane *intervals* of that day with enquiries and discussions of the affairs of *individuals*, for the purpose of curiosity or *malevolence*!

We have not yet exhausted the *hundredth* part of the subjects and persons, upon whom this unattaching and stupid accusation of *Jacobinism* has been flung. The judge of *military* tactics, who, judging on *scientific* principles, has discovered, that Bonaparte or Moreau are fine and accomplished *Generals*; that man is a *Jacobin*. The man, who, appreciating accurately the awful talents, which are required to conduct at a delicate crisis the affairs of a great nation, pauses before he can believe, that a Mr. Add*ngton, or a Mr. P*bus, is competent to the task; he is a *Jacobin*. To enumerate one tythe of instances would exhaust our readers and ourselves: since, in a word, *all* persons, and *all* things, to which these calumniators are *hostile* (and what can bound or describe the *infinite* malice and hostile feelings of hatred and calumny, or *count the number* of their *dislikes*?) these are *Jacobins* and *Jacobinical*. Not content with *living* names, they persecute and spoil the *dead*, with whom man should *not war*; and pass sentence of *Jacobinism backwards* upon such men as Milton, Sidney, Harrington, and Locke. It is sufficient, that these benefactors to mankind sought the happiness of their species in *ways* which *they* cannot *understand*. We have heard of *general lovers*, though we dislike the character: but these men are a sort of *general haters*, and discredit and cry down, at random, all that is *new*, and *good*, and *useful*. (*The Albion, and Evening Advertiser*, Tuesday, 30 June 1801, p. 3)

Note: Disguised names include Parr, Mackintosh, and Charles Pybus.

Notes

CHAPTER 1: STARTING OFF

1. *Elia*, 82.
2. *Elia*, 89.
3. It is interesting that the issue of the *London Magazine* just preceding that containing Lamb's 'Old Benchers of the Inner Temple' carried, in August 1821, a humorous poem in imitation of Spenser describing a man almost certainly Salt. This has been attributed with good reason to Lamb, who certainly knew the poem and even quoted a line from it in 'Old Benchers': 'Of building strong, albeit of Paper hight', a reference to the Temple's Paper Buildings. The protagonist of 'The Lawyer: A Picture' lived in the Paper Buildings, had a 'roguish clerk' and went into Parliament. He had little success there fighting 'Freedom's cause,' says the poet, and was a victim of ministerial 'Expediency' – i.e. that of William Pitt the Younger. References to 'proud Oppression's chains' and 'swol'n Corruption' show that Lamb in 1821 shared Salt's Whiggism, as we know he did from other sources. There is admiration as well as affection in the portrait of the man who died when Lamb was seventeen. See Hood (ed. Jerrold) 172–84.
4. Or possibly only the cobbler's widow and children. Perhaps they joined relatives already living in Lincoln, since John was one of the 'mountaineers' – says Lamb in 'Poor Relations' – from the higher and more fashionable part of the town as opposed to their humbler schoolboy rivals, the 'Below Boys' who dwelt down the hill. According to the essay one 'Mr. Billet', a 'poor relation', had been a schoolfellow of his father, John Lamb, and was a 'Below Boy'. See Charles Garton, 'Lamb's Paternal Forebears', *Notes and Queries*, Nov. 1969, 420, and *Elia*, 162.
5. M I, 52.
6. See Phyllis G. Mann, 'Notes by the Way', in *CLSB*, Jan. 1959, 221.
7. The picture we can put together from other evidence shows Elizabeth the more or less typical parent of the manic depressive – Mary – though Charles was also inclined to experience depressions, less severe. A dutiful mother, she lavished her *love* particularly on her elder son – and tended to be critical of Charles and Mary. Nevertheless, depression may run in families, and so may stammering – more usually called stuttering in the USA. (Some sources make a distinction between the two, but these are so varied as to be hardly worth recording; stammering, says one authority, is the polite word for stuttering.)

   In 1977 Gerald Jonas, himself a stutterer and a writer on science for the *New Yorker*, published a book called *Stuttering: The Disorder of Many Theories* (New York: Farrar, Straus, 1977). Mr Jonas is not entirely convinced by any theory but quotes a persuasive observation by the late Wendell Johnson of the Iowa Speech Clinic. Between ages three and five, says Johnson, the child 'learns to doubt that he can talk smoothly enough to please the people he talks to, mainly his parents. . . . He learns to fear what will happen if he doesn't. What this amounts to is that he learns to be afraid that "he will stutter". . . . Instead of just talking, he tries to talk "without stuttering", by doing things like pressing his lips together tightly, or holding his breath – but these are the things that he, and everyone else, calls his stuttering. Stuttering then is what the stutterer does by trying not to stutter' (p. 31).

A distinguished group of experts led by the editor, Dominick A. Barbara, a psychoanalyst specializing in speech disorders, wrote a book in 1965, *New Directions in Stuttering* (Springfield, Ill.: Thomas, 1965). They found, in nearly all cases of stuttering they had encountered, a dominant parent – critical, strict, tense, and either cool or overprotective – who managed to raise a great deal of anxiety in the child. The typical stuttering child tended, like Lamb, to be both shy and physically awkward.

Boys tend to stutter from four to eight times as often as girls because their role in our society is, from an early age, more competitive, especially in physical activity. Stuttering may start as the result of a severe emotional shock; more often it is the result of undue parental concentration on a child's minor and developmental speaking faults. Once started on his neurotic way, the severe stutterer develops an intense self-consciousness, a sense of inferiority, and, as in all neuroses, a number of serious frustrations breeding serious resentments. Such a situation surely explains some of Lamb's odd and hostile behaviour, particularly with strangers, who were coming upon his impediment for the first time. Some children do outgrow their early difficulty, or conquer it, or find that it grows less severe. Lamb's stammering late in life (but perhaps not early in life) was 'slight' according to a man who met him then, J. Fuller Russell: 'He spoke by fits and starts, and had a slight impediment in his utterance, which made him grunt once or twice before he began a sentence; but his tones were loud and rich' – and expressive in the reading of poetry, which was within his mature powers. (*Life*, 826.) Others described Lamb as speaking in little explosive bursts.

It is hard to tell what John Lamb's role in the family may have been; one does not feel that Lamb was very close to his father. A poem John wrote for his elder son suggests that he did take a hand in his children's moral education, at least that of the first child:

> Dear Grandmam,
> Pray to God to bless
> Your grandson dear with happiness;
> . . . .
> That as I do advance each year,
> I may be taught my God to fear,
> My little frame, from passion free,
> To man's estate, from infancy;
> From vice that leads a youth aside,
> And to have wisdom for my guide,
> That I may neither lie, nor swear,
> But in the path of virtue steer,
> My actions gen'rous, fair, and just,

> Be always true unto my trust;
> And then the Lord will ever bless
> Your grandson dear,
>   John L--b the Less.

(Life, 581)

8. *Elia*, 76.
9. *Life*, 46.
10. *Elia*, 152.
11. *Elia*, 103.

CHAPTER 2: A COMPANY OF WITCHES

1. Another of the elder John's sisters – he had at least two – may have lived south of the Thames, but we never hear of her directly.
2. *Elia*, 367.
3. *Chil.*, 319.
4. *Elia*, 66. In a first draft of his pseudo-Shakespearean tragedy, *John Woodvil*, the hero says,

> I can remember when a child the maids
> Would place me on their lap as they undrest me,
> As silly women use, and tell me stories
> Of Witches—Make me read "Glanvil on Witchcraft,"
> And in conclusion show me in the Bible,
> The old Family-Bible, with the pictures in it,
> The 'graving of the Witch raising up Samuel,
> Which so possest my fancy, being a child,
> That nightly in my dreams an old Hag came
> And sat upon my pillow.

(P, 364)

5. We know from Salt's bequest to Miss Peirson that it also contained the works of Pope, Swift, Shakespeare, Addison, and Steele.
6. *Chil.*, 318.
7. *Chil.*, 319.
8. *Elia*, 127.
9. *Misc.*, 47. Lamb found a folio revealing that Sycorax had rescued Algiers from the navy of Charles V by bringing on a storm, for which the citizens were naturally most grateful.
10. *Elia*, 65.
11. *Elia*, 68.
12. Virginia Woolf, *Second Common Reader*, (New York: Harcourt, Brace & World, Harvest Books, 1960) 160.
13. *Chil.*, 308.
14. *Misc.*, 344.

CHAPTER 3: DIVERSIONS

1. Mary Field, née Bruton, was baptized at Kimpton in 1713. She probably worked as a domestic in Hitchin before she married Edward Field, also employed in Hitchin, on 14 September 1736. She gave birth to Elizabeth within a year or two. Phyllis G. Mann, who has spent much time over many years researching the Lamb connections in Hertfordshire and elsewhere, has written four interesting articles for the *CLSB* on Charles and Mary's maternal relatives: July 1954, Jan. 1959, Apr. and July 1968. Mann tells us that she has not been able to find *proof* of Mrs Field's connection with the Plumers until 1773, when she witnessed a will; Mann therefore surmises that Mrs Field, in reduced circumstances after her husband's death in 1766, went soon after to the service of the Plumers. Her employment with the family would in this case have lasted only some twenty-five years, to her death in 1792.

   E. V. Lucas, however, pointed out (*Life*, 28) that it is 'on record that Mrs Field was for upwards of fifty years a servant in the Plumer family' – not naming the record. It is all too easy for even the questioning biographer to overlook a few words of Lamb himself in his letter of 13 June 1796 to Coleridge – Lucas's 'record' – as I did until the last minute. He tells Coleridge that 'my grandmother . . . lived housekeeper in a family the fifty or sixty last years of her life' (M 1, 30). I think we have to accept this word of Lamb's as truth; he had no reason at twenty-one in this serious letter to invent anything. Therefore Mrs Field (taking fifty years as the approximate length of her service) joined the Plumers in 1742 at age twenty-nine, or a little before, perhaps bringing her little girl with her. Note the fact that the Fields appear to have had only a single child, that Lamb never mentions his dead grandfather in the accounts of his grandmother, and that Edward, though alive in 1761, did not attend his daughter's wedding. On this point Mann says, 'The bride's father may have been detained in Hertfordshire by his employment as a gardener or by the terms of his service as a Militiaman rather than by estrangement from his wife' (*CLSB*, Jan. 1959, 221). But can we dismiss early estrangement as a likelihood, especially as Mann found all the records of Edward Field in Hitchin, not Widford? And might not Dorrell sooner cheat a family he rarely saw – i.e. one estranged from his wife's brother?

   By 1760, therefore, young Elizabeth Field, at age twenty plus, may well have been in service with the Plumers too, in their London house in Cavendish Square, Marylebone, her parish as given on her marriage certificate. Or she may have been employed nearby, but certainly in touch with the Plumers and their servants. It seems very likely, then, that she met John Lamb through Samuel Salt, the close friend of the Plumer family.

2. If he is the man of that name buried at Hitchin in 1765; it is known that he was alive until about that time. Note that his son (if such he was) survived him by only a year.

3. *Elia*, 28.

4. The original title and version of the poem 'Going or Gone', as published in William Hone's *Table Book*, 1827 (*P*, 319).

5. See *CLSB*, May 1959, 240, for Phyllis Mann's finding of Lovekin's coffin (she reports him to have been a tall man) at war-wrecked St. Bride's Church (since restored).

6. CL II, 73.
7. *Elia*, 97; in 'My First Play'.
8. See Phyllis Mann in *CLSB*, Apr. 1968, 590.
9. CL III, 67.
10. Compare *Elia*, 246–7.
11. James Gladman, her husband the substantial yeoman, had in fact died in 1769, before Charles was born. He left Aunt Ann (Phyllis Mann finds that she signed her name without the *e* sometimes accorded her) with three teen-aged sons, of whom Edward became the father of the charming Penelope whom Charles and Mary and their companion Barron Field met on their single return visit, in 1816. (Penelope was not the *youngest* Gladman daughter, though Lamb says so.) She married a Bruton, as Gladmans had done before, and Edward Bruton, her husband, was indeed substantial, the second largest ratepayer in the district. Besides Ann Gladman there was another Bruton sister, Lucey, who married a man called Crew and produced at least one cricketplayer. In 1806 four men bearing the names of Lamb connections played in an important cricket match; in 1814 two Sibleys and a Bruton played for Hertfordshire at Lord's. Mary Lamb presumably visited the Gladmans several times before she took Charles with her on their last visit, a year or so before Ann's death (on her earlier visits Charles was nonexistent or too young).
12. *Chil.*, 286.
13. *Chil.*, 287–8.
14. They went either that year, arriving by early May (the sheep-shearing would have been in June or early July), or in 1778, when Mrs Field's employer, old Mrs Plumer, died on 8 April and young John Lamb came out of school to look for a post. (See Phyllis Mann, *CLSB*, July 1968, 598.) If Elizabeth were needed by her mother in the upheaval that a death brings – two Plumer daughters had to be moved to another house (and at a time when the elder John was preoccupied with the younger) – Elizabeth may well have seized the opportunity to send little Charles away under Mary's care as he relates.
15. *Elia*, 155.
16. *Elia*, 157.
17. *Chil.*, 307.
18. *Elia*, 157.
19. *Elia*, 155.
20. Abraham Cowley, metaphysical poet of the seventeenth century.
21. *Elia*, 154–5.
22. *Elia*, 155.
23. *Elia*, 100.

THE TIMES: NO POPERY, 1780

1. (London: Fielding and Walker, 1780). Charles Dickens used this 62-page pamphlet as a main source for his novel of the riots, *Barnaby Rudge*; see Kathleen Tillotson's introduction to this work in the New Oxford Illustrated Dickens, 1954. (In summarizing this short pamphlet I include page references only for sizable extracts.)
2. Thompson, 72.

3. *Morning Post*, 9 June 1780, 2.
4. J. T. Smith, ed. G. W. Stonier, *Nollekens and His Times* (London: Turnstile Press, 1949) 14.
5. *A Plain and Succinct Narrative* . . . (Holcroft's pamphlet) 55.

CHAPTER 4: SCHOOLING AND SCHOOLFELLOWS

1. *Misc.*, 140 and 437.
2. Quoted in *Life*, 467.
3. Hood, 131.
4. The rate of inflation in 1979 makes it impossible to keep up with current money values. For the purposes of this book, the modern pound is translated at ten times its value in Lamb's lifetime (when such inflation as there was moved much more slowly), and the dollar at $2.25 per pound. But many other factors enter the picture for American readers; English salaries and English rents have traditionally been lower, for example.
5. *Misc.*, 301.
6. Hone, William (ed.), *The Every-Day Book*, Vol. 1, 1826 (New York and London, 1888) 463.
7. *Misc.*, 299.
8. *Misc.*, 300.
9. R. Brimley Johnson, xii.
10. R. Brimley Johnson, 5.
11. Hunt, 68.
12. In the rough draft of a letter to Lamb's biographer Thomas Noon Talfourd, recently found. It is the only original version known and has the virtue of immediacy; it includes details lacking in the previously published version. See *CLB*, April 1974, 116–18, 'The Old Familiar Faces', by Richard Madden. (The published version is used for the excerpt on p. 41.)
13. *Misc.*, 142–3.
14. *Elia*, 16–17.
15. The 'bridge' sounds circumstantial and has led some scholars to believe he may here have been visiting a second Lamb aunt. The Temple, where Aunt Hetty lived, and Christ's Hospital were both to the north of the Thames. I take the bridge to be Lamb embroidery and the 'good old aunt' to have been Hetty.
16. *Misc.*, 344.
17. So Lamb spelled his name. W. C. Hazlitt had it from the master's grandson that it was Fielde.
18. *Elia*, 19.
19. Hunt, 74.
20. *Elia*, 96.
21. *Elia*, 22.
22. Though Lamb does not say so directly, both Hunt's and Coleridge's accounts of the school indicate that Lamb would have been under Boyer in the Upper Grammar School. Ainger's edition of *Essays of Elia* notes that 'it is the tradition in Christ's Hospital that he was under Boyer's instruction some time before leaving school'. Alfred Ainger (ed.), *Essays of Elia*, 339.
23. Hunt, 107. Lamb's mother, however, signed his discharge.

THE TIMES: THE NEW MEN AND WOMEN

1. Now thought to be porphyria.
2. Son of a strong previous Prime Minister, the Earl of Chatham.
3. And Quakerism, though the sect was small by comparison.
4. Woodring, *Politics in English Romantic Poetry*, 33–4. This section is much indebted to Professor Woodring's book.
5. 'Citizen' Stanhope was later known to Lamb's circle, as we shall see. He was brother-in-law to Prime Minister Pitt and father of Lady Hester Stanhope, who left his protection to become Pitt's secretary. (Later she became a legendary settler in the Near East.) The lines between radical and Tory, friend and enemy, were always getting tangled in that so much smaller world. Pitt, for example, told Lady Hester that he sympathized with Tom Paine in some matters but as Prime Minister couldn't afford to show it; soon after he was advocating the gallows for Paine sympathizers.
6. Quoted by Charles W. Hagelman, Jr. (ed.), in introduction to Mary Wollstonecraft, *A Vindication of the Rights of Woman* (1792; New York: W. W. Norton, 1967) ii.
7. Quoted in Thompson, 79.
8. Cameron I, 328.
9. Moorman, 261.
10. The Jacobin clubs in France provided much popular support for Robespierre's extremist Montagnards.

CHAPTER 5: YOUNG CITY MAN

1. See *P*, 3. It was probably Lamb's to begin with, since it likened the 'shiv'ring joys' of her acting to the power of *witch* stories over a credulous infant, and since he mentions it in a proprietary manner to Coleridge. He did not reprint it in his *Works* of 1818, but it appeared in Coleridge's *Poems on Various Subjects* (1796) signed 'C. L.' and so in *Poems Second Edition* (1797), only to reappear as Coleridge's in *Poems Third Edition* (in which Lamb was not represented) in 1803. Presumably they had agreed, finally, it was to be Coleridge's.
2. *Life*, 87.
3. *Elia*, 80.
4. Blunden, *Charles Lamb and His Contemporaries*, 33.
5. Wollstonecraft, *A Vindication of the Rights of Woman*, op. cit., 36.
6. STCP, 543.
7. See pp. 163 and 233.
8. The spurious collection of 'Ossian' ballads, perpetrated by James Macpherson, was published and widely popular in the same year. We know that Lamb read Percy.
9. Carl Woodring estimates that some five thousand sonnets in English were printed in books, magazines, and newspapers between 1740 and 1800. *Wordsworth* (Cambridge, Mass.: Harvard University Press, 1965) 156.
10. *Elia*, 182.
11. *Elia*, 6.
12. If one compares the lives of the two humorous writers (Dickens was born in 1812) it is striking in how many ways Lamb is Dickens's spiritual and literary

progenitor, for all that Dickens was self-possessed, dashing, and fashionable, Lamb shy, modest, and drab. Both were deeply immersed in the London scene. Dickens the writer expanded on Lamb's kind of 'character' for a whole galaxy of portraits. Dickens grew up poor in London like Lamb, though Lamb, more fortunate in his parents, never knew the ultimate indignity of the blacking factory. Dickens, like Lamb, cared about the fate of the poor and was indignant at injustice. Dickens inherited Lamb's *friends* to an extraordinary degree. He dedicated *The Pickwick Papers*, his first substantial work, to T. N. Talfourd, Lamb's admirer and first biographer. John Forster, Harrison Ainsworth, Leigh Hunt, Daniel Maclise, and W. C. Macready the actor were all personal friends of Lamb, and then of Dickens. Both Dickens and Lamb adored the theatre. Dickens edited the autobiography of the great clown Joseph Grimaldi; Lamb's actress friend Fanny Kelly put on Grimaldi's final benefit performance and provided Dickens with her theatre for amateur theatricals. Dickens was twenty-two when Lamb died in 1834 and the two are not known to have met, but Dickens must have heard a good deal about Lamb from mutual friends. (The Dickens–Lamb connection has been previously noticed. See Houtchens, 70–71.)

13. Pronounced *Ellya*, as it would be in Italian. The pseudonym Elia, he said, was to avoid embarrassment to his brother, who rose to the position of Accountant in the South Sea House in 1805 and remained in it until his death in 1821. (It was also, Lamb told a friend, anagram for 'a lie'.) He claimed that the name was usurped from a South Sea House colleague of Italian blood, who sounds real enough in a letter of 1821 to John Taylor, the London publisher, though no one has found any other record of such a humble Elia. Lamb tells Taylor of having gone to 'laugh' with Elia over his use of the name, only to find he had 'died of consumption eleven months ago, and I knew not of it. So the name has fairly devolved to me, I think, and 'tis all he has left me' (CL II, 302). If Lamb was fooling Taylor, he also fooled Valentine Le Grice, who wrote in the rough draft already quoted, 'Are you aware of the derivation of Elia. I had it from his own mouth. There was a young Italian of that name studying Accountancy in the South Sea House.'

14. It will be recalled that this is a rough draft.

15. Guy Fawkes Day.

CHAPTER 6: ANN SIMMONS

1. To E. V. Lucas as well as the present author.

2. *Elia*, 305.

3. *Misc.*, 4.

4. His eyes have been variously described as hazel or brown.

5. *Misc.*, 15.

6. *Misc.*, 26.

7. *P*, 14.

8. This was the poem translated into French by the critic Charles-Augustin Sainte-Beuve (1804–1869). (*CLSB*, supplement of May, 1938.)

9. *P*, 8. Admired by Lamb's later friend the actor and playwright John Howard Payne, author of 'Home, Sweet Home'. Payne also told Lamb, 'the interest of *Rosamund Gray* appears to me the most inobtrusive and intense I know of. Some

of Mackenzie's stories try for the same effect, but this has a deeper character'
(CL III, 343).

10. *P*, 7.
11. If we continue to think with E. V. Lucas that Lamb went to his grandmother
between jobs.
12. *Elia*, 101.
13. M I, 18.
14. M I, 78.
15. Maria Bartram Coulson was 'notable for her skill in painting as well as her
attractive manners and great intelligence', says the *Dictionary of National
Biography* (under William Coulson).
16. WCH, 180.
17. *Misc.*, 33.
18. *P*, 21.
19. *Misc.*, 39.
20. *Elia*, 157.
21. *Elia*, 28.
22. There is no evidence whatever that Charles and Ann ever saw each other after
1799. But both lived in London, and anything is possible.

CHAPTER 7: COLERIDGE

1. See p. 319.
2. Mill, J. S., 'Coleridge', in *The Six Great Humanistic Essays of John Stuart Mill*
(New York: Washington Square Press, 1963), 76.
3. *Misc.*, 352.
4. Griggs I, 528.
5. Gunning, Henry, *Reminiscences of the University, Town, and County of Cambridge,
from the Year 1780*, Vol. I (London: George Bell, 1855), 274–5.
6. Moorman, 324.
7. Campbell, 47.
8. Quoted opposite frontispiece in Hanson. Dorothy Wordsworth, sister of the
poet, saw him thus at twenty-five:

He is a wonderful man. His conversation teems with soul, mind, and spirit.
Then he is so benevolent, so good tempered and cheerful. . . . At first I
thought him very plain, that is, for about three minutes: he is pale and thin,
has a wide mouth, thick lips, and not very good teeth, longish loose-growing
half-curling rough black hair. But if you hear him speak for five minutes you
think no more of them. His eye is large and full, not dark but grey; such an eye
as would receive from a heavy soul the dullest expression; but it speaks every
emotion of his animated mind; it has more of the 'poet's eye in a fine frenzy
rolling' than I ever witnessed. He has fine dark eyebrows, and an overhanging
forehead. (WL, 188–9)

9. Schneider, 224.
10. Cottle, 304.
11. Campbell, 28.
12. Griggs I, 63–4.

13. Even Boyer had perjured himself on Coleridge's account, or nearly, insinuating (said Coleridge's brother George) that he had given the miscreant leave to be away from college. 'God bless him,' said George, '—for a man of his disposition to descend to so amiable a fraud demands no trifling respect from us' (Griggs 1, 64).

14. Thompson, 132.

15. No evidence was ever found of plans to overthrow the government; the group, while exercising its right of free speech, was innocent of subversion.

16. In Edinburgh, where similar arrests were made for the same reason, two men were executed and several transported to Australia, in whose fate Coleridge, Southey, and their friends took a close interest. Only one of the transportees returned to England, the others soon dying under their hardships. Trevelyan says of the English acquittals: "This timely check saved England from a reign of terror and perhaps ultimately from a retributive revolution" (Trevelyan, 91).

17. Griggs 1, 113.

18. F. V. Morley, 82.

19. M 1, 32.

20. Griggs 1, 139.

21. Griggs 1, 138.

22. Griggs 1, 136.

23. Griggs 1, 147–8. This appears in STCP (p. 37) as 'To a Friend together with an unfinished poem'. The poem was 'Religious Musings', strongly political as well as religious. Lamb was soon a main testing-ground for the democratick poetry composed by his two Pantisocratic friends.

24. Quoted in Hester Burton, *Coleridge and the Wordsworths* (London: Oxford University Press, 1953) 55.

25. W. L. Bowles, 'Absence', in G. B. Woods (ed.), *English Poetry and Prose of the Romantic Movement* (Chicago: Scott, Foresman, 1929) 165.

26. References to these are so frequent in Lamb's writings that it is often forgotten how much they were admired by other Romantics as well.

27. Although in letters their prose styles were worlds apart, in criticism this was not always so. Edmund Blunden has pointed out that a piece by Coleridge on Sir Thomas Browne was for years thought to be Lamb's. 'It would be possible,' says Blunden, 'to produce a volume of critical notes by Coleridge and Lamb . . . as though by one writer.'—*Charles Lamb and His Contemporaries*, 102.

28. M 1, 78.

29. William Hazlitt, 'On the Living Poets', *Misc. Works* III, *Lectures on the English Poets*, 198–9.

30. Griggs 1, 405.

31. NL 1, 91.

THE TIMES: CHURCH, STATE AND THE YOUNG RADICALS

1. 'To be a Unitarian at that time,' writes Basil Willey,

meant also, almost as a matter of course, to be – if not an avowed republican in politics, at least a warm sympathiser with the French Revolution and a foe to aristocracy and the Established Church. Radicalism in politics and rationalism in religion went hand in hand. *Samuel Taylor Coleridge* (1971; New York: W. W. Norton, 1973) 16.

2. *Encyclopedia Britannica*, 1957, 'England, Church of', 471.

3. G. M. Trevelyan, *English Social History*, 3rd ed. (London: Longmans, Green, 1947) 359. Trevelyan provides the Gibbon quotation (on the same page) as well.

4. Ibid., 360.

5. In speaking of some journalism he had hoped to undertake, Lamb wrote, 'All my intention was but to make a little sport with such public & fair Game as Mr. Pitt, Mr. Wilberforce, . . . the Devil &c. . . . To have made free with these cattle, where was the Harm . . .' (M I, 191). Besides being a founder of the Society for the Suppression of Vice, Wilberforce wished to do away with Sunday newspapers. In an early letter (1796) Lamb speaks of piling ' "line upon line," out-Hannah-ing Hannah More', a prolific writer (M I, 78). Later, discussing her novel *Coelebs in Search of a Wife*, he says it has 'reach'd 8 Editions in so many weeks, yet literally it is one of the very poorest sort of common novels with the drawback of dull religion in it. Had the Religion been high and flavor'd, it would have been something' (M III, 14). He admired Clarkson – 'a good man' (M III, 233) – and not of the Clapham Sect.

6. Coleridge, *Lectures, 1795*, 64.

7. Thompson, 145.

CHAPTER 8: DIFFICULTIES

1. Blunden, *Lamb . . . Recorded*, 23.

2. Whether Lamb was a petitioner is uncertain. This material, and much in this chapter, is from Samuel McKechnie's excellent series, 'Charles Lamb of the India House' in *Notes and Queries* for 2, 16 and 30 Nov. and 14 and 28 Dec. 1946; 11 and 25 Jan., 8 and 15 Feb., and 8 March 1947.

3. Philips, 1.

4. J. M. Hope, 'Charles Lamb as a Business Man', unpublished MS in the Charles Lamb Library, Guildhall, read to the Charles Lamb Society 16 Jan. 1950, p. 5.

5. Quoted by McKechnie, op. cit., 30 Nov. 1946, 227.

6. I.e., 'amount of the hire' for shallow-water boats and sloops carrying goods from shore to ship.

7. Samuel McKechnie, 'Six of Charles Lamb's "True Works" Discovered', *CLSB*, Sept. 1955 (reprinted from *The Times*, 21 June 1955) 74.

8. M I, 79.

9. White was then perhaps still living at Mr Coventry's (see Blunden, *Lamb . . . Recorded*, 23) in the gloomy house near Serjeant's Inn, Fleet Street – that of the Old Bencher, frightener of children: no wonder Lamb knew so much about Coventry. The lawyer had taken the fifteen-year-old in after he left school, so that he might train for the school office.

10. *Elia*, 14.

11. The rough draft of it, as reported in *CLB*, Apr. 1974, 117.

12. Probably after White had left Coventry's.

13. White had a good head for business as well as a taste for drama, for he remained

at Christ's Hospital at least until 1808 – becoming an agent for provincial newspapers and conducting an advertising agency he founded about 1800 and
which still exists as R. F. White & Sons in Fleet Street, the oldest such business
in London. (He married Margaret Faulder, or Fauldes, daughter of a Bond
Street bookseller, and their descendants carried on the firm. See M 1, xxxvi.)
Robert Southey and V. Le Grice thought Lamb was 'joint author' of *Falstaff*
(see Blunden, *Lamb . . . Recorded*, 24); Lucas, however, does not.

14. M 1, 70.
15. NL 1, 112–13.
16. Coleridge also acknowledged, in that volume, four lines by Lamb in one of his
    own sonnets. The 1795 correspondence between the friends has disappeared.
17. Jackson, 34.
18. STCP, 538.
19. In his first surviving letter, evidently in answer to one from Coleridge, Lamb
    reports, for example, on the number of sonnets he had written 'since I saw you',
    suggesting that communication has just reopened.
20. M 1, 9. The Southey report (Norval) on p. 110 is from *Life*, 99.
21. M 1, 15.
22. Of which the following from this letter is characteristic:

> They are good imitative lines "he toild & toild, of toil to reap no end, but
> endless toil & never ending woe." 347 page Cruelty is such as Hogarth might
> have painted her. page 361 All the passage about Love (where he seems to
> confound conjugal love with Creating and Preserving love) is very confused &
> sickens me with a load of useless personifications. Else, that 9th book is the
> finest in the volume, an exquisite combination of the ludicrous and the
> terrible,—I have never read either even in translation, but such as I conceive
> to be the manner of Dante & Ariosto. . . . does not Southey use too often the
> expletives "did" and "does"? they have a good effect at times, but are too
> inconsiderable or rather become blemishes, when they mark a style. (M 1, 16)

23. M 1, 20.
24. M 1, 32.
25. M 1, 34.
26. M 1, 36.
27. M 1, 42.

CHAPTER 9: DISASTER

1. See Phyllis G. Mann's series on this Norris family in the *CLSB* of September,
   1953, Mar. 1954, and July 1955.
2. Griggs 1, 239.
3. The unnamed individuals cannot be identified.

CHAPTER 10: LONELINESS

1. At least from September to February, more fitfully thereafter.
2. M 1, 78.
3. See Griggs 1, 262.

4. M I, 96.
5. So in Marrs; Lucas gives the word as 'loss', which I take to be Lamb's meaning.
6. M I, 87.
7. M I, 84.
8. M I, 87.
9. Griggs I, 297.
10. M I, 89.
11. There is no evidence that one poet was influenced by the other.
12. Griggs I, 285–6. Elsewhere Coleridge attributed Lloyd's emotional disorder of March 1797 to her death. (See Griggs I, 318.)
13. M I, 74.
14. *P*, 6.
15. 'We were two pretty babes', 'Was it some sweet device', 'When last I roved' and the Margate sonnet.
16. The first edition had sold out by October, 1796.
17. M I, 60–1.
18. M I, 67.
19. M I, 62.
20. M I, 98.
21. Fish; perhaps food in general.
22. *Elia*, 47. The 'fanatic' described in the letter also figures in 'A Quakers' Meeting'. Lamb continues at some length about him to Coleridge.
23. *P*, 19–20.
24. Coleridge, in sending some lines on Charles Lloyd's melancholy to be published in the *Cambridge Intelligencer*, commiserated with a death in Benjamin Flower's family (he was its editor–publisher) by saying,

> The young Lady, who in a fit of frenzy killed her own mother, was the Sister of my dearest Friend, and herself dear to me as an only Sister. She is recovered, and is acquainted with what she has done, and is very calm. She was a truly pious young woman; and her Brother, whose soul is almost wrapped up in her, has had his heart purified by this horror of desolation, and prostrates his Spirit at the throne of God in believing Silence. The terrors of the Almighty are the whirlwind, the earthquake, and the Fire that precede the still small voice of his Love. . . . (11 Dec. 1796: Griggs I, 267)

25. LL, 38.
26. M I, 105.
27. There is still controversy on this point.
28. Fruman suggests that Lamb's 'dream' may have given Coleridge the idea of writing about a dream of his own – etc. See Norman Fruman, *Coleridge, The Damaged Archangel* (New York: Braziller, 1971) 345–6.
29. In C. C. Southey, 99.
30. STCP, 540.
31. STCP, 541.
32. See pp. 62–3.
33. Coleridge, Lamb, and Lloyd, *Poems, Second Edition*, 56.
34. M I, 114.

CHAPTER 11: TO NETHER STOWEY

1. Quoted in Thompson, 165.
2. An 1834 note in Coleridge's hand on the thirty-seven years which had elapsed since the visit – 'Ch. and Mary Lamb—dear to my heart, yea, as it were, my heart . . . ' – (STCP, 592) was found after Coleridge's death next to the poem 'This Lime-Tree Bower My Prison', the first version of which Coleridge wrote in the course of Lamb's stay. And a printed note on the poem as published describes it as having been inspired by the arrival of some 'long-expected friends' – which would again imply Mary's presence since the Wordsworths were not very long expected and had arrived a few days earlier. However, when Charles travelled with Mary he invariably spoke about her in letters, and often of 'we'. There are two letters, before and after this visit; in neither does he mention Mary or use any pronoun by 'I' regarding himself. And Coleridge speaks of his guest as 'Lamb' in a July letter (Griggs I, 197). Dykes Campbell, Coleridge's careful, scholarly editor and biographer, has a footnote on this matter (Campbell, 71) in which he says, 'There can be little doubt that Coleridge's memory . . . had failed him.' But the most decisive evidence is Charles Lamb's, when he writes to Coleridge in January, 1798, 'your invitation went to my very heart—but you have a power of exciting interest, of leading all hearts captive, too forcible to admit of Mary's being with you—. I consider her perpetually on the brink of madness—. I think, you would almost make her dance within an inch of the precipice—she must be with duller fancies, & cooler intellects' (M I, 127). 'I think you would almost make her dance': Lamb has not seen them together since the tragedy.
3. Chambers, 84.
4. Griggs I, 309.
5. Hazlitt, William, 'My First Acquaintance with Poets', *Misc. Works*, Vol. I, *Table Talk*, First Series, Part II, 154–5.
6. WL, 189.
7. De Quincey writes of Poole (*Lake Poets*, 35),

. . . as Coleridge afterwards remarked to me, he was almost an ideal model for a useful member of Parliament. He was a stout, plain-looking farmer, leading a bachelor life, in a rustic old-fashioned house; the house, however, upon further acquaintance, proving to be amply furnished with modern luxuries, and especially with a good library, superbly mounted in all departments bearing at all upon political philosophy; and the farmer turned out a polished and liberal Englishman, who had travelled extensively, and had so entirely dedicated himself to the service of his humble fellow countrymen, the hewers of wood and drawers of water in this southern region of Somersetshire, that for many miles round he was the arbiter of their disputes, the guide and counsellor of their daily lives; besides being appointed executor and guardian to his children by every third man who died in or about the town of Nether Stowey.

See also Sandford, *Thomas Poole and His Friends*, and Sara Coleridge (ed. Stephen Potter), *A Minnow Among Tritons* (London: Nonesuch Press, 1934).
8. Griggs I, 643.
9. Bate, 51.

10. In April Coleridge had had the following odd encounter relative to Burnett, described in a letter to a friend. It reflected not only Burnett's own view of his Pantisocratic experience – that Coleridge and Southey *owed* him something for having ruined him – but also the view many people, including some of his Nether Stowey neighbours, had of Coleridge at the time of Lamb's visit.

> My dear friend,
>   I am here [Stowey] after a most tiresome journey; in the course of which, a woman asked me if I knew one Coleridge, of Bristol. I answered, I had heard of him. 'Do you know, (quoth she) that that vile jacobin villain drew away a young man of our parish, one Burnet,' &c. and in this strain did the woman continue for near an hour; heaping on me every name of abuse that the parish of Billingsgate could supply. I listened very particularly; appeared to approve all she said, exclaiming, 'dear me!' two or three times, and, in fine, so completely won the woman's heart by my civilities, that I had not courage enough to undeceive her. . . .
>   S. T. Coleridge.
>   (Griggs I, 321)

11. Griggs I, 191.
12. In which 'My Sister & my Friends' of the last section becomes 'My Sara and my friends'.
13. As a number similar to this one are called.
14. STCP, 94.
15. When he had just missed meeting Lamb through Lamb's illness – see p. 111. It was a manuscript of *Salisbury Plain* that Coleridge had Lamb convey to Wordsworth (after reading it) but not, as it turned out, in person.
16. Burton R. Pollin, 'John Thelwall's Marginalia in a Copy of Coleridge's *Biographia Literaria*', 76.
17. See Moorman, 327–32, and S. T. Coleridge, *Biographia Literaria*, Chapter x, for the details. De Quincey reports the local gossip of the time:

> Some country gentlemen from the neighbourhood of Nether Stowey, upon a party happening to discuss the probabilities that Wordsworth and Coleridge might be traitors and in correspondence with the French Directory, answered thus:— 'Oh, as to that Coleridge, he's a rattle-brain, that will say more in a week than he will stand to in a twelvemonth. But Wordsworth—that's the traitor: why, God bless me, he's so close on the subject that, d—n me if you'll ever hear him open his lips on the subject from year's end to year's end!' (*Lake Poets*, 176–7)

18. E. V. Lucas believed that the Lambs had moved from Little Queen Street to Pentonville at the New Year; Professor Marrs deduces that the change took place after Lamb's return from Stowey, since he sends Coleridge the new address. For this writer the matter must remain in doubt. On the one hand, Coleridge sent written materials to Lamb's *office* and may have needed reminding of a newish home address, in effect perhaps earlier in 1797. On the other, since there is no previous indication of a move in Lamb's extant letters, Professor Marrs is possibly right.

CHAPTER 12: CHARLES LLOYD

1. M I, 119.
2. Griggs I, 236–7.
3. *Lake Poets*, 319.
4. *Lake Poets*, 322–3.
5. *Lake Poets*, 321.
6. He is so diagnosed by Dr Sam M. Seitz, psychiatrist.
7. M I, 123.
8. NL I, 160.
9. NL I, 144.
10. NL I, 152.
11. Jack, 23.
12. Griggs I, 268.
13. He wrote to Thelwall in October, 'Sara is in the way of repairing the ravages of war, as much as in her lies' (Griggs I, 349).
14. For a scholarly analysis of the Higginbottom sonnets, see David V. Erdman, 'Coleridge as Nehemiah Higginbottom', *Modern Language Notes*, Dec. 1958, 569–80. See Appendix A for the texts of 'Higginbottom'.
15. *Anti-Jacobin*, 20 Nov. 1797.
16. Griggs I, 410.

CHAPTER 13: THE TRAGIC POET

1. *P*, 20.
2. Its beginning, to his mother, is quoted on p. 10.
3. See Burton R. Pollin, 'Charles Lamb and Charles Lloyd as Jacobins and Anti-Jacobins', to which I am much indebted here and elsewhere.
4. E. V. Lucas places the poem in '?1798' but it may possibly have been written the preceding year, since it repeats and expands the anti-atheist motif of 'To Charles Lloyd' of August, 1797. Lamb did not publish it, however, until 1799, in Southey's *Annual Anthology*. Mary Wollstonecraft died 10 September 1797.
5. In 1796 Coleridge had meditated, as shown by his notebook of that period, an 'Epistle' to Mary Wollstonecraft, 'urging her to religion'; he had read, or proposed to read her 'Travels'; in talking to Hazlitt after her death he expressed admiration of her easy handling of the difficult Godwin, and of her conversation – though not of her writing. None of the friends named except Montagu were near enough to London to attend her funeral.
6. Quoted in Brown's *Godwin*, 131–2. Tuthill did not change his mind.
7. In his open 'Letter to Robert Southey' of 1823 (*Misc.*, 226–36).

CHAPTER 14: THE BREAK WITH COLERIDGE

1. Quoted in Hanson, 355.
2. M I, 97.
3. The critic George Whalley believed Lamb to have been an important source of inspiration for 'The Ancient Mariner'. See his 'Coleridge's Debt to Charles

Lamb', *Essays and Studies*, 1958, 68–85. He concludes his discussion with the image of Coleridge's 'way of mind' as like 'a cloud of starlings on the wing' which,

> at one moment a shapeless cloud, will suddenly turn like one bird, as though at a word of command imperiously uttered and with cheerful alacrity obeyed. In this way, Coleridge's mind, circling and wheeling in an indolent fancy, suddenly becomes intent, stoops, fascinated at the marvellous hint of a vision and the body of a vision; all its powers concentrated, at full stretch, responsive as a fiddle-string. Precisely how this happened we do not know, and shall never know. But one thing is sure: that Coleridge was launched forth upon his marvellous year with vision clarified and energies redirected by his fruitful nine-months' correspondence with Charles Lamb.

4. This would seem to contradict Professor Whalley's statement that the book did not appear until 28 October 1797. We know that Cottle had brought a copy to Southey in August.
5. NL I, 160.
6. CL I, 120.
7. CL I, 104.
8. In spite of Higginbottom, Coleridge and the Wordsworths saw something of Southey, whom Dorothy first met then, and for whom she had little enthusiasm: 'He is a young man of the most rigidly virtuous habits . . . but though his talents are certainly very remarkable for his years (as far as I can judge) I think them much inferior to the talents of Coleridge' (WL, 223).
9. As Lamb's French biographer Derocquigny believes.
10. Lamb claimed all his life to dislike music, though he admired the singing of John Braham, enjoyed *The Beggar's Opera*, and came to appreciate the playing of the organist Vincent Novello. From his essay on the subject, 'A Chapter on Ears', compare,

> I am constitutionally susceptible of noises. A carpenter's hammer, in a warm summer noon, will fret me into more than midsummer madness. But those unconnected, unset sounds, are nothing to the measured malice of music. . . . I have sat through an Italian Opera, till, for sheer pain, and inexplicable anguish, I have rushed out into the noisiest places of the crowded streets, to solace myself with sounds, which I was not obliged to follow . . . (*Elia*, 39)

11. See *Life*, 155.
12. 'Where are the snows of yesteryear?'
13. Lamb's own string of dots.
14. Ellipsis as in Marrs.
15. That roguery and folly were not in Lamb's eyes confined to the Church of England is apparent in his letter to Wordsworth of 19 October 1810, when he says, 'as glibly as Unitarian Belsham will discuss you the attributes of the word God in a Pulpit, and will talk of infinity with a tongue that dangles from a scull that never reached in thought and thorough imagination two inches, or further than from his hand to his mouth or from the vestry to the Sounding Board'

(M III, 58). Thomas Belsham followed Joseph Priestley in the pulpit of the Gravel Pit Chapel at Hackney and was later minister of the Essex Street Chapel, both of which Lamb attended at one time or another in his youth. He found discrepancies between faith and practice in the Quakers as well; see his essays, 'A Quakers' Meeting' and 'Imperfect Sympathies'. Since these were the two sects to which he felt closest, it is not hard to understand why he left the one and failed to join the other.

16. WCH, 164. Shelley was writing some twenty years later. Lamb, who knew Shelley's father-in-law, Godwin, well, did not, in general, care for Shelley's work and never got to know him, though the widowed Mary Shelley became a close friend of the Lambs.

17. Southey wrote to Joseph Cottle (publisher of *Edmund Oliver*) in January 1798, 'I have never told you how very *unhandsome* I think the conduct of Wordsworth and his sister to Charles Lloyd respecting the passage he has omitted. I never heard of so overbearing and mean an act of vanity' (NL I, 158). This interesting, puzzling statement suggests that the deletion requested concerned either Coleridge or even Wordsworth himself; it is possible that as new friends of Coleridge they did not yet know of the Comberback episode and failed to realize at that time the magnitude of the satire on Coleridge's life and habits. They did know of it after the book's publication in May, since Dorothy transcribed for Coleridge the copy of the letter to Lamb he kept. Cottle had sent a copy of *Edmund Oliver* to Wordsworth on publication, which he acknowledged on 9 May with the comment that he had not yet read it; but he reported Dorothy as thinking the novel contained 'a *very* great deal of excellent matter but bears the marks of a too hasty composition' (WL, 218). They seem not to have resented the Coleridge satire – or perhaps simply did not wish to go into this aspect of *Edmund Oliver* with Cottle. Priscilla Lloyd was to marry their brother Christopher and they may have been treading warily lest Cottle show the letter to Lloyd.

Sometime during these months Lloyd wrote to Dorothy (presumably before the book came out, since Coleridge managed to laugh it off) as described by Coleridge in a notebook entry of 1810:

Elucidation

If ever there was a time and circumstance in my life in which I behaved *perfectly* well, it was in that of C. Lloyd's mad quarrel & frantic ingratitude to me—He even wrote a letter to D. W., in which he not only called me a villian,but appealed to a conversation which had passed between him & *her*, as the grounds of it—and as proving that this was her opinion no less than his— She brought over the letter to me from Alfoxden with tears—I laughed at it— After this there succeeded on his side a series of wicked calumnies & irritations—infamous Lies to Southey & to poor dear Lamb—in short, a conduct which was not that of a friend, only because it was that of a madman. On my side, patience, gentleness, and good for evil—yet this supernatural effort injured me—what I did not suffer to act on my mind, preyed on my body—it prevented my finishing the Christabel—& at the retirement between Linton & Porlock was the first occasion of my having recourse to Opium/And all this was as well known to W. & D W., as to myself—(*Notebooks* III, No. 4006)

Coleridge always said that he had written 'Kubla Khan' during a brief stay at a farmhouse between Linton and Porlock, though he variously ascribed the time of its writing to the autumn of 1797 and the spring of 1798. Critics still differ as to which of his recollections was correct, E. L. Griggs, editor of his letters, favouring 1797. The claim of his last two Notebook lines above, that his first use of opium (for emotional reasons) was 'as well·known to W. & D W., as to myself' would be because he had told them so – with less than candour, though he may have persuaded himself that it was true.

18. Griggs I, 390.
19. Griggs points out (I, 403) that the year must be 1798, since *Edmund Oliver* is referred to. He thinks the month and day, as well as the year, may have been wrongly given by Lloyd, and that the 'odd letter' may refer to the long one written by Coleridge to Lamb in May. But Lloyd's mistaking all three elements (and naming a month still *ahead*) seem much less likely than his merely reverting to the previous year. Coleridge's May letter to Lamb begins with his learning from Dorothy Wordsworth that Lamb no longer intends to write to him. What Lloyd views as unkindness to Lamb on Coleridge's part must have preceded this in a letter now lost.
20. Hanson, 487.
21. *Life*, 158.
22. Griggs I, 403. The question has been raised as to whether the letter was actually sent. If not, however, why would Coleridge have showed it to Cottle without mentioning that fact? Why would he have showed it to Cottle at all? Lamb's next letter shows strong reaction to many aggravations, and I suspect this letter was one of them.
23. Cottle, 168.
24. Allsop, 152.
25. M I, 130.
26. Professor Marrs, on Lucas's cue, believes this letter to have been written between 23 May and 6 June, when Lamb was staying with Lloyd in Birmingham. But since Lamb was seeing Lloyd in London until both went, together – they were getting *Blank Verse* ready for the press, among other things – it could, I think, have been written earlier in the month of May, at any time after Coleridge's (undated) *Edmund Oliver* letter.
27. Lucas interprets this as 'The less shining virtues, savouring too much of man and earth' (CL I, 128).
28. See Moorman, 396.

CHAPTER 15: THE QUAKER LLOYDS

1. Francis Jeffrey (as 'Lord Jeffrey'), in *The Modern British Essayists*, Vol. VI (Philadelphia: Carey and Hart, 1846) 651.
2. A fact hitherto unnoticed, as far as I can learn. Bristol, where Cottle lived, was a wide detour on the London–Birmingham route, nor do we hear of any other such trip from Lamb in 1798. Cottle's 'one casual visit', below, is found in Cottle, 151.
3. Clarkson, though never a Friend himself, wrote a life of William Penn, a number of works on the slave trade, and the book for which he is most remembered, *A Portraiture of Quakerism* (1806).

4. Jeffrey, op. cit., 645.
5. Jeffrey, op. cit., 651.
6. Those called 'gay Quakers', such as the affluent family of young Elizabeth Gurney (later Elizabeth Fry), did not adhere to the Quaker dress, however.
7. *Anti-Jacobin Review and Magazine*, Aug. 1798, 177.
8. I am indebted to Mary Whiteman for letting me see Susanna Day's diary, which she has transcribed for the Society of Friends in London.
9. James too suffered a 'brain fever', but not until he was sixty-seven, after which he took no part in the bank's affairs until his death ten years later.
10. LL, 95.
11. LL, 99.
12. Anna became the only real 'ornament to the Society' – as he hoped all his children would be – that Charles Lloyd of Bingley produced. She married Isaac Braithwaite and became prominent as a Quaker 'minister' – one who takes a leadership role. She travelled as far as America when she felt called to, leaving her children behind in the care of her husband. Except among Friends few women could launch forth in this way and be considered respectable.
13. *Lake Poets*, 314.
14. This chapter owes much to *The Quaker Lloyds in the Industrial Revolution*, by Humphrey Lloyd, and to E. V. Lucas's *Charles Lamb and the Lloyds*.
15. He was forty-nine when Southey, his view perhaps coloured by Charles junior, wrote 'I do not like that old man. He is too civil—too fawning—too oily' (NL1, 160).
16. Lamb's string of dots.

CHAPTER 16: POLITICAL LAMB

1. William Hazlitt, *Misc. Works*, Vol. III, *The Spirit of the Age*, 47.
2. Pollin, 636.
3. Pollin, 636.
4. Pollin, 637.
5. I am indebted for this discussion and for much else in this chapter to 'Charles Lamb and Charles Lloyd as Jacobins and Anti-Jacobins', by Burton R. Pollin. Regarding *Blank Verse*, Professor Pollin says,

> In the poems that he ascribed specifically to himself, Lloyd continued this [radical] strain, so dangerous in the eyes of the anti-Jacobins, for in 'Lines to Mary Wollstonecraft Godwin' he cites Godwin's *Posthumous Works* of his wife (1797) for a kind of half-hearted disagreement 'with almost all her moral speculations' in which, however, he defends 'the heart and dignity of this excellent woman'. Even worse – he attacks her calumniators on the grounds that she had pure intentions and 'the individuality of an attachment constitutes its chastity'. His validation for this outrageous disdain for marriage compounds the fault by relying on the infamous *Memoirs of Emma Courtney* by Mary Hays (pp. 64–72). . . . One other slight poem, 'Address to Wealth' (pp. 53–54), might have seemed dissident in blaming wealth for all the evils of the world, rather than blaming the uncontrite heart of man. Nothing in Lamb's section of the small book could be reprehended save perhaps that it began with a poem 'To Charles Lloyd', purporting to express his sense of loss

at the absence of his 'well-known voice' and 'cordial look'. The invocation of the Deity here would not exculpate Lamb for such pernicious acquaintance.

It is certainly odd that on the one hand Lloyd should be striving to sweeten his reputation with the reviewers through the anti-Godwinian bias of the novel *Edmund Oliver* and virtually at the same time be publishing this relic of his admiration for pantisocracy and perfectibility. It appears as if a thrifty poet cannot forego using completed pieces for a book to which he is committed. (Pollin, 637)

6. Brown, 156.
7. *Critical Review*, Oct. 1798, 232–4.
8. *Analytical Review*, May 1798, 522.
9. *Anti-Jacobin Review*, Aug. 1798, 178.
10. See P. M. Zall, 'Epitaph for George Dyer', *CLB*, Jan. 1974, 107.
11. I summarize from Howard Mumford Jones, *Revolution and Romanticism*, (Cambridge, Mass.: Harvard University Press, 1974) 467–9.
12. Later George IV.
13. Quotation transcribed from cartoon, which see.
14. Brinton, 200.
15. Gillray did not close his scattered quotation-marks, which opened each of the last 26 lines, and are omitted here except for the first (and that at the beginning of the poem).
16. He is to be seen today in Russell Square, once part of his ancestral estate, memorialized in bronze and holding the implements of agriculture.
17. For a detailed discussion of the *Letter to a Noble Lord* as it relates to Gillray's cartoon, see Winifred F. Courtney, 'Lamb, Gillray and the Ghost of Edmund Burke' in *CLB*, Oct. 1975, 77–82.
18. Fox and Paine were an example: Fox had disliked the first part of *The Rights of Man* so much that he could not bring himself to read the second, but he fought unceasingly for freedom of the press.
19. Brinton says of the *Anti-Jacobin*:

In itself, even in its masterpiece of serious-mindedness, the *New Morality* of Canning, . . . it is really on the defensive; it is besieged in its own castle. What the Tories are defending is the state of things created by the revolution of 1688 by the Whig aristocracy and the wits and philosophers of Queen Anne's reign. One of the ways in which this state of things was attacked was through the [Romantic] literature we are to consider. (Brinton, 24)

20. When it reviewed the anonymous *Lyrical Ballads*, notably devoid of politics, it missed any connection with the despised new school and praised the Coleridge–Wordsworth collection whole-heartedly. For the 'New School' of poetry in the *Anti-Jacobin* I am indebted to William Haller (Haller, 231 and 268–75).
21. Haller, 273–90 *passim* and 285.
22. See pp. 325 and 334.
23. Griggs I, 541.
24. *Anti-Jacobin Review*, June 1799, 191.
25. Blunden, *Lamb . . . Recorded*, 29.

26. Pollin, 642.
27. *Anti-Jacobin Review*, Apr. 1799, 429.
28. *Elia*, 6.
29. NL I, 202–3.
30. Quoted by Fitzgerald in Talfourd, 270.
31. *Lit. Rem.* I, 96 and 107–8.
32. M II, 189.
33. *Lit. Rem.* I, 84.
34. *Lit. Rem.* I, 78.
35. Notable exceptions – because of his friendship for author or editor – were his review of Wordsworth's *Excursion* in the *Quarterly Review* (1814) and his contributions to John Stoddart's *New Times*.

CHAPTER 17: NEW FRIENDS: DYER AND SOUTHEY

1. 'Cornwall', 91.
2. William Hazlitt, *Misc. Works*, Vol. I, *Table Talk*, First Series, Part II, 139–40.
3. See, for example, Cone, 98, and Baker, 58.
4. See Griggs I, 218.
5. HCR, Morley, 4.
6. Williams, 82.
7. HCR, Morley, 4.
8. Wherry, 82.
9. CL II, 431–2.
10. See *Elia*, 314–15. For Mrs. Dyer's status see HCR, Sadler II, 472, correcting Crabb Robinson.
11. Crane Brinton says that having 'discovered that revolutionary principles had not made men good, he characteristically jumped to the conclusion that they had made men bad' (Brinton, 89).
12. M I, 32.
13. Many of the Romantics (and their readers) shared Lamb's fascination with the more obscure among earlier writers; Southey's prose style, too, was touched with their brush. W. C. Hazlitt has pointed out that his writing is sometimes hard to distinguish from Lamb's, citing among his examples a letter of 1801 from Southey to Coleridge: 'The sight of your handwriting did not give much pleasure: 'twas the leg of a lark to a hungry man—yet it was your handwriting' (WCH, 154). The two styles seem to have developed in parallel, for neither Lamb nor Southey had written much to the other in early days, nor had either published prose of this nature.
14. M I, 136; Quarles was the moral and religious poet of the seventeenth century.
15. M I, 139.
16. M I, 141.
17. Southey had, for example, earlier praised Coleridge's *Osorio* during one of his several quarrels with his brother-in-law. I do not impute to him the 'malice' his biographer Jack Simmons finds in the *Lyrical Ballads* review (Simmons, 77).
18. Simmons, 77.
19. Identified by Kenneth Curry, in 'The Contributors to the Annual Anthology', *Papers of the Bibliographical Society of America*, Vol. 42, First Quarter, 1948.
20. NL I, 211.

21. The artist's government pension, with its obvious indication that he was hired to attack, became an embarrassment, and in 1800 he was asked to discard six months' work on an illustrated edition of *Poetry of the Anti-Jacobin*, already in print unillustrated.

CHAPTER 18: ROBERT LLOYD AND *JOHN WOODVIL*

1. M I, 135.
2. M II, 37.
3. *P*, 365.
4. ML, 63.
5. James Dykes Campbell published an analysis of *John Woodvil*'s permutations in *The Athenaeum*, 1891. It is reprinted in Lucas's notes to the play, *Poems and Plays* (Vol. v of the Lambs' *Works*), 350–66.
6. As Clare abbreviated the title, without italics.
7. Lamb published the exchange that follows in the journal *Recreations in Agriculture* for November, 1800, as 'The General Lover'. With it appeared 'The Dying Lover', retitled 'Fragment of Dialogue'. (This was again retitled in Lucas's edition of Lamb's *Works* as 'Dramatic Fragment': *P*, 79–80,) Simon's 'hot amorist' speech in the scene appeared as a third contribution to the November *Recreations*, called there 'Description of a Forest Life'.
8. A modern verdict on *John Woodvil* is given by the drama historian Allardyce Nicoll (who admires Lamb's later play *Mr. H-----*):

   The very first scene gives some promise, but as the play progresses, all the worst faults of the romantic style become apparent. The theme . . . is slight in the extreme, and the conclusion strikes a note unutterably false. All that can be said of *John Woodvil* is that in it Lamb has played the sedulous ape to Beaumont and Fletcher and to Massinger, sprinkling his play, too, with reminiscences of Shakespearian romantic comedy. Beyond a few lines of beauty it does not rise. The characters are vague and shadowy. It is a dream called forth consequent upon the reading of older plays; of value for its time it has nothing. (Nicoll, 194)

9. Lamb, *Works*, 1818, I, viii–ix.

CHAPTER 19: CHEERFULNESS BREAKS IN

1. M I, 152.
2. The travellers saw one another again on the Continent for only a single day.
3. May had apparently once offered to help Lamb himself in this way – just how is not specified.
4. NL I, 192.
5. M I, 155.
6. M I, 155.
7. LML, 19.
8. M I, 156.
9. 'Compound': 'settle amicably', a legitimate, if rare, usage.

10. But soon after, in the words of George L. Barnett, it 'touched the hearts of the reviewers without exception' ('The History of Charles Lamb's Reputation', *CLB*, Apr.–July 1975, 26).
11. M I, 160.
12. LML, 27.
13. For further information on William Savery, see the *Life of William Savery of Philadelphia*, by Francis R. Taylor (New York: Macmillan, 1925), to which this account is indebted. The King's remark is quoted on p. 398. It is interesting to note, as an example of the close bonds which held the Society of Friends together, that young Charles Lloyd's sister Anna Lloyd Braithwaite had two grandchildren who married English Savorys of Hester's family.
14. Quoted in 'Hester Savory', an unpublished paper by Florence Reeves, read to the Charles Lamb Society 8 Sep. 1947. The Witch of Endor was, of course, the one consulted by Saul in the plate from Stackhouse which so frightened Lamb as a child.
15. M I, 248.

CHAPTER 20: MARY LAMB – AND COLERIDGE – COME HOME

1. Blunden, *Lamb . . . Recorded*, 30–1.
2. See 'The Lamb Tragedy and the Law', by H. G. L. King, *CLSB* Oct. 1942, p. 1, from which the quotations are taken.
3. Schizophrenia has been considered, but Mary's symptoms do not confirm it. Mary's early family experiences – the conscientious but not very loving mother – are more typical of the manic depressive. I am indebted for the analysis of Mary, and of Lamb's stammer, and of Charles Lloyd, to the psychiatrist Dr Sam M. Seitz.
4. Hutchinson, S. (ed. Kathleen Coburn), *The Letters of Sara Hutchinson* (London: Routledge & Kegan Paul, 1954) 134.
5. CL II, 267–8.
6. E. V. Lucas thought that it might have been James White, but this seems unlikely, since in Lamb's essay on Chimney Sweepers John Fenwick ('Bigod'), whom Lamb first met through Godwin in 1800, assists at the Smithfield dinners for the young sweepers – and these seem to have gone on for some years – together with Lamb and White.
7. *Misc.*, 352.
8. Lamb's dots.
9. M I, 171–2.
10. It was not *entirely* fair to Coleridge, who had taken out life insurance with Sara as beneficiary and had sent her money, though not enough for the family's needs.

CHAPTER 21: THOMAS MANNING

1. M I, 221.
2. *Gentleman's Magazine*, July 1840, 97.
3. HCR, Morley, 581.

4. Markham, clxiii–iv. For Manning in the Far East, see also E. C. Johnson, *Lamb Always Elia*, 39–75; Victor Allan, 'A Journey to Lhasa in 1811', *History Today*, Mar. 1962, 188–96; George Woodcock, *Into Tibet: The Early British Explorers* (London: Faber, 1971) 197–269. A biography is in preparation by Anne Lonsdale.
5. Miss Ruth B. Manning, his collateral descendant, has kindly provided family details.
6. *Gentleman's Magazine*, July 1840, 97.
7. WL, 296.
8. M I, 176.
9. LML, 35.
10. Markham, 278–9.
11. Lamb's dots.
12. LL, 106.
13. M I, 180.
14. M I, 183.
15. LML, 32.
16. Lamb's dots.
17. M I, 183.
18. Lamb's dots.
19. Protestants burned in the reign of Queen Mary I (1553–8).
20. M I, 188.
21. M I, 190.
22. M I, 191–2.
23. M I, 197.
24. Appearances are deceiving.
25. M I, 222.
26. The only reference to Manning in the Elia essays occurs in 'The Old and the New Schoolmaster': 'My friend *M*., with great painstaking, got me to think I understood the first proposition in Euclid, but gave me up in despair at the second' (*Elia*, 49).

CHAPTER 22: GODWIN

1. NL I, 246.
2. Brown, 160.
3. Griggs I, 588.
4. Brown, 1.
5. HCR, Morley, 14.
6. Professor Marrs, like Lucas, noting 'Saturday' at the top of Lamb's letter to Manning together with the absence of any other date and the omission of 'Dear Manning,' takes Saturday to be the date of the entire letter. Godwin, however, indicating that this is his first meeting with Lamb (he does not appear previously in Godwin's meticulous diary), says he saw Lamb at 'tea' at Coleridge's on Friday and dined with Coleridge at Lamb's on Saturday. So the sequence of Lamb's jottings has to be as I have described it. (See M I, 183.)
7. M I, 183.
8. HCR, Sadler I, 313.
9. *Life*, 334.

10. And Lamb's, as was Montagu; this was perhaps his first meeting with both. There is a reference to Tobin's blindness in Lamb's essay 'Detached Thoughts on Books and Reading'; references to Montagu occur in 'Oxford in the Vacation' and 'Newspapers Thirty-five Years Ago'. (See E. V. Lucas notes to these in *Works*.)

11. See Griggs 1, 567–8.

12. The remarkable sequel was that Montagu did repay his debts, becoming in time a highly respected lawyer and reformer of the law, a crusader against capital punishment and 'fermented liquors'. Lamb allowed him to reprint 'Confessions of a Drunkard' in a teetotal collection Montagu compiled. He was also the poet Shelley's legal assistant in trying to regain the guardianship of his and Harriet Shelley's children, and, through tactlessness, the cause of a serious break between Coleridge and Wordsworth in 1812.

13. It was over a year later; C. C. Southey, 536–7.

14. Griggs 1, 580.

15. M 1, 191.

16. M 1, 199.

17. Godwin's unpublished diary for Saturday, 26 Apr. 1800.

CHAPTER 23: THE MOVE TO LONDON

1. *Elia*, 73.

2. Leigh Hunt says of Canning at this time, 'I took him for nothing but a great sort of impudent Eton boy' (Hunt, 209).

3. Bryan Waller Procter.

4. All dots in this letter are Lamb's.

5. Lamb's dots.

6. M 1, 203–4.

7. George Dyer wrote a puzzling sentence to Southey on 29 July (1800) – 'Mr. Lamb is soon to be my neighbour in Southampton Buildings' (Williams, 34) – but Lamb's letter to Coleridge of 28 July (M 1, 215) makes it clear that he was already well settled in by then. The preoccupied George had probably not caught up with the Lambs' movements, or absent-mindedly forgot that they had moved earlier.

8. For 'saddening', as Marrs suggests?

9. M 1, 208.

10. Lamb's dots.

11. M 1, 216. (Lamb's dots within.)

12. A sociable had double seats facing each other.

13. M 11, 46.

14. M 1, 217–18.

15. Sophia gave birth in the neighbourhood of Birmingham. She had many children, all born far north of London, and never when Lamb and Manning *together* could have been present. Nor does it seem likely that either was so insensitive as to carouse noisily while Sophia was actually in labour.

16. As suggested to me by Sam M. Seitz, M.D.

17. To which Basil Montagu also contributed. Its editors, William Allen, a Quaker, and James Mill, the Utilitarian, were men of serious purpose. They edited Lamb more than he cared for.
18. There is no record, however, of drink being a problem in office hours.
19. *Life*, 294.

CHAPTER 24: LAMB AMONG THE LIONS

1. William Hazlitt, *Misc. Works*, Vol. II, *Table Talk*, Second Series. Part II, 50.
2. For those who wonder if incest was ever part of his close relationship with Mary, this writer would argue that it (quite emphatically) was not. Lamb was far too nervous of his sister's frenzies to have risked any action at all that would push her into one of her bad spells and burden both their sensitive consciences yet further. Mary's motherly early relationship with him, and her ten years' seniority would be other inhibiting factors. (We know he felt free to fall seriously in love with Fanny Kelly in 1819.) It would be rather odd than otherwise had either not experienced the occasional incestuous *impulse*, firmly suppressed.
3. M I, 231.
4. As 'Fragment in Dialogue'.
5. M I, 239.
6. *Elia*, 24.
7. Not previously scoured for Lamb's acquaintanceship, as far as I can learn.
8. The Irish Parliament, well bribed from the east, had voted its own dissolution. Ireland would now send representatives for Protestant landowners to the English Parliament.
9. The Whigs who sympathized with Ireland's troubles adored him. His daughter Amelia would one day companion Aaron Burr when the American paid a long visit to London in 1811 (dropping in on the Lambs), and she would paint the best known of the few portraits of Godwin's son-in-law Percy Bysshe Shelley.
10. T. Moore, (ed. Lord John Russell) *Memoirs, Journal, and Correspondence of Thomas Moore* (London, 1856) 5; and Cameron I, 410.
11. HCR, Morley II, 460.
12. Another encounter of Lamb's, soon after Cottle's wake in October, was not with a lion but a rattlesnake, on exhibition in London, occasion of an amusing letter to Manning. See M I, 241–2.
13. Southey wrote caustically, 'Why will he give his children such heathenish names? did he dip him in the river [Derwent] and baptize him in the name of the Stream God?' (NL I, 233). Coleridge claimed that his brothers' children had used up all the ordinary names.
14. D. Wordsworth (ed. Helen Darbishire) *Journals of Dorothy Wordsworth* (London: Oxford University Press, 1958) 57.
15. Griggs I, 624.
16. M II, 81.
17. Like Thomas Holcroft; see pp. 89–90.
18. His accomplishments cover nine pages in a recent *Dictionary of National Biography*.

19. *Encyclopedia Britannica*, 1957, 'Porson', 248.
20. Lucas, *Life* II, 1905 ed., 299.
21. Thornton, 167.
22. Baker, 90.
23. CL II, 460; William Hazlitt, *Misc. Works*, Vol. III, *The Spirit of the Age*, 65–7.
24. ML, 57.
25. *Dictionary of National Biography*, Perry.
26. *Elia*, 220.
27. CL I, 220.
28. M I, 21–2.
29. Stoddart, in the letter of 1838 quoted in part below, thought he had acted as messenger in April, 1800. But overwhelming evidence indicates that his visit to Keswick and Grasmere was in October–November of that year. See particularly WL, 320.
30. British Library, Add. MS 36878, f. 62 (1838).
31. HCR, Sadler II, 320.

THE TIMES: THEATRICAL INTERLUDE

1. Russell, 241.
2. Russell, 401.
3. Brander Matthews, professor and critic of the *New York Times*, admired Lamb's theatrical essays so much that he collected them in 1891 and wrote a warm introduction. Wayne McKenna, another professor and student of dramatic literature, has seconded this judgment in the 1970s in *Charles Lamb and the Theatre*. For other reassessments of Lamb as critic, see George L. Barnett, *Charles Lamb* (1976) Chapter 5 and notes.
4. J. Wordsworth, (ed. Carl H. Ketcham) *The Letters of John Wordsworth* (Ithaca: Cornell University Press, 1969) 79.
5. *Elia*, 295.
6. Scott and Moore on Kemble: Russell 248–9.
7. See p. 106.
8. HCR, Morley, 391.
9. Hunt, 133.
10. Russell, 226.
11. Holman, 11–12.
12. M. Kelly, *The Reminiscences of Michael Kelly* . . ., 2nd edn (1826; New York: Blom, 1969) 305–6.
13. *Elia*, 23.
14. D. M. R. Charnwood, *Call Back Yesterday* (London: Eyre & Spottiswoode, 1937) 129.

CHAPTER 25: ANTONIO

1. Cooper was Godwin's maid.
2. No relation to the American Barrymores, whose family substituted that name for their true one, Blythe, much later.
3. Paul II, 41–2.

4. Paul II, 43.
5. Brother of Jem (see p. 264). John Tobin died a few years after and his biography was written by the literary Miss Benger. Before he died he wrote a play called *The Honey Moon*, which proved a posthumous success and was still being acted forty years later – and seen by Crabb Robinson, who did not think much of it.
6. Cameron I, 241.
7. Paul II, 47.
8. Cameron I, 241.
9. M I, 251.
10. The Prologue has disappeared; we have the Epilogue only because of the letter to Manning, since on Lamb's advice neither was included with the published work.
11. M I, 253.
12. When he published this in *Essays of Elia* the *London* article was revised and broken into several essays, treating Kemble briefly at the end of 'On the Artificial Comedy of the Last Century' and omitting *Antonio* altogether. The account below is to be found in the Appendix to Lucas's *Elia* volume in Lamb's *Works*.
13. Cameron I, 364.
14. Monday's *Morning Post* said in part:

> Some hopes . . . must have been conceived from a play in which the female department could not have been filled with more splendid talent—for it was exclusively confined to Mrs. Siddons [as Elvira]—and in which Mr. Kemble, the hero of the piece, sustained the greater part of its burthen. These advantages . . . could not save the piece from condemnation. . . .
>
> If it had been the object of the author to have rendered the spirit of honour odious and disgustful, he could not have chosen a better personification of it than Antonio. . . . The dialogue is carried on through a dull series of *tête-à-têtes*, without incident, or variety in sentiment, or scene. . . . The disapproval gradually became general, and finally so great that Mr. Barrymore was not suffered to announce its further representation. A prologue and an epilogue [were] well suited to the piece, too bad to pass without censure, except when they pass without observation. (CL I, 229)

> The *Morning Chronicle* described the Epilogue, which had 'no more connection with the Tragedy than with the battle of Blenheim' as a 'trite and not humourous description of a tradesman, who neglects his shop to go to the Play'. And the *Porcupine*, William Cobbett's paper, stated that 'So gross an imposition on the public judgment has, perhaps, never been obtruded on the stage as the Tragedy of Antonio.' Miss Heard 'staggered on with evident emotion, to recite a pitiful Epilogue. Compassion listened to her with patience but had not a single plaudit to throw away' (M I, 260). Lamb's part in *Antonio* was of course also a secret.

15. Griggs I, 656–7.
16. Coleridge too had known her, and mourned her, but was too far away to attend her funeral.

CHAPTER 26: THE JOURNALIST

1. M I, 277.
2. There actually was a radical journalist called Daniel Lovell, but David V. Erdman, in notes lent me, has established that he could not have owned the *Albion* at this time.
3. A few earlier copies, before Lamb's day at the *Albion*, have also been located, by David Erdman. Those at Bath were first mentioned in print by Carl Woodring (*Politics in English Romantic Poetry*, 338, note 32).
4. By David Erdman, whose help on this chapter in article form has been immense. For a detailed account of Lamb's connection with the *Albion*, including probable Lamb contributions, see my series, 'New Lamb Texts from the *Albion*?' in the *Charles Lamb Bulletin* of January, April, and October, 1977.
5. M II, 21.
6. He limited his working hours and was steadily engaged in his own projects, nor does he record any *Albion* contributions in his careful diary.
7. E. V. Lucas included a number of similar 'paragraphs' which he thought (convincingly) to be Lamb's in his *Life* of the Lambs. These were from the period of Lamb's second stint on the *Morning Post* in 1803. (See *Life*, 264–6.)
8. Italics not Marvell's.
9. It now becomes the first published *essay* of Lamb's that we have.
10. I am indebted for this suggestion to Donald Reiman.
11. *Albion*, 7 July 1801, p. 2.
12. A fact newly discovered by David Erdman.
13. M II, 16.
14. M II, 16.
15. M II, 21.
16. M II, 41.
17. The piece he had tried to do against time was possibly that on Cooke's *Lear*, but it bears less obvious marks of his handiwork; M II, 45.
18. CL I, 295.
19 M II, 40.
20. M II, 45.
21. *Elia*, 224.

CHAPTER 27: LAMB & CO.: LIFE AND LETTERS, 1801–2

1. Not all the letters he wrote: those to Charles Lloyd and John Stoddart we know to have been destroyed, and there were no doubt others.
2. M I, 248.
3. God willing, and the devil not willing.
4. M I, 266.
5. M I, 268.
6. Brown, 202.
7. Lamb is mistaken: she had two children.
8. Brown, 207.
9. Brown, 207. Her daughter Claire Clairmont fled to the Continent in 1814 with the eloping Mary Godwin and Percy Bysshe Shelley. Besides complicating the relationship of these two, Claire later bore a daughter to Lord Byron.

10. M ii, 70.
11. He would later write a life of Daniel Defoe which included an essay on Defoe by Lamb.
12. Williams, 70–1.
13. M ii, 51.
14. M i, 39.
15. Williams, 59.
16. They were aided in the escape from Radicalism by their half-sister Hester Stanhope, who had long ago defected to Uncle Minister Pitt's camp, as had their elder brother; in the end Stanhope disinherited them all.
17. Lord Stanhope's house in Kent.
18. Williams, 63.
19. He had considered going to Manning in Paris, but Keswick proved more feasible.
20. Thomas Clarkson, the anti-slavery activist (see p. 177) and his wife, the former Catherine Buck, who would become close friends of the Lambs, as they were of the Wordsworths. Mrs Clarkson's sister, Ann Buck, had been on the coach to London with the Lambs on their return journey.
21. M ii, 66.
22. See Wordsworth's 1850 *Prelude*, lines 718 and 722–3.
23. Lamb and Stoddart: see Stoddart's recollections, pp. 289–90.
24. Stoddart was now Doctor of Civil Law and a member of the College of Advocates.

Selected Bibliography

Basic sources are the new edition of the Lambs' letters compiled by Edwin W. Marrs, Jr (incomplete at this writing but completed beyond 1802, where *Young Charles Lamb* ends) and E. V. Lucas's standard *Works* of the Lambs, collected in 1903–5 by an indefatigable Elian to whose *Life* of Lamb (5th edn, 1921) every biographer must be indebted. George L. Barnett has pointed out Lucas's weaknesses as editor of the previously standard *Letters*; Professor Marrs's careful continuing work and copious footnotes are invaluable. (On sound editorial advice, I have regretfully omitted his boldface, imitating Lamb's, in quotation.) I have drawn on the Lucas letters for some of his useful footnote material and in cases where Marrs's letters are as yet unpublished. The most recent general study of Lamb, in the Twayne English Authors Series, is George L. Barnett's excellent *Charles Lamb* (1976) by an authoritative Lamb scholar.

Since the Lucas *Works* are accessible to the general reader only in large libraries, while copies of *Essays and Last Essays of Elia* abound, I have chosen to abbreviate the *titles* of Lucas's four relevant volumes so that the layman will know what is in *Elia* and what is not, without trying to remember volume numbers. Articles in journals are listed by date to assist the reader seeking recent information. All abbreviations and short forms are listed separately and alphabetically in this list. (Further sources are cited in the footnotes.)

New works, well reviewed, that appeared too late for use and inclusion here are Roy Park (ed.), *Lamb as Critic*, Katharine Cooke's *Coleridge* and Don Locke's *A Fantasy of Reason: The Life and Thought of William Godwin* (all three London: Routledge & Kegan Paul, 1980, 1979 and 1980 respectively). Two recent book-length studies of Lamb concentrate on Elia essays beyond the scope of this book. They are Fred V. Randel's *The World of Elia* (Port Washington: Kennikat, 1975) and Robert D. Frank's *Don't Call Me Gentle Charles!* (Cornwallis: Oregon State University Press, 1976) which, with articles too numerous to list here, testify to the continuing interest of scholars in Lamb, as does Wayne McKenna on Lamb and the theatre, listed below.

The following are the works which were most useful to me: they are not exhaustive. The vast Lamb bibliography is best presented by George L. Barnett and Stuart M. Tave (which see); there are good bibliographies in Barnett's *Charles Lamb* (1976) and in Jack, Hine and Thomson, among others.

Adams, Martin Ray, *Studies in the Literary Background of English Radicalism, with Special Reference to the French Revolution* (1947; New York: Greenwood Press, 1968).

Ainger, Alfred, *Charles Lamb*, 2nd edn (London: Macmillan, 1888); (ed. with introd. and notes) Charles Lamb, *Essays of Elia* (New York: A. L. Burt, n.d.).

The Albion, or Evening Advertiser (ed. John Fenwick), ten issues of June–July, 1801.

Allsop: *Letters, Conversations, and Recollections of S. T. Coleridge*; *see* Coleridge.

American Psychiatric Association, Task Force on Nomenclature and Statistics, *Diagnostic and Statistical Manual of Mental Disorders*, 3rd edn, 1978.

Anon., 'Charles Lamb's Best Friend' [Mary Lamb], *Times Literary Supplement*, 24 May 1947.

Aspinall, A., *Politics and the Press, c. 1780–1850* (1949; New York: Harper & Row, 1974).

Baker, Herschel, *William Hazlitt* (Cambridge, Mass.: Harvard University Press, 1962).

Barnett, George L., *Charles Lamb: The Evolution of Elia* (1964; New York: Haskell House, 1973); *Charles Lamb* (Boston: Twayne, 1976).

Barnett, George L., and Stuart M. Tave, 'Charles Lamb', in C. W. and L. H. Houtchens (eds), *The English Romantic Poets and Essayists: A Review of Research and Criticism*, 2nd edn, pub. for the Modern Language Association of America (New York University Press, 1966) 37–74.

Bate, Walter Jackson, *Coleridge* (New York: Macmillan, 1968).

Beck, Aaron T., *Depression: Clinical, Experimental, and Theoretical Aspects* (Philadelphia: University of Pennsylvania Press, 1967).

Bernbaum, Ernest, 'Charles Lamb', in *Guide Through the Romantic Movement*, 2nd edn (New York: Ronald Press, 1949) 113–24.

BL: Coleridge's *Biographia Literaria*; *see* Coleridge.

Blunden, Edmund, *Charles Lamb and His Contemporaries* (Cambridge University Press, 1933); (ed.) *Charles Lamb: His Life Recorded by His Contemporaries* (1934, Folcroft, Pa.: Folcroft, 1975).

Brailsford, H. N., *Shelley, Godwin, and Their Circle* (1913; London: Williams & Norgate, n.d.).

Brinton, Crane, *The Political Ideas of the English Romanticists* (1926; Ann Arbor: University of Michigan Press, 1966).

Brown, Ford K., *The Life of William Godwin* (London: Dent, 1926).

Burton, Robert, *The Anatomy of Melancholy* . . . , 16th edn (London: B. Blake, 1838).

Cameron, Kenneth Neill (ed.), Carl H. Pforzheimer Library, *Shelley and His Circle, 1773–1822*, Vols. I–IV (Cambridge, Mass.: Harvard University Press, 1961–70).

Campbell, James Dykes, *Samuel Taylor Coleridge: A Narrative of the Events of His Life* (1894; Highgate: Lime Tree Bower Press, 1970); *see also* Coleridge.

Chambers, E. K., *Samuel Taylor Coleridge: A Biographical Study*, corr. edn (1938; Oxford, Clarendon Press, 1963).

Charles Lamb (Society) Bulletin, London. See *CLB, CLSB*.

Chil.: Books for Children, Lamb *Works* (ed. Lucas), Vol. III; *see* Lamb.

CL: Lamb *Letters* (ed. Lucas), 1935; *see* Lamb.

CLB: *Charles Lamb Bulletin* (London), new series, 1973–

CLSB Charles Lamb Society Bulletin (London), 1935–72.

Coleridge, Samuel Taylor, (Gen. Ed. Kathleen Coburn) *The Collected Works* (Princeton University Press, 1967–   ): of these, especially No. 1 (ed. Lewis Patton and Peter Mann), *Lectures 1795: On Politics and Religion* (1970), and introduction by David V. Erdman (ed.) to No. 3, *Essays on His Times* (3 vols, 1978); (ed. Kathleen Coburn) *Notebooks* (Princeton: Princeton University Press, 1957–   ); (ed. James Dykes Campbell) *Poetical Works* (London: Macmillan, 1893); (ed. George Watson) *Biographia Literaria, or Biographical Sketches of My Literary Life and Opinions*, 3rd edn (1817; London: Dent, 1965); (ed. Thomas Allsop) *Letters, Conversations, and Recollections of S. T. Coleridge*, 2nd edn (New York, 1847); (ed. Earl Leslie Griggs) *Collected Letters*, Vols. I and II, 1785–1806 (Oxford: Clarendon Press, 1966) ['Griggs' herein]; for *Poems* including some of Lamb's, *see* Lamb.

Cone, Carl B., *The English Jacobins: Reformers in Late Eighteenth-Century England* (New York: Scribner's, 1968).

'Cornwall, Barry' (Bryan Waller Procter), *Charles Lamb: A Memoir* (Boston: Roberts, 1866).

Cottle, Joseph, *Reminiscences of Samuel Taylor Coleridge and Robert Southey*, 2nd edn (1848; Highgate: Lime Tree Bower Press, 1970).

Cruse, Amy, *The Englishman and His Books in the Early Nineteenth Century* (1930; New York and London: Blom, 1968).

De Quincey, Thomas, *Literary Reminiscences* (Boston: Ticknor, Reed, and Fields, 1851); (ed. David Wright) *Recollections of the Lakes and the Lake Poets* [articles from *Tait's Edinburgh Magazine*] (Harmondsworth, Middlesex: Penguin, 1972).

Derocquigny, Jules, *Charles Lamb: sa vie et ses oeuvres* (Lille: Le Bigot, 1904).

Dobell, Bernard, *Sidelights on Charles Lamb* (New York: Scribner's, 1903).

Dobrée, B., and N. Davis (Gen. Eds.), *Oxford History of English Literature: 1789–1815* vol. by W. L. Renwick; *1815–1832* vol. by Ian Jack (London: Oxford University Press, 1963).

Downer, Alan S., *The British Drama: A Handbook and Brief Chronicle* (New York: Appleton-Century-Crofts, 1950) 268ff.

Elia: *Elia and the Last Essays of Elia*, Lamb *Works* (ed. Lucas), Vol. II; *see* Lamb.

Erdman, David V., introd. to S. T. Coleridge, *Essays on His Times* (ed. Erdman) in *Collected Works* of Coleridge; *see* Coleridge.

Gilchrist, Anne (ed. John H. Ingram), *The Life of Mary Lamb* (London, 1883).

Gillray, James (ed. with introd. by Draper Hill), *The Satirical Etchings of James Gillray* (New York: Dover, 1976).

Godwin, William, (abr. and ed. K. Codell Carter), *Enquiry Concerning Political Justice*, 3rd edn, *with Selections from Godwin's Other Writings* (1793, 1796, 3rd edn 1798; Oxford: Clarendon Press, 1971).

Griggs I and II: *Collected Letters* of Coleridge (ed. Earl Leslie Griggs); *see* Coleridge.

Griggs, Earl Leslie, *Thomas Clarkson, The Friend of Slaves* (1936; Westport, Conn.: Negro Universities Press, 1970).

Haller, William, *The Early Life of Robert Southey* (1917; New York: Octagon, 1967).

Hanson, Lawrence, *The Life of S. T. Coleridge: The Early Years* (1938; New York: Russell & Russell, 1962).

Harris, R. W., *Romanticism and the Social Order 1780–1830* (London: Blandford Press, 1969).

Hart, Roger, *English Life in the Eighteenth Century* (New York: Putnam's, 1970).

Hays, Mary (ed. A. F. Wedd), *The Love Letters of Mary Hays* (London: Methuen, 1925).

Hazlitt, W. Carew, *Mary and Charles Lamb: Poems, Letters, and Remains* (London: Chatto and Windus, 1874).

Hazlitt, William, *The Miscellaneous Works of William Hazlitt* (London: W. W. Gibbings, 1891); *see also* Holcroft.

HCR, Morley: *see* Henry Crabb Robinson, diary, etc.

HCR, Sadler: *see* Henry Crabb Robinson, diary, etc.

Hibbert, Christopher, *London: The Biography of a City* (New York: Morrow, 1969).

Hine, Reginald L., *Charles Lamb and His Hertfordshire* (London: Dent, 1949).

Holcroft, Thomas, and William Hazlitt, (ed. Eldridge Colby), *The Life of Thomas Holcroft, Written by Himself, Continued by William Hazlitt* (1925; New York: Blom, 1968).

Holman, L. E., *Lamb's 'Barbara S------': The Life of Frances Maria Kelly, Actress* (London: Methuen, 1935).

Hood, Thomas (ed. with additions by Walter Jerrold), *Thomas Hood and Charles Lamb* (London: Ernest Benn, 1930).

Houtchens, C. W. and L. H. (eds.), *The English Romantic Poets and Essayists*. *See* Barnett *and* Tave.

Howe, Will D., *Charles Lamb and His Friends* (New York: Bobbs-Merrill, 1944).

Hunt, L. (ed. J. E. Morpurgo), *The Autobiography of Leigh Hunt*, 2nd edn (1850, 2nd edn 1859; London: Cresset Press, 1949).

Jack, Ian. See Dobrée and Davis (eds), *Oxford History of English Literature, 1815–32*.

Jackson, J. R. de J. (ed.), *Coleridge: The Critical Heritage* (New York: Barnes & Noble, 1970).

Johnson, Edith Christina, *Lamb Always Elia* (London: Methuen, 1935).

Johnson, R. Brimley (ed.), *Christ's Hospital: Recollections of Lamb, Coleridge, and Leigh Hunt, with Some Account of Its Foundation* (London: George Allen, 1896).

Jones, Howard Mumford, *Revolution and Romanticism* (Cambridge, Mass.: Harvard University Press, 1974).

Jordan, Frank (ed.), *The English Romantic Poets: A Review of Research and Criticism*, 3rd rev. edn (New York: Modern Language Association of America, 1972).

Knight, Frida, *University Rebel: The Life of William Frend* (London: Gollancz, 1971).

Lake, Bernard, *A General Introduction to Charles Lamb: Together with a Special Study of His Relation to Robert Burton* (Leipzig, 1903).

Lake Poets: see De Quincey.

Lamb, Charles. Books he published or co-published, 1775–1802: (S. T. Coleridge's) *Poems on Various Subjects* (London and Bristol, 1796), contains 3–4 poems by Lamb; (Charles Lloyd's) *Poems on the Death of Priscilla Farmer* (Bristol, 1796), contains Lamb's 'The Grandame'; (S. T. Coleridge's) *Poems, Second Edition, to Which Are Now Added Poems by Charles Lamb, and Charles Lloyd* (Bristol and London, 1797), contains 15 poems by Lamb; (Lamb and Charles Lloyd) *Blank Verse* (London, 1798), contains 7 poems by Lamb; *A Tale of Rosamund Gray and Old Blind Margaret* (London and Birmingham, 1798), short novel; *John Woodvil: A Tragedy* (London, 1802), play, includes also 'Curious Fragments', 'Ballad from the German' and 'Helen', poem by Mary Lamb.

Lamb, Charles. Later editions: *The Works of Charles Lamb* (London: Ollier, 1818), 2 vols.; (ed. T. N. Talfourd), *The Works of Charles Lamb, to Which Are Prefixed, His Letters, and a Sketch of His Life* (New York: Harper, 1852), 2 vols.; (ed. William Macdonald), *The Works of Charles Lamb* (London and New York: Dent, and Dutton, 1903–4), 12 vols. (some useful notes); (ed. E. V. Lucas) *The Works of Charles and Mary Lamb* (London and New York: Methuen, and Putnam's 1903–5), 7 vols. The first five are the standard *Works* to date; the last two, of letters, have been superseded. Vol. i, *Miscellaneous Prose* ('*Misc.*' herein); Vol. ii, *Elia and The Last Essays of Elia* ('*Elia*' herein); Vol. iii, *Books for Children* ('*Chil.*' herein); Vol. iv, *Dramatic Specimens and Garrick Plays*; Vol. v, *Poems and Plays* ('*P*' herein); Vols vi and vii, the (superseded) *Letters*. *See also* Ainger.

Lamb, Charles. Letters: (ed. E. V. Lucas), *The Letters of Charles Lamb, to Which Are Added Those of His Sister Mary Lamb* (London: Dent, and Methuen, 1935), 3 vols., many useful notes, some inaccuracies ('CL' herein); (ed. Edwin W. Marrs, Jr.) *The Letters of Charles and Mary Anne Lamb* (Ithaca: Cornell University Press, 1975–   ), 6 vols, avail. through Vol. iii (to Oct. 1817) in 1980, careful, accurate, definitive – useful notes ('M' herein).

Lefebure, Molly, *Samuel Taylor Coleridge: A Bondage of Opium* (New York: Stein and Day, 1974).

Life: E. V. Lucas's *Life of Charles Lamb* (5th edn, 1921); see Lucas.

Lit. Rem.: *see* De Quincey, *Literary Reminiscences*.

LL: E. V. Lucas's *Charles Lamb and the Lloyds*; *see* Lucas.

Lloyd, Charles: *see* Lamb *and* Manning.

Lloyd, Humphrey, *The Quaker Lloyds in the Industrial Revolution* (London: Hutchinson, 1975).

LML: *The Lloyd–Manning Letters*; *see* Manning.

Lucas, E. V., *Charles Lamb and the Lloyds* (London: Smith, Elder, 1898); *The Life of Charles Lamb* (London: Methuen, 1905), 2 vols. – contains illustrations and appendices not in 5th edn; *The Life of Charles Lamb*, 5th edn (1921; New York: AMS Press, 1968) 2 vols. in one, unillustrated ('*Life*' herein); *At the Shrine of St. Charles: Stray Papers . . . for the Centenary of His Death . . .* (New York: Dutton, 1934); *see also* Lamb.

M (foll. by I, II, or III): Lamb *Letters* (ed. Marrs); *see* Lamb.

Manning, Thomas (ed. G. A. Anderson), *The Letters of Thomas Manning to Charles Lamb* (London: Secker, 1925); (ed. Frederick L. Beaty) *The Lloyd–Manning Letters* (Bloomington, Indiana, 1957); *see also* Markham.

Margetson, Stella, *Regency London* (New York: Praeger, 1971).

Markham, Clements R., *Narratives of the Mission of George Bogle to Tibet and of the Journey of Thomas Manning to Lhasa*, 2nd edn (London, 1879) – includes Manning's Far Eastern diary.

Martin, Benjamin Ellis, *In the Footprints of Charles Lamb* (London, 1891).

McKenna, Wayne, *Charles Lamb and the Theatre* (Gerrards Cross: Colin Smythe, 1978).

Mendels, Joseph, *Concepts of Depression* (New York: Wiley, 1970).

Misc.: *Miscellaneous Prose*, Lamb *Works* (ed. Lucas), Vol. I; *see* Lamb.

ML: *Letters of Thomas Manning to Charles Lamb*; *see* Manning.

Moorman, Mary, *William Wordsworth, A Biography: The Early Years, 1770–1803*, corr. edn (1957; Oxford: Clarendon Press, 1969).

Morley, F. V., *Lamb Before Elia* (London: Cape, 1932).

Nicoll, Allardyce, *A History of Early Nineteenth Century Drama* (Cambridge University Press, 1930).

NL: *New Letters of Robert Southey* (ed. Curry); *see* Southey.

P: *Poems and Plays*, Lamb *Works* (ed. Lucas), Vol. V; *see* Lamb.

Patmore, P. G., 'Charles Lamb', in Richard Henry Stoddard (ed.), *Personal Recollections of Lamb, Hazlitt, and Others* (New York: Scribner, Armstrong, 1875), 3–47.

Paul, Charles Kegan, *William Godwin, His Friends and Contemporaries* (London: Henry S. King, 1876).

Petry, Maude D. M., *The Ninth Lord Petre, or Pioneers of Roman Catholic Emancipation*, (London, 1928).

Philips, C. H., *The East India Company, 1784–1834*, 2nd edn (Manchester University Press, 1961).

Pollin, Burton R., 'Charles Lamb and Charles Lloyd as Jacobins and Anti-Jacobins', *Studies in Romanticism*, summer 1973, 633–47 ('Pollin' herein); 'John Thelwall's Marginalia in a Copy of Coleridge's *Biographia Literaria*', *New York Public Library Bulletin*, Feb. 1970, 73–94; and numerous articles on William Godwin and his circle.

Priestley, J. B., *The Prince of Pleasure and His Regency 1811–20* (1969; London: Sphere Books, 1971).

Procter, Bryan Waller: *see* 'Cornwall, Barry'.

Renwick, W. L.: *see* Dobrée and Davis (eds.), *Oxford History of English Literature 1789–1815*.

Robinson, Henry Crabb (ed. Thomas Sadler), *Diary, Reminiscences, and Correspondence of Henry Crabb Robinson* (Boston: Fields, Osgood, 1869); (ed. Edith J. Morley) *Henry Crabb Robinson on Books and Their Writers* (London: Dent, 1938)–from diary, travel journals, reminiscences.

Ross, Ernest C., *The Ordeal of Bridget Elia: A Chronicle of the Lambs* [on Mary Lamb] (Norman: University of Oklahoma Press, 1940).

Russell, W. Clark (ed.), *Representative Actors: A Collection of Criticisms, Anecdotes, . . . etc. . . .* (London: Warne, n.d. [c. 1900]).

Sandford, Elizabeth, *Thomas Poole and His Friends* (London, 1888).

Schneider, Ben Ross, Jr., *Wordsworth's Cambridge Education* (Cambridge University Press, 1957).

Seymour, William Kean, 'Charles Lamb as a Poet', *Essays by Divers Hands*, Mar. 1954, 103–25.

Simmons, Jack, *Southey* (London: Collins, 1945).

Smith, Elton E. and Esther G., *William Godwin* (New York: Twayne, 1965).

Southey, C. C., *The Life and Correspondence of Robert Southey* (1849–50; New York: Harper, 1851).

Southey, Robert (ed. Kenneth Curry), *New Letters of Robert Southey*, Vol. I *1792–1810*, Vol. II, *1811–1838* (New York and London: Columbia University Press, 1965).

STCP: Coleridge's *Poetical Works* (ed. Campbell), 1893; *see* Coleridge.

Talfourd, Thomas Noon (ed. Percy Fitzgerald), *Memoirs of Charles Lamb* (London: W. W. Gibbings, 1892); *see also* Lamb.

Thompson, E. P., *The Making of the English Working Class* (1963; New York: Vintage Books, n.d.).

Thornton, James (ed.), *Table Talk by Various Writers from Ben Jonson to Leigh Hunt* (London: Dent, 1934).

Tave, Stuart M.: *see* Barnett.

Thomson, J. C. *Bibliography of the Writings of Charles and Mary Lamb: A Literary History* (Hull: J. R. Tutin, 1908).

Tillotson, Geoffrey, 'The Historical Importance of Certain "Essays of Elia"', in Logan, Jordan, and Frye (eds), *Some British Romantics: A Collection of Essays* (Ohio State University Press, 1966) 89–118.

Tomalin, Claire: *The Life and Death of Mary Wollstonecraft* (New York and London: Harcourt, Brace, Jovanovich, 1974).

Trevelyan, G. M., *History of England*, Vol. III: *From Utrecht to Modern Times*, 3rd edn (Garden City, N.Y.: Doubleday, 1953).

Watson, E. Bradlee, *Sheridan to Robertson: A Study of the Nineteenth-Century London Stage* (Cambridge, Mass., 1926).

WCH: *see* W. Carew Hazlitt on the Lambs.

Wherry, George (ed.), *Cambridge and Charles Lamb* (Cambridge University Press, 1925).

Williams, Orlo, *Lamb's Friend the Census-Taker: Life and Letters of John Rickman* (London: Constable, 1912).

WL: Wordsworth *Letters* (ed. de Selincourt-Shaver); *see* Wordsworth.

Woodring, Carl, "Charles Lamb in the Harvard Library", *Harvard Library Bulletin*, 1956: spring, 208–39, autumn 367–402; *Politics in English Romantic Poetry* (Cambridge, Mass.: Harvard University Press, 1970) – especially 74–7 on Lamb.

Wordsworth, W. and D. (ed. Ernest de Selincourt, rev. Chester L. Shaver), *The Letters of William and Dorothy Wordsworth: The Early Years, 1787–1805*, 2nd edn (Oxford: Clarendon Press, 1967).

The Wordsworth Circle (ed. Marilyn Gaull, Temple University, Department of English, Philadelphia, Pa. 19122) – the American scholarly journal regularly concerned with Lamb.

Index

Abbreviations used are CL and ML for Charles and Mary Lamb, Col. for S. T. Coleridge, short-form Lloyd for Charles Lloyd Jr. Notes are indexed: when more than a single note 1 (for example) appears on a page the entry may show '362 n1a, 1b, 6b, 17'. In general, books listed in the Selected Bibliography are not indexed. Certain joint works are given separate main entries, cross-referenced. Birth dates are given for Lamb intimates for easy reference to their ages; for family birth dates consult the Genealogical Trees.